Demystifying Rising Inequality in Asia

Edited by

Bihong Huang, Peter J. Morgan, and Naoyuki Yoshino

ASIAN DEVELOPMENT BANK INSTITUTE

© 2019 Asian Development Bank Institute

All rights reserved. First printed in 2019.

ISBN 9784899741015 (Print)
ISBN 9784899741022 (PDF)

The views in this publication do not necessarily reflect the views and policies of the Asian Development Bank Institute (ADBI), its Advisory Council, ADB's Board or Governors, or the governments of ADB members.

ADBI does not guarantee the accuracy of the data included in this publication and accepts no responsibility for any consequence of their use. ADBI uses proper ADB member names and abbreviations throughout and any variation or inaccuracy, including in citations and references, should be read as referring to the correct name.

By making any designation of or reference to a particular territory or geographic area, or by using the term "recognize," "country," or other geographical names in this publication, ADBI does not intend to make any judgments as to the legal or other status of any territory or area.

Users are restricted from reselling, redistributing, or creating derivative works without the express, written consent of ADBI.

ADB recognizes "China" as the People's Republic of China.

Note: In this publication, "$" refers to US dollars.

Asian Development Bank Institute
Kasumigaseki Building 8F
3-2-5, Kasumigaseki, Chiyoda-ku
Tokyo 100-6008, Japan
www.adbi.org

Contents

Figures and Tables   v
Contributors   x
Abbreviations   xii

PART I: Income Inequality in Asia

1. **Introduction**   1
   Bihong Huang, Peter Morgan, and Naoyuki Yoshino

2. **Overview of Income Inequality in Asia: Profile, Drivers, and Consequences**   6
   Bihong Huang and Guanghua Wan

3. **Inclusive Growth, Decomposition, Incidence, and Policies: Lessons for Asia**   17
   Alexei Kireyev

4. **Different Faces of Income Inequality across Asia: Decomposition across Demographic Groups**   38
   Vladimir Hlasny

PART II: Drivers of Inequality

5. **Impact of Macroeconomic Factors on Income Inequality in Asian Countries**   111
   N.P. Ravindra Deyshappriya

6. **Education, Globalization, and Income Inequality in Asia**   132
   Kang H. Park

7. **Economic Growth and Income Distribution in Transition Economies of Central Asia: A Pure Empirical Study of the Post-Communist Development Era**   154
   Odiljon Komolov

8. **Middle-Class Composition and Growth in Middle-Income Countries**   166
   Riana Razafimandimby Andrianjaka

PART III: Country Case Studies

9. Growth Pro-Poorness from an Intertemporal Perspective with an Application to Indonesia, 1997–2007 — 199
   Florent Bresson, Jean-Yves Duclos, and Flaviana Palmisano

10. Spatial Dimensions of Expenditure Inequality in a Decentralized Indonesia — 226
    Takahiro Akita and Sachiko Miyata

11. The Sources of Income Inequality in Indonesia: Regression-Based Inequality Decomposition — 260
    Eko Wicaksono, Hidayat Amir, and Anda Nugroho

12. Intragenerational and Intergenerational Mobility in Viet Nam — 273
    Nguyen Tran Lam and Nguyen Viet Cuong

13. Foreign Direct Investment and Wage Inequality: Evidence from the People's Republic of China — 328
    Cen Chen, Hongmei Zhao, and Yunbo Zhou

14. Impacts of Rural Dual Economic Transformation on the Inverted-U Curve of Rural Income Inequality: An Empirical Study of Tianjin and Shandong Provinces in the People's Republic of China — 356
    Zongsheng Chen, Ting Wu, and Jian Kang

Index — 382

Figures and Tables

Figures

2.1	Within- and Between-Countries Income Inequality in Asia	6
3.1	Stylized Indicators of Inclusive Growth	20
3.2	Distributional Dimensions of Poverty	23
3.3	Consumption Growth by Welfare Groups (%)	24
3.4	Growth Incidence Curve for Total Population, 2001, 2005, 2011	25
3.5	Growth Incidence Curves for Urban Areas, 2001, 2005, 2011	26
3.6	Growth Incidence Curves for Rural Areas, 2001, 2005, 2011	27
3.7	Poverty Headcount Rate at International Poverty Line	29
3.8	Change in Poverty Rate	31
3.9	Factors Contributing to Pro-Poor Growth	32
5.1	Average Growth Rate of Gini Index (1990s–2000s) of Asian Countries by per Capita GDP Classification	115
6.1	Three Income Inequalities by Bourguignon and Morrisson (2002)	133
6.2	Average Years of Schooling by Education Level: Asia	136
6.3	Average Years of Schooling & Education Inequality: Asia	137
6.4	Education Gini and Average Years of Schooling, 2010	138
6.5	Average Years of Schooling and Standard Deviation, 2010	138
6.6	Gini Trend in the People's Republic of China	141
6.7	Gini Trend in Kyrgyz Republic	142
6.8	Asia Gini Coefficients, 2010	143
6.9	OECD Gini Coefficients, 2011	143
7.1	Net Income/Gini Index in Central Asian Economies, 1991–2013	157
7.2	Income Groups of Central Asian Economies in 2013, %	158
A7.1	Economic Growth Statistics of Central Asian Countries	162
A7.2	Income Distribution Statistics of Central Asian Countries	164
8.1	Middle-Class Subcategories (Average % Share of Population [a] and of Middle-Class [b] from 1985 to 2010)	173
8.2	Middle-Class Gini and Development Level 1981–2012	177
8.3	Overall Gini and Development Level 1981–2012	178
9.1	Sensitivity of IPP α,γ with respect to α and γ, Indonesia 1997–2007	217
10.1	Hierarchical Spatial Structure	228

v

10.2	Number of Districts by Region	237
10.3	Expenditure Inequalities by Theil Index L	238
10.4	Hierarchical Decomposition of Overall Expenditure Inequality: Urban or Rural Sector-District, Theil Index L	239
10.5	Expenditure Inequalities by Kuznets 20/20 Ratio	241
10.6a	Hierarchical Decomposition of Rural Expenditure Inequality: Region–Province–District, Theil Index L	244
10.6b	Hierarchical Decomposition of Urban Expenditure Inequality: Region–Province–District, Theil Index L	245
10.7a	Distribution of Districts in the Rural Sector by Within-District Inequality in 2010, Theil Index L	247
10.7b	Distribution of Districts in the Urban Sector by Within-District Inequality in 2010, Theil Index L	247
11.1	Poverty, Inequality and GDP per Capita in Indonesia	261
12.1	Income and Expenditure Inequality over Time	276
12.2	Per Capita Income by Urban/Rural and Ethnicity	277
12.3	Per Capita Income by Income Quintiles	277
12.4	Percentage of Households Moving up from the Lowest Income Quintile to a Higher Income Quintile	278
12.5	Percentage of People Moving from Unskilled to Skilled Occupation	288
12.6	Intergenerational Mobility from Unskilled Parents to Skilled Children	296
12.7	Intergenerational Elasticity between Father, Mother and Son, and Daughter	299
12.8	Intergenerational Elasticity by Rural/Urban and Ethnicity	300
12.9	Intergenerational Elasticity by Sex, Age, and Education	300
13.1	Effect of Labor Transfer on the Wage Gap	336
13.2	Image of $L\left(\dfrac{W_f}{W_d}\right)$	338
13.3	Effect of Technology Spillover on the Wage Gap	339
13.4	Shorter Lag between Two Effects	340
13.5	Longer Lag between Two Effects	340
14.1	Changes in Rural Income Inequality Gini and per Capita Income, 1994–2014	359
14.2	Changes in Comprehensive Dual Index in Tianjin, Shandong, and the People Republic of China, 1994–2013	363

Tables

2.1	Gini Coefficient in Asia	7
3.1	Senegal: Inequality Indicators, 1994–2011	22
3.2	Senegal: Poverty Indicators, 1994–2011	30
4.1	Quantile Decomposition for the PRC 2002, India 2004, Japan 2008, and Rep. of Korea 2006 by Rural/Urban Residence	42

4.2	Quantile Decomposition for the Russian Federation 2004, 2007, and 2010 by Rural/Urban Residence	53
4.3	Quantile Decomposition for Taipei,China 2005, 2007, and 2010 by Rural/Urban Residence	56
4.4	Quantile Decomposition for the PRC 2002, India 2004, Japan 2008, and Rep. of Korea 2006 by Disadvantaged/Advantaged Admin. Region	60
4.5	Quantile Decomposition for the Russian Federation 2004, 2007, and 2010, and Taipei,China 2005 by Disadvantaged/Advantaged Administrative Region	63
4.6	Quantile Decomposition for the PRC 2002, India 2004, Japan 2008, and Rep. of Korea 2006 by Less/More Educated Household Head	67
4.7	Quantile Decomposition for the Russian Federation 2004, 2007, and 2010 by Less/More Educated Household Head	70
4.8	Quantile Decomposition for Taipei,China 2005, 2007, and 2010 by Less/More Educated Household Head	73
4.9	Quantile Decomposition for the PRC 2002, India 2004, Japan 2008, and Rep. of Korea 2006 by Non-employed/Employed Household Head	76
4.10	Quantile Decomposition for the Russian Federation 2004, 2007, and 2010 by Non-employed/Employed Household Head	79
4.11	Quantile Decomposition for Taipei,China 2005, 2007, and 2010 by Non-employed/Employed Household Head	82
4.12	Quantile Decomposition for the PRC 2002, India 2004, Japan 2008, and Rep. of Korea 2006 by Female/Male Household Head	87
4.13	Quantile Decomposition for the Russian Federation 2004, 2007, and 2010 by Female/Male Household Head	90
4.14	Quantile Decomposition for Taipei,China 2005, 2007, and 2010 by Female/Male Household Head	93
A4.1	Distribution of Real Income	104
A4.2	Mean Disposable Household Income Per Capita and Share of Aggregate Income, by Quintile	105
A4.3	Means of Explanatory Variables of Interest	105
A4.4	Summary Statistics by Income Quintile	106
A4.5	Mean Disposable Household Income Per Capita by Demographic Group	107
5.1	Trend in Income Inequality of Selected Countries from 1980 to 2000	113
5.2	Description of Variables and Data Sources	119
5.3	Impacts of Macroeconomic, Political Economy, and Demographic Factors on Income Inequality	124

5.4	Impacts of Macroeconomic Factors on Income Share of Quantiles	126
6.1	Trends in Income Inequality in Asia	139
6.2	Regression of Income Inequality on Income	147
6.3	Regression of Income Inequality on Income and Education Variables	147
6.4	Regression of Income Inequality on Income, Education, and Globalization	148
8.1	Minimum, Mean, and Median Size and Economic Weight by Income Category	171
8.2	Ratio of the Upper and Higher Subgroups on the Floating and Lower Subgroups	174
8.3	Middle-Class Average Consumption per Capita by Income Category	175
8.4	Middle-Class Gini Indicator by Income Category	176
8.5	Middle-Class Configurations by Country Income Level	179
8.6	Middle-Class Configurations by Region	1811
8.7	Estimates of GDP per Capita (Constant 2005 $) on Middle-Class Indicators using FEGMM Estimator	185
A8.1	Data and Sources	193
A8.2	Countries by Region	194
9.1	Cross-sectional and Intertemporal EDE Gaps for Indonesia, 1997–2007	215
9.2	Values of the IPP Index for Indonesia, 1997–2007	217
9.3	Decomposition into Anonymous (AG) and Non-anonymous (M) for Indonesia, 1997–2007	218
9.4	Subperiod Contributions to the IPP Index for Indonesia, 1997–2007	219
9.5	Decomposition into Average Poverty Gap (ΔP c), Cross-sectional Inequality (Δc^c), Difference between Intertemporal and Unitemporal Inequality (M^c), and Variability (CV) for Indonesia, 1997–2007	220
9.6	Decomposition into Inequality Change (I), Reranking (R), and Pure Growth (PG) for Indonesia, 1997–2007	220
A10.1	Decomposition of Expenditure Inequality by Urban and Rural Sectors and by District in Each Sector, Theil Index L	256
A10.2	Hierarchical vs Non-Hierarchical Decomposition of Expenditure Inequality, Theil Index L	258
11.1	Summary Statistics of the Variables	264
11.2	The Estimated Income-Generating Function	266
11.3	Shapley Value Decomposition Results, 2000	268
11.4	Shapley Value Decomposition Results, 2007	269
11.5	Shapley Value Decomposition Results, 2014	269

12.1	Income Mobility of Households from 2010–2014	280
12.2	Regression of Income Mobility of Households from 2010–2014	282
12.3	Employment of Individuals Aged 15–60 over Time	287
12.4	Employment of Individuals Aged 15–60 in 2014	287
12.5	Employment Mobility of Individuals from 2010–2014	289
12.6	Regression of Employment Mobility of Individuals from 2010–2014	291
12.7	Intergenerational Mobility of Employment in 2014	296
12.8	Regression of Intergenerational Employment Mobility	301
A12.1	Income Mobility of Households from 2004–2008	310
A12.2	Regression of Income Mobility of Households from 2004–2008	312
A12.3	Employment Mobility of Individuals from 2004–2008	316
A12.4	Regression of Employment Mobility of Individuals from 2004–2008	318
A12.5	Intergenerational Mobility of Employment in 2004	322
A12.6	Regression of Log of Children's Wages on Father's and Mother's Wages	324
A12.7	Regression of Log of Children's Wages on Parent's Wages for Different Groups	325
A12.8	Regression of Log of Children's Wages on Parent's Wages for Different Groups	326
13.1	Descriptive Statistics	343
13.2	Results of $W_f/W_d, \eta, \eta^*, \eta^{**}$	344
13.3	Theil Index between Domestic Firms and Foreign Firms and All Companies' Average Wage	345
13.4	Results of Estimating Equation (13)	346
13.5	Factor Contributions to Inequality using the Shapley Method (%)	348
A13.1	Regression Results of Annual Cross-sectional Data	354
14.1	The Income Share (%) and Average Income (CNY) of Rural Households by Quintile	360
14.2	The Nonagricultural Income Share and Employment Share of Rural Residents	365
14.3	The Relationship between Rural Dual Transformation and Income Inequality	366
14.4	Regression Estimation Results	366
14.5	The Decomposition of Total Gini Coefficient by Sectoral Inequality in Tianjin and Shandong	369
14.6	Structural Effects and Distribution Effects of Dual Economic Transformation on Changes in Rural Income Inequality (Tianjin 1994–2002, 2003–2008; Shandong 2007–2009)	375

Contributors

Takahiro Akita is a specially appointed professor at the Graduate School of Business, Rikkyo University, Japan.

Hidayat Amir is a senior researcher at the Ministry of Finance of the Republic of Indonesia.

Riana Razafimandimby Andrianjaka is a PhD candidate in applied economics at the University of Bordeaux, France.

Florent Bresson is an associate professor at the Université d'Auvergne in Clermont-Ferrand, France.

Cen Chen is a postdoctoral research fellow at the Institute of Economics, School of Economics, Nankai University, Tianjin City, the People's Republic of China (PRC).

Zongsheng Chen is a professor of economics at Nankai School of Economics, Nankai University and former deputy secretary general of Tianjin Municipal People's Government, the PRC.

Nguyen Viet Cuong is affiliated with the National Economics University, Viet Nam.

N.P. Ravindra Deyshappriya is a a senior lecturer in economics at the Faculty of Management, Uva Wellassa University of Sri Lanka and PhD candidate at RMIT University, Australia.

Jean-Yves Duclos is a professor at Université Laval in Quebec, Canada.

Vladimir Hlasny is an associate professor of economics at Ewha Womans University, Seoul, Republic of Korea.

Bihong Huang is a research fellow at the Asian Development Bank Institute, Tokyo, Japan.

Jian Kang is a PhD candidate at Nankai Institute of Economics, Nankai University, Tianjin, the PRC.

Alexei Kireyev is a senior economist at the International Monetary Fund.

Odiljon Komolov is a professor at the Department of Finance, Tashkent Financial Institute, Uzbekistan.

Nguyen Tran Lam is a policy research specialist at Oxfam in Viet Nam.

Sachiko Miyata is an associate professor at the College of Business, Ritsumeikan University, Japan.

Peter Morgan is senior consulting economist and vice chair of research, Asian Development Bank Institute, Tokyo, Japan.

Anda Nugroho is a researcher at the Ministry of Finance of the Republic of Indonesia.

Flaviana Palmisano is an assistant professor at Universita di Roma "La Sapienza", Rome, Italy.

Kang H. Park is a professor of economics, at Missouri State University, United States.

Guanghua Wan is a director at the Institute of World Economy, Fudan University, the PRC.

Eko Wicaksono is a researcher at the Ministry of Finance, Republic of Indonesia.

Naoyuki Yoshino is dean of the Asian Development Bank Institute, Tokyo, Japan

Ting Wu is a lecturer of economics at the Party School of Communist Party of China, Tianjin Binhai New District, the PRC.

Hongmei Zhao is an associate professor at the Institute of Econometrics and Statistics, School of Economics, Nankai University, Tianjin City, the PRC.

Yunbo Zhou is a professor at the Institute of Economics, School of Economics, Nankai University, Tianjin City, the PRC.

Abbreviations

AR1	first-order autocorrelation
AR2	second-order autocorrelation
BLT	unconditional cash transfers
EDE	equally distributed equivalent
ESAM	Enquête Sénégalaise Auprès des Ménages
ESPS	Enquête Suivi de la Pauvreté au Sénégal
FDI	foreign direct investment
G20	Group of Twenty
GDP	gross domestic product
GMM	generalized method of moments
GNI	gross national income
GRDE	gross regional domestic expenditure
GRDP	gross regional domestic product
GSO	General Statistics Office
HDI	Human Development Index
HIC	high-income countries
IFLS	Indonesian Family Life Survey
IMF	International Monetary Fund
INFL	inflation
IPP	intertemporal pro-poorness
LFP	labor force participation
LIC	low-income countries
LIS	Luxembourg Income Study
LMIC	lower middle-income countries
MLD	mean log deviation
NBSC	National Bureau of Statistics of the PRC
ODA	official development assistance
OECD	Organisation for Economic Co-operation and Development
OLS	ordinary least squares
PPP	purchasing power parity
PRC	People's Republic of China
RIF	re-centered influence function
RPPG	rate of pro-poor growth
SSA	sub-Saharan African
UMIC	upper-middle-income countries
UNCTAD	United Nations Conference on Trade and Development
UNDP	United Nations Development Program

UNEMP	unemployment
UQR	unconditional quantile regression
US	United States
VHLSS	Viet Nam Household Living Standard Surveys
WAEMU	West African Economic and Monetary Union
WDI	World Development Indicators
WIID	World Income Inequality Database

PART I
Income Inequality in Asia

1

Introduction

Bihong Huang, Peter Morgan, and Naoyuki Yoshino

Income inequality is one of the most profound social, economic, and political challenges of our time. A survey conducted by Pew Research Center (2014) found that more than 60% of worldwide respondents regard the gap between the rich and the poor as a major concern. Piketty (2014) draws an unequivocal conclusion that growing inequality between rich and poor — between the owners of capital and the rest of society — is the normal state of affairs under capitalism; periods of decreasing inequality, such as during the post-war boom, are the exception, not the rule. The gap is at its highest level in decades for advanced economies (Dabla-Norris et al. 2015), while the inequality trend has been rising in many developing countries. In Asia, despite recent economic growth, income distribution has been worsening as well.

This book contributes to the existing literature on inequality in Asia by focusing on three broad themes, corresponding to three parts of the volume. Part I offers an overview of inequality in Asia. Chapter 2 profiles income inequality in Asia, discusses its drivers and consequences, and provides policy recommendations. Chapter 3 examines the dynamic measures of growth inclusiveness derived from incidence curves that identify the extent to which each decile of households benefits from growth. The main features of growth incidence curves, their design, computation, data requirements, and interpretation are discussed. The use of growth incidence curves are illustrated with a case study, which can be applied to Asia, in particular its low- and middle-income countries. Employing Luxembourg Income Study, Chapter 4 evaluates inequality in household incomes per capita across various demographic groups in six middle- and high-income economies across Asia: the PRC, India, Japan, Republic of Korea, the Russian Federation, and Taipei,China. It describes patterns in overall inequality, inequality in various quantiles of national income distributions, and income differentials across various demographic groups. Income gaps due to households' rural/urban residence, administrative region, education and employment status, and gender are assessed at various income quantiles using unconditional quantile regressions, and are decomposed into parts due to differentials in household endowments and parts due to differentials in returns to those endowments. Japan; Taipei,China; and Republic of Korea have very low degrees of overall income inequality by world standards, while India and the PRC have high levels. The Russian Federation has a medium degree of inequality, sluggishly improving over time.

Part II focuses on the drivers of rising inequality in Asia. Chapter 5 assesses the macroeconomic determinants of income inequality over the period of 1990–2013 across 33 Asian countries by using dynamic panel data analysis and Generalized Method of Moments. The study found an inverted U-shaped (parabolic) relationship between gross domestic product (GDP) and inequality, supporting the well-known concept, the Kuznets curve. Apart from that, official development assistance (ODA), education, and labor force participation reduce inequality while higher inflation, political risk, terms of trade, and unemployment increase inequality in Asian countries. Chapter 6 examines the effects of education and globalization on income inequality in Asia. The analysis indicates that a higher level of education achieved by the population aged 15 and over has improved income distribution in Asia, while educational inequality, measured by the education Gini index, has a negative effect on income distribution. Higher levels of globalization are correlated with higher levels of income inequality, while freedom, either political or economic, has marginal effects on the level of inequity in income distribution. Chapter 7 analyzes the economic growth and income inequality paths of Central Asian countries and proposes recommendations. It suggests that labor market policy should keep pace with economic development and the global labor market environment; reducing tuition payments at private and public primary, secondary, and tertiary education institutions ensures accessibility and inclusion; and creating a tax-friendly environment for labor relations may result in more favorable conditions for productivity. Chapter 8 investigates the composition of the middle class by computing various statistical features of the distribution of income and of consumption: the incidence, the depth (the average consumption), and the heterogeneity of the middle class for a panel of 120 countries from 1985 to 2012. The bulk of bottom middle classes is found to be negatively linked to growth, whereas the composition of the middle class in those countries reveals a still large share of floating and lower middle classes, confirming the size of a unique middle class alone is not enough to comprehend the complex mechanisms through which the expansion of the middle class impacts on growth.

Finally, Part III presents country case studies. Chapter 9 adopts a longitudinal perspective to evaluate the relative contribution of intertemporal poverty and horizontal mobility on the pro-poorness of distributional changes. Several decompositions are introduced to evaluate the relative contribution of each of these effects on the pro-poorness of distributional changes. An empirical illustration performed on Indonesian data for the period 1997–2007 shows that growth can be deemed intertemporally pro-poor in Indonesia during this period. Chapter 10 analyzes the spatial dimensions of expenditure inequality under decentralization in Indonesia with the hierarchical decomposition method and finds urban–rural disparity constitutes 15%–25% of overall expenditure inequality. At the same time, a large difference between urban and rural areas in the magnitude of inequality among districts. After controlling for the urban–rural difference, inequality among districts accounts for 15%–25% of overall inequality. Given unequal geographic distributions of resource endowments, public infrastructure, and economic activities, some spatial inequalities are inevitable. Chapter 11 employs the household-level data and regression-based inequality decomposition approach to investigate the source of income inequality in Indonesia. The results show that education, wealth, and employment are significant contributors to income inequality in Indonesia. These findings suggest that any policy aimed at reducing unequal access to education and finance is important to improve income inequality in the future.

Chapter 12 examines intra-generational and intergenerational mobility of employment and income in Viet Nam during 2004–2008 and 2010–2014 and finds rather high mobility across income quintiles. There was high mobility of individuals by occupational skills but less mobility by employment status and sectors. The upward mobility of occupation increased over time because of the increase in skilled occupation. The intergenerational elasticity of earnings for parents and children is estimated at around 0.36. The intergenerational elasticity is very similar for 2004 and 2014. Education plays an important role in improving intergenerational mobility. The intergenerational elasticity for children without education degrees and those with post-secondary degrees is 0.51 and 0.17, respectively. With a postsecondary degree, 80% of people whose parents are unskilled have skilled or nonmanual occupation. Chapter 13 uses the Chinese Industrial Enterprises Database to measure the effects of FDI on the wage gap between foreign and domestic firms in the host country. The theoretical analysis shows that the wage gap in the host country caused by FDI through the labor transfer and technology spillover effect tends to initially increase and then decrease, implying an inverted-U curve. The empirical results indicate that FDI has significant effects on the wage gap in the PRC during the period under study. Chapter 14 explores the sources of income inequality in rural PRC, especially how rural dual structural transformation leads to the inverted-U curve. The case studies about rural Tianjin and Shandong provinces suggest that changes in rural income inequality are roughly consistent with the changes in dual economic transformation in different regions. A marginal decomposition analysis on the Gini coefficient changes of income inequality shows that the distribution effect always accounts for the dominant position and determines the inequality change direction. The dual transformation is sure to affect and change the sectoral labor participation rate directly, and then affect and change the within-sector income inequality, and further to make total income inequality go up or down.

References

Dabla-Norris, E., K. Kochhar, F. Ricka, N. Suphaphiphat, and E. Tsounta 2015. Causes and Consequences of Income Inequality: A Global Perspective. IMF Working Paper SDN/15/13. Washington, DC: International Monetary Fund.

Pew Research Center 2014. 2014 Global Attitude Survey. Available at: http://www.pewresearch.org/wp-content/uploads/sites/2/2014/10/Pew-Research-Center-Inequality-Report-FINAL-October-17-2014.pdf

Piketty, T. 2014. Capital in the Twenty-First Century, Harvard University Press, Cambridge.

2

Overview of Income Inequality in Asia: Profile, Drivers and Consequences

Bihong Huang and Guanghua Wan

Despite the remarkable economic growth achieved in Asia in the last few decades, rising income inequality is one of the most profound challenges in the region. This chapter profiles income inequality in Asia, disentangles its drives and provides policy recommendations.

2.1 Profile of Income Inequality in Asia

Figure 2.1 presents the overall inequality in Asia from the mid-1990s to 2008, as measured by the Theil index. The regional inequality consists of inequality within individual economies (the within component) and

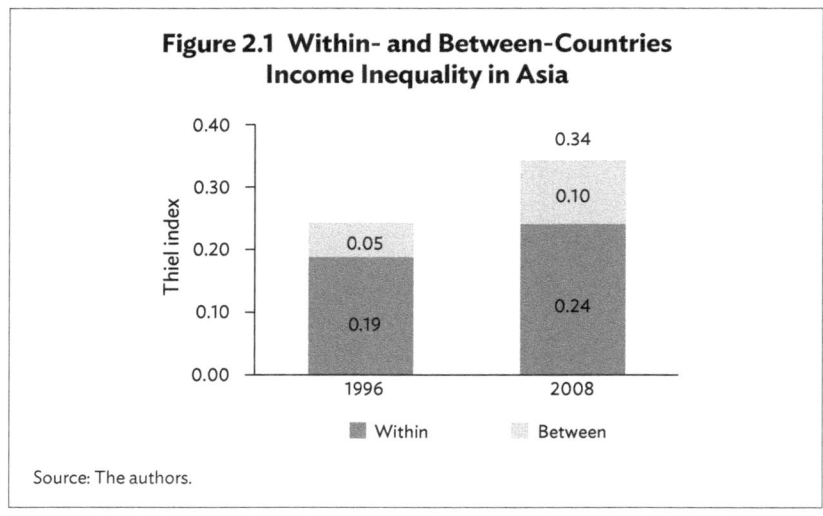

Figure 2.1 Within- and Between-Countries Income Inequality in Asia

Source: The authors.

also of income gaps across countries (the between component). Clearly, inequality for the Asian region as a whole grew significantly, rising by almost 42% in around 2 decades. More importantly, both the within- and between-component have increased. The latter exactly doubled.

Figure 2.1 also indicates that inequalities within economies dominate the regional income distribution, accounting for more than 70% of the total. To explore this component, we turn our attention to inequality trends in individual economies in Asia, using the Gini coefficient. Table 2.1 shows the Gini coefficient and its average annual growth rate in the 1990s and 2000s, calculated using both net income (income after taxes and transfers) and gross income data.

According to Table 2.1, 18 of the 32 Asian economies now have a Gini coefficient of gross income equal to or greater than 40. Based on net income, only 10 economies have their Gini coefficients above 40, suggesting that taxes and transfers moderate the income gap. Although the Gini coefficients in developing Asia are on average lower than sub-Saharan Africa, Latin America, and the Caribbean, the growth rate of inequality has surpassed these regions. In terms of inequality trends, 16 of the 32 Asian economies exhibited an increase (worsening distribution) in the Gini coefficient in the past two decades, covering around 80% of the region's population. In particular, the People's Republic of China (PRC) and India, with the largest populations in the world, have the highest Gini coefficients of around 0.5.

Table 2.1 Gini Coefficient in Asia

Economy	Initial year	Final year	Gini_net 1990s	Gini_net 2000s	Annualized growth rate (%)	Gini_market 1990s	Gini_market 2000s	Annualized growth rate (%)
Central Asia								
Armenia	1994	2008	36.125	33.757	−0.468	34.967	34.840	−0.026
Azerbaijan	1994	2008	35.503	32.669	−0.570	42.183	31.786	−1.760
Georgia	1994	2008	37.312	41.173	0.739	34.466	45.952	2.380
Kazakhstan	1994	2008	32.803	31.009	−0.391	37.870	29.177	−1.640
Kyrgyz Republic	1994	2008	47.848	35.685	−1.816	55.493	36.463	−2.450
Tajikistan	1994	2008	31.184	32.902	0.393	34.358	33.804	−0.115
Turkmenistan	1994	2005	34.172	39.286	1.360	35.763	42.792	1.787
Uzbekistan	1994	2005	34.603	34.232	−0.097	36.590	33.716	−0.714

continued on next page

Table 2.1 continued

Economy	Initial year	Final year	Gini_net 1990s	Gini_net 2000s	Annualized growth rate (%)	Gini_market 1990s	Gini_market 2000s	Annualized growth rate (%)
East Asia								
PRC	1994	2008	39.370	51.990	2.290	38.873	49.684	1.986
Hong Kong, China	1994	2008	40.103	49.199	1.620	44.186	53.008	1.426
Taipei,China	1994	2008	28.361	31.461	0.781	30.793	32.059	0.294
Japan	1994	2008	27.263	30.220	0.775	36.087	45.090	1.782
Republic of Korea	1994	2008	30.662	31.543	0.205	34.774	33.904	-0.179
Mongolia	1994	2008	33.870	33.097	-0.163	34.419	35.096	0.141
South Asia								
Bangladesh	1994	2008	37.055	42.949	1.136	39.298	45.740	1.171
Bhutan	2003	2008	51.882	38.617	-5.113	45.542	40.565	-2.186
India	1994	2008	48.926	49.371	0.065	45.199	50.000	0.759
Maldives	1998	2008	63.120	39.144	-3.799	61.438	40.696	-3.376
Nepal	1995	2008	39.362	37.709	-0.323	43.800	41.086	-0.477
Pakistan	1994	2008	32.587	32.422	-0.036	32.942	37.285	0.942
Sri Lanka	1994	2008	38.771	41.730	0.545	39.455	42.325	0.520
Southeast Asia								
Cambodia	1994	2008	37.827	39.351	0.288	43.108	39.176	-0.652
Indonesia	1994	2008	36.204	35.952	-0.050	37.538	42.158	0.879
Lao PDR	1994	2008	33.080	39.063	1.292	34.321	38.965	0.966
Malaysia	1994	2008	42.819	41.637	-0.197	47.342	42.634	-0.710
Philippines	1994	2008	43.496	42.431	-0.175	46.832	45.268	-0.238
Singapore	1994	2008	35.576	39.969	0.882	39.590	46.763	1.294
Thailand	1994	2008	43.478	42.103	-0.226	46.190	42.493	-0.572
Viet Nam	1994	2008	36.333	39.344	0.592	38.174	41.708	0.661
Pacific								
Fiji	1994	2008	38.319	33.116	-0.970	44.785	36.255	-1.361
Papua New Guinea	1995	2005	42.674	53.706	2.585	42.212	54.906	3.007
Timor-Leste	2001	2007	40.639	31.844	-3.607	41.553	35.803	-2.306

Lao PDR = Lao People's Democratic Republic, PRC = People's Republic of China.
Source: World Income Inequality Database (accessed July 2016).

It is useful to highlight the case of the PRC, which is now the second-largest economy in the world and has been experiencing rapid rises in income inequality. Even in terms of net income, the PRC's Gini coefficient has increased from 39.37 in 1994 to 51.99 in 2008. These very high inequalities can undermine social stability. They also contribute to the slowdown of the economy and to the global imbalance (Lin, Wan, and Morgan 2016). Despite recent declines in PRC inequality (Wan and Zhuang 2015), income distribution remains a serious issue.

The situation in India is similar to that in the PRC. Starting in the 1980s, average incomes in India grew faster than ever before, but most of the gains went to the super-rich. According to the International Monetary Fund (2016), India's Gini coefficient rose from 45 in 1990 to 51 in 2013, mainly due to the rising gap between urban and rural areas, as well as within urban areas.

2.2 Drivers of Income Inequality

Many factors such as globalization, technological change, financial development, and demographic changes, among others, have been identified as drivers of growing income inequality.

Globalization: Although globalization spurs economic growth, it can also affect income distribution in that trade increases differentials in returns to education and skills, globalization marginalizes certain groups of people or geographic regions, and liberalization is not complemented by development of adequate institutions and governance. For example, Wan, Lu, and Chen (2007) found that trade and foreign direct investment (FDI) account for around 22% of regional inequality in the PRC. In addition, when industrial countries shift parts of the production process to developing countries, increased employment and higher wages tend to benefit skilled workers more than their unskilled counterparts.

Financial deepening: In most emerging economies, financial deepening, measured as the relative share of the banking and stock market sectors in the economy, has been associated with growing inequality, meaning it benefits mainly higher-income groups in these economies (IMF 2015). However, in Asia, particularly India, Malaysia, the Philippines, and Thailand, financial deepening moderates income inequality because successful policies of financial inclusion have allowed financial services to reach the lower end of the income distribution with an increased geographical reach (IMF 2016; Anand, Tulin, and Kumar 2014).

Technological change: Improvements in technology have dramatically augmented productivity. However, they have also affected income distribution by altering the rate of return on assets, favoring capital over labor, as well as skilled labor over unskilled labor. While increased automation has eliminated the need for many manual or low-skilled jobs, technological progress has driven demand for skilled labor and increased the skill premium disproportionately (Card and DiNardo 2002; Acemoglu 1998). Compared to other regions, skill premium has played a much greater role in explaining income inequality in Asia, with a contribution that is three times larger in Asia than elsewhere (IMF 2016).

Labor market imperfections: Flexible labor markets promote economic dynamism through reallocation of resources from less-productive to more-productive firms. However, greater flexibility can increase risks disproportionately more for low-skilled workers (Alvaredo et al. 2013), exacerbating income inequality. In the Republic of Korea and Japan, for instance, the duality between regular and nonregular employment has been the most important driver of wage inequality, with nonregular employment accounting for around one-third of the labor force in 2013 (IMF 2016). Moreover, in certain developing countries such as India, rigid hiring and firing laws and high employment protection have led to expansion of the informal sector and adoption of capital-intensive production methods that, in turn, fuel wage inequality (IMF 2015).

Education: Education is often seen as the primary engine for upward mobility. However, unequal access to education has increased income inequalities in countries where the rich continue to get access to premium education while the poor drop out or fail. Moreover, it has also been found that children from less affluent backgrounds are more likely to drop out if they live in places where the income gap is large. In quite a few emerging Asian countries such as Bhutan, Cambodia, India, and Nepal, the percentage of people with fewer than 4 years of schooling is much higher for the poorest quintile than for the richest quintile (IMF 2016).

Fiscal policy: Progressive taxation, usually measured by the top corporate tax rate or top personal tax rate, is associated with lower income inequality in Asia (IMF 2016). However, in some Asian countries such as the Philippines, poor administration has significantly constrained government tax collection (ADB 2009), which, in turn, has impacted public spending and driven up inequality. Moreover, poorly targeted policies may have reduced the equalizing effects of expenditure. Indeed, due to the low coverage of spending policies and disproportionate allocation of the benefits toward the rich, education and social services are found to be associated with higher income inequality in Asia (IMF 2016).

2.3 Consequences of Growing Income Inequality

Economic consequences of income inequality

High and persistent income inequality can significantly impede growth, cause crises, and weaken demand (IMF 2015). Specifically, a 1 percentage point increase in the income share of the top 20 percent is associated with a 0.08 percentage point decrease in gross domestic product growth in the following 5 years. By contrast, the same percentage increase in the income share of the bottom 20% is related to a 0.38 percentage point growth. In addition, the length of growth spells is also found to be shorter in more unequal countries. A study by Ostry and Berg (2011) found that a 10-percentage point percentage point decrease in inequality increases the expected length of a growth spell by 50%.

Empirical evidence provided by Wan, Lu, and Chen (2006) unequivocally points to the negative effects of inequality on growth in the short, medium, and long runs in the PRC. The negative effects stem from the strong and negative influence of inequality on physical investment. The causal effects of a prolonged period of rising inequality on crises have been identified by a growing body of research (Kumhof and Ranciere 2015; Kumhof et al. 2012).

The negative relationship between inequality and growth may be attributed to two reasons. On the one hand, a higher concentration of income reduces the chances for lower-income households to accumulate physical and human capital such as land, education, or good health, which will consequently lower the labor productivity and growth potential of the economy. Kanbur, Rhee, and Zhuang (2014) found that if inequality had been stable within Asian countries from 1990 to 2010, the same levels of economic growth would have lifted about 240 million more Asians (6.5% of the population) out of poverty. On the other hand, an enlarged income gap undermines growth by dampening aggregate demand because the consumption propensity of the affluent is much lower than that of the poor. In addition, income inequality may generate unsustainable consumption outcomes for the poor. Relative income is seen to be an important determinant of sustainable consumption.

Quite a few Asian economies have joined the World Bank's group of middle-income countries. But there is no guarantee that buoyant economic growth in Asia will continue. The possibility for middle-income countries to fall into the "middle-income trap" is real (ADB 2011). If that occurs, Asia's share of world gross domestic product by 2050 would be 32%, only a small increase from 27.4% in 2010. A middle-income trap could occur not only if a country fails to augment its productivity, but also if there is a worsening of income distribution, which itself is related to economic structural changes. Worsening income inequality would cause social unrest and become a drag on economic growth. Also, income inequality is related to the limits of "human development" (UNDP 2011). Abundance of educated and healthy workers is key for a high-value-added and knowledge-based economy. However, an enlarged income gap will result in a large cohort of low-income households that are less likely to be able to afford education and healthcare, and hence are less likely to engage in productivity-driven industries. Moreover, low-income households tend to pay little attention to environmental protection, which would harm sustainability (Egawa 2013).

Social and political consequences of income inequality

Growing disparities can entail huge social costs by undermining individuals' education and occupational choices, damaging trust and eroding social cohesion, undermining the quality of governance, and increasing pressure for inefficient populist policies. This is because inequality is frequently associated with rent seeking, which has a corrosive effect on morale, societal solidarity, and fairness.

Moreover, income distribution affects a country's political structure. If high inequality prevents lower-income groups from influencing political decisions, it may result in loss of trust and generate political instability (Alesina and Perotti 1996; Keefer and Knack 2002). In other cases, high inequality could lead to poor public policies that may hurt growth in the long run. The lower-income voters may demand higher taxation and regulation, which may negatively affect investment in the country (Persson and Tabellini 1994). Political backlash due to high inequality may force governments to enact populist measures and protectionist measures, which, in the short term, benefit the lower end of the income distribution, but are detrimental to long-term growth (Alesina and Rodrik 1994). Political influence from the elite may also adversely affect provision of public services such as education, healthcare, and infrastructure.

Lack of trust in business groups and rising deprivation among lower-income groups may increase crime and violence, further affecting the investment climate and political environment in the country (Fajnzylber,

Lederman, and Loayza 2002). When people crowd at the top and bottom of the economic ladder, there may be a hollowing out of the middle class, which is important in maintaining stability and economic growth. In general, the clustering of population, often referred to as polarization, can have more damaging impacts than income inequality (Wang and Wan 2015).

Individuals at the lower level of incomes in unequal societies may try to compare and imitate consumption patterns of the rich. This phenomenon of conspicuous consumption, i.e., when lower-income groups prioritize luxury goods over necessities to signal higher status, has been found to have large environmental costs. Further, inequality is also found to have a negative linkage with nutrition. Pickett et al. (2005) found that the proportion of obese people in the total population was higher for more unequal countries.

2.4 Confronting Income Inequality in Asia

Income inequality is not only itself an important dimension of development, but it also has implications for governments' efforts to fight poverty, sustain growth, and keep social cohesion. As the Nobel Laureate Joseph E. Stiglitz said, "The only true and sustainable prosperity is shared prosperity". Hence, it is pertinent to adopt appropriate policy measures.

First, differences in educational and human capital attainments explain a large proportion of inequality in Asia. Efficient fiscal policies that ensure equal access to education and improve human capital and skills for the poor can help moderate income inequality. Other measures include providing transfers to poor families for health and education purposes, expanding social protection schemes, and improving tax administration. Further, fiscal transfers from richer regions to poorer regions can lead to reductions in spatial gaps. This also includes developing transport and communication infrastructure in rural and inland areas to increase connectivity with the economic hubs.

Second, urbanization can lead to the narrowing of the urban–rural gap and hence in turn helps reduce national income inequality (Wan and Zhuang 2015). Urbanization is regarded by the classical developmental theories as a key step in reshaping emerging economies dichotomized by a subsistence rural sector and an industrializing urban sector. According to the famous inverse-U shaped curve hypothesized by Kuznets, as more people move from lower-income rural sectors to higher-income urban sectors, overall income inequality will first increase and then decrease. It is believed that quite a few Asian economies such as the PRC have already passed the turning point; therefore, urbanization should help alleviate income inequality.

Finally, policy measures that create equality of opportunity, equal access to public goods and services, reduce corruption, and improve the quality of institutions and governance can reduce income inequalities within countries.

References

Acemoglu, D. 1998. Why Do New Technologies Complement Skills? Directed Technical Change and Wage Inequality. *Quarterly Journal of Economics* 1055–1089.

Alesina, A., and D. Rodrik. 1994. Distributive Politics and Economic Growth. *The Quarterly Journal of Economics* 109(2): 465–490.

Alesina, A., and R. Perotti. 1996. Income Distribution, Political Instability, and Investment. *European Economic Review* 40(6): 1203–1228.

Alvaredo, F., A. B. Atkinson, T. Piketty, and E. Saez. 2013. The Top 1 Percent in International and Historical Perspective. *The Journal of Economic Perspectives* 27(3): 3–20.

Anand, R., V. Tulin, and N. Kumar. 2014. India: Defining and Explaining Inclusive Growth and Poverty Reduction. IMF Working Paper 14/63. Washington, DC: International Monetary Fund.

Asian Development Bank (ADB). 2009. *Philippines: Critical Development Constraints*. Manila: Asian Development Bank.

ADB. 2011. *Asia 2050: Realizing the Asian Century*. Manila: Asian Development Bank.

Card, D., and J. E. DiNardo. 2002. Skill Biased Technological Change and Rising Wage Inequality: Some Problems and Puzzles. *Journal of Labor Economics* 20(4): 733–783.

Egawa, A. 2013. Will Income Inequality Cause a Middle-income Trap in Asia? Bruegel Working Paper 2013/06.

Fajnzylber, P., D. Lederman, and N. Loayza. 2002. What Causes Violent Crime? *European Economic Review* 46(7): 1323–1357.

International Monetary Fund (IMF). 2015. *Regional Economic Outlook: Asia and Pacific*. Washington, DC: International Monetary Fund.

International Monetary Fund (IMF). 2016. *Regional Economic Outlook: Asia and Pacific*. Washington, DC: International Monetary Fund.

Kanbur, R., C. Rhee, and J. Zhuang. 2014. *Inequality in Asia and the Pacific: Trends, Drivers, and Policy Implications*. Routledge.

Keefer, P., and S. Knack. 2002. Polarization, Politics and Property Rights: Links Between Inequality and Growth. *Public Choice* 111(1–2): 127–154.

Lin, J. Y., G. Wan, and P. J. Morgan. 2016. Prospects for a Re-acceleration of Growth in China. *Journal of Comparative Economics* 44: 842–853.

Ostry, J. D., and A. Berg. 2011. *Inequality and Unsustainable Growth: Two Sides of the Same Coin?* (No. 11/08). International Monetary Fund.

Persson, T., and G. Tabellini. 1994. Is Inequality Harmful for Growth? *The American Economic Review*: 600–621.

Pickett K. E., S. Kelly, E. Brunner, T. Lobstein, and R. G. Wilkinson 2005. Wider Income Gaps, Wider Waistbands? An Ecological Study of Obesity and Income Inequality. *Journal of Epidemiology & Community Health* 59(8): 670–674.

United Nations Development Program (UNDP). 2011. *Human Development Report 2011–Sustainability and Equity: A Better Future for All*. New York: UNDP.

Wan, G., M. Lu, and Z. Chen. 2006. The Inequality-Growth Nexus in the Short and Long Runs: Empirical Evidence from China. *Journal of Comparative Economics* 34(4): 654–67.

Wan, G., M. Lu, and Z. Chen. 2007. Globalization and Regional Income Inequality: Empirical Evidence from within China. *Review of Income and Wealth* 53(1): 35–59.

Wan, G. and J. Zhuang. 2015. Making Growth More Inclusive. In *Managing the Middle Income Transition–Challenges Facing the People's Republic of China* edited by J. Zhuang, P. Vandenberg, and Y. Huang. UK: Edward Elgar.

Wang, C. and G. Wan. 2015. Income Polarization in China: Trends and Changes. *China Economic Review* 36(c): 58–72.

3

Inclusive Growth: Decomposition, Incidence, and Policies—Lessons for Asia

Alexei Kireyev*

3.1 Inclusiveness of Growth

3.1.1 Theoretical Considerations

Growth is usually considered inclusive if its benefits are widely shared across the population. Although there is no commonly accepted definition, inclusive growth usually refers to the goal of fostering high growth while providing productive employment and equal opportunities, so that all segments of society can share in the growth and employment, while redressing inequalities in outcomes, particularly those experienced by the poor (see IMF 2013, for an overview). For analytical purposes, growth is usually considered inclusive if it is high, sustained over time, and broad-based across sectors; creates productive employment opportunities; and includes a large part of a country's labor force. Additional dimensions of inclusive growth include gender, regional diversification, and empowerment of the poor, including through inclusive institutions. This chapter focuses only on the distributional characteristics of growth. Therefore, in this chapter, growth is considered inclusive if it helps improve equality.

Inclusive growth should simultaneously reduce poverty and inequality. Growth reduces poverty if the mean income of the poor rises. Growth reduces inequality if it helps straighten the Lorenz curve, which plots the percentage of total income earned by various portions of the population when the population is ordered by the size of their incomes. More formally, starting from Ravallion and Chen (2003), the growth incidence curve, which traces out variability of consumption

---

* The views expressed herein are those of the author and should not be attributed to the IMF, its Executive Board, or its management.

or expenditure growth by the percentile of the population, can be defined as

$$g_t(p) = \frac{L'_t(p)}{L'_{t-1}(p)}(\gamma_t + 1) - 1 \qquad (1.1)$$

where $L'_t(p)$ is the rate of change (slope) of the Lorenz curve,[1] p is the decile of the population, and γ_t is the growth rate of its mean.

For illustration, assume that the ratio of the rate of change of the Lorenz curve is linear

$$\frac{L'_t(p)}{L'_{t-1}(p)} = \alpha + \beta p \qquad (1.2)$$

Then

$$g_t(p) = (\alpha + \beta p)(\gamma_t + 1) - 1 \qquad (1.3)$$

Or

$$g_t(p) = \alpha(\gamma_t + 1) - 1 + \beta(\gamma_t + 1)p \qquad (1.4)$$

Obviously, shifts up or down by $g_t(p)$ and changes its slope depending on β.

From equation (1) it follows that
- $g_t(p) = \gamma_t$, if $L'_t(p) = L'_{t-1}(p)$ growth at each decile of incidence curve will be equal to the average growth of the distribution at each decile of population, if the slope of the Lorenz curve does not change over time.
- $g_t(p) = \gamma_t$, if $L'_t(p) = L'_{t-1}(p)$: growth at each decile of the incidence curve will be higher than the average growth of the distribution at each decile of population, if the slope of the Lorenz curve increases over time;
- $g_t(p) = \gamma_t$, if $L'_t(p) = L'_{t-1}(p)$: growth at each decile of the incidence curve will be lower than the average growth of the distribution at each decile of population, if the slope of the Lorenz curve decreases over time;

---

[1] $L_t(p)$ is the fraction at time t of total income that the holders of the lowest pth fraction of incomes possess. This varies from zero to one, $0 \le p \le 1$, presented as the inverse of the cumulative distribution function.

- The slope of the incidence curve is positive if

$$g'_t(p) = \frac{L''_t L'_{t-1} - L'_t L''_{t-1}}{(L'_{t-1})^2} > 1.$$

- The slope of the incidence curve is negative if

$$g'_t(p) = \frac{L''_t L'_{t-1} - L'_t L''_{t-1}}{(L'_{t-1})^2} < 1.$$

Therefore, based on the incidence curve, pro-poor and inclusive growth can be derived as follows.

Assuming for simplicity of illustration that the incidence curve is linear (Figure 3.1), (i) pro-poor growth shifts the mean expenditure (or consumption) of the poor up; the slope of the incidence curve is irrelevant and may be positive, suggesting that growth is not inclusive; (ii) pro-poor inclusive growth shifts the mean expenditure up while the incidence curve is negatively sloped; (iii) accelerations of pro-poor growth just shift the median income further up, while the slope of the incidence curve may remain positive, suggesting the growth remains noninclusive; (iv) an increase in the inclusiveness of growth suggests that the incidence curve becomes negatively sloped (g), the slope increases (g'), and/or the whole curve shifts to g'' as inequality declines.

From an operational perspective, to assess inclusiveness of growth, a country should take a number of actions: (i) establish the slope of the incidence curve based on the information of at least two sequential household surveys; (ii) if the slope is positive, suggesting that growth has not been inclusive, identify measures that could increase income and spending of the lowest deciles, while increasing the mean growth rate, that is, not at the expense of higher deciles; (iii) if the slope of the incidence curve is negative, suggesting growth has been inclusive, identify measures to increase the slope by making growth of consumption of lower deciles even faster, without hampering any other deciles; (iv) alternatively or in addition, find a measure to reduce inequality in the Lorenz curve coefficient in the next period that would shift the entire incidence curve up.

The growth incidence curve assesses how consumption at each percentile changes over time. The part of the curve above zero points at the deciles that benefit from growth, and the part below zero points at the deciles that lose because of growth. The part of the curve that is above its own mean points at the deciles of the population that benefit

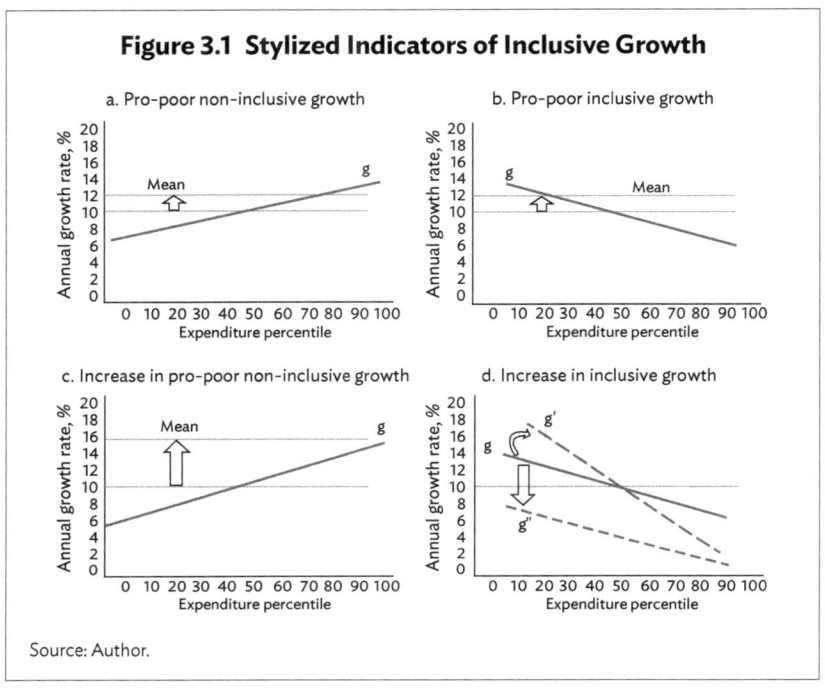

Figure 3.1 Stylized Indicators of Inclusive Growth

a. Pro-poor non-inclusive growth
b. Pro-poor inclusive growth
c. Increase in pro-poor non-inclusive growth
d. Increase in inclusive growth

Source: Author.

from growth relatively more than an average household. The part of the curve below the mean, but still above zero, points at the deciles that also benefit from growth but less than an average household. A negatively sloping growth incidence curve suggests that income or spending of the poorer deciles of the population grows faster than income or spending of the richer deciles. Because, in this case, the poorer groups of the population are catching up with the richer, a negatively sloping growth incidence curve can be viewed as one of the indications of inclusiveness of growth. Improvements in the degree of inclusiveness of growth would be signaled by the growth incidence curve changing the slope from positive to negative, and progress in poverty reduction would lead to the mean of the growth incidence curve and the curve itself moving up.

The linear form of the growth incidence curve is a simplification assumption taken to illustrate better its key properties. In reality, growth incidence curves usually have complex shapes, reflecting growth in consumption or expenditure at each decile of the population. The analysis for the purposes of public policies should be performed on carefully constructed growth incidence curves based on the two most recent household surveys.

3.1.2 Measures of Equality and Data Issues

Several statistical metrics allow evaluation of different aspects of inclusiveness in this narrow definition. The squared poverty gap[2] assesses inequality as it captures differences in the severity of poverty among the poor. The Watts index[3] is a distribution-sensitive poverty measure because it reflects the fact that an increase in income of a poor household reduces poverty more than a comparable increase in income of a rich household. The Gini coefficient shows a deviation of income per decile from the perfect equality line. The mean log deviation (MLD) index[4] is more sensitive to changes at the lower end of the income distribution. The decile ratio is the ratio of the average consumption of income of the richest 10% of the population divided by the average income of the poorest 10%. Finally, in dynamic terms the increase of income of the bottom deciles can be compared with the average income increase or the income increase in the highest deciles of the population. If the income of the bottom decile in the distribution tends to rise proportionately or faster than the average income, growth would be considered inclusive. Although the squared poverty gap and the Watts index take into account the distributional characteristics of growth indirectly, all other methods measure equality directly.

The quality of the analysis of growth inclusiveness depends on data availability and quality. Such analysis requires at least two household surveys based on a comparable methodology, as well as data on income and consumption by households, which is difficult to collect in many countries because most of the population is employed in the informal sector (Foster et al. 2013). The data may include outliers at both tails of the distribution. Although the outliers have been routinely corrected in national household surveys, they may lead to negative growth rates of the incidence curve for both tails of the distribution in some years (see below). Also, some parameters, such as the size of households and other

---

[2] The squared poverty gap index averages the squares of the poverty gaps relative to the poverty line. It takes into account not only the distance separating the poor from the poverty line (the poverty gap), but also the inequality among the poor because it places a higher weight on households further away from the poverty line.

[3] The Watts index is defined as a logarithm of the quotient of the poverty line and a geometric mean of an income standard applied to the censored distribution.

[4] An index of inequality is given by the mean across the population of the log of the overall mean divided by individual income.

sociodemographic variables (household head, education level, marital status, employment sector, place of residence, regional distribution, etc.), can vary from survey to survey, affecting poverty measures. Finally, the timing and the definitions of key variables, including the coverage of rural and urban areas, should be the same in different surveys to achieve consistent poverty estimates.

3.2 Growth and Poverty Reduction: The Case of Senegal

3.2.1 Income Inequality

Using Senegal as example, different statistical measures suggest that, although poverty declined, overall inequality remains broadly unchanged. In 1994–2011, the squared poverty gap shrank by more than half, suggesting that poverty among the poorest people became less severe (Table 3.1). The Watts index also dropped substantially, suggesting a relatively faster improvement in the situation of people with the lowest incomes. At the same time, both the Gini coefficient and the MLD index declined a bit in 1994–2005 and increased again in 2005–2011, suggesting no major changes in the overall level of inequality.

Table 3.1 Senegal: Inequality Indicators, 1994–2011

	Square Poverty Gap	Watts Index	Gini Coefficient	MLD Index
1994	9.09	0.27	41.44	0.30
2001	6.18	0.19	41.25	0.29
2005	4.67	0.15	39.19	0.26
2011	3.77	0.12	40.30	0.27

MLD = mean log deviation, an index of inequality given by the mean across the population of the log of the overall mean divided by individual income.

Note: Purchasing power parity (PPP)-based calculations. The Gini index and income shares may differ from the aggregates used for the national poverty lines. The Gini index based on Enquête Suivi de la Pauvreté au Sénégal (ESPS) 2005–2006 and ESPS 2011 household surveys was 39.2 in 2001, 38.1 in 2005, and 37.8 in 2011. All income/consumption shares by decile are based on estimated Lorenz curves. Households are ranked by income or consumption per person. Distributions are population (household size and sampling expansion factor) weighted.

Source: World Bank. PovcalNet. 2013.

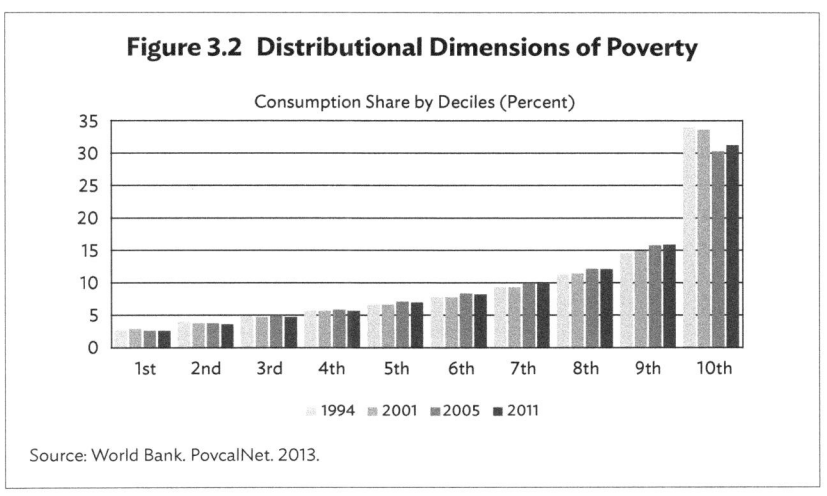

Figure 3.2 Distributional Dimensions of Poverty

Source: World Bank. PovcalNet. 2013.

A simple decile ratio also suggests that the level of inequality remained broadly unchanged. The ratio of consumption in the top decile relative to the bottom decile of the population did not change much between 1994 and 2011. It stood at 12.9 in 1994, declined to about 11.8 in both 2001 and 2005, but increased again to 12.5 in 2011, suggesting the richest consume on average 12–13 times more than the poorest. The richest two deciles of the population consume about half the goods and services in the country, roughly the same amount as the seven bottom deciles of the population (Figure 3.2), suggesting a substantial level of income disparity and inequality, although lower than the average for sub-Saharan Africa.

Growth in the level of consumption in 2006–2011 was positive but low and almost equal among different deciles of the population (Figure 3.3). No significant changes occurred in inequality during this period, because growth in consumption of the bottom deciles was only slightly higher than that of the top deciles. In contrast, in 2001–2005, the poorest fifth of the population experienced a decline in consumption, while all middle deciles registered significant growth in consumption, although the increase of the consumption level of the richest groups was insignificant.

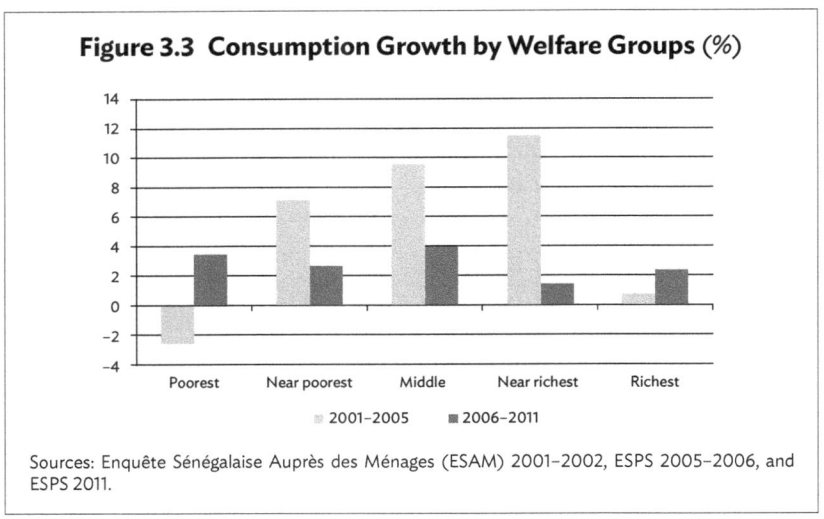

Figure 3.3 Consumption Growth by Welfare Groups (%)

Sources: Enquête Sénégalaise Auprès des Ménages (ESAM) 2001–2002, ESPS 2005–2006, and ESPS 2011.

3.2.2 Growth Incidence Curves

A dynamic measure of inclusiveness of growth can be derived from the growth incidence curve.

Although the growth incidence curves give somewhat conflicting signals on distributional shifts in Senegal, they seem to confirm that growth benefited most people in the middle of the income distribution. Between 2001 and 2005 (Figure 3.4), consumption increased on average because the mean of the growth incidence curve is above zero, driven by the middle of the distribution (from the 3rd to the 8th deciles). The growth incidence curve is positively sloped, suggesting some increase in inequality during this period. Between 2005 and 2011, the mean of the growth incidence curve is above zero; but the curve is broadly flat, suggesting no clear trend in changes in inequality. On average, for 2001–2011, a clear increase in mean consumption confirms the decline in poverty, as the middle class improved their relative position. However, for 2001–2011 as a whole, the growth incidence curve has a slightly positive slope, which may point to some worsening of inclusiveness. This trend may not be statistically significant, indicating no substantial distributional changes during this period other than the improvement in the relative position of the middle class. This overall result, however, masks significant differences in growth inclusiveness between urban and rural areas.

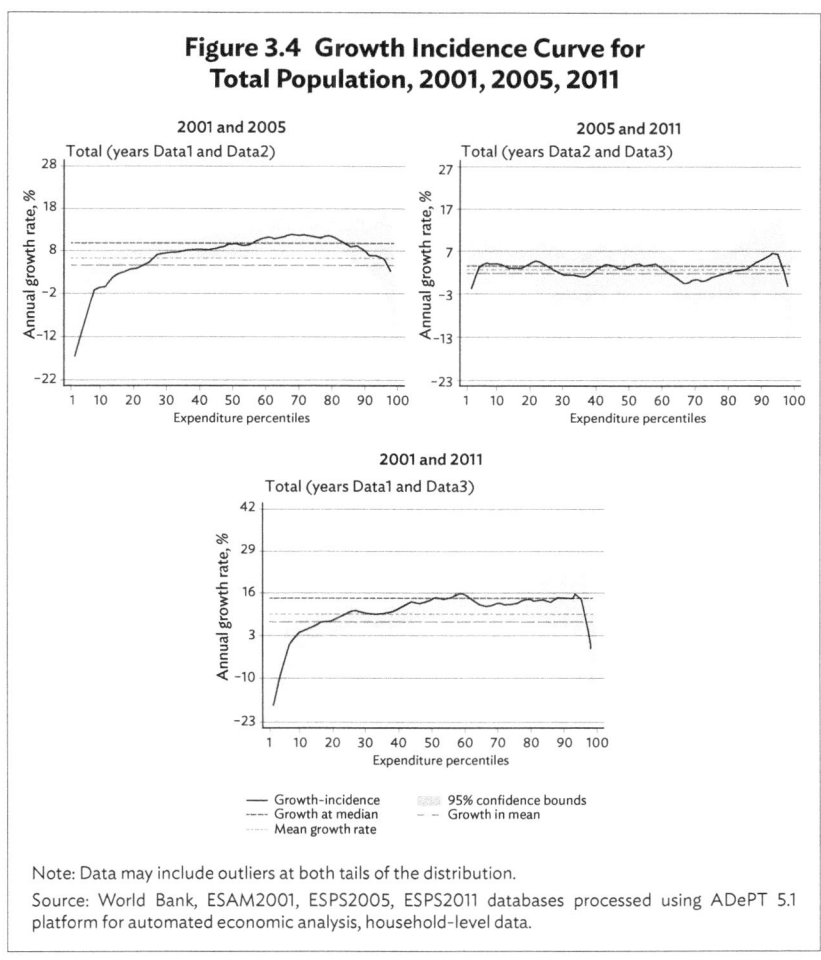

Figure 3.4 Growth Incidence Curve for Total Population, 2001, 2005, 2011

Note: Data may include outliers at both tails of the distribution.
Source: World Bank, ESAM2001, ESPS2005, ESPS2011 databases processed using ADePT 5.1 platform for automated economic analysis, household-level data.

In urban areas, people in the middle of the distribution seem to have benefited the most from growth. Between 2001 and 2005, the growth incidence curve for urban areas is substantially above the mean for the whole distribution other than the top decile; but it slopes down a little, suggesting somewhat reduced disparity between the rich and the poor (Figure 3.5). For 2005–2011, however, the incidence curve hovers around zero and is upward sloping, pointing to some worsening of inclusiveness. For 2001–2011 overall, again there is no clear trend, although growth of consumption of the middle decile was very strong. Although the

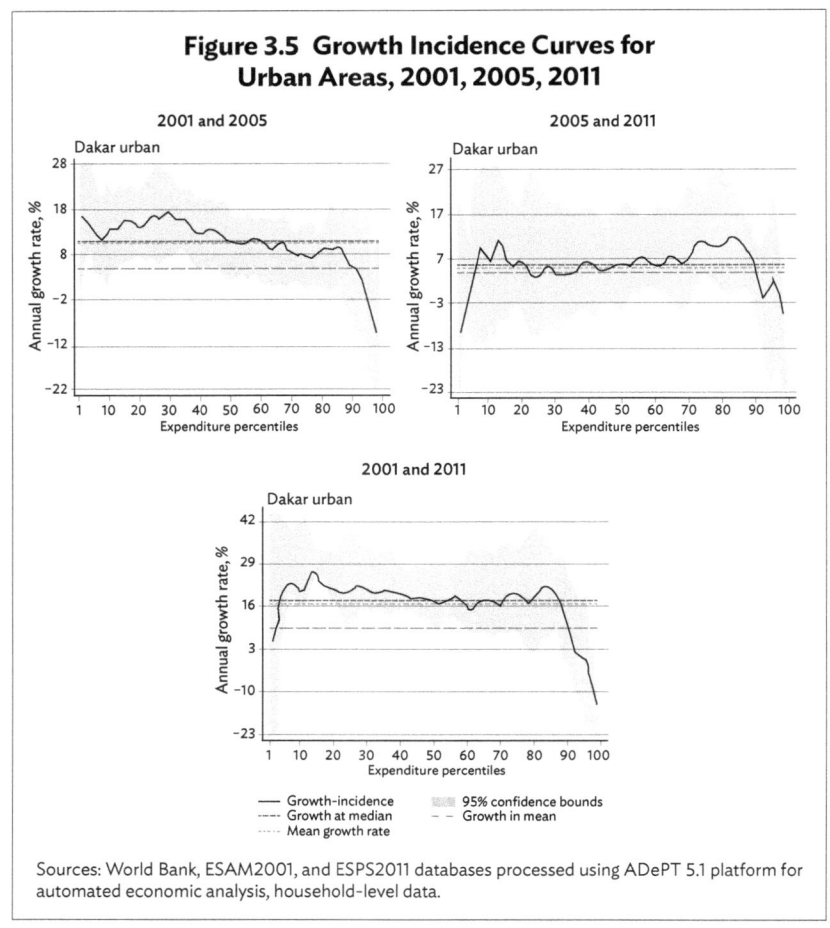

Figure 3.5 Growth Incidence Curves for Urban Areas, 2001, 2005, 2011

Sources: World Bank, ESAM2001, and ESPS2011 databases processed using ADePT 5.1 platform for automated economic analysis, household-level data.

incidence curve is above zero it looks broadly flat, pointing to unchanged inclusiveness.

In rural areas, inclusiveness of growth may have worsened, and the improvement of the middle class was not very pronounced. Between 2001 and 2005, a clear trend of growing inequality is seen in rural areas because the incidence curve is positively sloped and actually below zero for the first two deciles of the population (Figure 3.6). Again, there is no clear trend in 2005–2011, neither in terms of inclusiveness (the incidence curve is broadly flat) nor in terms of poverty reduction (the mean is about zero). Overall, in 2001–2011, the incidence curve is

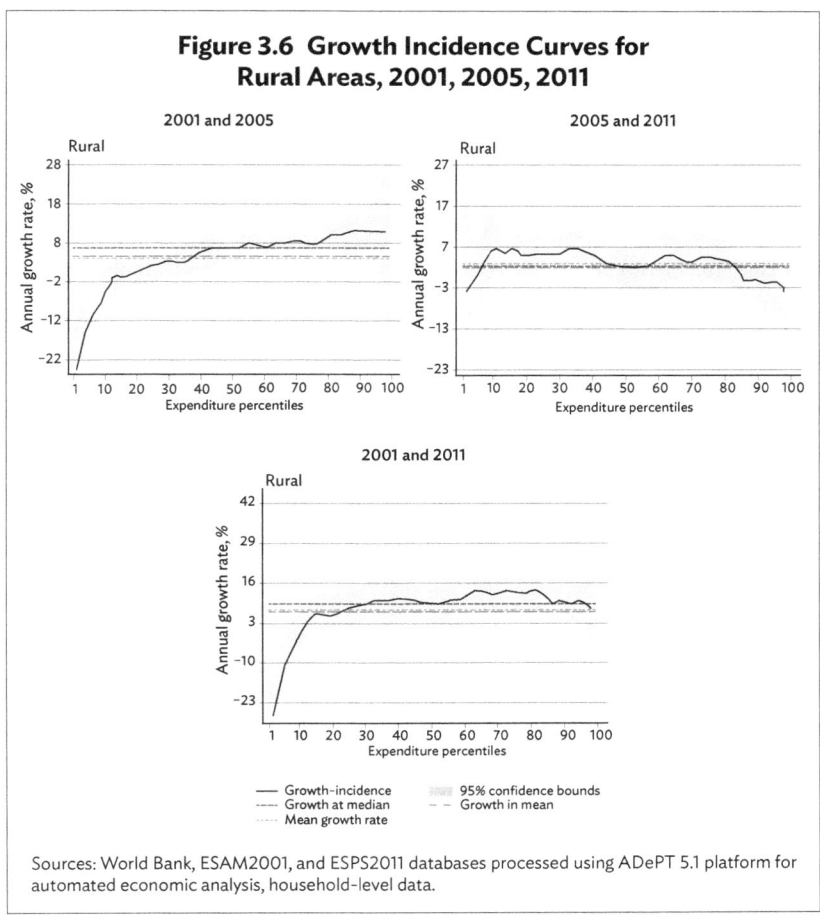

Figure 3.6 Growth Incidence Curves for Rural Areas, 2001, 2005, 2011

Sources: World Bank, ESAM2001, and ESPS2011 databases processed using ADePT 5.1 platform for automated economic analysis, household-level data.

positively sloped at low deciles but is broadly flat in the middle, with the growth rate in the lower deciles substantially lower than growth in the median and highest deciles. This may point to an increasing gap between the poor and the rich in some rural areas.

The degree of inclusiveness of growth in rural areas has an important impact on the degree of inclusiveness of growth in Senegal as a whole. The difference between the median growth rates of spending by households in rural areas is closer to the mean growth rate than in urban areas. This may suggest that the overall change in the distribution of households' consumption is heavily influenced by the changes in the distribution in rural areas and that it is skewed to the right, because most households are relatively poorer than the mean household in the country. On the contrary, in urban areas, the impact of changes in growth rates of consumption of relatively rich households on the overall inclusiveness of growth is less significant, because the distribution in urban areas is skewed to the left—most households are relatively richer than the mean household in the country.

Although available indicators sometimes give conflicting signals on distributional shifts, the statistical analysis of the distributional characteristics of growth suggests the following: (i) poverty in Senegal has fallen in the last 2 decades, although poverty reduction has slowed in recent years; (ii) although available indicators sometimes give conflicting signals on distributional shifts, growth seems to have benefited most people in the middle of the income distribution; (iii) the middle class has benefited from growth, mainly in urban areas, while both the poorest and the richest have lost ground; (iv) growth in rural areas has been less inclusive than in urban areas.

The overall poverty level is relatively lower in Senegal than in most other sub-Saharan African (SSA) countries. At the revised international poverty line, which usually differs somewhat from the national poverty line, Senegal is in the top quarter of SSA countries for which data are available (Figure 3.7). At the $1.25 a day poverty line (in 2005 prices), Senegal in 2011 was comparable to Ethiopia and Ghana but was behind other countries in the region such as Gabon, Cameroon, and Côte d'Ivoire.[5]

The 2011 household survey in Senegal indicated that poverty remains high, although it declined in the most recent 2 decades. More than 6 million people were living on a household income below the national poverty line. In 1994–2001, gross domestic product (GDP) growth in Senegal was about 5% a year; the poverty rate fell significantly, from 68% in 1994/1995 to 55% in 2001/2002. In 2002–2005, GDP growth reached 4.7%, allowing the poverty rate to decline further to about 48.5%. However, since 2005–2006, repeated shocks have contributed to reducing per capita income growth to little more than the rate of population growth. The 2011 household survey suggests that in the past 5 years poverty incidence has declined by only 1.8 percentage points to 46.7%.

---

[5] Most comparisons in this chapter are based on the data from household surveys. The most recent survey for Senegal was conducted in 2011, whereas for most SSA countries the latest surveys were published in 2005–2010.

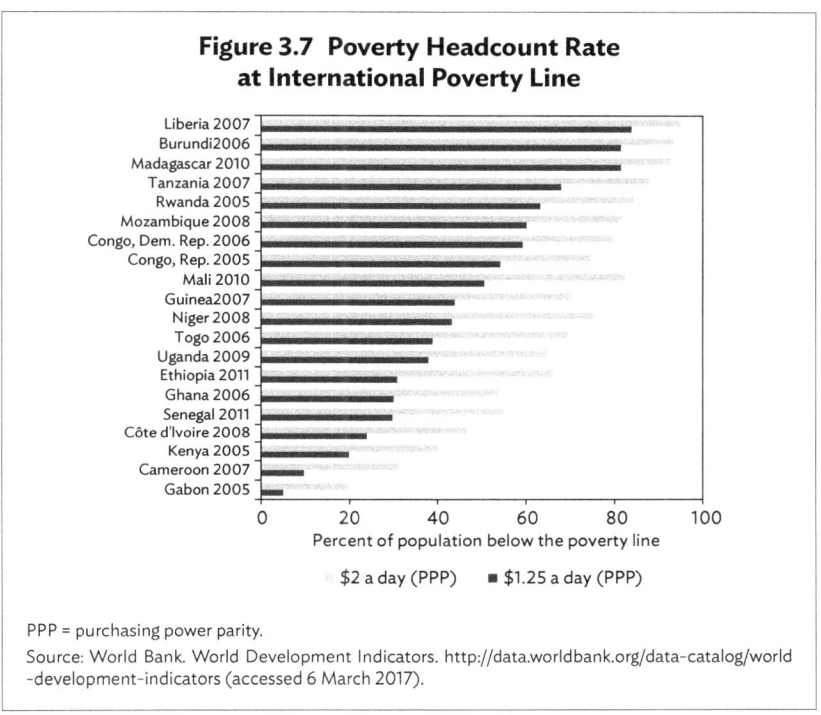

Figure 3.7 Poverty Headcount Rate at International Poverty Line

PPP = purchasing power parity.
Source: World Bank. World Development Indicators. http://data.worldbank.org/data-catalog/world-development-indicators (accessed 6 March 2017).

3.2.3 Poverty and Inequality Estimates

This chapter uses both national and international estimates of poverty and inequality in Senegal. The distributional and poverty-related data are drawn from nationally representative household surveys published by the National Statistical and Demographic Agency of Senegal (Agence Nationale de la Statistique et de la Démographie). However, for international comparisons, the chapter uses the data published by the World Bank, including in PovcalNet (World Bank, PovcalNet), an interactive computational tool that allows calculating poverty measures comparable among countries. In PovcalNet, all poverty rates are based on the international poverty line of $1.25 per day in 2005 purchasing power parity (PPP) at 2005 prices, which is different from the poverty line in Senegal. Therefore, the poverty rate calculated based on this poverty line is not directly comparable with the national poverty rate. Moreover, because PovcalNet uses grouped data for each income group, there might be differences from the national data in the Gini index, poverty headcount ratios, consumption by decile of population, and other poverty indicators.[6]

Growth is usually defined as pro-poor if it reduces poverty. Several metrics are used to measure the change in poverty: the change in the share of population living below the poverty line, monthly per capita consumption, income, or expenditure; and the change in the poverty gap. The poverty line is the minimum level of income deemed adequate for meeting basic consumption needs in a given country, and it differs from country to country. For international comparison, two poverty lines are usually used: daily income of $1.25 and $2 at 2005 PPP. The poverty gap is the mean distance from the poverty line (counting the non-poor as having zero shortfall), expressed as a percentage of the poverty line. This measure reflects the depth of poverty and its incidence.

The recent prolonged episode of growth has led to a significant reduction in poverty. Based on several household surveys,[7] poverty in Senegal—defined as the share of people below the national poverty line—declined from 55.2% in 2001 to 46.7% in 2011 (Table 3.2). The poverty gap declined from 17.2 to 14.5; other metrics also point to a continued trend in the reduction in poverty, although the pace of improvement declined during the second half of the decade and may not be statistically significant between 2006 and 2011.

Table 3.2 Senegal: Poverty Indicators, 1994–2011

	2001	2005	2011
Poverty incidence	55.2	48.3	46.7
Confidence interval (95%)	52.9–57.5	46.1–50.6	44.1–49.3
Poverty gap	17.3	15.5	14.5

Source: Agence Nationale de la Statistique et de la Démographie. 2012. www.ansd.sn

Progress achieved in poverty reduction has been more pronounced in Senegal than in some regional peers. In 1994–2005, the

---

[6] Methodological differences between national and internationally comparable poverty-related estimates are documented and discussed in detail on the World Bank PovcalNet site at http://iresearch.worldbank.org/PovcalNet

[7] Based on data from income, expenditure, household, and budgetary surveys conducted by Senegal's authorities in 1991–2011 and processed by the World Bank through PovcalNet, an online poverty calculation tool (http://iresearch.worldbank.org/PovCalNet).

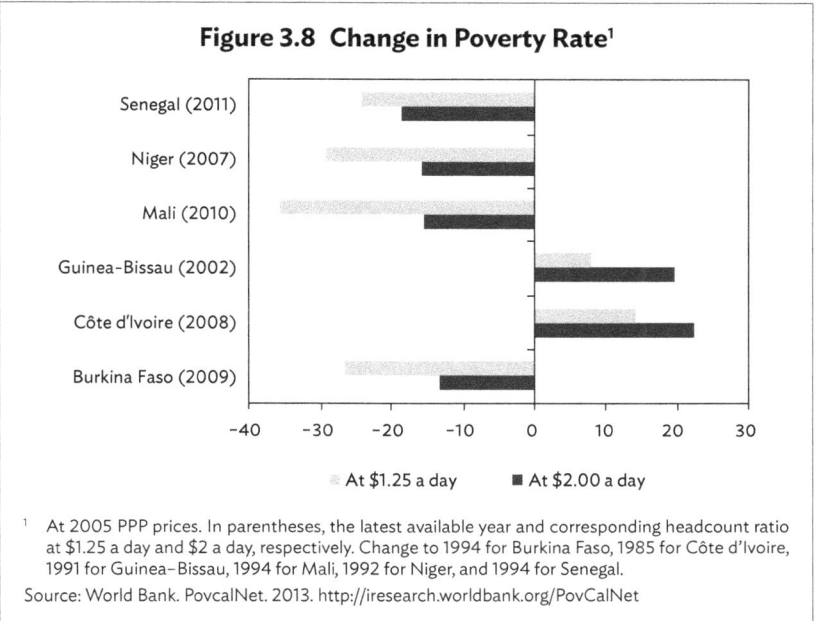

Figure 3.8 Change in Poverty Rate[1]

[1] At 2005 PPP prices. In parentheses, the latest available year and corresponding headcount ratio at $1.25 a day and $2 a day, respectively. Change to 1994 for Burkina Faso, 1985 for Côte d'Ivoire, 1991 for Guinea–Bissau, 1994 for Mali, 1992 for Niger, and 1994 for Senegal.
Source: World Bank. PovcalNet. 2013. http://iresearch.worldbank.org/PovCalNet

share of population living on less than $1.25 a day declined by about 20 percentage points, and for people living on less than $2 a day by about 19 percentage points (Figure 3.8). By the latter metric, which may be more appropriate for Senegal given its per capita income, Senegal's poverty dropped faster than in other West African Economic and Monetary Union (WAEMU) countries (15 percentage points) in approximately the same period. The dynamics of poverty reduction in the region have been significantly affected by an increase in poverty in Guinea–Bissau and Côte d'Ivoire during political crises in these countries.

The level of poverty also differs significantly among different regions of Senegal. In 2011, for example, the poverty incidence in the poorest regions (Kolda, Fatick, and Ziguinchor) was 67%–73%, whereas it was only 26% in Dakar.

This outcome reflects higher growth and a higher sensitivity to growth of poverty reduction in Senegal. Unlike a number of countries in the WAEMU, particularly those affected by internal conflicts or crises (e.g., Guinea–Bissau and Côte d'Ivoire in the 2000s), real per capita GDP growth in Senegal was always positive in 1995–2011 and in some years quite significant (Figure 3.9a). In addition, the elasticity of poverty

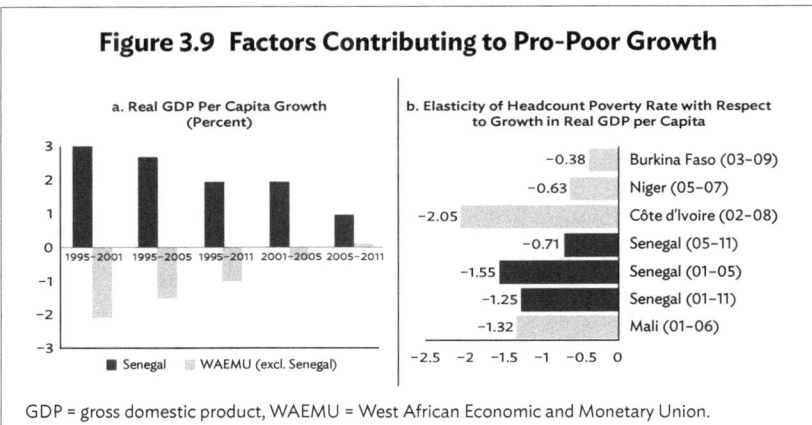

Figure 3.9 Factors Contributing to Pro-Poor Growth

GDP = gross domestic product, WAEMU = West African Economic and Monetary Union.
Sources: World Bank. World Development Indicators; International Monetary Fund (IMF). World Economic Outlook; Agence Nationale de la Statistique et de la Démographie; and IMF staff estimates.

reduction to per capita income growth has been significant in Senegal in regional comparisons. In 2001–2011, this elasticity was about –1.3 in Senegal, above that of some other fast-growing WAEMU countries (e.g., Burkina Faso) (Figure 3.9b).

Although growth seems to have been a major factor behind the reduction of poverty, this conclusion should be treated with caution. First, an increase in real GDP per capita does not necessarily imply a reduction of poverty and requires supplementary information on the distribution of this additional income among different groups of the population. If the initial distribution of income is highly unequal, the impact of growth on poverty may not be significant. In an extreme case, if all benefits of higher growth were captured by the wealthiest part of the population, the impact of growth on poverty reduction may be negative. Second, the elasticity of poverty reduction to growth in per capita income depends on the shape of income or consumption distribution and on the position of the poverty line with respect to this distribution. Normally, the closer the poverty line is to the median of the distribution, the higher will be the elasticity of the poverty rate to real per capita growth. Finally, more regular household surveys based on a similar methodology are needed to assess the evolution of growth inclusiveness through time. This impact assessment would be better served by the use of more advanced econometric techniques, which is difficult in the absence of high-frequency poverty data sets.

3.3 Policies to Increase Growth Inclusiveness: Lessons for Asia

Based on the theoretical consideration and the case study discussed above, the following lessons can be drawn on how to increase growth inclusiveness in Asia, in particular in low- and middle-income countries.

First, sustained overall economic growth is a precondition for poverty reduction and inclusiveness. A number of studies confirm that sustained growth is a key factor in enhancing inclusiveness. Kraay (2004) showed that in developing countries, growth of average income explains 70% of the variation in poverty reduction in the short run. Berg and Ostry (2011) argued that longer growth spells are robustly associated with more equality in the income distribution. Lopez and Servén (2006) suggested that for a given inequality level, the poorer the country the more important is the growth component in explaining poverty reduction. Affandi and Peiris (2012) showed that growth is in general pro-poor, with growth leading to significant declines in poverty across economies and time periods. Specifically, a 1% increase in real per capita income leads to a decline of about 2% in the poverty headcount ratio. Therefore, any successful pro-poor growth strategy should have at its core measures to achieve sustained and rapid economic growth. Senegal's experience is consistent with this cross-country evidence.

Second, special attention should be given to the distributional dimension of growth. An increase in inequality may offset and even exceed the beneficial impact on poverty reduction of the same increase in income (Affandi and Peiris 2012). According to recent estimates, about two-thirds of poverty reduction within a country comes from growth, and greater equality contributes the other third. A 1% increase in incomes in the most unequal countries produces a mere 0.6% reduction in poverty, while in the most equal countries it yields a 4.3% cut (Ravallion 2013). Because inclusiveness of growth is associated with a number of macroeconomic outcomes and policies, it is important to analyze growth and inclusiveness simultaneously. Increased inequality may dampen growth, but at the same time poorly designed measures to increase inclusiveness could undermine growth. For instance, increasing farm productivity and broadening rural job opportunities is important in addressing rural poverty. In the long run, attention to inclusiveness can bring significant benefits for growth.

Third, well-designed public policies are critical for promoting growth inclusiveness. The Poverty and Social Impact Analysis for Asian countries regularly performed by the International Monetary Fund in cooperation with the World Bank is a useful tool. It suggests that poorer households could be protected against food and fuel price increases in the short term at a lower budgetary cost and more effectively by redirecting resources to better-targeted measures: poor groups can be targeted through measures such as school lunches and public works programs and better-targeted tariffs for small quantities of electricity to protect some of the urban poor. In the medium term, a well-targeted and conditional cash transfer system is the best option for assistance for the poorest.

Fourth, strong growth in agriculture is probably the single most important factor in improving inclusiveness of growth. The strong performance of agriculture in 2008–2010 helps explain the improvement in consumption levels of the poor during this period in spite of low overall GDP growth.

Fifth, structural policies promoting employment and productivity increases, in particular in agriculture, could also help increase inclusiveness. According to the World Bank (2010), several policies have been successful in increasing the agricultural earnings of the poor in other low-income countries. These policies could be applicable in Asia. They include improving market access and lowering transaction costs; strengthening property rights for land; creating an incentive framework that benefits all farmers; expanding the technology available to smallholder producers; and helping poorer and smaller producers handle risk. To expand nonagricultural and urban employment opportunities for poor households, other SSA countries took steps to improve the investment climate; expand access to secondary and girls' education; design labor market regulations to create attractive employment opportunities; and increase access to infrastructure, especially roads and electricity.

Sixth, inclusive institutions have also been found important for growth inclusiveness. Acemoglu and Robinson (2012) argued that rich countries are rich by virtue of having inclusive institutions, that is, economic and political institutions that include the large majority of the population in the political and economic community. An initial set of inclusive economic institutions would include secure property rights, rule of law, public services, and freedom to contract. The role of the state would be to impose law and order, enforce contracts, and prevent theft and fraud. When the state fails to provide such a set of institutions, growth becomes extractive.

Seventh, coherent labor market policies are also needed for increasing inclusiveness. The challenges of growth, job creation, and inclusion are closely linked, because creating productive employment opportunities throughout the economy is an important way to generate inclusive growth (IMF 2013). In low-income countries, creation of employment opportunities and increasing productivity in rural areas, in particular in agriculture, would prompt higher consumption growth among poorer households. For example, the stronger per capita consumption growth observed in Cameroon and Uganda at the poorest levels seems to relate to high agricultural employment growth (IMF 2011). By contrast, rural agricultural employment fell in Mozambique and Zambia where the poorest experienced weaker or negative per capita consumption growth.

Finally, deepening the finance sector through policies that give better access to the poor for financial services would increase inclusiveness. A number of studies found that financial development generally increases incomes of the poorest households (Claessens 2005), whereas unequal access to financial markets can reduce incomes by impeding investments in human and physical capital. These barriers are widespread in low-income countries, where most people lack access to the formal financial system. At the same time, microfinance and other rural finance and expanding credit information sharing could significantly expand credit availability.

References

Acemoglu, D., and J. Robinson. 2012. *Why Nations Fail: The Origins of Power, Prosperity, and Poverty*. New York, NY: Crown Business.

Affandi, Y., and S. Peiris. 2012. Building Inclusive Growth in the Philippines. IMF Country Report 12/50. Washington, DC: International Monetary Fund.

Agence Nationale de la Statistique et de la Démographie (ANSD). 2011. *Situation Economique et Sociale du Sénégal*. Décembre. Dakar: ANSD.

Agence Nationale de la Statistique et de la Démographie. www.ansd.sn.

Arze del Granado, J. F., and I. Adenauer. 2011. Burkina Faso—Policies to Protect the Poor from the Impact of Food and Energy Price Increases. IMF Working Paper 11/202. Washington, DC: International Monetary Fund.

Azam, J., M. Dia, C. Tsimpo, and Q. Wodon. 2007. Has Growth in Senegal after the 1994 Devaluation Been Pro-Poor? In Growth and Poverty Reduction: Case Studies from West Africa. World Bank Working Paper 79: 45–67. Washington, DC: The World Bank.

Berg, A., and J. Ostry. 2011. Inequality and Unsustainable Growth: Two Sides of the Same Coin? IMF Staff Discussion Note SDN/11/08. 8 April. Washington, DC: International Monetary Fund.

Chandy L., N. Ledlie, and V. Penciakova. 2013. The Final Countdown: Prospects for Ending Extreme Poverty by 2030. Brookings Institution Policy Paper 2013-04. Washington, DC: Brookings Institution.

Claessens, S. 2005. Access to Financial Services: A Review of the Issues and Public Policy Objectives. Policy Research Working Paper 3589. Washington, DC: The World Bank.

David, A., and M. Petri. 2013. Inclusive Growth and the Incidence of Fiscal Policy in Mauritius—Much Progress, but More Could Be Done. IMF Working Paper 13/116. Washington, DC: International Monetary Fund.

Economist. 2013. Towards the End of Poverty. 1 June.

Enquête Suivi de la Pauvreté au Sénégal (ESPS)-II 2010–2011. 2012. Dakar: Agence Nationale de la Statistique et de la Démographie.

Foster, J., S. Seth, M. Lokshin, and Z. Sajaia. 2013. *A Unified Approach to Measuring Poverty and Inequality: Theory and Practice*. Washington, DC: The World Bank.

Garcia, M., and C. Moore. 2012. *The Cash Dividend: The Rise of Cash Transfer Programs in Sub-Saharan Africa*. Washington, DC: The World Bank.

Gastwirth, J. 1971. A General Definition of the Lorenz Curve. *Econometrica* 39(6): 1037–1039.

Ianchovichina, E., and S. Gable. 2012. What is Inclusive Growth? In *Commodity Price Volatility and Inclusive Growth in Low Income Countries,* edited by Arezki et al. Washington, DC: International Monetary Fund.

International Labor Organization (ILO). 2012. *Understanding Deficits of Productive Employment and Setting Targets: A Methodological Guide.* Geneva, Switzerland: International Labor Organization.

International Monetary Fund (IMF). 2008. Senegal: Selected Issues: Policies to Protect the Poor from Rising Energy and Prices in Senegal. IMF Country Report 2008/221. Washington, DC: International Monetary Fund.

———. 2011. How Inclusive Has Africa's Recent High-Growth Episode Been? Regional Economic Outlook: Sub-Saharan Africa. October. Washington, DC: International Monetary Fund.

———. 2013. Jobs and Growth: Analytical and Operational Considerations for the Fund. Washington, DC: International Monetary Fund.

Kraay, A. 2004. When Is Growth Pro-Poor? Cross-Country Evidence. IMF Working Paper 2004/12. Washington, DC: International Monetary Fund.

Lopez, H., and L. Servén. 2006. A Normal Relationship? Poverty, Growth, and Inequality. Policy Research Working Paper 3814. Washington, DC: The World Bank.

McKinsey & Company. 2012. *Africa at Work: Job Creation and Inclusive Growth.* New York, NY and London: McKinsey Global Institute.

Ravallion, M. 2013. How Long Will It Take to Lift One Billion People Out of Poverty? World Bank Policy Research Working Paper 6325. Washington, DC: The World Bank.

———. 2012. Pro-Poor Growth: A Primer. www.wds.worldbank.org

Ravallion, M., and S. Chen. 2003. Measuring Pro-Poor Growth. *Economics Letters* (78): 93–99.

World Bank. 2013. Senegal: Social Safety Net Assessment. 10 July. Washington, DC: The World Bank.

———. 2010. *Pro-Poor Growth in the 1990s: Lessons and Insights from 14 Countries.* Washington, DC: The World Bank.

———. 2007. Senegal: Looking for Work: The Road to Prosperity. Country Economic Memorandum. Washington, DC: The World Bank.

———. PovcalNet. http://iresearch.worldbank.org/PovcalNet/home.aspx

4

Different Faces of Inequality across Asia: Decomposition of Income Gaps across Demographic Groups

Vladimir Hlasny

4.1 Motivation

Household income surveys have traditionally been used to evaluate income inequality, but the focus was limited to an aggregate measure of inequality or decomposition of inequality around the mean of the income distribution. Less is known about the distribution of incomes at lower and upper ends of countries' income distributions even in industrialized nations. Our knowledge is sparser yet in regard to developing countries. At the same time, understanding the income differentials among the bottom and top income households is important in all countries, because their influence on estimates of overall inequality, poverty, and polarization is substantial. This is particularly important today given the calls for action in countries worldwide in response to inequality, social injustice, and polarization of societies. Evidence in upper- and middle-income countries around the world shows that the aggregate-income share of top-income households has risen significantly in recent years, that the middle class may be shrinking, and that low-income households have seen stagnation or deterioration in their living standards.

In the Asia and the Pacific region including India, economic inequality has been found to be growing (UNESCAP 2015), and some dimensions including rural–urban inequality are high and persistent (Imai and Malaeb 2016). Economic inequality is not limited to inequality in outcomes, but more worryingly extends to inequality in opportunities for proper nutrition, health, education, other human development, and access to public resources and markets. These inequalities jointly contribute to the observed inequality in economic outcomes, including that in income, consumption, wealth, life expectancy, and life satisfaction. This is of particular concern in developing economes in Asia, where disadvantaged households are held in a perpetual deprivation trap by fragmented markets, lack of infrastructure, inapt or corrupt local governments, and households' lack of resources and information necessary for upward mobility.

In the People's Republic of China (PRC), economic growth and integration into the world economy through the opening of trade and foreign direct investment have increased inequality. The role of economic privatization and market capitalization has become more important in driving inequality over time, while that of geographic and demographic factors has diminished (Wan 2004; Wan and Zhou 2004; Wan, Lu, and Zhao 2007). Structural differences between regions have been found to persist, but regional inequality fell on account of improvements in factor mobility (Heshmati 2004). An important facet of inequality in the PRC involves the ethnicity and residence registration (*hukou*) dimensions. Chinese non-Han ethnic groups have traditionally fared worse than the Han, due to poor backgrounds, limited opportunities, and discrimination. Residents with agricultural *hukou* have been denied education, employment, and residence opportunities outside of their region of registration. In a bid to preempt domestic instability and separatism, and to integrate regional factor markets, the Central PRC government has in recent years aimed to remove *hukou*-based restrictions and to promote the welfare of ethnic minorities (Jeong and Hlasny 2016), but the efforts have been weak.

In the Russian Federation, cross-region inequality had been rising until the 1990s due to natural and structural differences and shocks (Heshmati 2004), but recent evidence points to a decrease in inequality since then on account of local economic growth (Guriev and Vakulenko 2012). Nevertheless, the level of inter-regional inequality remains high (Mahler 2011; also refer to studies evaluated by Gluschenko 2010, 2011), suggesting that opportunities for labor mobility are improving only slowly, and that inadequate regional housing options, transportation infrastructure and social policy may play a role in it (Gluschenko 2010). These findings have implications for regional as well as national socio-economic policy.

In India, substantial inequality between urban and rural areas was identified as driving inter-regional disparities and their growth over time (Sachs et al. 2002; Heshmati 2004; Chamarbagwala 2010). Urban districts are richer and growing faster on account of strong performance of services and knowledge-intensive industries there, and inflow of skills and capital (Brar et al. 2014). Northern and urban districts also exhibit lower inequality in educational opportunities (Asadullah and Yalonetzky 2012). Trade expansion and liberalization of the services sector have had some effect on inequality growth, in part through their effect on inequality in returns to education (Kijima 2006), but employment reallocations for other reasons have played a greater role (Mehta and Hasan 2012).

In Japan; the Republic of Korea; and Taipei,China, much lower degrees of income inequality were identified, but were found to be systematic and persistent (Kang and Yun 2008; Higashikata 2013). One dimension involves disparity between incomes of regular and irregular workers (Sato and Imai 2011; Tarohmaru 2014; Hlasny 2016b). In the Republic of Korea, increases in inequality since the 1990s were blamed on inequality in returns to skills (Kang and Yun 2008; Nahm 2008; Chang and England 2011), on demographic change—particularly aging (Lee, Kim, and Cin 2013), and on unionization (studies cited by Ghosh and Lee 2016). In Japan it was observed that the return to skills stagnated or fell for lower- and middle-income workers while it rose for high-income male workers, contributing to gender gaps (Yokoyama, Kodama, and Higuchi 2016). In both countries, structural factors in the economy—including labor market reforms and skill-biased technological change—effectively led to relegation of disadvantaged workers to lower quality industries and jobs (Kang and Yun 2008; Park and Mah 2011). In Taipei,China, gender gaps are low, while rural–urban and educational gaps are responsible for much of inequality (Chang 2012; Chen 2014).

Persistent and systematic inequality is not only a fairness and social-justice concern but also a problem for countries' development. High inequality hampers economic growth and increases government costs for ensuring minimum levels of security (ECA, ILO, UNCTAD, UNDESA, and UNICEF 2012). Above a certain threshold, inequality undermines sustainable growth and poverty alleviation efforts (Chambers and Krause 2010; Berg and Ostry 2011). Between-group inequality is particularly worrying as it may yield intergenerational transmission of inequality, poverty traps for entire social groups, polarization, social tension, and political instability (Stewart and Langer 2007; Kabeer 2010; UNDP 2013). All these factors may yield social and political instability as well as outbreaks of conflict, as the events in the Middle East in 2011–2013, and recently in Latin America show.

Proper measurement, understanding, and eradication of inter-group inequalities are thus priorities for regional organizations and policy makers. However, existing knowledge is limited and inconclusive with respect to inter-group comparisons for vulnerable demographic groups such as rural or uneducated households. Hence, this paper contributes to the empirical literature on developing economies worldwide and particularly in Asia by measuring inter-group inequalities within six economies, decomposing the inequalities by source, and evaluating trends in the inequalities and their sources over time. Inequalities between different geographic areas and demographic groups are measured to estimate the effect of household endowments on overall inequality.

4.2 Contributions of this Study

Inter-group inequality is thought to be driven by differences in households' human capital, demographic characteristics, and geographic access to markets. Differences in households' endowments such as human capital, demographic characteristics, geographic location, and residence are evaluated as main determinants explaining the income differentials between social groups. In particular, income differentials across rural/urban areas, disadvantaged/advantaged administrative regions, and households with less/more educated, non-employed/employed, and female/male heads are evaluated using 10 Asian household income surveys included in the Luxembourg Income Study database. The 10 surveys are for six middle- and high-income economies from across Asia that were harmonized and made available by Luxembourg Income Study (LIS).

The six economies evaluated in this study differ significantly in the levels of income as well as in the within-economy degree and form of inequality in incomes. India and the PRC have the lowest distribution of incomes, whose mean and median are less than one-tenth of the levels in the highest-income economy in the sample, Japan (Table 4.1). The Republic of Korea's distribution of income is near Japan's level, while Taipei,China is midway between the levels in the PRC and India, and those in Japan. The Russian Federation has been making fast progress from income levels just twice as high as the PRC, to near those of Taipei,China.

Inequality gauged by the Gini index shows that Japan, the Republic of Korea, and Taipei,China have modest inequality by world standards, at or below the world mean of national Ginis. The Russian Federation's Gini is 5 percentage points higher, or approximately one standard deviation above the world mean. Finally, the PRC and India have Ginis 20 percentage points above the levels in Japan and Taipei,China, in the high end of the worldwide distribution of Ginis.[1] Aggregate income shares held by population quintiles in each economy exhibits equivalent trends (Tables A4.1 and A4.2).

---

[1] In fact, the Ginis for the PRC and India are just short of estimates of the Gini in middle- and high-income countries worldwide, of 54.6 using LIS data, and that is before these Ginis are corrected for various sampling and measurement issues that could lead to further adjustments upward by 3–7 percentage points (Hlasny and Verme 2015; Hlasny 2016a).

Table 4.1 Quantile Decomposition for the PRC 2002, India 2004, Japan 2008, and Republic of Korea 2006 by Rural/Urban Residence

		PRC 02			India 04		
		10th pctile	50th pctile	90th pctile	10th pctile	50th pctile	90th pctile
	Treatment group	5.858***	6.915***	7.833***	5.845***	6.847***	8.015***
		(0.018)	(0.009)	(0.013)	(0.010)	(0.006)	(0.010)
	Control group	7.650***	8.381***	9.106***	6.613***	7.652***	8.729***
		(0.011)	(0.008)	(0.013)	(0.011)	(0.009)	(0.013)
	Overall Gap	−1.792***	−1.466***	−1.274***	−0.768***	−0.805***	−0.714***
		(0.021)	(0.012)	(0.018)	(0.015)	(0.011)	(0.016)
	Endowment	0.200***	0.004	−0.121***	−0.286***	−0.343***	−0.580***
		(0.046)	(0.023)	(0.032)	(0.017)	(0.010)	(0.017)
	Returns	−1.992***	−1.470***	−1.152***	−0.482***	−0.462***	−0.135***
		(0.050)	(0.025)	(0.036)	(0.022)	(0.013)	(0.021)
Endowment Effects (Explained)	Characteristics of hhd. head	0.158***	0.049***	−0.033*	0.009***	0.013***	0.022***
		(0.029)	(0.014)	(0.020)	(0.002)	(0.002)	(0.003)
	Head education	−0.013	−0.032**	0.014	−0.045***	−0.123***	−0.330***
		(0.026)	(0.013)	(0.018)	(0.008)	(0.005)	(0.010)
	Head employment	0.080***	0.055***	0.013	−0.180***	−0.152***	−0.153***
		(0.022)	(0.011)	(0.015)	(0.011)	(0.006)	(0.010)
	Household composition	0.013	−0.018*	−0.029**	−0.016***	−0.010***	−0.000
		(0.019)	(0.009)	(0.013)	(0.005)	(0.003)	(0.004)
	Geographic location	−0.040***	−0.051***	−0.086***	−0.053***	−0.071***	−0.119***
		(0.009)	(0.005)	(0.007)	(0.011)	(0.006)	(0.011)
Returns Effects (Unexplained)	Characteristics of hhd. head	0.250	−0.397	−0.366	0.002	0.034	0.022
		(0.631)	(0.335)	(0.498)	(0.311)	(0.209)	(0.319)
	Head education	0.184**	0.221***	0.451***	−0.175***	−0.235***	0.166***
		(0.086)	(0.044)	(0.063)	(0.029)	(0.020)	(0.030)
	Head employment	−0.250***	−0.080**	−0.059	0.160***	0.094***	0.034
		(0.068)	(0.036)	(0.052)	(0.040)	(0.026)	(0.040)
	Household composition	0.127	0.016	−0.079	0.179*	0.144**	0.346***
		(0.106)	(0.058)	(0.087)	(0.095)	(0.063)	(0.097)
	Geographic location	−0.160***	−0.093***	0.021	−0.040	0.064***	0.202***
		(0.035)	(0.019)	(0.030)	(0.024)	(0.016)	(0.025)
	Constant	−2.143***	−1.137***	−1.120**	−0.608*	−0.563**	−0.904***
		(0.658)	(0.349)	(0.518)	(0.325)	(0.219)	(0.334)
	Observations		17,029			41,004	

continued on next page

Table 4.1 continued

		Japan 08			Rep. of Korea 06		
		10th pctile	50th pctile	90th pctile	10th pctile	50th pctile	90th pctile
	Treatment group	9.406***	10.140***	10.700***	8.857***	9.864***	10.560***
		(0.111)	(0.032)	(0.051)	(0.0221)	(0.011)	(0.015)
	Control group	9.496***	10.220***	10.860***	9.263***	10.050***	10.660**
		(0.021)	(0.012)	(0.017)	(0.0131)	(0.007)	(0.008)
	Overall Gap	−0.090	−0.076**	−0.156***	−0.406***	−0.182***	−0.101***
		(0.113)	(0.034)	(0.054)	(0.0256)	(0.013)	(0.017)
	Endowment	−0.136**	−0.055***	−0.051*	−0.419***	−0.243***	−0.166***
		(0.064)	(0.020)	(0.029)	(0.0241)	(0.012)	(0.017)
	Returns	0.046	−0.022	−0.106*	0.0125	0.061***	0.065***
		(0.118)	(0.033)	(0.056)	(0.0323)	(0.015)	(0.023)
Endowment Effects (Explained)	Characteristics of hhd. head	−0.042	−0.011	0.004	−0.065***	−0.000	0.029**
		(0.039)	(0.009)	(0.015)	(0.020)	(0.009)	(0.014)
	Head education	−0.111**	−0.027**	−0.039**	−0.119***	−0.105***	−0.119***
		(0.044)	(0.012)	(0.019)	(0.017)	(0.008)	(0.013)
	Head employment	0.008	−0.006	−0.006	−0.249***	−0.102***	−0.049***
		(0.024)	(0.007)	(0.009)	(0.022)	(0.010)	(0.015)
	Household composition	0.024	0.014	0.014	0.0028	−0.041***	−0.030**
		(0.034)	(0.011)	(0.017)	(0.017)	(0.008)	(0.013)
	Geographic location	−0.015	−0.025***	−0.023	0.010**	0.004**	0.004**
		(0.031)	(0.009)	(0.014)	(0.0049)	(0.002)	(0.002)
Returns Effects (Unexplained)	Characteristics of hhd. head	−1.818	−0.097	−0.409	1.076**	0.607***	0.113
		(1.315)	(0.376)	(0.629)	(0.491)	(0.235)	(0.347)
	Head education	0.727**	0.112	0.125	−0.407***	0.003	0.052
		(0.355)	(0.103)	(0.172)	(0.136)	(0.067)	(0.094)
	Head employment	0.076	−0.076	−0.019	−0.115*	0.068**	0.062
		(0.213)	(0.061)	(0.101)	(0.069)	(0.033)	(0.049)
	Household composition	0.002	0.268**	−0.140	0.484	−0.133	0.043
		(0.397)	(0.114)	(0.190)	(0.333)	(0.159)	(0.236)
	Geographic location	0.141	0.091	0.124	−0.431***	−0.188***	−0.194***
		(0.224)	(0.065)	(0.109)	(0.055)	(0.026)	(0.040)
	Constant	0.919	−0.319	0.214	−0.595	−0.296	−0.010
		(1.440)	(0.412)	(0.690)	(0.416)	(0.199)	(0.294)
	Observations		3,318			15,081	

PRC = People's Republic of China, pctile = percentile, hhd. = household.
Notes: Standard errors computed using the delta method are in parentheses. *** $p<0.01$, ** $p<0.05$, * $p<0.1$.
Source: Author's analysis of LIS data.

Our study offers several contributions to the existing literature on inequality in the developing world, and specifically in developing Asia. First, a recent estimation technique—unconditional quantile regression combined with the Blinder–Oaxaca decomposition—is used to estimate income gaps across demographic groups at various quantiles of national income distributions, and to explain them using differences in endowments as well as differences in the returns to those endowments. This approach has not been utilized adequately in decomposing inequality in developing Asian economies. The analysis was conducted in part on site at the LIS office in Luxembourg using offline access to LIS database. This allowed us to review all data carefully and use add-on statistical programs, which would have been cumbersome using online access alone.

The second contribution is that we use a novel set of household surveys that are harmonized across economies and time. The fact that these economies range from lower-middle-income (India), through upper-middle-income (the PRC, the Russian Federation) and recently industrialized (Taipei,China; Republic of Korea), to high-income countries (Japan) is viewed as a strength. It allows us to comment on the socio-economic conditions in economies at different stages of development, allows robustness checks, and facilitates comparisons that can inform policy makers regarding prospects for economies on their respective growth paths.

The third contribution is that this study assesses multiple, non-traditional dimensions of inequality. Beside income gaps between rural versus urban residential groups and between disadvantaged versus advantaged regions, this study assesses income gaps across households with less versus more educated, non-employed versus employed, and female versus male heads. Therefore, this study tells a different story than that in existing literature regarding the form and evolution of inequality in developing Asia. The study is organized as follows. The next section reviews several methods commonly used in the empirical welfare-economic literature to decompose economic inequality by its dimensions. The following section presents the data and describes how variables were combined and formatted in the empirical analysis. Empirical results are presented next. Finally, Section V concludes with a discussion of main lessons, their robustness and their implications for policy making.

4.3 Methods

Existing literature relies on a variety of approaches to decompose inequality and analyze its determinants. One method that helps to identify the causes of between-group inequality is the regression-based

Blinder–Oaxaca decomposition (Blinder 1973; Oaxaca 1973), which distinguishes the role of differentials in endowments, and differentials in the returns to those endowments between pairs of demographic groups. One limitation of the standard Blinder–Oaxaca decomposition is that it only estimates the mean effect of a given variable on the gap in economic outcomes. In fact, the effects of covariates typically differ systematically along the income (or expenditure or wage) distribution. One method that allows estimating the impact of explanatory variables at different points on the welfare-aggregate distribution is the unconditional quantile regression (UQR) technique (Fournier and Koske 2012).

This chapter uses UQR decomposition to study income gaps across the entire population distribution and decompose them by source. The UQR is implemented by a recently developed re-centered influence function (RIF) method (Firpo et al. 2009; Fortin et al. 2010). The UQR technique estimates the impacts of explanatory variables on individual quantiles of the unconditional distribution of an outcome variable—annual disposable household income per adult-equivalent here. It measures how various quantiles of the distribution, not only the average, of the outcome variable will be affected by changes in explanatory variables.

The RIF method is a regression-based procedure facilitating decomposition of different distributional statistics across the unconditional distribution of total incomes per capita. The RIF is used in this paper to decompose the distribution of total income by households' rural/urban residence and disadvantaged/advantaged region, and households with less/more educated, non-employed/employed, and female/male head. The method consists of two stages. The first stage entails estimating the UQR on log annual household income per capita of the two groups of interest,[2] then constructing a counterfactual distribution that would prevail if group 1 (e.g., rural households) received the returns that pertained to the second group (urban households, respectively). The comparison between the counterfactual and the empirical distribution allows us to estimate the part of the income gap attributable to differences in household characteristics (*endowment effect*) and the part attributable to differences in returns to these characteristics (*returns effect*).

The method can be expressed as using the following influence function re-centered so that its mean corresponds to the th quantile of *y*, log annual income per capita:

---

[2] In our case: rural/urban households, and households with female/male, uneducated/educated and non-employed/employed heads.

$$RIF(y, Q_\theta) = X\beta + \varepsilon \qquad (1)$$

$RIF(y,Q_\theta)$ is estimated by computing the sample quantile and deriving the density of y at that point by use of the Kernel method. X is a matrix of regressors that can be divided into five groups. The first group consists of household-head characteristics including age, age squared, gender, and marital status. The second group consists of three binary indicators for the education level of the head. The third group includes binary indicators for the employment status and employment sector of the household head. The fourth group contains household characteristics including household size and ratio of those below 14 years and those above 65 years of age in the household. Finally, the fifth group includes geographic location indicators.

After estimating the RIF equation for individual deciles from the 10th percentile to the 90th percentile of the population, the predicted values for individual demographic groups are decomposed into the endowment and returns effects as follows:

$$\hat{Q}_\theta^i - \hat{Q}_\theta^j = \{\hat{Q}_\theta^i - \hat{Q}_\theta^*\} + \{\hat{Q}_\theta^* - \hat{Q}_\theta^j\} =$$
$$(\bar{X}^i - \bar{X}^j)\hat{\beta}_\theta^i + \bar{X}^j(\hat{\beta}_\theta^i - \hat{\beta}_\theta^j) \qquad (2)$$

for i/j pairs: rural/urban, female/male head, uneducated/educated head, non-employed/employed head.
*= counterfactual values.

Here $\hat{Q}_\theta$ is the θth unconditional quantile of log annual income per capita, $\bar{X}$ is the vector of the means of covariates, and $\hat{\beta}_\theta^k$ is the estimate of the unconditional quantile partial effects of group k. $\hat{Q}_\theta^* = X^j \hat{\beta}^i$ is the θth quantile of the unconditional counterfactual distribution that would have prevailed for group j if they received group i's returns to their characteristics.

The first term in equation 2, $(\bar{X}^i - \bar{X}^j)\hat{\beta}_\theta^i$, is the endowment effect. It is the contribution of the differences in distributions of household characteristics to inequality at the θth unconditional quantile. The second term, $\bar{X}^j(\hat{\beta}_\theta^i - \hat{\beta}_\theta^j)$, is the returns effect—the inequality due to differences in the returns to household characteristics at the θth unconditional quantile.

4.4 Data

4.4.1 Selection of Surveys

This study relies on 10 household surveys for six economies from across Asia collected and harmonized by LIS. As of October 2015, LIS offered public access to over 250 income distributions for 45 economies, and additional surveys are being added several times a year. The datasets are harmonized and can be studied jointly both across years and across economies. In this study, only the most recent waves of national surveys are used, to focus on inequality at its level in recent times, and to ensure comparability. The 10 surveys are for years 2002–2010. For the Russian Federation and Taipei,China, two older survey waves are used to evaluate robustness of results and comment on evolution over time.[3]

The original microdata for the 10 surveys were provided by the Chinese Household Income Survey Project provided by the Beijing Inter-University Consortium for Political and Social Research, University of Michigan; India Human Development Survey, provided by the Data Sharing for Demographic Research—Carolina Population Center at the University of North Carolina—Chapel Hill; Japan Household Panel Survey run by the Keio University Joint Research Center for Panel Studies; Korean Household Income and Expenditure Survey and Farm Household Income and Expenditure Survey conducted by Statistics Korea; Russia Longitudinal Monitoring Survey run by the Higher School of Economics and provided also by the Carolina Population Center; Taipei,China Survey of Family Income and Expenditure—Taipei,China Area, administered by the Directorate General of Budget, Accounting and Statistics.

The Russian Federation is included among Asian economies evaluated here because 76.8% of its territory (13.1 mil. km²), 26.3% of population (37.6 mil.), and three of its eight federal districts (Ural, Siberian, and Far Eastern) are in Asia.[4] The Russian Federation is also

---

[3] LIS database additionally includes the year-2000 survey for the Russian Federation, and the 1981, 1986, 1991, 1995, 1997, and 2000 waves for Taipei,China, not evaluated here.

[4] These numbers are prior to the annexation of Crimea in 2014. Russian surveys in LIS database includes eight regions: Moscow and St. Petersburg; Northern and North Western; Central and Central Black-Earth; Volgo–Vyatski and Volga Basin; North Caucasian; Ural; Western Siberia; Eastern Siberia and Far East. This differs slightly from the Russian Federation's federal districts—Center (including Moscow/St. Petersburg); South; North West (including North); Far East; Siberia; Ural; Volga; Northern Caucasus.

sometimes classified as a Central Asian (or Central Eurasian) economy, because the Russian economy and households may be thought of as facing similar industrial, institutional, and cultural conditions as those in surrounding Central Asian countries around the Ural mountain range.

4.4.2 Variables for the Analysis

In the LIS database of national surveys, we use information from both the household and the personal record files. Information on demographic characteristics and employment status of household heads is merged with information for households including their residence, administrative region, and disposable income per capita.

Specifically, the following variables are used to identify income inequality across demographic groups: disposable household income *dhi*, administrative region *region_c*, residence type *rural*, employment status *emp*, highest attended education level *educlev*, and *sex*. Other variables used in the estimation include: *age*; industry classification *ind1*, farming activity status *farming*, cohabitation with partner *hpartner*; household composition *hhtype*; household size *nhhmem*; number of household members 13 or younger *nhhmem13*, and 65 or older *nhhmem65*; relationship to household head *relation*; and normalized household sampling weights *hwgt*. Finally, currency conversion rates and gross domestic product deflators are adopted from the World Bank Development Indicators database (World Bank 2015a, 2015b). Table A4.1 presents selected summary statistics for the 10 surveys.

4.4.3 Treatment versus Control Groups

Inequality in incomes within economies is decomposed into between-group components using several delineations of treatment versus control groups—households with rural versus urban residence, in disadvantaged versus advantaged administrative regions, and with heads who are less versus more educated, non-employed versus employed, and female versus male. Tables A4.3 and A4.4 show that there are substantial differences in demographic composition of population across the six economies and that, perhaps more importantly, the composition differs very systematically across income-quantile groups in national populations.

Rural versus urban residence: First we identify inequality between households with urban versus rural residence. In the PRC, India, Japan, and the Russian Federation, an appropriate indicator *rural* is used to this end. In the Republic of Korea and Taipei,China, however, identification problems arise. In the 2007 and 2010 waves of the

Taipei,China survey, an indicator for urban/rural residence—or any other subnational geographic indicator—is missing for all households. The closest variable that can be used to distinguish rural and urban households is *farming* (and an identical variable *farm* in 2007). In this study, Taipei,China households with *farming* set to "runs a farming activity" are classified as rural households, and those that do not run a farming activity are classified as urban households. Similarly, 3,074 households in the Republic of Korea survey have the residence indicator missing. The closest variable that can be used to distinguish rural and urban households is the industry classification—in this study, Korean households with residence indicator missing are classified as rural if their industry is agriculture (classification done for 2,745 households).[5] One potential problem with this classification in Taipei,China and the Republic of Korea is that only economically active household heads may be classified as rural, while both active and inactive heads may be classified as urban. The results, however, do not appear to show any pro-rural bias.

Disadvantaged versus advantaged administrative regions: To decompose inequality within each economy by geography, we use administrative-region disaggregation available in the LIS database. In the PRC, we distinguish the predominantly agricultural northwest, west, and southwest regions—including Anhui, Gansu, Guangxi, Guizhou, Hebei, Henan, Hubei, Hunan, Jiangxi, Shaanxi, Shanxi, Sichuan, Xinjiang, and Yunnan provinces—from the industrialized east coast—including Beijing, Chongqing, Guangdong, Jiangsu, Jilin, Liaoning, Shandong, and Zhejiang provinces.

In India, we distinguish the country's less developed states, mostly in India's interior and east—from the states in the industrialized and developed southwest and north. This classification also relies on categorization of regions according to economic development by Brar et al. (2014).

In Japan, regions are split between those on all but Honshu island (Hokkaido, Kyushu, Shikoku islands), and Honshu Island (Chubo, Chugoku, Kanto, Kinki, Tohoku regions). In the Russian Federation, we distinguish the mineral-extraction reliant Asian districts—Ural, Siberia, and Far East—from the industrialized European regions—including Moscow and St. Petersburg, Northern and North Western, Central

---

[5] Another problem in the Republic of Korea and Taipei,China is that even for respondents with known residence and region indicators, inequality between rural versus urban residences, and that between disadvantaged versus advantaged regions, will be estimated imprecisely, because *Seoul Metropolitan Area* and *Taipei Municipality* are entirely urban regions.

and Central Black–Earth, Volgo–Vyatski and Volga Basin, and North Caucasian regions. In the Republic of Korea, for lack of more precise regional disaggregation, we distinguish the non-capital area of the country (both urban and rural), and Seoul Metropolitan Area (all urban). Similarly, in Taipei,China we distinguish Taipei province and Kaohsiung municipality, as a disadvantaged region, from Taipei Municipality, the advantaged region.

Decompositions are further performed for households with uneducated (less than complete secondary school) versus educated (complete secondary or higher) heads; non-employed (not currently employed) versus employed heads; and female versus male heads.

4.4.4 Other Explanatory Variables: Households' Endowments

In regressions decomposing inequality across other, non-geographic dimensions, we account for households' residence in different regions as their endowment on which they receive returns. In India, we distinguish four regions: the most developed region, the above-median region, the median region, and the least developed region. This again relies on categorization of regions according to economic development by Brar et al. (2014).

Additional endowments including household heads' age, age squared, gender, status as married, education status (illiterate, primary, lower secondary/preparatory, secondary, postsecondary through tertiary, bachelor's or higher), employment status and sector (agriculture, industry, services, undistinguishable), household size, dependents (proportion of persons below 14, proportion of persons above 65), specific household composition (one-person household, couple without children, couple with children, one parent with children, couple without children and relatives, head, and other members), administrative region, and residence type (rural/urban) are used.

4.5 Results

Tables 4.1–4.14 present the main results of this study. To provide an overall range of estimated log-incomes and income effects in the population, the tables report the statistics for the first, the fifth (median), and the ninth income deciles. The first two rows in these tables report the predicted values of log incomes for the two comparison groups—the treatment (or disadvantaged) group and the control (or advantaged) group, less the overall constant term. Because these statistics are not of central interest here, their discussion will be omitted to save space. The third row reports on the composite income differential between the two groups, and rows 4 and 5 report the portions attributable to systematic differences in various endowments across the treatment and control groups, and the portion attributable to the differential returns to these endowments. For household endowments, we use all observable household characteristics that may have bearing on households' earning capacity or that may be valued by markets, with the exception of the characteristic defining the treatment versus control group. For instance, in the analysis of the rural/urban income differential, characteristics of household heads (age, age squared, gender, marriage, education and employment status, and sector of employment), household size and specific composition, and administrative region of residence are used. These characteristics may affect income directly if human-capital markets value them or offer allowances for them, or if they imply more working people in the household. The effects of each of these (groups of) endowments on the income differential are shown in rows 6–10.

Row 5 reports on the portion of the income differential that cannot be explained by systematic endowment differences between the treatment and the control groups, and is thus attributed to the differential returns to all endowments, assuming that no important endowments were omitted from the analysis, in agreement with the tradition in the literature using this technique (Belhaj Hassine 2014; Ramadan et al. 2015). The last large block of rows, rows 11–15 in the lower half of Tables 4.1–4.14, shows the effects of differential returns to individual (groups of) endowments on the income gaps. Finally, the bottom row of Tables 4.1–4.14 shows the overall constant terms in the regressions.

4.5.1 Rural/Urban Income Gap

The first two rows in Tables 4.1–4.14 confirm that the PRC and India are at the lower end among the evaluated economies in terms of income levels across each pair of comparison groups (rural/urban, disadvantaged/advantaged region, less/more educated, non-employed/employed, female/male), and across income quantiles, while Japan and the Republic of Korea are in the upper end.

Tables 4.1–4.3 show the results for the rural/urban gap in each survey. Row 3 confirms that the PRC has substantial income differentials between rural and urban households, followed by India and the Russian Federation, and then by Taipei,China and the Republic of Korea, while such a differential is largely missing in Japan. In the PRC, the Russian Federation, and the Republic of Korea, the rural/urban gap is largest among the poorest households, suggesting that the rural poor are trapped in a desperate position. In India and Taipei,China, the gap is similar across income quantiles, while in Japan the gap increases only in the highest income quantiles. Over time, the rural/urban gap in the Russian Federation has been gradually diminishing across all population quantiles, and in Taipei,China there was a significant improvement in rural/urban inequality between 2005 and 2007.

Decomposing the composite income differential into endowment and returns effects, in rows 4–5 of Tables 4.1–4.3, indicates that the endowment effect between rural and urban households is nearly non-existent in the PRC, suggesting similar household characteristics, including education and household composition. The rural rich have slightly lower sets of endowments (demographics of household head, household composition, and access to geographic markets) than the urban rich, while the rural poor have even higher endowments (demographics of household head and employment) than their urban counterparts. The returns effect, however, is consistently negative and much larger, affecting particularly low-income rural households. The rural poor receive much lower returns on their endowments, including sector of employment and access to geographic markets, than similarly endowed urban households. This could be due to discrimination, to various barriers including state-regulated ones, as well as to market fragmentation under which employers and workers are not matched efficiently. In India, a different pattern emerges. Both the endowment effect and the returns effect are consistently negative, but while the endowment effect is largest among richer households—suggesting a particular shortfall in education, employment sector, and access to geographic markets among the rural rich—the returns effect is large among median and poor households—suggesting discrimination or lack of market access among the rural poor that lowers their return to education. In Japan, some evidence exists of a shortfall in endowments (particularly education) among the rural poor, while the rural rich are affected more by lower returns to their endowments (particularly household-head demographics) than their urban counterparts. In the Republic of Korea, significant shortfalls in endowments including household-head demographics, education, and employment are found among rural households, particularly among the rural poor, while rural households receive slightly higher returns on their endowments (demographics and employment sector), significant among households in the middle and at the top of the income distribution.

Table 4.2 Quantile Decomposition for the Russian Federation 2004, 2007, and 2010 by Rural/Urban Residence

		Russian Federation 04		
		10th pctile	50th pctile	90th pctile
	Treatment group	6.978***	8.040***	8.990***
		(0.083)	(0.034)	(0.050)
	Control group	7.676***	8.543***	9.449***
		(0.028)	(0.019)	(0.026)
	Overall Gap	−0.698***	−0.503***	−0.459***
		(0.087)	(0.039)	(0.057)
	Endowment	0.112	−0.068*	−0.151**
		(0.099)	(0.041)	(0.060)
	Returns	−0.810***	−0.436***	−0.309***
		(0.126)	(0.053)	(0.079)
Endowment Effects (Explained)	Characteristics of hhd. head	0.041	0.026**	0.0117
		(0.031)	(0.013)	(0.017)
	Head education	−0.006	−0.042**	−0.040
		(0.046)	(0.019)	(0.029)
	Head employment	0.058	−0.041*	−0.027
		(0.058)	(0.024)	(0.036)
	Household composition	0.087**	0.036**	0.040*
		(0.041)	(0.017)	(0.024)
	Residence	−0.068	−0.047*	−0.136***
		(0.069)	(0.028)	(0.042)
Returns Effects (Unexplained)	Characteristics of hhd. head	0.611	0.458	0.839
		(1.055)	(0.450)	(0.680)
	Head education	−0.323	−0.090	0.134
		(0.410)	(0.188)	(0.284)
	Head employment	−0.223	−0.049	0.057
		(0.148)	(0.064)	(0.096)
	Household composition	0.401	−0.010	−0.122
		(0.272)	(0.118)	(0.178)
	Residence	0.363**	0.073	0.068
		(0.175)	(0.076)	(0.115)
	Constant	−1.639	−0.818*	−1.285*
		(1.158)	(0.497)	(0.750)
	Observations		3,086	

continued on next page

Table 4.2 continued

		Russian Federation 07		
		10th pctile	50th pctile	90th pctile
	Treatment group	7.513***	8.650***	9.558***
		(0.075)	(0.037)	(0.035)
	Control group	8.186***	9.125***	9.901***
		(0.024)	(0.018)	(0.020)
	Overall Gap	−0.673***	−0.475***	−0.343***
		(0.079)	(0.041)	(0.040)
	Endowment	−0.185**	−0.186***	−0.173***
		(0.080)	(0.039)	(0.037)
	Returns	−0.488***	−0.288***	−0.170***
		(0.105)	(0.051)	(0.052)
Endowment Effects (Explained)	Characteristics of hhd. head	0.036	0.031**	0.019
		(0.029)	(0.016)	(0.014)
	Head education	−0.102**	−0.118***	−0.079***
		(0.042)	(0.022)	(0.021)
	Head employment	−0.061	−0.056**	−0.084***
		(0.048)	(0.023)	(0.023)
	Household composition	−0.017	−0.014	−0.002
		(0.035)	(0.016)	(0.013)
	Residence	−0.042	−0.030	−0.027
		(0.041)	(0.021)	(0.019)
Returns Effects (Unexplained)	Characteristics of hhd. head	0.291	−0.175	0.797
		(0.910)	(0.447)	(0.464)
	Head education	−0.155	0.323	0.319
		(0.448)	(0.237)	(0.258)
	Head employment	0.192	−0.030	0.001
		(0.124)	(0.061)	(0.064)
	Household composition	−0.243	0.066	−0.040
		(0.236)	(0.118)	(0.123)
	Residence	0.563***	0.217***	0.050
		(0.157)	(0.079)	(0.083)
	Constant	−1.136	−0.690	−1.299**
		(1.024)	(0.509)	(0.533)
	Observations		3,370	

continued on next page

Table 4.2 continued

		Russian Federation 10		
		10th pctile	50th pctile	90th pctile
	Treatment group	8.196***	9.171***	9.998***
		(0.060)	(0.019)	(0.029)
	Control group	8.742***	9.513***	10.280***
		(0.018)	(0.012)	(0.016)
	Overall Gap	−0.547***	−0.342***	−0.280***
		(0.062)	(0.023)	(0.033)
	Endowment	−0.243***	−0.127***	−0.055*
		(0.062)	(0.021)	(0.030)
	Returns	−0.303***	−0.215***	−0.225***
		(0.082)	(0.027)	(0.042)
Endowment Effects (Explained)	Characteristics of hhd. head	0.002	0.018**	0.004
		(0.028)	(0.009)	(0.014)
	Head education	−0.138***	−0.085***	−0.068***
		(0.032)	(0.011)	(0.015)
	Head employment	−0.079**	−0.023**	0.001
		(0.035)	(0.010)	(0.016)
	Household composition	−0.021	0.004	0.058***
		(0.032)	(0.011)	(0.016)
	Residence	−0.007	−0.041***	−0.051***
		(0.034)	(0.011)	(0.017)
Returns Effects (Unexplained)	Characteristics of hhd. head	0.652	0.505**	1.095***
		(0.738)	(0.246)	(0.381)
	Head education	−0.082	0.113	0.362
		(0.411)	(0.165)	(0.249)
	Head employment	0.407***	−0.072**	−0.029
		(0.099)	(0.034)	(0.053)
	Household composition	0.013	0.145**	0.218**
		(0.18)	(0.062)	(0.095)
	Residence	0.121	0.118***	0.121*
		(0.125)	(0.044)	(0.067)
	Constant	−1.415*	−1.024***	−1.992***
		(0.831)	(0.291)	(0.446)
	Observations		5,713	

pctile = percentile, hhd. = household.
Notes: Standard errors computed using the delta method are in parentheses. *** $p<0.01$, ** $p<0.05$, * $p<0.1$.
Source: Author's analysis of LIS data.

Table 4.3 Quantile Decomposition for Taipei,China 2005, 2007, and 2010 by Rural/Urban Residence

		Taipei,China 05		
		10th pctile	50th pctile	90th pctile
	Treatment group	8.390***	9.045***	9.692***
		(0.050)	(0.040)	(0.035)
	Control group	8.853***	9.517***	10.210***
		(0.009)	(0.006)	(0.008)
	Overall Gap	−0.463***	−0.472***	−0.521***
		(0.051)	(0.041)	(0.036)
	Endowment	−0.233	−0.363**	−0.171
		(0.181)	(0.151)	(0.143)
	Returns	−0.230	−0.109	−0.351**
		(0.184)	(0.154)	(0.147)
Endowment Effects (Explained)	Characteristics of hhd. head	0.041	0.069**	0.0126
		(0.033)	(0.029)	(0.026)
	Head education	−0.123	−0.276*	−0.140
		(0.175)	(0.147)	(0.139)
	Head employment	−0.083	−0.105**	−0.010
		(0.057)	(0.048)	(0.045)
	Household composition	−0.068*	−0.052	−0.033
		(0.038)	(0.033)	(0.027)
Returns Effects (Unexplained)	Characteristics of hhd. head	2.079*	−0.345	−1.645*
		(1.090)	(0.900)	(0.880)
	Head education	−0.424*	0.373*	−0.105
		(0.237)	(0.197)	(0.190)
	Head employment	−0.779***	0.211	−0.138
		(0.174)	(0.144)	(0.140)
	Household composition	−0.431	0.835	0.520
		(0.974)	(0.804)	(0.787)
	Constant	−0.675	−1.182**	1.018**
		(0.639)	(0.530)	(0.513)
	Observations		13,679	

continued on next page

Table 4.3 *continued*

		Taipei,China 07		
		10th pctile	50th pctile	90th pctile
	Treatment group	8.585***	9.244***	9.921***
		(0.029)	(0.019)	(0.031)
	Control group	8.808***	9.498***	10.220***
		(0.010)	(0.006)	(0.009)
	Overall Gap	−0.223***	−0.254***	−0.298***
		(0.030)	(0.020)	(0.032)
	Endowment	−0.082	−0.124*	−0.295***
		(0.099)	(0.063)	(0.109)
	Returns	−0.141	−0.130**	−0.003
		(0.102)	(0.065)	(0.112)
Endowment Effects (Explained)	Characteristics of hhd. head	0.035	0.066*	0.091
		(0.056)	(0.036)	(0.061)
	Head education	−0.033	−0.118***	−0.295***
		(0.028)	(0.019)	(0.033)
	Head employment	−0.061	−0.038	−0.055
		(0.096)	(0.061)	(0.106)
	Household composition	−0.023	−0.034	−0.035
		(0.056)	(0.036)	(0.061)
Returns Effects (Unexplained)	Characteristics of hhd. head	−0.354	−0.423	0.245
		(0.661)	(0.419)	(0.715)
	Head education	−0.795***	−0.047	0.456***
		(0.124)	(0.078)	(0.133)
	Head employment	−0.257	−0.018	−0.112
		(0.823)	(0.523)	(0.902)
	Household composition	−0.204	0.083	0.270
		(0.525)	(0.333)	(0.566)
	Constant	1.467	0.275	−0.863
		(1.037)	(0.659)	(1.135)
	Observations		13,774	

continued on next page

Table 4.3 continued

		Taipei,China 10		
		10th pctile	50th pctile	90th pctile
	Treatment group	8.534***	9.273***	9.955***
		(0.029)	(0.020)	(0.031)
	Control group	8.749***	9.503***	10.220***
		(0.010)	(0.006)	(0.008)
	Overall Gap	−0.215***	−0.230***	−0.265***
		(0.031)	(0.021)	(0.032)
	Endowment	0.016	−0.064	−0.203**
		(0.079)	(0.052)	(0.084)
	Returns	−0.230***	−0.167***	−0.062
		(0.083)	(0.054)	(0.088)
Endowment Effects (Explained)	Characteristics of hhd. head	0.050	0.011	0.087**
		(0.041)	(0.027)	(0.044)
	Head education	−0.050*	−0.114***	−0.277***
		(0.027)	(0.019)	(0.031)
	Head employment	0.055	−0.014	−0.035
		(0.074)	(0.049)	(0.079)
	Household composition	−0.040	0.054*	0.021
		(0.042)	(0.029)	(0.045)
Returns Effects (Unexplained)	Characteristics of hhd. head	0.098	−0.697*	−0.232
		(0.621)	(0.399)	(0.644)
	Head education	−1.011***	−0.062	0.076
		(0.163)	(0.105)	(0.171)
	Head employment	0.439	−0.171	−0.210
		(0.560)	(0.368)	(0.598)
	Household composition	0.154	0.602*	0.665
		(0.498)	(0.318)	(0.512)
	Constant	0.091	0.161	−0.361
		(0.793)	(0.519)	(0.844)
	Observations		14,843	

pctile = percentile, hhd. = household.
Notes: Standard errors computed using the delta method are in parentheses. *** p<0.01, ** p<0.05, * p<0.1. Residence unavailable.
Source: Author's analysis of LIS data.

In the Russian Federation (Table 4.2), rural households have lower endowments than urban households, particularly in their educational achievement, employment sector, and access to geographic markets. Over time, this shortfall fluctuates for households in the middle and top, while it systematically grows in size among the poorest households. The returns effect is consistently strongly negative among rural households, and strongest among the poorest households, but it gradually abates over time. In Taipei,China (Table 4.3), rural households are systematically less educated than urban households, and the returns to education and other endowments are systematically lower among rural households, but the effects are insignificant in one half of all cases, and there are no clear patterns across income quantiles or over time.

In most of the surveys evaluated in Tables 4.1–4.3, the endowment effect is as large as or larger than the returns effect, suggesting that rural households are less endowed with characteristics that are associated with higher earning capacity than urban households. Rural households may still receive lower returns on their stock of endowments than urban households. The policy priority, however, should be to increase the endowments of rural households because the lack of endowments such as marketable skills is a primary driver of the rural/urban income gap.

4.5.2 Disadvantaged/Advantaged Region Gap

Regarding regional inequality, assessed in Tables 4.4–4.5, the differential in row 3 appears smaller than the rural/urban gap, suggesting that in most economies spatial inequality is due more to gaps along the local rural/urban dimension than to gaps across larger national regions. In the PRC and the Russian Federation the differential is greatest in the middle and top of the income distribution. In India; Japan; and Taipei,China (2005) all income quantiles see a similar level of regional inequality that cannot be ranked.[6] In the Republic of Korea, the income differential is large only among the poorest decile of the population. Over time, surprisingly, regional inequality in the Russian Federation increases systematically across the 3 years and across all income quantiles. This calls into question reports in existing studies that regional incomes have been converging in the Russian Federation (Guriev and Vakulenko 2012), as the increases in regional gaps are very consistent.

Decomposing the gap into the endowment and returns effects in the PRC, we find the endowment effect to be of a similar magnitude as

---

[6] Years other than '05 cannot be evaluated for Taipei,China for lack of regional indicators in the respective survey waves.

the returns effect. Households in disadvantaged western provinces tend to be less educated (most notably households in the upper half of the income distribution) and reside in rural areas, away from major centers of economic activity. They also receive significantly lower returns on their education, on their household composition, and on their type of residence—particularly households in the lower half of the income distribution.

For most of the other evaluated surveys—specifically Japan, the Russian Federation, and Taipei,China (and to some degree in India)—the decomposition suggests that the returns effects are more important to the regional income gaps than the endowment effects. In India, households in disadvantaged states are slightly less educated, work in inferior sectors, have a less advantageous household composition, and have an inferior access to urban markets compared to households in privileged states, limiting their earning potential. They receive substantially lower returns on their demographic characteristics such as age and marital status, education, and economically advantageous household composition.

In Japan, the Russian Federation, and Taipei,China the endowment effects are small, implying that across regions households are similarly endowed with characteristics that are associated with earning capacity. In disadvantaged regions, the income shortfall is thus due to unexplained factors such as a shortfall in returns to the available stock of endowments—the return to household heads' age and marital status in Japan and the Russian Federation.

Table 4.4 Quantile Decomposition for the PRC 2002, India 2004, Japan 2008, and Republic of Korea 2006 by Disadvantaged/Advantaged Admin. Region

	PRC 02			India 04		
	10th pctile	50th pctile	90th pctile	10th pctile	50th pctile	90th pctile
Treatment group	6.047***	7.172***	8.434***	5.894***	6.911***	8.156***
	(0.016)	(0.012)	(0.012)	(0.010)	(0.007)	(0.011)
Control group	6.300***	7.899***	9.021***	6.222***	7.348***	8.514***
	(0.027)	(0.019)	(0.016)	(0.014)	(0.010)	(0.012)
Overall Gap	−0.253***	−0.727***	−0.587***	−0.328***	−0.437***	−0.358***
	(0.032)	(0.023)	(0.020)	(0.017)	(0.012)	(0.016)
Endowment	−0.137***	−0.331***	−0.264***	−0.087***	−0.171***	−0.238***
	(0.011)	(0.014)	(0.013)	(0.007)	(0.006)	(0.010)

continued on next page

Table 4.4 continued

		PRC 02			India 04		
		10th pctile	50th pctile	90th pctile	10th pctile	50th pctile	90th pctile
Endowment Effects (Explained)	Returns	−0.116***	−0.396***	−0.323***	−0.241***	−0.266***	−0.120***
		(0.031)	(0.018)	(0.019)	(0.017)	(0.011)	(0.016)
	Characteristics of hhd. head	0.016***	0.005	−0.033***	0.005**	−0.006***	−0.017***
		(0.005)	(0.003)	(0.004)	(0.002)	(0.002)	(0.003)
	Head education	−0.001	−0.015***	−0.064***	−0.010***	−0.051***	−0.103***
		(0.005)	(0.003)	(0.007)	(0.003)	(0.003)	(0.007)
	Head employment	0.035***	0.008**	−0.007*	−0.014***	−0.017***	−0.006**
		(0.007)	(0.004)	(0.004)	(0.003)	(0.002)	(0.003)
	Household composition	−0.006	−0.025***	−0.006	−0.024***	−0.023***	−0.019***
		(0.007)	(0.005)	(0.005)	(0.004)	(0.003)	(0.004)
	Residence	−0.182***	−0.304***	−0.153***	−0.044***	−0.074***	−0.093***
		(0.012)	(0.013)	(0.009)	(0.004)	(0.003)	(0.005)
Returns Effects (Unexplained)	Characteristics of hhd. head	1.078	−1.042**	0.398	−1.209***	−0.292	−0.184
		(0.874)	(0.473)	(0.514)	(0.331)	(0.213)	(0.297)
	Head education	−0.622**	−0.520***	0.006	−0.212***	−0.073***	0.153***
		(0.260)	(0.138)	(0.150)	(0.028)	(0.018)	(0.025)
	Head employment	−0.018	0.005	−0.159***	0.052	−0.013	0.073*
		(0.092)	(0.050)	(0.054)	(0.043)	(0.028)	(0.039)
	Household composition	−0.203	−0.041	−0.273***	−0.163	−0.176***	−0.074
		(0.137)	(0.075)	(0.081)	(0.104)	(0.067)	(0.094)
	Residence	−0.378***	−0.242***	0.156***	−0.004	0.019*	0.130***
		(0.044)	(0.024)	(0.026)	(0.015)	(0.010)	(0.014)
	Constant	0.027	1.445***	−0.452	1.296***	0.270	−0.217
		(0.924)	(0.499)	(0.542)	(0.346)	(0.223)	(0.310)
Observations		17,029			41,004		

	Japan 08			Rep. of Korea 06		
	10th pctile	50th pctile	90th pctile	10th pctile	50th pctile	90th pctile
Treatment group	9.390***	10.080***	10.690***	9.122***	10.000***	10.650***
	(0.041)	(0.025)	(0.037)	(0.014)	(0.006)	(0.007)
Control group	9.530***	10.240***	10.870***	9.327***	10.060***	10.690***
	(0.024)	(0.012)	(0.018)	(0.031)	(0.016)	(0.021)
Overall Gap	−0.140***	−0.163***	−0.178***	−0.205***	−0.056***	−0.049**
	(0.048)	(0.028)	(0.041)	(0.034)	(0.017)	(0.022)

continued on next page

Table 4.4 *continued*

		Japan 08			Rep. of Korea 06		
		10th pctile	50th pctile	90th pctile	10th pctile	50th pctile	90th pctile
Endowment Effects (Explained)	Endowment	-0.021	-0.041***	-0.043**	-0.128***	-0.071***	-0.063***
		(0.021)	(0.014)	(0.018)	(0.018)	(0.007)	(0.007)
	Returns	-0.119**	-0.122***	-0.135***	-0.077**	0.015	0.015
		(0.048)	(0.028)	(0.041)	(0.031)	(0.016)	(0.021)
	Characteristics of hhd. head	-0.016	-0.012	-0.008	0.007	0.017***	0.018***
		(0.016)	(0.009)	(0.013)	(0.007)	(0.004)	(0.005)
	Head education	-0.016	-0.012**	-0.016**	-0.075***	-0.060***	-0.064***
		(0.012)	(0.006)	(0.008)	(0.008)	(0.006)	(0.006)
	Head employment	-0.006	-0.004	0.001	-0.015	-0.004	-0.003
		(0.011)	(0.006)	(0.008)	(0.009)	(0.002)	(0.002)
	Household composition	0.021	-0.001	-0.013	-0.046***	-0.024***	-0.014***
		(0.018)	(0.013)	(0.016)	(0.008)	(0.004)	(0.005)
	Residence	-0.003	-0.012**	-0.008	–	–	–
		(0.007)	(0.005)	(0.007)			
Returns Effects (Unexplained)	Characteristics of hhd. head	-1.110**	-0.352	-1.027**	0.445	0.756**	0.939**
		(0.561)	(0.329)	(0.485)	(0.584)	(0.298)	(0.404)
	Head education	0.330**	0.104	0.136	-0.0415	-0.0799	-0.098
		(0.160)	(0.093)	(0.137)	(0.262)	(0.136)	(0.184)
	Head employment	0.036	-0.028	0.024	0.132	-0.030	0.025
		(0.086)	(0.050)	(0.074)	(0.095)	(0.049)	(0.066)
	Household composition	0.171	-0.055	-0.244*	0.112	-0.182	-0.452*
		(0.166)	(0.097)	(0.143)	(0.359)	(0.183)	(0.248)
	Residence	0.0357	0.125*	0.0155	–	–	–
		(0.126)	(0.072)	(0.106)			
	Constant	0.418	0.084	0.960*	-0.724	-0.450*	-0.399
		(0.626)	(0.367)	(0.541)	(0.503)	(0.256)	(0.348)
	Observations		3,318			15,448	

PRC = People's Republic of China, pctile = percentile, hhd. = household.
.Notes: Standard errors computed using the delta method are in parentheses. *** $p<0.01$, ** $p<0.05$, * $p<0.1$. – variables unavailable.
Source: Author's analysis of LIS data.

Table 4.5 Quantile Decomposition for the Russian Federation 2004, 2007, and 2010, and Taipei,China 2005 by Disadvantaged/Advantaged Administrative Region

		Russian Federation 04			Russian Federation 07		
		10th pctile	50th pctile	90th pctile	10th pctile	50th pctile	90th pctile
	Treatment group	7.438***	8.325***	9.247***	7.931***	8.892***	9.665***
		(0.049)	(0.025)	(0.036)	(0.049)	(0.024)	(0.028)
	Control group	7.478***	8.454***	9.403***	8.054***	9.060***	9.888***
		(0.035)	(0.022)	(0.029)	(0.028)	(0.020)	(0.022)
	Overall Gap	−0.040	−0.130***	−0.156***	−0.123**	−0.169***	−0.222***
		(0.061)	(0.034)	(0.046)	(0.056)	(0.031)	(0.035)
	Endowment	−0.060**	0.014	0.004	−0.071***	−0.049***	−0.020
		(0.030)	(0.017)	(0.016)	(0.026)	(0.016)	(0.012)
	Returns	0.021	−0.144***	−0.159***	−0.052	−0.119***	−0.203***
		(0.059)	(0.031)	(0.047)	(0.055)	(0.029)	(0.035)
Endowment Effects (Explained)	Characteristics of hhd. head	−0.007	−0.023	−0.013	−0.021	0.008	0.025
		(0.036)	(0.019)	(0.027)	(0.026)	(0.010)	(0.026)
	Head education	0.0006	0.000	−0.001	−0.021*	−0.016**	−0.010*
		(0.008)	(0.006)	(0.007)	(0.011)	(0.006)	(0.006)
	Head employment	0.029**	0.015**	0.008	−0.005	−0.007	−0.003
		(0.013)	(0.007)	(0.005)	(0.011)	(0.008)	(0.006)
	Household composition	−0.038	0.041	0.019	0.010	−0.019*	−0.025
		(0.043)	(0.025)	(0.034)	(0.031)	(0.011)	(0.025)
	Residence	−0.045***	−0.019***	−0.008*	−0.033**	−0.016***	−0.007*
		(0.017)	(0.007)	(0.005)	(0.013)	(0.006)	(0.004)
Returns Effects (Unexplained)	Characteristics of hhd. head	−1.075	−0.526	−1.277*	0.266	−0.579	1.224**
		(0.986)	(0.507)	(0.771)	(0.826)	(0.430)	(0.530)
	Head education	−0.078	0.064	0.165	−0.438	−0.056	0.132
		(0.335)	(0.174)	(0.263)	(0.383)	(0.201)	(0.247)
	Head employment	0.285***	0.057	−0.034	−0.053	−0.031	0.022
		(0.090)	(0.047)	(0.071)	(0.083)	(0.043)	(0.053)
	Household composition	0.079	0.159	1.338**	0.704	0.227	−0.927**
		(0.812)	(0.409)	(0.629)	(0.643)	(0.329)	(0.408)
	Residence	0.193*	−0.024	−0.105	0.211**	−0.002	−0.009
		(0.101)	(0.053)	(0.080)	(0.095)	(0.050)	(0.061)
	Constant	0.616	0.127	−0.246	−0.742	0.322	−0.644
		(0.706)	(0.372)	(0.558)	(0.682)	(0.359)	(0.441)
	Observations		3,086			3,370	

continued on next page

Table 4.5 continued

		Russian Federation 10			Taipei,China 05		
		10th pctile	50th pctile	90th pctile	10th pctile	50th pctile	90th pctile
	Treatment group	8.465***	9.305***	10.050***	8.788***	9.457***	10.120***
		(0.046)	(0.015)	(0.024)	(0.010)	(0.006)	(0.008)
	Control group	8.640***	9.485***	10.280***	9.278***	9.956***	10.560***
		(0.022)	(0.014)	(0.018)	(0.020)	(0.016)	(0.017)
	Overall Gap	−0.175***	−0.180***	−0.231***	−0.490***	−0.499***	−0.437***
		(0.051)	(0.021)	(0.030)	(0.023)	(0.016)	(0.019)
	Endowment	−0.075***	−0.040***	−0.018	−0.072***	−0.133***	−0.224***
		(0.025)	(0.010)	(0.011)	(0.017)	(0.008)	(0.012)
	Returns	−0.100**	−0.140***	−0.213***	−0.418***	−0.366***	−0.214***
		(0.051)	(0.019)	(0.030)	(0.022)	(0.015)	(0.020)
Endowment Effects (Explained)	Characteristics of hhd. head	−0.080**	−0.008	−0.005	−0.054**	0.006	−0.014
		(0.034)	(0.008)	(0.012)	(0.023)	(0.013)	(0.020)
	Head education	−0.018*	−0.008*	−0.009*	−0.094***	−0.123***	−0.198***
		(0.011)	(0.005)	(0.005)	(0.007)	(0.006)	(0.011)
	Head employment	0.016	0.005	0.003	0.019	−0.014***	−0.011**
		(0.011)	(0.004)	(0.004)	(0.014)	(0.004)	(0.005)
	Household composition	0.020	−0.023**	−0.002	0.058**	−0.002	−0.001
		(0.039)	(0.009)	(0.015)	(0.023)	(0.013)	(0.020)
	Residence	−0.013*	−0.006*	−0.005*	–	–	–
		(0.008)	(0.003)	(0.003)			
Returns Effects (Unexplained)	Characteristics of hhd. head	−1.424**	−0.019	−0.020	−0.447	0.352	−0.225
		(0.726)	(0.271)	(0.428)	(0.592)	(0.429)	(0.538)
	Head education	0.109	0.112	−0.004	0.0515	0.113	0.237
		(0.493)	(0.177)	(0.284)	(0.182)	(0.135)	(0.165)
	Head employment	0.062	−0.049*	−0.028	0.810***	−0.051	0.037
		(0.076)	(0.029)	(0.046)	(0.083)	(0.059)	(0.075)
	Household composition	1.291**	0.011	0.315	0.764	−0.598	−0.112
		(0.555)	(0.201)	(0.321)	(0.541)	(0.391)	(0.492)
	Residence	0.163*	0.006	0.026	–	–	–
		(0.086)	(0.033)	(0.051)			
	Constant	−0.300	−0.201	−0.502	−1.596***	−0.182	−0.151
		(0.682)	(0.255)	(0.403)	(0.353)	(0.258)	(0.321)
	Observations		5,713			13,679	

pctile = percentile, hhd. = household.
Notes: Standard errors computed using the delta method are in parentheses. *** $p<0.01$, ** $p<0.05$, * $p<0.1$.
– variables unavailable.
Source: Author's analysis of LIS data.

In the Republic of Korea, the endowment effect exceeds the returns effect which is around zero, suggesting that workers outside of Seoul have as good an access to earning opportunities as workers in the capital, and the same returns on this characteristic, but they lack important characteristics to be eligible for those opportunities, including education and favorable household composition. This may in turn suggest the existence of inequality of opportunities for quality education, housing, and family planning.

To summarize, in disadvantaged regions in Japan, the Russian Federation, and Taipei,China (and to some degree in India), markets may not exist to utilize workers' skills efficiently, or workers face discrimination compared to relatively endowed workers from more advantaged regions. To promote equalization of living conditions across administrative regions, regulators at the regional and federal levels should strive to integrate markets better, and facilitate better matches between employers and workers. In the PRC, development policy should strive both to improve skills of workers in disadvantaged regions as well as to afford them better access to markets and provide protection from discrimination.

4.5.3 Less/More Educated Gap

Tables 4.6–4.8 present the decomposition of income gaps between households with less versus more educated heads. Row 3 shows that income differentials between households with less than high-school education and those with completed high school or more are very high across all economies. Perhaps as a surprise, even here we find that the gaps are larger in India and the PRC (in that order), followed by Taipei,China; the Republic of Korea; and the Russian Federation, and are smallest in Japan. This presumably reflects polarization of society in developing economies where skilled workers concentrate in cities, and rural population does not invest in education at all, perhaps in the face of barriers or in expectation of low returns. Over time, education gaps further significantly grow at the bottom of the income distribution in the Russian Federation and Taipei,China, while remaining similar at the high end. This disagrees with previous findings for urban India and for Japan that the returns to education in the 1990s increased mostly at the top of the income distribution while stagnating for lower-income households (Azam 2012; Aza and Bhatt 2016; Yokoyama, Kodama, and Higuchi 2016).

Decomposing the education gap into the endowment and returns effects yields diverging results across economis. In the PRC, the Republic of Korea, and the first waves of the Russian Federation and Taipei,China surveys (2004 and 2005, respectively), the two effects are similar among the bottom income quantile groups. This suggests that the stock of non-education related endowments as well as the returns to them generate the income differential between less and more educated households. In the PRC, the returns effect is limited among higher income-level groups, and the income gap becomes mostly due to the endowment effect (i.e., inferior non-education related characteristics among less educated households). In Japan, the Republic of Korea, and Taipei,China, on the other hand, the endowment effect vanishes among the median and higher quantile households, and it is mostly the returns effect that explains education gaps. Among these households, highly educated households receive higher returns to non-education related characteristics than lower-educated households. In the Russian Federation, a significant transformation occurs across the three survey waves. The endowment effect starts as large in 2004, disfavoring all less educated households, particularly in the top half of the income distribution. At the same time, the returns effect is evident only among non-top income households. Over time, the endowment effect rises gradually in magnitude among bottom-income households and shrinks among top-income households, so that by 2010 it is similar across all income quantiles. The returns effect, on the other hand, rises sharply in magnitude over time among bottom-income and top-income households, while remaining similar in the middle of the income distribution.

In the PRC, households with less educated heads tend to be located further from urban market centers (significantly inferior geographic location), receive lower returns on their work in their economic sector, and significantly lower returns on their location of residence. In India, households with less educated heads are employed in inferior sectors, and reside further from urban market centers. They receive substantially higher returns on advantageous forms of household composition, and lower returns on their employment in the services and industry sectors. The return to their residence near markets disadvantages unskilled households in the bottom of the income distribution, while helping unskilled households in the middle and top of the income distribution.

In Japan and the Republic of Korea, less educated workers have similar characteristics as more educated workers, although they work in somewhat inferior economic sectors. Their incomes are negatively affected by their lower return on their demographic characteristics, in the case of Japan, and lower return on their proximity to markets (or geographic location), in the case of the Republic of Korea. Other endowment and returns effects do not have consistent signs or degrees of significance across income quantiles.

In the Russian Federation, the rising endowment effects among bottom-income less educated households are due to deteriorating employment status and residence among poor households with less educated heads relative to their more educated counterparts. The less educated poor households fell behind during 2004–2007 and remained in that state until 2010. The shrinking endowment effects among top-income households have to do with the relative improvement of their employment status and proximity to markets compared to more educated households (diminution of the respective endowment effects).

Incomes of less educated Russian households also suffer from significant unexplained or returns effects. The returns to household-head characteristics, education, employment, household composition, and residence have a mixed ranking across less- and more-educated households, across income quantiles and across years.

Finally, in Taipei,China, education gaps are mostly due to large negative unexplained or returns effects, which increase with the households' income quantile (Table 4.8, row 5). These returns effects persist across the years. Negative endowment effects are also observable among lower-income households, but vanish by the middle of the income distribution and turn positive among above-median income households. Less educated households in Taipei,China thus appear to receive lower returns on some of their characteristics, but among the characteristics evaluated here, none of their returns effects are systematically strongly negative (bottom of Table 4.8, rows 11–15). Nevertheless, large endowment effects are also found among the poorest households, attributable to inferior employment status and household composition among poor less educated households relative to their more educated peers. Less educated households also appear to reside further from economic centers, which adversely affects their earnings. This effect may be larger among higher-income households.

Table 4.6 Quantile Decomposition for the PRC 2002, India 2004, Japan 2008, and Republic of Korea 2006 by Less/More Educated Household Head

	PRC 02			India 04		
	10th pctile	50th pctile	90th pctile	10th pctile	50th pctile	90th pctile
Treatment group	6.002***	7.127***	8.353***	5.937***	6.961***	8.101***
	(0.017)	(0.011)	(0.015)	(0.009)	(0.006)	(0.008)
Control group	6.493***	8.137***	9.043***	6.517***	8.056***	9.061***
	(0.031)	(0.015)	(0.015)	(0.030)	(0.015)	(0.020)
Overall Gap	−0.491***	−1.009***	−0.690***	−0.580***	−1.095***	−0.959***
	(0.036)	(0.019)	(0.021)	(0.031)	(0.016)	(0.021)

continued on next page

Table 4.6 *continued*

		PRC 02			India 04		
		10th pctile	50th pctile	90th pctile	10th pctile	50th pctile	90th pctile
	Endowment	−0.322***	−0.613***	−0.770***	−0.244***	−0.273***	−0.245***
		(0.021)	(0.015)	(0.021)	(0.010)	(0.008)	(0.010)
	Returns	−0.169***	−0.396***	0.080***	−0.337***	−0.822***	−0.714***
		(0.040)	(0.019)	(0.025)	(0.031)	(0.015)	(0.022)
Endowment Effects (Explained)	Characteristics of hhd. head	0.008	−0.006	−0.032***	−0.029***	−0.005	0.030***
		(0.011)	(0.006)	(0.009)	(0.011)	(0.007)	(0.010)
	Head education	–	–	–	–	–	–
	Head employment	0.049***	−0.016*	−0.028**	−0.140***	−0.127***	−0.094***
		(0.015)	(0.008)	(0.011)	(0.007)	(0.005)	(0.006)
	Household composition	0.019**	−0.014***	0.021***	0.009	0.011	−0.003
		(0.010)	(0.005)	(0.007)	(0.011)	(0.007)	(0.010)
	Geographic location	−0.397***	−0.576***	−0.731***	−0.083***	−0.151***	−0.178***
		(0.024)	(0.016)	(0.021)	(0.008)	(0.006)	(0.008)
Returns Effects (Unexplained)	Characteristics of hhd. head	0.607	0.183	0.447	1.147	−0.396	−0.933
		(0.989)	(0.432)	(0.559)	(0.872)	(0.417)	(0.611)
	Head education	–	–	–	–	–	–
	Head employment	−0.237**	−0.079*	−0.028	−0.364***	−0.134***	−0.043
		(0.107)	(0.047)	(0.062)	(0.090)	(0.043)	(0.064)
	Household composition	0.055	0.066	−0.119	0.379**	0.261***	0.576***
		(0.160)	(0.070)	(0.091)	(0.176)	(0.085)	(0.126)
	Geographic location	−1.135***	−0.188***	0.735***	−0.171***	0.077***	0.145***
		(0.083)	(0.037)	(0.048)	(0.058)	(0.028)	(0.041)
	Constant	0.541	−0.380	−0.956*	−1.327	−0.630	−0.459
		(1.005)	(0.439)	(0.569)	(0.882)	(0.421)	(0.617)
	Observations		17,006			40,840	

continued on next page

Table 4.6 continued

		Japan 08			Rep. of Korea 06		
		10th pctile	50th pctile	90th pctile	10th pctile	50th pctile	90th pctile
	Treatment group	9.212***	10.040***	10.670***	8.720***	9.689***	10.440***
		(0.050)	(0.029)	(0.032)	(0.017)	(0.011)	(0.012)
	Control group	9.548***	10.240***	10.870***	9.403***	10.100***	10.710***
		(0.023)	(0.012)	(0.017)	(0.011)	(0.006)	(0.009)
	Overall Gap	−0.336***	−0.198***	−0.201***	−0.682***	−0.409***	−0.272***
		(0.055)	(0.031)	(0.036)	(0.020)	(0.013)	(0.015)
	Endowment	−0.077***	−0.046***	−0.022	−0.190***	−0.002	0.037*
		(0.029)	(0.017)	(0.017)	(0.031)	(0.019)	(0.021)
	Returns	−0.259***	−0.152***	−0.179***	−0.493***	−0.407***	−0.309***
		(0.056)	(0.032)	(0.037)	(0.036)	(0.022)	(0.026)
Endowment Effects (Explained)	Characteristics of hhd. head	−0.061*	−0.015	0.034*	−0.058	0.059**	−0.040
		(0.032)	(0.016)	(0.019)	(0.041)	(0.024)	(0.028)
	Head education	–	–	–	–	–	–
	Head employment	−0.013	−0.017**	−0.024**	−0.073**	−0.104***	−0.051**
		(0.014)	(0.008)	(0.010)	(0.031)	(0.018)	(0.021)
	Household composition	0.002	−0.014	−0.020	−0.002	0.022	0.073***
		(0.025)	(0.016)	(0.017)	(0.034)	(0.021)	(0.024)
	Geographic location	−0.005	−0.001	−0.012*	−0.056*	0.021	0.054***
		(0.013)	(0.008)	(0.007)	(0.030)	(0.018)	(0.021)
Returns Effects (Unexplained)	Characteristics of hhd. head	−1.160*	−0.735**	−1.161***	0.748*	0.623***	−0.440
		(0.628)	(0.352)	(0.421)	(0.396)	(0.238)	(0.293)
	Head education	–	–	–	–	–	–
	Head employment	−0.199**	−0.036	0.119*	−0.086	0.147***	−0.025
		(0.097)	(0.054)	(0.065)	(0.056)	(0.034)	(0.043)
	Household composition	−0.088	0.213*	0.040	0.589***	0.211*	−0.034
		(0.197)	(0.111)	(0.132)	(0.189)	(0.114)	(0.142)
	Geographic location	0.279	0.019	0.133	−0.331	−0.355**	−0.168
		(0.273)	(0.152)	(0.184)	(0.276)	(0.167)	(0.214)
	Constant	0.910	0.387	0.690	−1.413***	−1.033***	0.357
		(0.733)	(0.411)	(0.491)	(0.470)	(0.284)	(0.351)
	Observations		3,318			15,081	

PRC = People's Republic of China, pctile = percentile; hhd. = household.
Notes: Standard errors computed using the delta method are in parentheses. *** $p<0.01$, ** $p<0.05$, * $p<0.1$.
Source: Author's analysis of LIS data.

Table 4.7 Quantile Decomposition for the Russian Federation 2004, 2007, and 2010 by Less/More Educated Household Head

		Russian Federation 04		
		10th pctile	50th pctile	90th pctile
	Treatment group	7.270***	8.109***	9.068***
		(0.044)	(0.025)	(0.042)
	Control group	7.566***	8.525***	9.419***
		(0.034)	(0.020)	(0.027)
	Overall Gap	−0.296***	−0.417***	−0.351***
		(0.055)	(0.032)	(0.050)
	Endowment	−0.102**	−0.237***	−0.346***
		(0.047)	(0.028)	(0.046)
	Returns	−0.194***	−0.180***	−0.005
		(0.068)	(0.037)	(0.061)
Endowment Effects (Explained)	Characteristics of hhd. head	0.119*	0.069*	0.070
		(0.068)	(0.037)	(0.063)
	Head education	–	–	–
	Head employment	−0.138***	−0.147***	−0.246***
		(0.042)	(0.024)	(0.041)
	Household composition	0.055	−0.069*	−0.074
		(0.064)	(0.037)	(0.060)
	Residence	−0.138***	−0.091***	−0.097***
		(0.024)	(0.014)	(0.024)
Returns Effects (Unexplained)	Characteristics of hhd. head	1.764**	0.384	−1.505**
		(0.776)	(0.422)	(0.672)
	Head education	–	–	–
	Head employment	−0.025	0.060	0.362***
		(0.097)	(0.053)	(0.085)
	Household composition	0.247	0.676**	1.455***
		(0.521)	(0.283)	(0.449)
	Residence	−0.257*	−0.089	−0.026
		(0.138)	(0.075)	(0.120)
	Constant	−1.923***	−1.211***	−0.291
		(0.647)	(0.351)	(0.564)
	Observations		3,086	

continued on next page

Table 4.7 continued

		Russian Federation 07		
		10th pctile	50th pctile	90th pctile
	Treatment group	7.617***	8.561***	9.505***
		(0.093)	(0.031)	(0.047)
	Control group	8.145***	9.106***	9.878***
		(0.027)	(0.018)	(0.020)
	Overall Gap	−0.528***	−0.545***	−0.373***
		(0.097)	(0.036)	(0.051)
	Endowment	−0.110	−0.237***	−0.217***
		(0.092)	(0.031)	(0.046)
	Returns	−0.417***	−0.308***	−0.156**
		(0.121)	(0.040)	(0.061)
Endowment Effects (Explained)	Characteristics of hhd. head	−0.058	0.016	−0.203**
		(0.129)	(0.040)	(0.082)
	Head education	–	–	–
	Head employment	−0.387***	−0.156***	−0.086**
		(0.084)	(0.027)	(0.041)
	Household composition	0.539***	0.001	0.178**
		(0.128)	(0.039)	(0.077)
	Residence	−0.204***	−0.098***	−0.107***
		(0.043)	(0.016)	(0.025)
Returns Effects (Unexplained)	Characteristics of hhd. head	2.756**	0.334	2.175***
		(1.265)	(0.465)	(0.674)
	Head education	–	–	–
	Head employment	0.391**	−0.002	−0.015
		(0.161)	(0.056)	(0.084)
	Household composition	−1.798**	0.116	−1.765***
		(0.841)	(0.324)	(0.458)
	Residence	0.388	0.038	0.306**
		(0.238)	(0.085)	(0.125)
	Constant	−2.154*	−0.793**	−0.857
		(1.158)	(0.401)	(0.601)
	Observations		**3,370**	

continued on next page

Table 4.7 continued

		Russian Federation 10		
		10th pctile	50th pctile	90th pctile
	Treatment group	8.122***	9.139***	9.985***
		(0.069)	(0.022)	(0.029)
	Control group	8.682***	9.477***	10.250***
		(0.018)	(0.011)	(0.016)
	Overall Gap	−0.560***	−0.339***	−0.268***
		(0.071)	(0.025)	(0.033)
	Endowment	−0.137*	−0.134***	−0.107***
		(0.073)	(0.023)	(0.031)
	Returns	−0.423***	−0.205***	−0.160***
		(0.094)	(0.030)	(0.042)
Endowment Effects (Explained)	Characteristics of hhd. head	0.458***	0.089***	−0.023
		(0.101)	(0.028)	(0.038)
	Head education	–	–	–
	Head employment	−0.351***	−0.096***	−0.060**
		(0.065)	(0.020)	(0.027)
	Household composition	−0.076	−0.031	0.032
		(0.095)	(0.028)	(0.037)
	Residence	−0.169***	−0.097***	−0.057***
		(0.036)	(0.013)	(0.017)
Returns Effects (Unexplained)	Characteristics of hhd. head	−1.437	−0.086	1.396***
		(0.990)	(0.326)	(0.458)
	Head education	–	–	–
	Head employment	0.383***	−0.045	0.007
		(0.119)	(0.040)	(0.055)
	Household composition	1.761**	0.611***	−0.393
		(0.686)	(0.227)	(0.319)
	Residence	−0.073	0.031	−0.069
		(0.179)	(0.060)	(0.084)
	Constant	−1.057	−0.716***	−1.101***
		(0.795)	(0.263)	(0.369)
	Observations		5,713	

pctile = percentile, hhd. = household.
Notes: Standard errors computed using the delta method are in parentheses. *** $p<0.01$, ** $p<0.05$, * $p<0.1$.
Source: Author's analysis of LIS data.

Table 4.8 Quantile Decomposition for Taipei,China 2005, 2007, and 2010 by Less/More Educated Household Head

		Taipei,China 05		
		10th pctile	50th pctile	90th pctile
	Treatment group	8.578***	9.298***	9.928***
		(0.015)	(0.008)	(0.011)
	Control group	9.052***	9.636***	10.320***
		(0.009)	(0.007)	(0.010)
	Overall Gap	−0.474***	−0.338***	−0.396***
		(0.017)	(0.011)	(0.015)
	Endowment	−0.226***	−0.029***	0.011
		(0.016)	(0.009)	(0.012)
	Returns	−0.248***	−0.310***	−0.407***
		(0.020)	(0.012)	(0.018)
Endowment Effects (Explained)	Characteristics of hhd. head	0.022	0.068***	0.138***
		(0.020)	(0.011)	(0.017)
	Head education	–	–	–
	Head employment	−0.190***	−0.072***	−0.055***
		(0.012)	(0.005)	(0.007)
	Household composition	−0.018	0.005	−0.022*
		(0.016)	(0.009)	(0.014)
	Residence	−0.040***	−0.030***	−0.050***
		(0.006)	(0.003)	(0.005)
Returns Effects (Unexplained)	Characteristics of hhd. head	−0.999**	−0.013	0.370
		(0.468)	(0.317)	(0.468)
	Head education	–	–	–
	Head employment	0.705***	0.025	−0.212***
		(0.067)	(0.046)	(0.068)
	Household composition	0.493	0.393	0.012
		(0.427)	(0.294)	(0.434)
	Residence	−0.106	−0.063	−0.114
		(0.110)	(0.081)	(0.120)
	Constant	−0.341	−0.651***	−0.464*
		(0.265)	(0.173)	(0.256)
	Observations		13,679	

continued on next page

Table 4.8 continued

		Taipei,China 07		
		10th pctile	50th pctile	90th pctile
	Treatment group	8.519***	9.276***	9.930***
		(0.014)	(0.009)	(0.012)
	Control group	8.997***	9.593***	10.310***
		(0.009)	(0.007)	(0.010)
	Overall Gap	−0.477***	−0.316***	−0.375***
		(0.016)	(0.011)	(0.015)
	Endowment	−0.155***	−0.003	0.071***
		(0.014)	(0.009)	(0.012)
	Returns	−0.322***	−0.313***	−0.447***
		(0.019)	(0.012)	(0.018)
Endowment Effects (Explained)	Characteristics of hhd. head	0.034**	0.103***	0.161***
		(0.016)	(0.010)	(0.014)
	Head education	–	–	–
	Head employment	−0.142***	−0.067***	−0.050***
		(0.011)	(0.006)	(0.008)
	Household composition	−0.045***	−0.030***	−0.027***
		(0.011)	(0.007)	(0.010)
	Residence	−0.002	−0.009***	−0.012***
		(0.005)	(0.003)	(0.004)
Returns Effects (Unexplained)	Characteristics of hhd. head	−0.709*	0.486*	0.124
		(0.394)	(0.274)	(0.401)
	Head education	–	–	–
	Head employment	0.551***	0.125***	−0.040
		(0.066)	(0.047)	(0.068)
	Household composition	0.142	0.039	0.602*
		(0.344)	(0.244)	(0.356)
	Residence	−0.133**	−0.047	0.116*
		(0.064)	(0.045)	(0.065)
	Constant	−0.173	−0.916***	−1.249***
		(0.255)	(0.170)	(0.250)
	Observations		13,774	

continued on next page

Table 4.8 continued

		Taipei,China 10		
		10th pctile	50th pctile	90th pctile
	Treatment group	8.417***	9.242***	9.888***
		(0.017)	(0.010)	(0.011)
	Control group	8.933***	9.587***	10.290***
		(0.009)	(0.007)	(0.009)
	Overall Gap	−0.515***	−0.344***	−0.401***
		(0.019)	(0.012)	(0.014)
	Endowment	−0.209***	−0.009	0.055***
		(0.019)	(0.012)	(0.013)
	Returns	−0.307***	−0.335***	−0.456***
		(0.024)	(0.015)	(0.019)
Endowment Effects (Explained)	Characteristics of hhd. head	0.039	0.123***	0.157***
		(0.025)	(0.015)	(0.018)
	Head education	–	–	–
	Head employment	−0.209***	−0.110***	−0.054***
		(0.014)	(0.007)	(0.008)
	Household composition	−0.031*	−0.013	−0.044***
		(0.018)	(0.011)	(0.013)
	Residence	−0.008	−0.009***	−0.004
		(0.005)	(0.003)	(0.004)
Returns Effects (Unexplained)	Characteristics of hhd. head	0.272	0.948***	0.494
		(0.491)	(0.316)	(0.419)
	Head education	–	–	–
	Head employment	0.553***	0.142***	−0.183***
		(0.071)	(0.046)	(0.061)
	Household composition	−0.670	−0.164	−0.133
		(0.434)	(0.282)	(0.377)
	Residence	−0.003	−0.017	−0.087
		(0.073)	(0.046)	(0.061)
	Constant	−0.459	−1.244***	−0.548**
		(0.304)	(0.189)	(0.244)
	Observations		**14,843**	

pctile = percentile, hhd. = household.
Notes: Standard errors computed using the delta method are in parentheses. *** $p<0.01$, ** $p<0.05$, * $p<0.1$.
Source: Author's analysis of LIS data.

4.5.4 Non-employed/Employed Gap

Table 4.9 row 3 shows that the income gap due to the employment status of household heads is high in the Republic of Korea and non-negligible in Japan, particularly in the lower half of the income distribution. In the PRC and India, households with non-employed heads receive a premium, particularly in the lower half of the income distribution in the PRC, and in the upper half of the income distribution in India. This is puzzling, but may reflect the significance of the shadow economy and informal resource markets across the PRC and India, or high prevalence among households of relying on saved wealth and capital earnings rather than labor earnings for income. Another possible explanation has to do with the contributions or remittances from household members and relatives other than household head. To the extent that households with high flows of incomes from other household members have higher reported incomes and their heads may be less likely to work, this may explain the puzzle. This reaches to the highest echelons of society in both countries. In fact, Table A4.4 in the Appendix shows that the employment rate in the PRC, and slightly more weakly in India, is highest among the poorest households. The evidence for the PRC in Table 4.9 should thus be interpreted as comparing labor class (control group) versus leisure class (treatment group).

Table 4.9 Quantile Decomposition for the PRC 2002, India 2004, Japan 2008, and Republic of Korea 2006 by Non-employed/Employed Household Head

	PRC 02			India 04		
	10th pctile	50th pctile	90th pctile	10th pctile	50th pctile	90th pctile
Treatment group	6.589***	8.138***	8.949***	5.871***	7.293***	8.473***
	(0.046)	(0.020)	(0.020)	(0.031)	(0.015)	(0.023)
Control group	6.082***	7.293***	8.661***	5.985***	7.008***	8.270***
	(0.014)	(0.012)	(0.012)	(0.008)	(0.006)	(0.009)
Overall Gap	0.507***	0.845***	0.288***	−0.114***	0.285***	0.203***
	(0.048)	(0.023)	(0.023)	(0.032)	(0.016)	(0.024)
Endowment	1.214***	0.650***	0.214***	0.433***	0.285***	0.380***
	(0.065)	(0.028)	(0.029)	(0.046)	(0.022)	(0.033)
Returns	−0.707***	0.195***	0.074**	−0.546***	−0.000	−0.177***
	(0.072)	(0.031)	(0.035)	(0.054)	(0.025)	(0.039)

continued on next page

Table 4.9 continued

		PRC 02			India 04		
		10th pctile	50th pctile	90th pctile	10th pctile	50th pctile	90th pctile
Endowment Effects (Explained)	Characteristics of hhd. head	−0.043	0.217***	0.137***	0.051	0.130***	0.237***
		(0.075)	(0.031)	(0.036)	(0.092)	(0.042)	(0.065)
	Head education	0.003	0.0002	0.006	−0.016***	−0.029***	−0.025***
		(0.006)	(0.005)	(0.006)	(0.005)	(0.005)	(0.008)
	Head employment	–	–	–	–	–	–
	Household composition	0.001	0.007	−0.025	0.313***	0.094**	0.107*
		(0.051)	(0.021)	(0.024)	(0.085)	(0.038)	(0.060)
	Geographic location	1.253***	0.425***	0.096***	0.085***	0.089***	0.062***
		(0.057)	(0.023)	(0.024)	(0.011)	(0.006)	(0.008)
Returns Effects (Unexplained)	Characteristics of hhd. head	−2.344**	1.809***	0.528	1.323**	−0.160	0.404
		(1.010)	(0.481)	(0.559)	(0.590)	(0.280)	(0.437)
	Head education	−0.019	0.368***	0.057	0.038	0.120***	0.043
		(0.224)	(0.107)	(0.124)	(0.045)	(0.021)	(0.033)
	Head employment	–	–	–	–	–	–
	Household composition	−0.028	0.071	0.253**	0.669***	0.102	0.173
		(0.187)	(0.086)	(0.099)	(0.201)	(0.094)	(0.147)
	Geographic location	0.815***	−0.154***	−0.235***	0.039	−0.009	−0.110***
		(0.075)	(0.034)	(0.039)	(0.048)	(0.023)	(0.035)
	Constant	0.870	−1.898***	−0.529	−2.615***	−0.052	−0.687
		(1.068)	(0.506)	(0.587)	(0.636)	(0.301)	(0.469)
Observations		17,029			41,004		

		Japan 08			Rep. of Korea 06		
		10th pctile	50th pctile	90th pctile	10th pctile	50th pctile	90th pctile
	Treatment group	9.269***	10.060***	10.750***	8.360***	9.420***	10.45***
		(0.038)	(0.020)	(0.037)	(0.039)	(0.019)	(0.031)
	Control group	9.593***	10.270***	10.870***	9.351***	10.060***	10.670***
		(0.021)	(0.013)	(0.019)	(0.009)	(0.006)	(0.007)
	Overall Gap	−0.325***	−0.212***	−0.122***	−0.991***	−0.640***	−0.216***
		(0.044)	(0.023)	(0.042)	(0.040)	(0.019)	(0.032)

continued on next page

Table 4.9 *continued*

		Japan 08			Rep. of Korea 06		
		10th pctile	50th pctile	90th pctile	10th pctile	50th pctile	90th pctile
Endowment Effects (Explained)	Endowment	0.040	−0.009	−0.014	−0.055	−0.219***	−0.126***
		(0.044)	(0.023)	(0.043)	(0.052)	(0.025)	(0.041)
	Returns	−0.365***	−0.203***	−0.108*	−0.936***	−0.421***	−0.090*
		(0.061)	(0.031)	(0.058)	(0.065)	(0.029)	(0.050)
	Characteristics of hhd. head	0.125**	0.080***	0.136***	0.405**	−0.206**	0.311**
		(0.053)	(0.027)	(0.050)	(0.186)	(0.083)	(0.144)
	Head education	−0.046***	−0.010	−0.038**	−0.098***	−0.188***	−0.201***
		(0.016)	(0.008)	(0.015)	(0.028)	(0.014)	(0.023)
	Head employment	–	–	–	–	–	–
	Household composition	−0.039	−0.077***	−0.112***	−0.360*	0.175**	−0.232
		(0.031)	(0.017)	(0.031)	(0.184)	(0.082)	(0.142)
	Geographic location	−0.000	−0.001	0.000	−0.003	−0.001	−0.004*
		(0.005)	(0.003)	(0.003)	(0.003)	(0.001)	(0.002)
Returns Effects (Unexplained)	Characteristics of hhd. head	−1.127**	−0.774***	−0.147	−0.680	0.755**	0.437
		(0.522)	(0.272)	(0.494)	(0.700)	(0.318)	(0.542)
	Head education	0.015	−0.115	0.024	−0.150	0.458***	0.302**
		(0.144)	(0.076)	(0.134)	(0.165)	(0.078)	(0.129)
	Head employment	–	–	–	–	–	–
	Household composition	−0.030	0.153*	0.276*	1.486***	−0.341	0.921**
		(0.162)	(0.084)	(0.154)	(0.515)	(0.232)	(0.398)
	Geographic location	0.116	0.009	0.020	0.062	0.032	0.153**
		(0.161)	(0.084)	(0.153)	(0.080)	(0.036)	(0.062)
	Constant	0.662	0.523*	−0.280	−1.654***	−1.325***	−1.904***
		(0.598)	(0.311)	(0.566)	(0.538)	(0.247)	(0.417)
	Observations	3,318			15,081		

PRC = People's Republic of China, pctile = percentile, hhd. = household.
Notes: Standard errors computed using the delta method are in parentheses. *** $p<0.01$, ** $p<0.05$, * $p<0.1$.
Source: Author's analysis of LIS data.

Table 4.10 Quantile Decomposition for the Russian Federation 2004, 2007, and 2010 by Non-employed/Employed Household Head

		Russian Federation 04		
		10th pctile	50th pctile	90th pctile
	Treatment group	7.330***	8.121***	9.066***
		(0.039)	(0.019)	(0.033)
	Control group	7.565***	8.587***	9.465***
		(0.040)	(0.023)	(0.030)
	Overall Gap	−0.235***	−0.467***	−0.399***
		(0.056)	(0.030)	(0.045)
	Endowment	0.097**	−0.128***	−0.272***
		(0.047)	(0.023)	(0.039)
	Returns	−0.332***	−0.339***	−0.127**
		(0.069)	(0.033)	(0.055)
Endowment Effects (Explained)	Characteristics of hhd. head	0.119	0.078**	−0.226***
		(0.087)	(0.039)	(0.077)
	Head education	−0.072***	−0.069***	−0.078***
		(0.028)	(0.013)	(0.023)
	Head employment	–	–	–
	Household composition	0.091	−0.111***	0.062
		(0.077)	(0.035)	(0.068)
	Residence	−0.042***	−0.027***	−0.031**
		(0.014)	(0.008)	(0.013)
Returns Effects (Unexplained)	Characteristics of hhd. head	1.370	0.585	1.767***
		(0.878)	(0.446)	(0.683)
	Head education	0.189	−0.505	0.003
		(0.796)	(0.431)	(0.602)
	Head employment	–	–	–
	Household composition	0.323	−0.208	−0.349
		(0.583)	(0.292)	(0.457)
	Residence	−0.252*	−0.181***	−0.112
		(0.138)	(0.069)	(0.108)
	Constant	−1.962*	−0.030	−1.437*
		(1.024)	(0.542)	(0.783)
	Observations		3,086	

continued on next page

Table 4.10 *continued*

		Russian Federation 07		
		10th pctile	50th pctile	90th pctile
	Treatment group	7.785***	8.659***	9.576***
		(0.042)	(0.025)	(0.027)
	Control group	8.234***	9.196***	9.933***
		(0.035)	(0.019)	(0.023)
	Overall Gap	−0.448***	−0.537***	−0.358***
		(0.054)	(0.032)	(0.035)
	Endowment	0.063	−0.133***	−0.103***
		(0.049)	(0.030)	(0.032)
	Returns	−0.512***	−0.404***	−0.255***
		(0.069)	(0.039)	(0.044)
Endowment Effects (Explained)	Characteristics of hhd. head	−0.069	0.028	−0.249***
		(0.122)	(0.070)	(0.083)
	Head education	−0.090***	−0.081***	−0.076***
		(0.027)	(0.016)	(0.017)
	Head employment	–	–	–
	Household composition	0.274**	−0.054	0.226***
		(0.115)	(0.066)	(0.079)
	Residence	−0.051***	−0.026***	−0.004
		(0.016)	(0.010)	(0.011)
Returns Effects (Unexplained)	Characteristics of hhd. head	1.229	−0.824	0.877
		(0.920)	(0.509)	(0.589)
	Head education	0.486	−0.146	0.528
		(2.439)	(1.269)	(1.575)
	Head employment	–	–	–
	Household composition	−0.657	0.489	−0.603
		(0.712)	(0.400)	(0.456)
	Residence	−0.184	−0.148*	−0.159*
		(0.139)	(0.077)	(0.089)
	Constant	−1.385	0.224	−0.899
		(2.508)	(1.309)	(1.619)
	Observations		3,370	

continued on next page

Table 4.10 continued

		Russian Federation 10		
		10th pctile	50th pctile	90th pctile
	Treatment group	8.317***	9.232***	10.010***
		(0.035)	(0.013)	(0.024)
	Control group	8.721***	9.558***	10.290***
		(0.021)	(0.013)	(0.018)
	Overall Gap	−0.404***	−0.327***	−0.280***
		(0.041)	(0.019)	(0.030)
	Endowment	0.227***	−0.015	−0.109***
		(0.040)	(0.015)	(0.027)
	Returns	−0.631***	−0.311***	−0.171***
		(0.053)	(0.021)	(0.037)
Endowment Effects (Explained)	Characteristics of hhd. head	0.240***	0.094***	−0.005
		(0.081)	(0.028)	(0.055)
	Head education	−0.083***	−0.058***	−0.092***
		(0.021)	(0.007)	(0.014)
	Head employment	−	−	−
	Household composition	0.099	−0.037	−0.007
		(0.073)	(0.026)	(0.049)
	Residence	−0.029***	−0.015***	−0.005
		(0.010)	(0.005)	(0.009)
Returns Effects (Unexplained)	Characteristics of hhd. head	1.339**	0.194	0.660
		(0.631)	(0.270)	(0.452)
	Head education	0.070	1.059	0.277
		(1.945)	(1.183)	(1.648)
	Head employment	−	−	−
	Household composition	−0.553	0.529***	0.127
		(0.503)	(0.199)	(0.350)
	Residence	−0.045	−0.033	−0.064
		(0.102)	(0.044)	(0.074)
	Constant	−1.441	−2.060*	−1.170
		(1.980)	(1.194)	(1.670)
	Observations		5,713	

'pctile = percentile, hhd. = household.
Notes: Standard errors computed using the delta method are in parentheses. *** $p<0.01$, ** $p<0.05$, * $p<0.1$.
Source: Author's analysis of LIS data.

Table 4.11 Quantile Decomposition for Taipei,China 2005, 2007, and 2010 by Non-employed/Employed Household Head

		Taipei,China 05		
		10th pctile	50th pctile	90th pctile
	Treatment group	8.086***	8.788***	9.759***
		(0.021)	(0.016)	(0.022)
	Control group	8.967***	9.549***	10.230***
		(0.007)	(0.006)	(0.008)
	Overall Gap	−0.881***	−0.762***	−0.470***
		(0.022)	(0.017)	(0.024)
	Endowment	0.241***	0.055	−0.045
		(0.056)	(0.039)	(0.055)
	Returns	−1.122***	−0.817***	−0.425***
		(0.060)	(0.041)	(0.058)
Endowment Effects (Explained)	Characteristics of hhd. head	0.149*	0.236***	0.021
		(0.089)	(0.061)	(0.085)
	Head education	−0.078***	−0.190***	−0.170***
		(0.018)	(0.014)	(0.020)
	Head employment	−	−	−
	Household composition	0.155*	−0.015	0.078
		(0.084)	(0.058)	(0.081)
	Residence	0.014***	0.024***	0.026***
		(0.004)	(0.005)	(0.006)
Returns Effects (Unexplained)	Characteristics of hhd. head	0.167	−0.312	0.967
		(0.744)	(0.515)	(0.730)
	Head education	−0.212***	0.186***	0.003
		(0.077)	(0.055)	(0.080)
	Head employment	−	−	−
	Household composition	−0.946	0.258	−0.237
		(0.663)	(0.459)	(0.651)
	Residence	−0.337**	0.125	0.044
		(0.133)	(0.092)	(0.131)
	Constant	0.207	−1.073***	−1.201***
		(0.432)	(0.299)	(0.424)
	Observations		13,679	

continued on next page

Table 4.11 *continued*

		Taipei,China 07		
		10th pctile	50th pctile	90th pctile
	Treatment group	8.108***	8.853***	9.814***
		(0.021)	(0.018)	(0.023)
	Control group	8.904***	9.512***	10.220***
		(0.008)	(0.006)	(0.009)
	Overall Gap	−0.796***	−0.659***	−0.405***
		(0.022)	(0.019)	(0.024)
	Endowment	0.081	−0.122*	0.023
		(0.088)	(0.068)	(0.089)
	Returns	−0.877***	−0.537***	−0.428***
		(0.090)	(0.069)	(0.091)
Endowment Effects (Explained)	Characteristics of hhd. head	0.267***	0.326***	0.242***
		(0.063)	(0.049)	(0.063)
	Head education	−0.145***	−0.242***	−0.183***
		(0.019)	(0.017)	(0.021)
	Head employment	−	−	−
	Household composition	0.003	−0.202***	−0.051
		(0.058)	(0.045)	(0.058)
	Residence	−0.044	−0.004	0.015
		(0.066)	(0.051)	(0.066)
Returns Effects (Unexplained)	Characteristics of hhd. head	−0.063	0.768**	0.842**
		(0.397)	(0.303)	(0.403)
	Head education	0.026	0.455***	0.035
		(0.079)	(0.058)	(0.084)
	Head employment	−	−	−
	Household composition	−0.122	0.230*	0.448**
		(0.180)	(0.138)	(0.181)
	Residence	−0.714	−0.202	0.062
		(0.662)	(0.510)	(0.664)
	Constant	−0.003	−1.788***	−1.815**
		(0.856)	(0.657)	(0.861)
	Observations		**13,774**	

continued on next page

Table 4.11 *continued*

		Taipei,China 10		
		10th pctile	50th pctile	90th pctile
	Treatment group	7.934***	8.824***	9.880***
		(0.025)	(0.018)	(0.023)
	Control group	8.874***	9.527***	10.220***
		(0.008)	(0.006)	(0.009)
	Overall Gap	−0.940***	−0.703***	−0.343***
		(0.026)	(0.019)	(0.024)
	Endowment	0.221**	−0.019	−0.027
		(0.090)	(0.059)	(0.077)
	Returns	−1.161***	−0.685***	−0.315***
		(0.094)	(0.061)	(0.079)
Endowment Effects (Explained)	Characteristics of hhd. head	0.014	0.134*	−0.179*
		(0.105)	(0.069)	(0.097)
	Head education	−0.110***	−0.284***	−0.239***
		(0.022)	(0.017)	(0.021)
	Head employment	–	–	–
	Household composition	0.342***	0.091	0.376***
		(0.098)	(0.064)	(0.092)
	Residence	−0.025	0.040	0.015
		(0.056)	(0.036)	(0.047)
Returns Effects (Unexplained)	Characteristics of hhd. head	−1.365	0.675	3.181***
		(0.832)	(0.543)	(0.722)
	Head education	−0.267**	0.548***	0.142
		(0.115)	(0.077)	(0.113)
	Head employment	–	–	–
	Household composition	−0.789	−1.008**	−2.984***
		(0.704)	(0.460)	(0.613)
	Residence	−0.513	0.280	0.050
		(0.597)	(0.388)	(0.506)
	Constant	1.773**	−1.180**	−0.703
		(0.851)	(0.554)	(0.728)
	Observations		14,843	

pctile = percentile, hhd. = household.
Notes: Standard errors computed using the delta method are in parentheses. *** $p<0.01$, ** $p<0.05$, * $p<0.1$.
Source: Author's analysis of LIS data.

In the Russian Federation and especially in Taipei,China (Tables 4.10 and 4.11), the employment gap is large negative, particularly among the poorest households. The non-employed poor are thus particularly disadvantaged relative to their employed peers. Across the three waves of Russian and Taipei,China surveys, the employment gap fluctuates over time, perhaps even slightly growing among the poorest households, and falling among the richest households.

Decomposing the non-employment/employment gap into the endowment and returns effects also yields divergent trends across the 10 surveys. In the PRC and India, the non-employed households' income premium is almost entirely due to the high (positive) endowment effects, as non-employed household heads have more advantageous characteristics and geographic residence than their working peers, particularly among the first through fifth income-decile households. In India they also have more advantageous household composition, and these surpluses in endowments offset significant shortages in educational attainment among non-employed household heads. The returns effect is negative among households in the bottom three income-deciles, and vanishes to essentially zero among higher-decile groups. This suggests that non-employed households in the PRC, particularly those in the bottom half of the income distribution have higher endowments than their employed counterparts. Even though these non-employed households also receive lower returns on their endowments than the employed households, in the composite the earnings of the non-employed group are higher.

Hence, the returns effects further favor non-employed median- and high-income households in the PRC, while they favor working households in India, and working householders among the poor in the PRC. Across individual household endowments and income quantiles, the returns effects are not consistent qualitatively or quantitatively. The most significant finding is that the return to geographic location favors non-working households among the poor, while it favors working households in the middle and upper half of the income distribution.

In Japan and Republic of Korea, both the endowment and returns effects have the expected negative signs, favoring households with working heads. The returns effects are consistently larger in absolute value than the endowment effects, and particularly large among the lowest income-quantile groups. The endowment effects are near zero—balancing the contrary signs of the differentials in the returns to householders' characteristics, and to education and household composition between working and non-working households—and only become significant at richer income quantiles in Republic of Korea. The strong negative composite effects are caused by the differentials in returns to householder characteristics, in the case of Japan, and by differentials in returns to various endowments, in the Korean case. In Japan, non-working households receive systematically lower returns on householder characteristics than their working counterparts, while in both countries non-working households appear to receive higher returns on education and household composition.

In the Russian Federation, the endowment component of the employment gap is positive among poor households, suggesting that poor non-employed households are more endowed with marketable characteristics than the working poor (most notably characteristics of household heads), while richer non-employed households are less endowed than their employed counterparts. The returns effects are significantly negative and larger in magnitude among lower-income households, exerting the greatest harm on poor non-working households. This is due to a differential in the returns to the proximity to markets between working and non-working households.

In Taipei,China, the endowment component of the employment gap is largely nonexistent across years and income quantiles, even though it is consistently positive among the lowest-decile group. Non-employed households appear to have heads with more favorable demographic characteristics and more favorable household composition, but they are also less educated. On balance, these endowment effects cancel out (except among the lowest decile). The returns component drives most of the employment gap in incomes. Non-working households appear to face lower returns on their composition.

4.5.5 Female/Male Income Gap

The final dimension along which we decompose inequality is gender of the household head. The third row in Tables 4.12–4.14 shows that gender gap in favor of male households is high among the poorest households in India, the Republic of Korea, and Taipei,China, and much smaller (but still favoring male households) among households with median or high incomes. In the PRC, like with the employment gap, gender gap is very high positive, meaning that female households receive a large premium compared with male-headed households. Once again this could be explained by the existence of remittances from partners or ex-husbands who are not present in the household but contribute to household income (Ramadan et al. 2015). This pro-female income differential in the PRC is high across all income quantiles, particularly among low and median income groups, suggesting that while the unusual arrangements are widespread even among the richest households, perhaps they are most prevalent among business-owning families in the middle class, and among poor rural households with migrant bread-winners living temporarily in cities.

In Japan and the Russian Federation, the gap is relatively small across the board, and only statistically significant among richer households.[7] Over time, gender gap gradually increases in the Russian Federation, while it stays relatively unchanged in Taipei,China.

Decomposing this gender gap into the endowment and the returns effects, we also find divergent results across the six economies. In the PRC, the pro-female gap is due equally to a large positive endowment effect and a large positive returns effect (except for a large negative returns effect among the poorest decile). Female households appear to have higher education, and more advantageous geographic location. They also receive higher returns to their employment, to the characteristics of their household head and possibly to their education than male households.

Table 4.12 Quantile Decomposition for the PRC 2002, India 2004, Japan 2008, and Republic of Korea 2006 by Female/Male Household Head

	The PRC 02			India 04		
	10th pctile	50th pctile	90th pctile	10th pctile	50th pctile	90th pctile
Treatment group	6.957***	8.345***	9.141***	5.622***	6.935***	8.212***
	(0.058)	(0.016)	(0.025)	(0.032)	(0.020)	(0.024)
Control group	6.074***	7.256***	8.589***	6.005***	7.051***	8.318***
	(0.014)	(0.011)	(0.012)	(0.008)	(0.006)	(0.009)
Overall Gap	0.883***	1.089***	0.553***	−0.383***	−0.116***	−0.106***
	(0.060)	(0.019)	(0.028)	(0.033)	(0.021)	(0.025)
Endowment	3.324***	0.497***	0.293***	−0.662***	0.060	−0.126
	(0.089)	(0.026)	(0.044)	(0.187)	(0.108)	(0.131)

continued on next page

---

[7] The results for Japan and the Republic of Korea provide an interesting picture about the manifestation of gender gaps across the income distribution—while the Republic of Korea has significantly graver gender gaps overall, these gaps fall below those in Japan in the upper tail of the income distribution. This possibly corroborates evidence by Youm and Yamaguchi (2016) that glass-ceiling discrimination against female managers is high in Japan, and that by mid-2000s this problem had reached similar levels in the Republic of Korea.

Table 4.12 *continued*

		The PRC 02			India 04		
		10th pctile	50th pctile	90th pctile	10th pctile	50th pctile	90th pctile
Endowment Effects (Explained)	Returns	−2.441***	0.592***	0.259***	0.279	−0.176	0.020
		(0.089)	(0.029)	(0.050)	(0.189)	(0.109)	(0.133)
	Characteristics of hhd. head	−0.037	−0.060***	−0.038	−0.764	−0.367	−0.849
		(0.053)	(0.017)	(0.030)	(1.270)	(0.733)	(0.891)
	Head education	0.0084	0.105***	0.103***	−0.117***	−0.207***	−0.383***
		(0.028)	(0.010)	(0.016)	(0.028)	(0.017)	(0.022)
	Head employment	−0.054	−0.037**	−0.050	−0.139***	−0.002	−0.017
		(0.054)	(0.018)	(0.031)	(0.025)	(0.015)	(0.018)
	Household composition	0.084	0.021	0.025	0.336	0.612	1.114
		(0.071)	(0.023)	(0.041)	(1.249)	(0.722)	(0.877)
	Geographic location	3.323***	0.469***	0.253***	0.021***	0.024***	0.010**
		(0.106)	(0.031)	(0.055)	(0.006)	(0.005)	(0.004)
Returns Effects (Unexplained)	Characteristics of hhd. head	0.359	0.976**	0.174	2.517*	0.979	0.622
		(0.991)	(0.403)	(0.612)	(1.407)	(0.816)	(1.001)
	Head education	0.447	0.300***	−0.034	0.118**	0.139***	0.286***
		(0.274)	(0.104)	(0.165)	(0.051)	(0.030)	(0.037)
	Head employment	0.140	0.141***	0.196**	−0.017	−0.108***	−0.082
		(0.128)	(0.049)	(0.078)	(0.067)	(0.040)	(0.050)
	Household composition	−0.389	0.058	−0.019	0.074	−0.120	−0.780
		(0.242)	(0.086)	(0.143)	(1.277)	(0.738)	(0.897)
	Geographic location	1.514***	−0.126***	−0.240***	−0.155***	−0.011	−0.046
		(0.092)	(0.032)	(0.053)	(0.050)	(0.029)	(0.036)
	Constant	−4.511***	−0.756*	0.182	−2.259***	−1.055***	0.019
		(1.073)	(0.429)	(0.658)	(0.561)	(0.334)	(0.430)
	Observations		17,029			41,004	

continued on next page

Table 4.12 *continued*

		Japan 08			Rep. of Korea 06		
		10th pctile	50th pctile	90th pctile	10th pctile	50th pctile	90th pctile
	Treatment group	9.406***	10.140***	10.700***	8.807***	9.747***	10.550***
		(0.111)	(0.032)	(0.051)	(0.023)	(0.014)	(0.016)
	Control group	9.496***	10.220***	10.860***	9.282***	10.060***	10.670***
		(0.021)	(0.012)	(0.017)	(0.012)	(0.006)	(0.008)
	Overall Gap	−0.090	−0.076**	−0.156***	−0.475***	−0.311***	−0.120***
		(0.113)	(0.034)	(0.054)	(0.026)	(0.015)	(0.018)
	Endowment	−0.136**	−0.055***	−0.051*	−0.190***	−0.141***	−0.079***
		(0.064)	(0.020)	(0.029)	(0.042)	(0.026)	(0.030)
	Returns	0.046	−0.022	−0.106*	−0.285***	−0.170***	−0.041
		(0.118)	(0.033)	(0.056)	(0.047)	(0.029)	(0.034)
Endowment Effects (Explained)	Characteristics of hhd. head	−0.042	−0.011	0.004	−0.273	0.024	−0.339**
		(0.039)	(0.009)	(0.015)	(0.223)	(0.136)	(0.160)
	Head education	−0.111**	−0.027**	−0.039**	−0.055***	−0.142***	−0.163***
		(0.044)	(0.012)	(0.019)	(0.018)	(0.012)	(0.014)
	Head employment	0.008	−0.006	−0.006	−0.101***	−0.044***	0.025
		(0.024)	(0.007)	(0.009)	(0.021)	(0.013)	(0.015)
	Household composition	0.024	0.014	0.014	0.226	0.038	0.395**
		(0.034)	(0.011)	(0.017)	(0.221)	(0.135)	(0.159)
	Geographic location	−0.015	−0.025***	−0.023	0.014	−0.016	0.003
		(0.031)	(0.009)	(0.014)	(0.016)	(0.010)	(0.011)
Returns Effects (Unexplained)	Characteristics of hhd. head	−1.818	−0.097	−0.409	0.519	0.308	0.687**
		(1.315)	(0.376)	(0.629)	(0.478)	(0.277)	(0.338)
	Head education	0.727**	0.112	0.125	−0.327**	0.264***	0.186*
		(0.355)	(0.103)	(0.172)	(0.138)	(0.077)	(0.097)
	Head employment	0.076	−0.076	−0.019	−0.759***	−0.095**	−0.164***
		(0.213)	(0.061)	(0.101)	(0.067)	(0.038)	(0.047)
	Household composition	0.0024	0.268**	−0.140	−0.473	0.327	−0.136
		(0.397)	(0.114)	(0.190)	(0.370)	(0.216)	(0.263)
	Geographic location	0.141	0.091	0.124	−0.262	−0.306	0.364
		(0.224)	(0.065)	(0.109)	(0.343)	(0.200)	(0.243)
	Constant	0.919	−0.319	0.214	1.018**	−0.670**	−0.977***
		(1.440)	(0.412)	(0.690)	(0.500)	(0.288)	(0.353)
	Observations		3,318			15,081	

PRC = People's Republic of China, pctile = percentile, hhd. = household.
Notes: Standard errors computed using the delta method are in parentheses. *** p<0.01, ** p<0.05, * p<0.1.
Source: Author's analysis of LIS data.

Table 4.13 Quantile Decomposition for the Russian Federation 2004, 2007, and 2010 by Female/Male Household Head

		Russian Federation 04		
		10th pctile	50th pctile	90th pctile
	Treatment group	7.484***	8.406***	9.341***
		(0.029)	(0.019)	(0.022)
	Control group	7.281***	8.423***	9.411***
		(0.092)	(0.057)	(0.074)
	Overall Gap	0.203**	−0.017	−0.070
		(0.096)	(0.060)	(0.077)
	Endowment	0.028	0.045	−0.028
		(0.037)	(0.032)	(0.030)
	Returns	0.176*	−0.061	−0.041
		(0.095)	(0.055)	(0.075)
Endowment Effects (Explained)	Characteristics of hhd. head	−0.007	−0.012	0.017
		(0.011)	(0.009)	(0.026)
	Head education	−0.003	0.020*	0.012
		(0.012)	(0.011)	(0.008)
	Head employment	0.012	−0.007	−0.027*
		(0.018)	(0.013)	(0.014)
	Household composition	0.000	0.053***	−0.018
		(0.023)	(0.020)	(0.026)
	Residence	0.025	−0.010	−0.012
		(0.021)	(0.017)	(0.017)
Returns Effects (Unexplained)	Characteristics of hhd. head	−0.341	1.471**	1.291
		(1.200)	(0.692)	(0.943)
	Head education	0.841*	−0.109	−0.102
		(0.454)	(0.261)	(0.356)
	Head employment	−0.318*	−0.292***	−0.375***
		(0.169)	(0.098)	(0.133)
	Household composition	0.523	−0.737	−0.713
		(0.878)	(0.506)	(0.690)
	Residence	−0.284	−0.160	−0.053
		(0.286)	(0.164)	(0.225)
	Constant	−0.246	−0.234	−0.089
		(1.053)	(0.607)	(0.827)
	Observations		3,086	

continued on next page

Table 4.13 continued

		Russian Federation 07		
		10th pctile	50th pctile	90th pctile
	Treatment group	8.006***	8.992***	9.808***
		(0.026)	(0.017)	(0.019)
	Control group	8.039***	9.096***	9.943***
		(0.059)	(0.066)	(0.043)
	Overall Gap	−0.033	−0.104	−0.135***
		(0.064)	(0.068)	(0.047)
	Endowment	−0.036	−0.004	−0.048*
		(0.033)	(0.028)	(0.027)
	Returns	0.003	−0.100*	−0.088*
		(0.064)	(0.059)	(0.046)
Endowment Effects (Explained)	Characteristics of hhd. head	−0.006	−0.006	0.005
		(0.020)	(0.015)	(0.009)
	Head education	0.005	−0.007	−0.008
		(0.013)	(0.008)	(0.009)
	Head employment	0.024	−0.003	−0.002
		(0.016)	(0.012)	(0.010)
	Household composition	−0.026	0.054***	0.013
		(0.018)	(0.015)	(0.012)
	Residence	−0.033**	−0.042***	−0.056***
		(0.017)	(0.015)	(0.018)
Returns Effects (Unexplained)	Characteristics of hhd. head	−0.603	−0.604	0.131
		(0.599)	(0.525)	(0.438)
	Head education	0.458	−0.072	0.024
		(0.372)	(0.325)	(0.272)
	Head employment	−0.121	−0.524***	−0.064
		(0.096)	(0.088)	(0.070)
	Household composition	0.263	0.420*	−0.101
		(0.260)	(0.232)	(0.190)
	Residence	0.377**	0.054	0.033
		(0.164)	(0.147)	(0.120)
	Constant	−0.371	0.626	−0.112
		(0.668)	(0.581)	(0.488)
	Observations		**3,370**	

continued on next page

Table 4.13 *continued*

		Russian Federation 10		
		10th pctile	50th pctile	90th pctile
	Treatment group	8.561***	9.404***	10.200***
		(0.022)	(0.011)	(0.014)
	Control group	8.689***	9.517***	10.390***
		(0.049)	(0.034)	(0.056)
	Overall Gap	−0.128**	−0.113***	−0.187***
		(0.054)	(0.036)	(0.057)
	Endowment	−0.067**	−0.037**	−0.058***
		(0.026)	(0.017)	(0.019)
	Returns	−0.061	−0.076**	−0.129**
		(0.054)	(0.033)	(0.054)
Endowment Effects (Explained)	Characteristics of hhd. head	−0.016	−0.018***	−0.011
		(0.012)	(0.007)	(0.007)
	Head education	0.010	0.0015	−0.008
		(0.010)	(0.006)	(0.006)
	Head employment	−0.020	−0.013*	−0.008
		(0.015)	(0.007)	(0.007)
	Household composition	−0.037**	0.014	0.008
		(0.015)	(0.009)	(0.009)
	Residence	−0.004	−0.022**	−0.039***
		(0.012)	(0.010)	(0.013)
Returns Effects (Unexplained)	Characteristics of hhd. head	−0.723	−0.364	2.317***
		(0.787)	(0.480)	(0.810)
	Head education	0.328	0.226	−0.720**
		(0.362)	(0.215)	(0.357)
	Head employment	−0.124	−0.217***	−0.320***
		(0.089)	(0.054)	(0.090)
	Household composition	0.431	0.334	−1.533**
		(0.693)	(0.427)	(0.725)
	Residence	0.366***	0.089	0.095
		(0.142)	(0.086)	(0.145)
	Constant	−0.339	−0.143	0.032
		(0.562)	(0.332)	(0.552)
	Observations		5,713	

pctile = percentile, hhd. = household.
Notes: Standard errors computed using the delta method are in parentheses. *** $p<0.01$, ** $p<0.05$, * $p<0.1$.
Source: Author's analysis of LIS data.

Table 4.14 Quantile Decomposition for Taipei,China 2005, 2007, and 2010 by Female/Male Household Head

		Taipei,China 05		
		10th pctile	50th pctile	90th pctile
	Treatment group	8.654***	9.415***	10.180***
		(0.019)	(0.013)	(0.017)
	Control group	8.886***	9.522***	10.210***
		(0.010)	(0.006)	(0.009)
	Overall Gap	−0.232***	−0.107***	−0.029
		(0.022)	(0.015)	(0.019)
	Endowment	−0.122***	−0.054***	−0.076***
		(0.022)	(0.016)	(0.020)
	Returns	−0.110***	−0.054***	0.047*
		(0.026)	(0.018)	(0.025)
Endowment Effects (Explained)	Characteristics of hhd. head	−0.099***	−0.012	−0.043
		(0.035)	(0.025)	(0.035)
	Head education	−0.038***	−0.013*	−0.000
		(0.007)	(0.007)	(0.008)
	Head employment	−0.087***	0.015**	0.001
		(0.014)	(0.007)	(0.009)
	Household composition	0.088**	−0.061**	−0.055
		(0.035)	(0.025)	(0.034)
	Residence	0.013***	0.017***	0.022***
		(0.003)	(0.003)	(0.004)
Returns Effects (Unexplained)	Characteristics of hhd. head	0.488**	0.619***	−0.097
		(0.236)	(0.163)	(0.231)
	Head education	−0.308***	0.194***	0.070
		(0.088)	(0.061)	(0.086)
	Head employment	0.139**	−0.033	−0.219***
		(0.069)	(0.047)	(0.067)
	Household composition	−0.217***	0.116**	0.196***
		(0.076)	(0.053)	(0.075)
	Residence	−0.000	0.078	−0.093
		(0.139)	(0.098)	(0.137)
	Constant	−0.212	−1.028***	0.190
		(0.280)	(0.194)	(0.275)
	Observations		13,679	

continued on next page

Table 4.14 continued

		Taipei,China 07		
		10th pctile	50th pctile	90th pctile
	Treatment group	8.595***	9.365***	10.170***
		(0.018)	(0.013)	(0.021)
	Control group	8.834***	9.499***	10.210***
		(0.010)	(0.006)	(0.009)
	Overall Gap	−0.239***	−0.135***	−0.043*
		(0.020)	(0.014)	(0.023)
	Endowment	−0.124***	−0.097***	−0.131***
		(0.021)	(0.016)	(0.025)
	Returns	−0.115***	−0.037**	0.088***
		(0.026)	(0.019)	(0.031)
Endowment Effects (Explained)	Characteristics of hhd. head	−0.091	−0.164	0.130
		(0.182)	(0.132)	(0.221)
	Head education	−0.035***	−0.008	−0.005
		(0.007)	(0.007)	(0.011)
	Head employment	−0.037***	0.007	0.002
		(0.010)	(0.007)	(0.010)
	Household composition	0.051	0.067	−0.263
		(0.183)	(0.133)	(0.223)
	Residence	−0.012***	0.001	0.005
		(0.004)	(0.003)	(0.005)
Returns Effects (Unexplained)	Characteristics of hhd. head	1.043**	1.147***	−0.261
		(0.469)	(0.327)	(0.541)
	Head education	−0.086	0.179***	0.250**
		(0.091)	(0.063)	(0.104)
	Head employment	−0.247***	−0.066	−0.078
		(0.071)	(0.050)	(0.082)
	Household composition	−0.562	0.001	1.095**
		(0.434)	(0.302)	(0.500)
	Residence	−0.292***	−0.102	0.082
		(0.089)	(0.063)	(0.105)
	Constant	0.028	−1.196***	−1.000***
		(0.274)	(0.192)	(0.317)
	Observations		13,774	

continued on next page

Table 4.14 *continued*

		Taipei,China 10		
		10th pctile	50th pctile	90th pctile
	Treatment group	8.567***	9.390***	10.180***
		(0.018)	(0.013)	(0.016)
	Control group	8.791***	9.504***	10.210***
		(0.011)	(0.006)	(0.009)
	Overall Gap	−0.224***	−0.115***	−0.024
		(0.021)	(0.014)	(0.019)
	Endowment	−0.077***	−0.059***	−0.116***
		(0.021)	(0.015)	(0.018)
	Returns	−0.148***	−0.056***	0.092***
		(0.026)	(0.018)	(0.024)
Endowment Effects (Explained)	Characteristics of hhd. head	−0.095**	−0.021	0.009
		(0.045)	(0.032)	(0.042)
	Head education	−0.020***	−0.002	0.003
		(0.007)	(0.007)	(0.008)
	Head employment	−0.049***	0.000	0.006
		(0.012)	(0.007)	(0.009)
	Household composition	0.084*	−0.046	−0.142***
		(0.044)	(0.031)	(0.040)
	Residence	0.003	0.010***	0.009**
		(0.004)	(0.003)	(0.004)
Returns Effects (Unexplained)	Characteristics of hhd. head	0.726***	0.730***	0.221
		(0.256)	(0.171)	(0.238)
	Head education	−0.570***	0.208***	0.115
		(0.120)	(0.078)	(0.112)
	Head employment	−0.167**	0.051	−0.154**
		(0.072)	(0.047)	(0.067)
	Household composition	−0.158	0.073	0.321***
		(0.104)	(0.071)	(0.097)
	Residence	0.050	0.133**	0.095
		(0.096)	(0.066)	(0.089)
	Constant	−0.028	−1.250***	−0.506*
		(0.295)	(0.196)	(0.274)
	Observations		14,843	

pctile = percentile, hhd. = household.
Notes: Standard errors computed using the delta method are in parentheses. *** p<0.01, ** p<0.05, * p<0.1.
Source: Author's analysis of LIS data.

In India, the pro-male gender gap is apparently due to the endowment effects among poor and rich households, while at the center of the income distribution, the returns effect dominates and drives the pro-male gap. Female Indian households are less educated, have an inferior employment status, and inferior demographic characteristics to male households, even though they have a superior location or access to markets. Female households receive higher returns to their demographic characteristics and to education, while they receive lower returns to their employment status and location. On balance, these returns effects essentially cancel out, for a low insignificant composite returns effect.

In Japan, the pro-male gap is driven by the endowment effects, as female households are less educated and have poorer geographic access to markets. The returns effects contribute only among the highest deciles, through a lower return to demographic characteristics earned by female heads relative to males. In the Republic of Korea, both the endowment and returns effects work to harm female households, particularly in the lower half of the income distribution. Female households have less desirable demographic characteristics and employment status, and lower education than male households. Female heads also receive a lower return on their employment status (significant), although higher-income female heads may receive higher returns on their demographic characteristics and education.

In the Russian Federation, the overall gender gap rose substantially between 2004 and 2010, especially among poorer households. In 2004, the endowment effect was essentially nonexistent, with female households having very similar characteristics as male households across all income quantiles. The returns effect was actually positive in the lowest decile group, thanks to a higher return to education (and to household composition) among poor female households relative to poor male households. Female households received lower returns on their employment status and geographic residence, but these were counteracted by higher returns on demographic characteristics among richer female households. By 2007, the composite endowment effect became consistently negative for all quantile groups (significant only in the top decile), and the returns effect became negative significant among the middle and high-income groups, leading to an overall pro-male gap among households in the middle and top of the income distribution. Female households are now found to reside in significantly inferior locations relative to male households, affecting their earning capacity. At the same time, female households receive a lower return on their employment status and on their demographic characteristics, which trumps small premiums in their returns to household composition and geographic location.

Finally, in 2010, the composite endowment effects became negative significant across all income quantiles, and the returns effect turned more negative and significant. The differentials in individual endowments and returns to them still carry the same signs as in 2007 but are larger and more significant. Hence, female households are hurt by deterioration in their endowment of marketable characteristics as well as by deterioration in the market valuation of their characteristics relative to men's. Whether these trends are due to deprivation traps, corrosion of social welfare nets, market discrimination, or other structural marginalization of female workers is unclear, but clearly public policy should tackle the degradation of the living conditions of female-led households on both fronts.

In Taipei,China, the gender gap has been larger among poorer households, and has stagnated at the year-2005 levels to 2010. The gap has been made up approximately equally of the endowment and returns effects, with the exception of the richest quantile, where a pro-female returns effect has inexplicably been offsetting nearly two-thirds of the pro-male endowment effect.

Female household heads attain slightly lower education than their male counterparts in Taipei,China, and have slightly less market-desirable demographic characteristics. They earn lower returns on their employment status, but higher returns on their demographic characteristics. A divergence is apparent in the returns effects between poorer and richer households. While poorer female households receive lower returns on their education and household composition than their poor male counterparts, richer female households receive a premium in their return to these attributes. This is what drives the pro-female composite returns effect and what makes the overall gender gap small at the top of the income distribution. The precise source of this phenomenon is presently unclear and deserves future scrutiny.

Conclusions

This study has used 10 national household surveys to investigate the level, composition, and evolution of income inequality among six Asian economies in different stages of development—the PRC; India; Japan; the Republic of Korea; the Russian Federation; and Taipei,China. To estimate the effects of various household characteristics and the returns to them on household income at different income quantiles, we have used advanced methods including the Blinder–Oaxaca decomposition and the unconditional quantile regressions estimated using a recently developed re-centered influence function estimation procedure.

The results indicate that Japan; Taipei,China; and the Republic of Korea have very low degrees of income inequality, while India and the PRC have very high levels, followed by the Russian Federation. There is evidence of rural/urban and regional income gaps across all of the evaluated economies, but they are particularly high in India; the PRC; and the Russian Federation, and account for a large portion of the overall inequality. While the rural/urban gap has been going away in the Russian Federation and Taipei,China, regional gaps remain strong in Taipei,China and appear to further grow in the Russian Federation, disagreeing with claims in recent Russian reports that Russian factor markets have become more integrated and that the level of economic development has been converging across Russian regions.

Education gap is an important component in overall inequality across most economies. Some evidence exists of polarization of societies whereby a small group of households accumulate large stocks of education and non-education endowments, and concentrate near markets—in cities and advantaged regions—to receive high returns on all these endowments. The rest of the national population, most notably in India, lacks resources to invest in the various endowments and falls behind.

Urban/rural gap is due to education and employment status of urban versus rural households, and because rural households receive a significantly lower return on their education. These point to a lack of employment opportunities in rural areas, particularly for skilled workers. Education gap is due in part to the fact that less educated workers have a harder time finding employment. In other words, workers who are less formally educated receive lower credit for their other endowments—such as residence closer to main labor markets—and are not given a chance to prove themselves. Female-headed households are less educated and are viewed in the market as having inferior personal characteristics (age, marital status), leading to a lower propensity to be employed. Even when employed, they work in irregular positions or are self-employed, and suffer a substantial reduction in earnings, interpreted as a penalty for inconvenience that female workers cause to employers.

Overall, education and the return to it, geographic location, and household composition play an important role in driving economic inequality—and suggest a viable way to control it—across demographic groups. These findings have important implications for public policy in developing Asia. For one, education reform and better welfare nets are needed to provide basic opportunities for workers to improve their skills. Family planning and residence support programs, such as public housing or relaxation of national-registration laws (i.e., *hukou*), could help ameliorate regional and rural/urban inequality. Empowering authorities and organizations in disadvantaged regions to support workers, and to help them acquire skills and be matched to quality employment would also work to loosen the grip of the deprivation trap (Chambers 1983). The role of public policy should be to open opportunities to workers in all regions and circumstances, and to facilitate quality matches between workers and employers. There is hope that appropriate policy reforms will not only increase the aggregate level of wealth, but will bring more equal prosperity to all corners of the societies in developing Asia.

References

Asadullah, M. N., and G. Yalonetzky. 2012. Inequality of Educational Opportunity in India: Changes over Time and Across States. *World Development* 40(6): 1151–1163.

Azam, M. 2012. Changes in Wage Structure in Urban India, 1983–2004: A Quantile Regression Decomposition. *World Development* 40(6): 1135–1150.

Azam, M., and V. Bhatt. 2016. Spatial Income Inequality in India, 1993–2011: A District Level Decomposition. IZA Discussion Paper 9892. Fukuoka, Japan: Institute of Labor Economics.

Belhaj Hassine, N. 2014. Economic Inequality in the Arab Region. World Bank Policy Research Working Paper WPS-6911. Washington, DC: The World Bank.

Berg, A., and J. Ostry. 2011. Inequality and Unsustainable Growth: Two Sides of the Same Coin? IMF Staff Discussion Note. Washington, DC: International Monetary Fund.

Blinder, A. 1973. Wage Discrimination: Reduced Form and Structural Estimates. *Journal of Human Resources* 8(4): 436–455.

Brar, J., S. Gupta, A. Madgavkar, B. C. Maitra, S. Rohra, and M. Sundar. 2014. India's Economic Geography in 2025: States, Clusters and Cities. Insights India Report. McKinsey & Company, October.

Chamarbagwala, R. 2010. Economic Liberalization and Urban–Rural Inequality in India: A Quantile Regression Analysis. *Empirical Economics* 39(2): 371–394.

Chambers, D., and A. Krause. 2010. Is The Relationship Between Inequality and Growth Affected by Physical and Human Capital Accumulation? *Journal of Economic Inequality* 8(2): 153–172.

Chambers, R. 1983. *Rural Development: Putting the Last First*. Harlow, United Kingdom: Prentice Hall.

Chang, C., and P. England. 2011. Gender Inequality in Earnings in Industrialized East Asia. *Social Science Research* 40(1): 1–14.

Chang, H. 2012. A Decomposition Analysis of Differences in Distribution. *Agricultural Economics* 43(5): 487–498.

Chen, C.-L. 2014. http://bit.ly/2lIg38n 44(2): 1–44.

ECA, ILO, UNCTAD, UNDESA, and UNICEF. 2012. Social Protection: A Development Priority on the Post 2015 UN Development Agenda. UN System Task Team on the Post 2015 UN Development Agenda.

Firpo, S., N. M. Fortin, and T. Lemieux. 2009. Unconditional Quantile Regressions. *Econometrica* 77(3): 953–973.

Fortin, N. M., T. Lemieux, and S. Firpo. 2010. Decomposition Methods in Economics. NBER Working Paper 16045. Cambridge, MA: National Bureau of Economic Research.

Fournier, J.-M., and I. Koske. 2012. The Determinants of Earnings Inequality: Evidence from Quantile Regressions. *OECD Journal: Economic Studies* 2012/1: 7–36. Paris: Organisation for Economic Co-operation and Development.

Ghosh, P. K., and J. Y. Lee. 2016. Decomposition of the Changes in Korean Wage Inequality during the Period 1998–2007. *Journal of Labor Research* 37(1): 1–28.

Gluschenko, K. P. 2010. Methodologies of Analyzing Inter-Regional Income Inequality and Their Applications to Russia (1 April). William Davidson Institute Working Paper 984. Ann Arbor, MI: William Davidson Institute, University of Michigan.

———. 2011. Studies on Income Inequality among Russian Regions: Variations in Social-Economic Development by Region. *Regional Research of Russia* 1(4): 319–330.

Guriev, S., and E. Vakulenko. 2012. Convergence between Russian Regions. CEFIR/ES Working Paper 180. Moscow: Center for Economic and Financial Research.

Heshmati, A. 2004. Regional Income Inequality in Selected Large Countries. IZA Discussion Paper 1307. Fukuoka, Japan: Institute of Labor Economics.

Higashikata, T. 2013. Factor Decomposition of Income Inequality Change: Japan's Regional Income Disparity from 1955 to 1998. IDE Discussion Paper 400.2013.3. Tokyo: Institute of Developing Economies, Japan External Trade Organization.

Hlasny, V. 2016a. Unit Nonresponse Bias to Inequality Measurement: Worldwide Analysis Using Luxembourg Income Study Database. Luxembourg Income Study Technical Working Paper 8. March.

———. 2016b. Labor Market Rigidities and Social Inequality in Korea: The Role of Legal, Economic and Social Governance. On Korea Academic Paper Series 10. Washington, DC: Korea Economic Institute of America.

Hlasny, V., and P. Verme. 2015. Top Incomes and the Measurement of Inequality: A Comparative Analysis of Correction Methods Using EU and US Survey Data. World Bank Policy Research Working Paper Series. Forthcoming.

Imai, K. S., and B. Malaeb. 2016. Asia's Rural–Urban Disparity in the Context of Growing Inequality. Kobe University RIEB Discussion Paper DP2016-29. Kobe, Japan: Research Institute for Economics and Business Administration, University of Kobe.

Jeong, J., and V. Hlasny. 2016. Co-opting Separatists: Social Welfare to Cross-Border Minorities in Xinjiang. Ewha Womans University Working Paper. Seoul: Ewha Womans University.

Kabeer, N. 2010. *Can the MDGs Provide a Pathway to Social Justice? The Challenges of Intersecting Inequalities.* New York, NY:

UN MDG Achievement Fund; Brighton, United Kingdom: Institute of Development Studies, University of Sussex.

Kang, B.-G., and M.-S. Yun. 2008. Changes in Korean Wage Inequality, 1980–2005. IZA Discussion Paper 3780. Fukuoka, Japan: Institute of Labor Economics.

Kijima, Y. 2006. Why Did Wage Inequality Increase? Evidence from Urban India 1983–99, *Journal of Development Economics* 81: 97–117.

Lee, H.-Y., J. Kim, and B. C. Cin. 2013. Empirical Analysis on the Determinants of Income Inequality in Korea. *International Journal of Advanced Science and Technology* 53(April): 95–109.

Mahler, C. 2011. Diverging Fortunes: Recent Developments in Income Inequality across Russian Regions. *Opticon 1826* 10(Spring).

Mehta, A., and R. Hasan. 2012. The Effects of Trade and Services Liberalization on Wage Inequality in India. *International Review of Economics and Finance* 23: 75–90.

Nahm, J. 2008. Shrinking Middle Class and Changing Income Distribution of Korea: 1995–2005. *Korean Economic Review* 24(2): 345–365.

Oaxaca, R. 1973. Male–Female Wage Differentials in Urban Labor Markets. *International Economic Review* 14(3): 693–709.

Panel Data Research Center (PDRC). 2015. Survey Methodology: Keio Household Panel Survey and Japan Household Panel Survey Data. Unpublished manuscript. Tokyo: Keio University.

Park, J., and J. S. Mah. 2011. Neo-liberal Reform and Bipolarisation of Income in Korea. *Journal of Contemporary Asia* 41(2): 249–265.

Ramadan, R., V. Hlasny, and V. Intini. 2015. Inequality Decomposition in the Arab Region: Application to Jordan, Egypt, Palestine, Sudan and Tunisia. UN ESCWA Working Paper 9. Beirut: United Nations Economic and Social Commission for West Asia.

Sachs, J. D., N. Bajpai, and A. Ramiah. 2002. Understanding Regional Economic Growth in India. *Asian Economic Papers* 1(3): 32–62.

Sato, Y., and J. Imai (eds.). 2011. *Japan's New Inequality: Intersection of Employment Reforms and Welfare Arrangements*. Melbourne, Australia: Trans Pacific Press.

Stewart, F., and A. Langer. 2007. Horizontal Inequalities: Explaining Persistence and Change. Centre for Research on Inequality, Human Security and Ethnicity. Working Paper 39. Oxford, United Kingdom: University of Oxford.

Tarohmaru, H. 2014. Factors in the Wage Differential between Standard and Nonstandard Employment. In *Transformation of the Intimate and the Public in Asian Modernity*, edited by E. Ochiai and L. Aoi Hosoya. Leiden, The Netherlands: Brill Publishers.

United Nations Development Programme (UNDP). 2013. *Humanity Divided: Confronting Inequality in Developing Countries*. New York, NY: United Nations Development Programme.

United Nations Statistics Division (UNSD). 2015. Millennium Development Goals Indicators: Purchasing Power Parities (PPP) Conversion Factor, Local Currency Unit to International Dollar, 1990–2012. Updated 6 July.

Wan, G. 2004. Accounting for Income Inequality in Rural China: A Regression-based Approach. *Journal of Comparative Economics* 32(2): 348–363.

Wan, G., and Z. Zhou. 2004. Income Inequality in Rural China: Regression-Based Decomposition Using Household Data. UNU–WIDER Research Paper 2004/51. Tokyo: United Nations University World Institute for Development Economics Research.

Wan, G., M. Lu, and C. Zhao. 2007. Globalization and Regional Income Inequality: Empirical Evidence From Within China. *Review of Income and Wealth* 53(1): 35–59.

———. 2015a. Inflation: GDP Deflator (annual %), World Bank national accounts data, and OECD National Accounts data, World Development Indicators catalog. http://data.worldbank.org/indicator/NY.GDP.DEFL.KD.ZG.

———. 2015b. PPP conversion factor, GDP (LCU per international $), International Comparison Program database, World Development Indicators catalog. http://data.worldbank.org/indicator/PA.NUS.PPP.

Yokoyama, I., N. Kodama, and Y. Higuchi. 2016. What Happened to Wage Inequality in Japan during the Last 25 Years? Evidence from the FFL Decomposition Method. RIETI Discussion Paper 16-E-081. Tokyo: Research Institute of Economy, Trade and Industry.

Youm, Y., and K. Yamaguchi. 2016. Gender Gaps in Japan and Korea: A Comparative Study on the Rates of Promotions to Managing Positions. RIETI Discussion Paper 16-E-011. Tokyo: Research Institute of Economy, Trade and Industry.

Appendix

Table A4.1 Distribution of Real Income (2005 $)

Economy	Income Ref. Year	LIS dname	Curr= 2005$1	Net/Mixed/ Gross	Sample Size
PRC	2002	cn02	2.898cny	M: tax., contr. insuf. captured	17,124
India	2004	in04	11.531inr	N: tax, contrib. not collected	41,554
Japan	2008	jp08	108.300jpy	G: tax, contrib. imputed	4,022
Rep. of Korea	2006	kr06	749.176krw	G: taxes, contrib. fully captured	15,532
Russian Federation	2004	ru07	13.216rub	N: taxes, contrib. not collected	3,394
	2007	ru07	13.216rub		3,933
	2010	ru10	14.372rub		6,323
Taipei,China	2005	tw05	31.022twd	G: taxes, contrib. fully captured	13,681
	2007	tw07	31.030twd	G: taxes, contrib. collected	13,776
	2010	tw10	29.263twd		14,853

Economy	Avg. Inc. ($)	Median Inc. ($)	Gini[a]
PRC	2,706*	1,646	50.72 (0.28)
India	1,905**	1,144	50.84 (0.43)
Japan	30,730	27,199	30.18 (0.52)
Rep. of Korea	24,894	22,319	31.02 (0.27)
Russian Federation	5,912*	4,474	40.45 (0.63)
	9,752*	8,090	37.05 (0.51)
	15,111*	12,252	35.71 (0.59)
Taipei,China	15,826	13,437	30.53 (0.25)
	15,385	13,069	31.03 (0.25)
	15,395	13,150	31.80 (0.24)

US = United States, LIS = Luxembourg Income Survey, PRC = People's Republic of China.
* – classified by LIS as upper-middle, ** – lower-middle, rest – high-income.

[a] LIS winsorizing method is partly adopted: Keep only disposable incomes of $1 or greater, and positive weights; no top/bottom coding is performed; Adult equivalence scale is square root of household members; for analytical weight, count of household members is used. For clarity, Ginis and their jack-knife estimated standard errors are multiplied by 100.

Source: Author's analysis of LIS data; $ gross domestic product deflators, currency conversion rates, and income-status from the World Bank.

Different Faces of Inequality across Asia:
Decomposition of Income Gaps across Demographic Groups   105

Table A4.2 Mean Disposable Household Income Per Capita and Share of Aggregate Income, by Quintile (2005 $, %)

Quintile	cn02	in04	jp08	kr06	ru04	ru07	ru10	tw05	tw07	tw10
1	488	391	11,957	7,317	1,471	2,489	4,652	5,815	5,533	5,187
	[3.19]	[3.88]	[7.90]	[7.12]	[5.38]	[5.68]	[6.42]	[8.22]	[8.05]	[7.59]
2	1,137	807	20,224	14,340	2,818	4,756	8,521	9,562	9,207	9,036
	[7.03]	[7.77]	[13.39]	[13.17]	[10.38]	[10.97]	[11.88]	[13.11]	[12.96]	[12.83]
3	2,114	1,304	26,714	20,699	4,073	7,222	11,527	12,887	12,523	12,613
	[12.41]	[12.13]	[17.65]	[17.94]	[15.23]	[16.72]	[16.41]	[17.04]	[17.00]	[17.15]
4	3,681	2,259	34,807	28,260	6,166	10,770	16,169	17,514	17,069	17,236
	[23.25]	[20.51]	[22.88]	[23.63]	[22.98]	[24.17]	[22.99]	[22.62]	[22.58]	[22.81]
5	7,830	5,942	58,427	46,748	12,816	19,619	30,354	30,709	30,236	30,416
	[54.13]	[55.71]	[38.18]	[38.15]	[46.03]	[42.46]	[42.31]	[39.00]	[39.40]	[39.62]

Notes: Currency conversion rates and gross domestic product deflators from World Bank (2015a, 2015b). Summary statistics account for household sampling weights and household size.
Source: Author.

Table A4.3 Means of Explanatory Variables of Interest (% of households with binary variable=1)

	cn02	in04	jp08	kr06	ru04	ru07	ru10	tw05	tw07	tw10
Urban	46.44	35.23	90.27	80.79	74.55	74.90	74.96	97.16	92.09	92.85
Advantaged region	38.49	37.49	81.04	13.07	66.26	67.19	66.37	14.62	–	–
Household head characteristics										
Cohabiting	95.03	85.51	72.98	73.07	54.31	53.78	55.59	69.41	68.10	64.29
Employed	85.15	85.71	68.97	83.15	55.37	55.16	57.85	82.86	83.31	81.45
Complete upper secondary educat.	36.75	13.34	87.14	60.83	72.54	75.58	80.06	57.44	59.02	64.07
Male	83.68	90.26	48.51	77.11	12.46	12.00	13.23	77.93	76.44	73.44
Prime working-age (30–50yo)	63.11	56.30	35.95	49.02	40.52	37.78	37.39	52.67	51.49	48.93
Industry classification										
Service	34.31	35.34	13.51	51.39	70.86	71.90	75.21	55.50	56.53	55.88
Industry	28.88	19.61	65.38	27.01	23.68	24.09	20.37	36.64	36.13	37.11
Agriculture	33.32	45.07	21.96	21.60	5.46	4.01	4.42	7.87	7.34	7.02

cn = People's Republic of China, in = India, jp = Japan, kr = Republic of Korea, ru = Russian Federation, tw = Taipei,China, yo = years old.
Note: In tw07 and tw10, urban is inferred from "not running a farming activity." Cohabiting entails "head living with partner," "married couple," or "non-married cohabiting couple" as opposed to "head not living with partner." Age ranges from 16 to 104.
Source: Author.

Table A4.4 Summary Statistics by Income Quintile (% of households)

Quintile	cn02	in04	jp08	kr06	ru04	ru07	ru10	tw05	tw07	tw10
Urban										
1	0.67	12.29	88.39	53.97	54.05	59.70	59.23	92.29	85.92	88.14
2	8.92	21.03	88.84	63.57	70.81	70.77	70.78	96.89	89.73	90.33
3	46.13	34.15	89.73	67.97	75.85	74.78	78.28	98.28	92.81	93.26
4	82.34	47.18	91.07	71.60	82.79	83.23	80.55	98.72	95.35	95.49
5	94.16	61.53	93.3	73.66	89.3	86.05	85.99	99.63	96.66	97.00
Advantaged region										
1	31.57	24.38	75.15	6.99	66.18	62.22	61.33	3.47	–	–
2	32.35	30.70	78.42	10.16	64.03	65.43	61.07	7.02	–	–
3	34.04	39.28	79.91	10.58	62.88	63.06	64.83	11.62	–	–
4	38.26	45.87	85.27	12.17	66.23	68.69	68.29	17.54	–	–
5	56.25	47.22	86.46	12.52	71.96	76.56	76.36	33.46	–	–
Complete upper secondary education										
1	17.43	3.73	68.90	31.91	55.34	56.44	67.98	23.14	24.28	31.19
2	19.15	3.91	80.95	53.62	65.00	68.25	73.84	47.88	52.45	57.33
3	28.46	6.51	83.04	64.82	72.29	78.04	81.29	60.42	61.89	67.65
4	50.25	13.31	87.35	73.98	82.95	84.27	87.74	70.54	71.80	76.05
5	68.64	39.41	88.39	78.83	87.84	91.25	91.24	85.27	84.71	88.21
Employed										
1	93.78	85.04	54.72	56.67	39.12	28.49	42.64	47.00	52.09	48.37
2	92.60	90.22	63.83	83.79	35.00	35.76	43.31	86.84	86.32	84.94
3	86.14	87.56	69.72	90.36	54.46	57.27	53.10	92.36	92.56	89.82
4	78.12	84.16	78.36	92.98	70.94	71.66	71.67	92.80	91.54	92.12
5	74.91	82.45	81.79	93.56	81.36	80.56	79.68	95.36	94.12	92.28
Male										
1	95.45	86.49	44.35	60.55	14.56	10.37	11.02	68.27	66.72	63.99
2	95.01	90.70	48.96	73.46	10.32	10.39	10.59	77.56	74.41	71.47
3	87.18	91.11	49.55	80.29	11.67	10.53	12.76	80.74	79.46	77.80
4	75.03	91.04	51.34	85.47	11.36	10.68	13.50	81.80	80.87	77.43
5	65.59	92.16	53.27	86.05	13.94	15.43	16.20	81.28	80.76	76.45

cn = People's Republic of China, in = India, jp = Japan, kr = Republic of Korea, ru = Russian Federation, tw = Taipei,China.
Note: In tw07 and tw10, urban is inferred from "not running a farming activity."
Source: Author's analysis of LIS income surveys.

Table A4.5 Mean Disposable Household Income Per Capita by Demographic Group

	cn02	in04	jp08	kr06	ru04	ru07	ru10	tw05	tw07	tw10
Urban	5,181	3,050	31,013	25,650	6,657	10,702	16,378	15,972	15,673	15,685
Rural	1,319	1,496	28,084	21,786	3,989	7,167	11,716	9,670	12,205	11,963
Advantaged region	3,826	2,408	31,594	26,014	6,211	10,317	16,086	23,344	–	–
Disadvantaged	2,016	1,663	26,980	24,827	5,321	8,535	13,107	14,820	–	–
Employed	2,518	1,849	32,335	26,112	6,748	11,300	16,689	16,511	15,990	16,069
Non-employed	3,975	2,259	26,467	16,773	4,534	7,325	12,357	9,015	9,443	9,545
Complete upper secondary education	4,223	4,303	31,767	27,212	6,429	10,544	15,935	18,111	17,397	17,197
Less educated	1,919	1,612	23,167	18,644	4,334	6,925	11,399	12,325	12,018	11,580
Male	2,351	1,925	31,307	25,958	6,196	10,913	17,755	16,056	15,665	15,674
Female	4,937	1,654	30,168	20,347	5,879	9,633	14,786	14,711	14,163	14,382

cn = People's Republic of China, in = India, jp = Japan, kr = Republic of Korea, ru = Russian Federation, tw = Taipei,China.
Note: Currency conversion rates and gross domestic product deflators from World Bank (2015a, 2015b). Summary statistics account for household sampling weights and household size.
Source: Author.

PART II
Drivers of Inequality

5

Impact of Macroeconomic Factors on Income Inequality and Income Distribution in Asian Countries

N.P. Ravindra Deyshappriya

5.1 Introduction

Income inequality, which adversely affects the living standard of people, is a multifaceted issue that is deeply rooted in most of the Asian countries. Consequently, countries such as the People's Republic of China (PRC) and India are still labeled "developing" countries, despite their significantly high economic growth. This scenario further heated the discussion on growth and equity, focusing more on the concepts of inclusive growth and shared prosperity. Apart from its dramatic growth process, the poverty reduction mechanism in Asia has achieved remarkable levels, more than any other region in the world. However, income disparity is considerably higher and the majority of people live in countries with relatively high inequality. Furthermore, as Alesina and Perotti (1996) and Persson and Tebellini (1994) indicated, inequality considerably slows down the overall economic growth as existence of inequality restricts utilizing available resources equally and efficiently. In turn, inequality reduces the pace at which growth translates into poverty reduction as well (Bourguignon 2004; Kakwani 1993). Thus, Asian countries would have achieved much more progress in growth and poverty reduction than they have achieved, had inequality been lower.

According to empirical investigations, factors that drive Asia's accelerated economic growth have themselves caused inequality. According to Zhuang et al. (2014), technological improvements, market-oriented reforms, and globalization are the key forces that accelerated growth especially in developing Asia. However, Zhuang et al. (2014) further explained that these drivers increase inequality by widening the gap between owners of capital and laborers, skilled and unskilled workers, and urban and rural sectors. In fact, policy makers and government authorities cannot restrict these three drivers to reduce inequality, as they are the key determinants of higher productivity. Apart from that, weaknesses of fiscal policy, particularly in tax structure, also cause growing inequality in the region. The tax systems of most of the countries in the region depend highly on consumption taxes, which place large burdens on low- and middle-income groups. Similarly, the tax system is likely to concentrate the wealth of higher-income groups, as the taxes are highly partial to labor income rather than capital gain and properties. Additionally, unequal access to basic services, such as education, health, and finance; institutional weaknesses; and social exclusion due to religion and cultural factors are also crucial in explaining regional inequality in Asia.

In fact, the available scholarly works that specifically address the link between macroeconomic factors and inequality are very limited in the economic literature. Similarly, even existing studies have ended with mixed findings—therefore, there is no consensus on the relationship between macro factors and inequality. Specifically, Kuznets (1955) highlighted the parabolic relationship between income and inequality by introducing the well-known concept of the Kuznets Curve. However, the idea of Kuznetz curve was argued by Bruno et al. (1996), Fishlow (1995), and Deininger and Squire (1997). They highlighted that there is no significant relationship between income and inequality. Similarly, some studies have considered the impacts of only very limited macroeconomic factors such as inflation, exchange rate (Bulir and Gulde 1995), and government debt (You and Dutt 1996). Apart from that, most studies are based on individual countries (Cole and Towe 1996; Razin and Sadka 1996) or a small group of countries by applying conventional time-series or cross-sectional methods. Hence, the mentioned weaknesses attached to existing literature highlight the gaps, which appropriate scholarly works should fill.

The main objective of the current study is to examine the determinants of income inequality in Asian countries, highlighting the impacts of macroeconomic factors. Specifically, the study quantifies the impact of macroeconomic factors on income inequality and also on the income share of each income quantile. Apart from the macroeconomic factors, political economy variables and demographic variables are also considered to provide more realistic and appropriate policy recommendations. The current study analyzes the situation of 33 Asian countries over 1990–2013 in a dynamic panel data setting. The applied dynamic longitudinal method essentially overcomes econometric issues attached to time-series and cross-country analysis; in turn, the current study expects to provide more methodologically solid empirical findings. The next sections of the study expound on trends of inequality in Asia, reviews of existing empirical studies, methodology and model specification, and results and discussion, followed by the conclusion and recommendations.

5.2 Trends in Income Inequality in Asia

This section describes the recent trends in inequality in Asia based on the Gini coefficient during the past 2 decades. Table 5.1 summarizes the average Gini coefficient, which was calculated using all available data points during 1980–2013 for 33 Asian countries. In the 1980s, the highest averaged Gini was recorded in Malaysia (48.1) followed by Turkey (46.6). Similarly Maldives (63.3) and Singapore (47.1) account for the highest inequality in the 1990s and 2000s, respectively. Apart from that, the average Gini coefficient in Asia increased from 34.5 in the 1980s to 38.8 by the 1990s, but it plunged slightly to 38.3 by the 2000s. In the 2000s, the inequality of 16 countries out of the selected 33 Asian countries is higher than the average inequality of the Asian region (38.3).

Table 5.1 Trend in Income Inequality of Selected Countries from 1980 to 2000

Country	Average Gini Index			Country	Average Gini Index		
	1980s	1990s	2000s		1980s	1990s	2000s
Asia (Avg)	34.5	38.8	38.3	Asia (Avg)	34.5	38.8	38.3
Armenia	26.7	42.1	41.3	Malaysia	48.1	46.9	44.2
Azerbaijan	29.1	42.5	41.3	Maldives	–	63.3	37.8
Bangladesh	32.1	36.1	40.6	Mongolia	–	31.9	34.0
Cambodia	–	40.3	40.0	Nepal	38.0	43.3	41.3
PRC	24.0	30.5	41.3	Pakistan	32.9	32.0	31.0
Cyprus	–	29.0	28.8	Philippines	43.1	45.5	45.6
Georgia	28.3	41.5	41.5	Russian Federation	26.0	40.8	42.3
India	32.1	32.2	39.2	Singapore	42.9	44.6	47.1
Indonesia	32.2	32.8	36.8	Sri Lanka	39.9	39.1	43.4
Iran	45.2	43.4	35.7	Tajikistan	28.5	36.9	32.6
Israel	39.5	39.5	41.6	Thailand	45.4	47.2	42.1
Japan	30.4	31.4	37.0	Turkey	46.6	46.4	40.7
Jordan	35.4	40.7	37.4	Turkmenistan	–	27.6	30.2

continued on next page

Table 5.1 *continued*

Country	Average Gini Index			Country	Average Gini Index		
	1980s	1990s	2000s		1980s	1990s	2000s
Kazakhstan	27.5	38.6	33.0	Uzbekistan	27.7	36.7	37.6
Korea, Republic of	35.4	33.7	32.4	Viet Nam	–	35.2	36.0
Latvia	25.0	31.9	35.6	Yemen	–	31.6	37.7
Lebanon	–	43.5	37.0				

– = not available, Avg = average, PRC = People's Republic of China.
Note: The average Gini index was calculated using all available data points during 1980–2013.
Source: Calculated by the author based on the United Nations University World Institute for Development Economics Research (UNU-WIDER), World Income Inequality Database.

There are three inequality patterns that can be identified in Table 5.1. First, there are some countries, such as Japan, the Russian Federation, Israel, Singapore, Sri Lanka, the PRC, India, Latvia, Bangladesh, and Indonesia, in which the level of inequality has been increasing over time. Specifically, most of the high-income countries in Asia, such as Japan, Singapore, the Russian Federation, and Israel also account for increasing income inequality. Second, the inequality level of some other countries—Iran, Republic of Korea, Malaysia, Turkey, and Pakistan—has been declining continuously over the past 2 decades. Third, inequality in the rest of the countries in Table 5.1 reached a peak during the 1990s and has been declining since.

Figure 5.1 depicts the rate of change of the Gini coefficient of Asian countries during 1990–2000 and the figure further categorizes these countries into four groups—high income, low income, lower-middle income, and upper-middle income—based on the per capita income of each country. The calculated average growth rates of the Gini index (shown by reference lines in each graph) for high-income, low-income, lower-middle income, and upper-middle-income countries are 4.6%, –8.9%, 7.7%, and –4.2%, respectively. Thus, it is apparent that lower-middle-income countries accounted for a relatively high inequality growth rate followed by high-income countries during 1990–2000. Particularly, within the group of lower-middle-income countries, India (23.0%), Yemen (19.4%), and Indonesia (12.4%) have the fastest growing Gini indexes, respectively. Furthermore, within the group of higher-income countries, Japan (17.9%) has the highest Gini growth rate, while Republic of Korea (–3.9%) has the lowest. The majority of the upper-middle-income countries have a negative growth rate of the Gini index, indicating the possibility of having a more equal income distribution in the future. However, the PRC (35.7%), which accounted for the highest

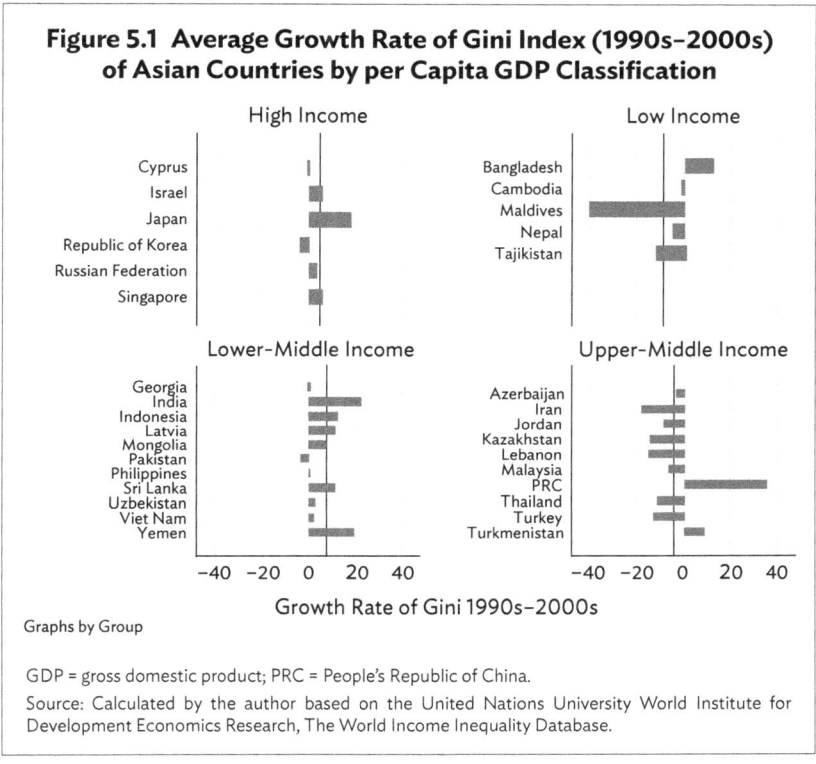

Figure 5.1 Average Growth Rate of Gini Index (1990s–2000s) of Asian Countries by per Capita GDP Classification

GDP = gross domestic product; PRC = People's Republic of China.
Source: Calculated by the author based on the United Nations University World Institute for Development Economics Research, The World Income Inequality Database.

Gini growth rate across the region, can be considered an outlier within and among the group(s). In contrast, inequality in the Maldives dropped by 40% during 1990–2000, although inequality in the Maldives is considerably higher. Overall, inequality has become a critical issue that hinders the effectiveness of growth and poverty reduction policies of Asian countries, irrespective of their development status.

5.3 Review of Existing Knowledge

Lack of inequality-related data historically restricted conducting inequality-related research. The recent development of inequality data allows researchers to construct their analyses in a more flexible environment. However, existing empirical studies have used different inequality data sets, over different time periods, across different countries, and also applied different methodologies and in turn the existing knowledge is highly diverse and complex. Consequently, this section provides a comprehensive understanding on existing empirical work, and particularly focuses on inequality and its macroeconomic factors. In fact, growth is one of the most significant macroeconomic factors and, hence, many researchers have widely examined the inequality–growth nexus; however, there is no consensus yet. The well-known work by Kuznets (1955), which highlighted a parabolic relationship between income and inequality, has provided a historical approach for the discussion. The parabolic relationship indicates that an increase in income serves to widen inequality up to some extent and reduces inequality thereafter. However, this relationship is investigated by researchers such as Persson and Tabellini (1994), Alesina and Rodrik (1994), and Alesina and Perotti (1996) who found a negative relationship between income and inequality. Conversely, Barro (2000) supported a nonlinear relationship between economic growth and inequality and stressed that economic growth negatively affects poor countries and positively affects rich countries. Apart from that, Bruno et al. (1996), Fishlow (1995), Ravallion (1995), and Deininger and Squire (1997) stated that there is no significant relationship between income and inequality.

The impacts of government expenditure on inequity were addressed by Calderon and Serven (2004) who observed that government expenditure on infrastructure stimulates economic growth and, in turn, the expenditure on infrastructure has a significant effect on reducing inequality. But Calderon and Serven (2004) examined this relationship based on a panel of Latin American countries, where inequality is highest. Thus, it is not rational to extend this finding for countries with a low or moderate level of inequality. Apart from that, Chatterjee and Turnovsky (2012) also confirmed that government expenditure may reduce inequality in the short run while increasing inequality in the long run. Furthermore, a study based on the Philippines by Blejer and Guerrero (1988) highlighted that government expenditure strongly increases inequality in the context of the Philippines. Similarly, Maestri and Roventini (2012) also discovered that a higher level of government expenditure is associated with higher income inequality, particularly in some European countries. Maestri and Roventini (2012) further found that government expenditure Granger causes earning inequality in countries such as the Netherlands, Canada, and the United Kingdom. In contrast, Sarel (1997) proved cross-sectionally that government expenditure has no significant impact on income inequality.

The impacts of globalization and trade have also been widely discussed in literature. Dollar and Kraay (2004) emphasized that globalization and the openness of economies tend to benefit the poor and in turn reduce inequality. Conversely, Milanovic (2005) argued that the poor in more open countries with higher trade liberalizations are more likely to be worse off as the benefits of trade are unevenly distributed. This notion is also supported by Barro (2000) and Bourguignon and Morrisson (1990), and indicates that richer groups in society absorb the benefits of international trade more so than lower-income groups and, hence, trade may cause higher income inequality. However, Marrewijk (2007) expressed that openness and international trade lower inequality in labor-abundant poor countries, while increasing inequality in rich countries with a higher level of capital stock. A time-series study by Maestri and Roventini (2012) examined the impact of inflation and unemployment on income inequality in a set of member countries of the Organisation for Economic Co-operation and Development (OECD), and found that inflation increases income inequality in countries such as Germany, Sweden, and the United States, while reducing inequality in Canada. Further, the current study found that unemployment in the United Kingdom and in the United States reduces consumption inequality. Similar results were obtained by Stiglitz (2011) and Kumhof and Ranciere (2010). Furthermore, Jantti and Jenkins (2001) in a time-series analysis based on the United Kingdom over the period 1961–1991 argued that unemployment may reduce the income share of the third income quantile to the richest quantile while increasing the income share of the poorest quantile and the second. Moreover, Jantti and Jenkins (2001) highlighted that both inflation and the real interest rate have negative impacts on the income share of the income quantiles from the poorest to the fourth, and a positive impact on the fourth and richest quantiles. However, Sarel (1997) concluded that inflation has no significant impact on the income distribution of many countries.

Not only macroeconomic factors, but several demographic factors too—such as education, employment structure, and population growth—have been identified as crucial determinants of income inequality. A cross-sectional analysis based on both developed and developing countries by Breen and Garcia–Penalosa (1999) stressed that higher educational attainment, particularly at least up to secondary level, greatly reduces income inequality. Similarly, Gunatilaka and Chotikapanich (2005), Barro (2000), Li et al. (1998), and De Gregorio and Lee (2002) also found that average years of schooling or any other educational attainment leads economies toward more equal income distribution. Apart from education, Garcia–Penalosa (1999) investigated the impact of employment in agriculture on income inequality in both developed and developing countries and found that a higher level of employment in the agriculture sector accounts for the lower level of income inequality, as lower-income groups are able to increase their income through agricultural output. Similar results were observed by Alderson and Nielsen (1995), who expressed that a higher rural population with more employed in the agriculture sector leads to lower income inequality. Apart from that, Alderson and Nielsen (1995) indicated that a relatively high population growth may increase income inequality. In addition to demographic factors, politically related factors such as democratization have been observed as important for income inequality (Rodrik 1999; Milanovic 2004; Dreher and Gaston 2008). In particular, Rodrik (1999) and Milanovic (2004) expressed that democratization reduced inequality through higher wages for labor and fair distribution, respectively. However, Dreher and Gaston (2008) indicated that inequality may increase with higher levels of democratization in some OECD countries. The impact of foreign aid on income inequality was also checked by Herzer and Nunnenkamp (2012) and Bjornskov (2010), who concluded that foreign aid may widen the income gap as the distribution process of foreign aid is highly politicized, especially in developing countries.

The reviewed existing literature clearly highlights the lack of consensus on the linkages between inequality and its determinants. Similarly, most of the studies are purely based on conventional time series and cross-sectionals, which have significant methodological issues as well. Consequently, the current study attempts to conduct a rigorous analysis that can overcome the weaknesses and contradictory ideas in the literature. The International Monetary Fund working paper by Sarel (1997) highlighted particularly two main modifications that need to be considered by future researchers. The first is to include fiscal policy variables and demographic variables such as tax and education, respectively. The second is to expand the empirical framework from cross-sectional analysis to panel data analysis. I strongly believe that the current study has adequately addressed the modifications highlighted by Sarel (1997).

5.4 Methodology and Model Specification

5.4.1 Data and Variables

The study is based on the longitudinal data set, which consists of 33 Asian countries over 1990–2013. These countries were selected based on the availability of the data for selected variables. Table 5.2 explains the variables and sources of the data used for the study.

In particular, the Gini index and income shares owned by quantiles were used as the dependent variables in Model 1 and Model 2, respectively, and data were collected by the World Income Inequality Database. Similarly, the Corruption Perception Index and Political Risk

Table 5.2 Description of Variables and Data Sources

Variable Name	Variable Used for the Study	Data Source
Inequality	Gini Index	UNU–WIDER The World Income Inequality Database (WIID)
Income Distribution	Income Shares owned by Quantiles	UNU–WIDER (WIID)
National Production	Gross Domestic Product	World Bank Data
Investment	Capital Formation	World Bank Data
Changes in Price Level	Inflation	World Bank Data
Unemployment	Unemployment	World Bank Data
Trade	Terms of Trade	World Bank Data
Debt Level	Government Debt as Percentage of GDP	World Bank Data
Corruption	Corruption Perception Index	Transparency International
Political Instability	Political Risk Index	The PRS Group (www.prsgroup.com)
Development Assistance	Official Development Assistance	World Bank Data
Education	Gross Enrollment Ratio Secondary Education	World Bank Data
	Labor Force Participation	World Bank Data
Population	Population Growth Rate	World Bank Data

GDP = gross domestic product, UNU–WIDER = United Nations University World Institute for Development Economics Research.
Source: Author.

Index published by Transparency International and the PRS Group (www.prsgroup.com) were employed to approximate corruption and political instability. The Corruption Perception Index captures the domestic public sector corruption of countries and the index scores of countries on a scale of 0 to 10, with zero indicating high levels of corruption, and 10 low levels. The Political Risk Index accounts for the overall risk of a country and the methodology of the index considers the risk attached to turmoil, financial transfers, direct investments, and export markets. The higher index values are attached to low-risk countries while lower index values represent higher political risk. Data for the rest of the variables were collected from the World Bank data series.

5.4.2 Empirical Models

The current study applies panel data analysis to accomplish the study's objectives. Specifically, the empirical model, which is presented in Equation 1, was used to model the macroeconomic determinants of income inequality of selected Asian countries. The growth rate of the Gini index was used as the dependent variable of Model 1, along with the set of explanatory variables.

$$GRGini_{i,t} = \beta_1'X_{i,t} + \beta_2'Y_{i,t} + \beta_2'Z_{i,t} + \delta_{1,i} + \epsilon_{1i,t} \qquad (1)$$

To have a clearer understanding of how the macroeconomic factors affect inequality, the second model was constructed. The main objective of the second model is to quantify the impact of macroeconomic variables on the income share of each income quantile. Thus, the income shares of each quantile were used as the dependent variable of Model 2.

$$(Q1)_{i,t}......(Q5)_{i,t} = \beta_1'X_{i,t} + \beta_2'Y_{i,t} + \beta_2'Z_{i,t} + \delta_{1,i} + \epsilon_{1i,t} \qquad (2)$$

Apart from the macroeconomic variables, political economy and demographic variables are also included in both models to obtain more accurate estimates by minimizing the residual part. In both models, $X_{i,t}$, $Y_{i,t}$, and $Z_{i,t}$ are vectors of macroeconomic variables, political economy variables, and demographic variables, respectively, while δ is the unobserved country-specific effect, and ε explains the error term of both models. The vector of macroeconomic variables includes the log of gross domestic product (lnGDP), growth rate of capital formation (GRCF), inflation (INFL), unemployment (UNEMP), growth rate of terms of trade (GRToT), and growth rate of debt as a percentage of GDP (GRDEBT). The vector of political economy includes variables such as corruption, political risk, and the growth rate of official development assistance (GRODA). Similarly, education, labor force participation, and growth rate of population (GRPOP) are considered the vector of demographic variables.

5.4.3 Estimation Techniques

The process of model estimation considered all 33 countries as one set of data, although the selected 33 countries included high-income, low-income, lower-middle-income, and upper-middle-income countries. In fact, any attempt to categorize the data set into the mentioned income criteria essentially restricts the sample size of high-income and low-income countries to six and five, respectively. It absolutely affects the statistical significance and accuracy of estimated coefficients. As the current study applies dynamic panel data analysis based on the generalized method of moment (GMM), consideration of all 33 countries as a whole does not lead to misleading findings as in a time-series and cross-sectional analysis. In fact, the instruments involved in GMM, and taking the first difference of the regression equation are the possible remedies, which overcome the issue of country-specific omitted variable bias.

The empirical models expressed in Equations (1) and (2) were estimated using dynamic panel data, which specifically used the GMM estimation technique developed by Arellano and Bond (1991) and Arellano and Bover (1995). In fact, application of panel data analysis has a number of advantages over both cross-country and time-series analysis. On one hand, cross-country analysis treats countries with different characteristics as a homogeneous group and, on the other hand, it hinders the country-specific effects, which may lead to higher error terms. Similarly, results of a time-series analysis cannot be generalized and also have the issue of simultaneity. In particular, the GMM estimation technique overcomes econometric issues such as endogeneity and country-specific omitted variable bias by introducing appropriate instruments and first difference of the regression equation, respectively. Application of the GMM method to empirical models (1) and (2) can be detailed as follows:

$$GRGini_{i,t} - GRGini_{i,t-1} = \alpha_1 GRGini_{i,t-1} + \beta_1'^{X_{i,t}} + \beta_2'^{Y_{i,t}} + \beta_2'^{Z_{i,t}} + \delta_{1,i} + \epsilon_{1i,t} \quad (3)$$

$$(Q1_{i,t} - Q2_{i,t-1}) \ldots (Q4_{i,t} - Q5_{i,t-1}) = \alpha_2 (Q1 \ldots Q5)_{i,t-1} + \beta_1' X_{i,t} + \beta_2' Y_{i,t} + \beta_2' Z_{i,t} + \delta_{1,i} \quad (4)$$

Rearranging the above equations (3) and (4),

$$g_{i,t} = \alpha_1 GRGini_{i,t-1} + \beta_1' X_{i,t} + \beta_2' Y_{i,t} + \beta_2' Z_{i,t} + \delta_{1,i} + \epsilon_{1i,t} \quad (5)$$

Where $GRGini_{i,t} - GRGini_{i,t-1} = g_{i,t}$

$$q_{i,t} = \alpha_2 (Q1 \ldots Q5)_{i,t-1} + \beta_1'^{X_{i,t}} + \beta_2'^{Y_{i,t}} + \beta_2' Z_{i,t} + \delta_{1,i} + \epsilon_{1i,t} \quad (6)$$

Where $(Q1_{i,t} - Q2_{i,t-1}) \ldots (Q4_{i,t} - Q5_{i,t-1}) = q_{i,t}$

The first difference of equations (5) and (6) were constructed to eliminate the unobserved country-specific effects.

$$g_{i,t} - g_{i,t-1} = \alpha_1(GRGini_{i,t-1} - GRGini_{i,t-2}) + \beta_1'(X_{i,t} - X_{i,t-1}) + \beta_2'(Y_{i,t} - Y_{i,t-1}) + \beta_2'(Z_{i,t} - Z_{i,t-1}) + (\epsilon_{1i,t} - \epsilon_{1i,t-1}) \quad (7)$$

$$q_{i,t} - q_{i,t-1} = \alpha_2((Q1\ldots Q5)_{i,t-1} - (Q1\ldots Q5)_{i,t-2}) + \beta_1'(X_{i,t} - X_{i,t-1}) + \beta_2'(Y_{i,t} - Y_{i,t-1}) + \beta_2'(Z_{i,t} - Z_{i,t-1}) + (\epsilon_{1i,t} - \epsilon_{1i,t-1}) \quad (8)$$

To avoid endogeneity problems related to the regressors, instruments were used. In accordance with the GMM difference estimators, the lag values of the regressors were used as the instruments based on the following moment conditions.

$$E[GRGini_{i,t-s}(e_{1i,t} - e_{1i,t-1})] = 0 \; for \; s \geq 2; t = 3, \ldots T \quad (9)$$

$$E[X_{i,t-s}(e_{2i,t} - e_{2i,t-1})] == 0 \; for \; s \geq 2; t = 3, \ldots T \quad (10)$$

$$E[Y_{i,t-s}(e_{2i,t} - e_{2i,t-1})] = 0 \; for \; s \geq 2; t = 3, \ldots T \quad (11)$$

$$E[Z_{i,t-s}(e_{2i,t} - e_{2i,t-1})] = 0 \; for \; s \geq 2; t = 3, \ldots T \quad (12)$$

$$E[(Q1\ldots Q5)_{i,t-s}(e_{2i,t} - e_{2i,t-1})] = 0 \; for \; s \geq 2; t = 3, \ldots T \quad (13)$$

The Sargan test and Serial Correlation test were employed to test the validity of the instruments used and the existence of serial correlation in the estimated models.

5.5 Results and Discussion

This section elaborates results that were empirically estimated based on dynamic panel data analysis, explained in the previous section. Initially, the impacts of macroeconomics, political economy, and demographic factors on income inequality are summarized in Table 5.3. Model 1 specified in Table 5.3, quantifies the link between income inequality and macroeconomic factors alone, while Model 2 and 3 take the impacts of macroeconomic factors on income inequality along with the political economy and demographic factors. In fact, variables were gradually added into the model and estimated for the expanded model in three steps to check the robustness of the estimated coefficient of macroeconomic factors.

According to the table, GDP is one of the crucial factors of income inequality in the Asian region. The lnGDP (log of GDP) in particular, positively affects income inequality, while the square of lnGDP has a negative effect on all three models with higher levels of statistical significance. This relationship clearly indicates the existence of a parabolic linkage between GDP and income inequality. In particular, income inequality initially increases with the increase of GDP, and reduces thereafter, with further increase of GDP. Thus, this finding is consistent with Kuznets (1955) and Barro (2000). In fact, most economic activities are highly concentrated in the urban areas of many Asian countries at the early and middle stages of the economic expansion process, and therefore an initial increase in GDP widens the spatial income gap, followed by a higher overall income inequality as well. However, further increases in GDP in the long run allow the redistribution of economic activities fairly across the country and, as a result, income inequality may decrease.

Apart from that, the study found that inflation and unemployment increase income inequality in Asian countries, and the result is statistically significant, even after the inclusion of political and demographic variables. In fact, higher inflation adversely affects the purchasing power of poor people more than their rich counterparts and, in turn, widens the income gap between poorer and richer groups. Similarly, unemployment essentially restricts access to the income sources of lower-income groups who have no or lack accumulated wealth compared with higher-income groups. Consequently, inflation and unemployment increase income inequality, and the findings are aligned with those of Jantti and Jenkins (2001). Conversely, the growth rate of terms of trade increases the income gap of Asian countries. In fact, trade flows in many developing and emerging countries largely benefit higher-income groups rather than lower-income groups and, in turn, benefits from trade may increase the income gap among people. Nevertheless, macroeconomic factors, such as capital formation and debt, have not succeeded in explaining income inequality in Asia.

In addition to the macroeconomic factors, political economic variables such as political risk and official development assistance also significantly affect income inequality. In particular, an increase in the political risk of economies tends to increase income inequality while decreasing official development assistance. Moreover, official development assistance plays a major role, especially in developing Asian

Table 5.3 Impacts of Macroeconomic, Political Economy, and Demographic Factors on Income Inequality

Dependent Variable	Growth Rate of Gini Index		
	Model 1	Model 2	Model 3
GRGINI(-1)	0.5309***	0.4625**	0.3761***
	(0.1440)	(0.2014)	(0.0948)
Macroeconomic Variables			
lnGDP	0.3492**	0.0432**	0.0674**
	(0.1647)	(0.0178)	(0.0295)
(lnGDP)^2	-0.0269**	-0.0172**	-0.0302***
	(0.0128)	(0.0077)	(0.0043)
GRCF	0.0032	0.4017	0.7302
	(0.0563)	(0.3050)	(0.5432)
INFL	0.0608**	0.2431**	0.2701**
	(0.0251)	(0.0942)	(0.1131)
UNEMP	0.0917**	0.4424*	0.0287**
	(0.0431)	(0.2570)	(0.0112)
GRToT	0.0198***	0.0573**	0.0201**
	(0.0051)	(0.0242)	(0.0098)
GRDEBT	0.0007	0.0010	0.0417
	(0.0033)	(0.0063)	(0.3526)
Political Economy Variables			
Corruption		-0.5218	-0.4023
		(1.0231)	(0.4271)
Political Risk		0.0243*	0.1732*
		(0.0123)	(0.0898)
GRODA		-0.8768*	-0.9076**
		(0.4588)	(0.3524)
Demographic Variables			
Education			-2.431**
			(0.9231)
LFP			-0.0290*
			(0.0148)
GRPOP			-0.7864
			(0.9843)
Diagnostic Statistics			
Observations	410	430	465
Instrument Rank	31.0000	27.0000	32.0000
J Statistics	15.9511	22.8710	25.0809
Sargan Test (P - value)[1]	0.8573	0.2230	0.4013
Serial Correlation (P - Value)[2]	0.0991	0.2999	0.6031

ln = logarithm, GDP = gross domestic product, GRCF = growth rate of capital formation, GRDEBT = growth rate of debt, GRGINI = growth rate of GINI Index, GRODA = growth rate of official development assistance, GRPOP = growth rate of population, GRToT = growth rate of terms of trade, INFL = inflation, LFP = labor force participation, UNEMP = unemployment.

[1] Sargan Test has the null hypothesis that the over-identified restrictions are valid.
[2] Serial Correlation Test has the null hypothesis that error terms are not serially correlated.
Note: * Significant at 10%, ** Significant at 5%, *** Significant at 1%.
Source: Author.

countries, by promoting infrastructure and employment opportunities for spatially discriminated low-income groups. From a demographic point of view, the study empirically confirmed that education is the key factor that hinders income inequality. Higher educational attainments essentially create efficient and easy access to better employment opportunities, and also open new avenues for important networking that is especially crucial in the globalized world. Studies by De Gregorio and Lee (2000), Li, Squire, and Zou (1998). and Barro (2000) also discussed the importance of education for more equal income distribution. Apart from that, labor force participation also marginally reduces income inequality, as higher labor force participation ensures stable income, especially for vulnerable groups and, consequently, it is possible that it may decrease income inequality.

The goodness-of-fit of the model was evaluated using the Sargan test and the Serial Correlation test. These tests respectively verify the appropriateness of the instruments and nonexistence of the serial correlation among error terms. The higher p-values attached to these tests clearly indicate acceptance of the null hypotheses that explain that over-identified restrictions are valid, and error terms are not serially correlated, respectively.

Table 5.4 summarizes the results, which were estimated by taking the income shares of each income quantile into account. Thus, this analysis provides a better understanding of how macroeconomic factors affect the income distribution of Asian countries. Further, education as a demographic factor was also included in the model as it was highly significant in explaining income inequality. As the result indicates, an increase in GDP may initially redistribute income from poor people (first and second quantiles) to the middle class (third and fourth quantiles) or richest groups (fifth quantile). However, further increases in GDP (considering lnGDP) decrease the income share of the richest group and increase the income shares of all other quantiles. Education also has a similar impact on the income share of the quantiles and, hence, both education and further increases in GDP redistribute the income from the richest group to middle- and poor-income groups. The findings are consistent with the previous works by Breen and Garcia–Penalosa (1999) and Jantti and Jenkins (2001).

Apart from that, inflation negatively affects the income share of the bottom 20% of people while it benefits only the richest group. In particular, the lower-income groups who spend a higher percentage of their income on the consumption of essential items, such as foods, are adversely affected by price hikes due to inflation. At the same time, a price hike essentially transfers a significant share of the income of lower-income groups to higher-income groups, as the higher-income

Table 5.4 Impacts of Macroeconomic Factors on Income Share of Quantiles

	Q1 (Poorest)	Q2	Q3	Q4	Q5 (Richest)
Q1(−1)	0.5481* (0.2748)	0.0247 (0.0733)	0.1620** (0.0750)	0.8920 (0.9190)	1.9843*** (0.6314)
lnGDP	−0.0254** (0.0106)	−0.0301** (0.0141)	0.1207** (0.0518)	0.1071** (0.0481)	0.0471* (0.0245)
(lnGDP)^a	0.1450*** (0.0301)	0.2073*** (0.0231)	0.1321** (0.0621)	0.0223** (0.0109)	−0.0195** (0.0095)
GRINFL	−0.0832* (0.0427)	−0.0635** (0.0292)	−0.0521 (0.0348)	−0.0274 (0.0182)	0.2072** (0.0804)
GRUNEMP	−0.1027** (0.0448)	−0.2387** (0.1027)	−0.1982* (0.1021)	−0.0787* (0.0413)	−0.0163 (0.0975)
GRToT	−0.0089 (0.1024)	−0.0367 (0.0213)	−1.2035 (0.8321)	0.2192 (0.1341)	0.0412* (0.0207)
Education	0.1056** (0.0457)	0.0374 (0.0741)	0.2014** (0.0924)	0.4082 (0.5127)	−0.0242** (0.0098)
GRODA	0.4571 (0.5409)	1.3071 (0.8231)	0.6523* (0.3403)	−0.2103 (0.1321)	−0.0625 (0.0924)
Diagnostic Statistics					
Observations	321	321	321	321	321
Instrument Rank	18.3911	14.2618	22.2627	19.3101	23.2191
J Statistics	12.7612	10.3637	16.2721	14.2028	13.2781
Sargan Test (P-value)^b	0.3523	0.3310	0.4561	0.3218	08321
Serial Correlation (P-Value)^2	0.2031	0.1521	0.3407	0.0928	0.2312

ln = logarithm, education = gross enrollment ratio secondary education, GDP = gross domestic product, GRODA = growth rate of official development assistance, GRINFL = growth rate Inflation, GRToT = growth rate of terms of trade, GRUNEMP = growth rate of unemployment.
^{a} Serial Correlation Test has the null hypothesis that error terms are not serially correlated.
^{b} Sargan Test has the null hypothesis that the over-identified restrictions are valid.
Note: *** Significant at 1%, ** Significant at 5%, * Significant at 10%.
Source: Author.

groups are the ultimate beneficiaries of increased prices (Jantti and Jenkins 2001). However, unlike inflation, unemployment causes a reduction in the income share of all quantiles except the richest group, and the impact of unemployment is relatively higher for the second, third, and first quantiles. Additionally, the benefits of trade and official development assistance (ODA) marginally increase the income shares only for the richest and third quantiles, respectively. The goodness-of-fit of the model explained in Table 5.3 is also at a higher level than that verified by both the Sargan and Serial Correlation tests.

5.6 Conclusion and Policy Recommendations

This empirical study attempts to quantify the impacts of macroeconomic factors on income inequality and income distribution in Asian countries. Further, the study focuses on the impacts of the political economy and demographic factors as well. The study applies dynamic panel data analysis over 1990–2013 across 33 Asian countries, and the employed methodology essentially overcomes the major weaknesses attached to the literature. The descriptive analysis identified that the inequality of countries—such as Japan, the Russian Federation, Israel, Singapore, Sri Lanka, the PRC, India, Latvia, Bangladesh, and Indonesia—has been continuously increasing since the 1990s. In contrast, countries such as Iran, Republic of Korea, Malaysia, Turkey, and Pakistan have been experiencing declining inequality.

The analysis focused on the impact of macroeconomic factors on income inequality and observed an inverted-U-shaped (parabolic) relationship between GDP and income inequality, which is similar to Kuznets (1955), leading to the formulation of the well-known Kuznets curve. Thus, the findings of this research in particular highlighted that income inequality in Asian countries increases with the expansion of GDP up to some extent and reduces thereafter with a further increase of GDP. However, the study further highlighted that macroeconomic factors, such as higher inflation, terms of trade, and unemployment, increase inequality in Asian countries. In addition to the macroeconomic factors, political economy and demographic factors—such as ODA, education, and labor force participation—reduce income equality significantly in Asian countries, while political risk may marginally increase income inequality. Furthermore, the study highlighted that there is no statistically significant link between income inequality and factors such as the growth rate of capital formation, the growth rate of debt, corruption, and the growth rate of population.

The analysis based on the distribution of income among the different quantiles indicates that an initial increase in GDP may cause the redistribution of income from poor people to the middle class or the richest groups. However, further increases in GDP decrease the income share of the richest group, while increasing the income share for all other quantiles. Education also has a similar impact on the income share of quantiles and, hence, both education and further increases in GDP indicate redistribution of income from the wealthiest groups to middle-income and poor-income groups. Apart from that, inflation negatively affects the income share of the bottom 20% of people, while it benefits only the richest group. However, unlike inflation, unemployment reduces the income share of all quantiles except the richest group, whereas the benefits from trade and ODA marginally increase the income shares only for the richest and third quantiles, respectively. The study recommends ensuring that higher and steady long-term economic growth is generated while efficient fiscal instruments are deployed that can fairly redistribute the growth and trade benefits among lower-income groups. Similarly, for more equal income distribution, it is crucial to enhance access to education, employment, and other income-generating activities, while maintaining price stability and political stability in economies.

References

Alderson, A. S., and F. Nielsen. 1995. Income Inequality, Development and Dualism: Results from an Unbalanced Cross-national Panel. *American Sociological Review* 60: 674–701.

Alesina, A., and R. Perotti. 1994. The Political Economy of Budget Deficits. NBER Working Paper 4637. Cambridge, MA: National Bureau of Economic Research.

Alesina, A., and R. Perotti. 1996. Income Distribution, Political Instability, and Investment. *European Economic Review* 40(6): 1203–1228.

Alesina, A., and R. Perotti. 1997. Fiscal Adjustments in OECD Countries: Composition and Macroeconomic Effects. *Staff Papers* 44(2): 210–248.

Arellano, M., and S. Bond. 1991. Some Tests of Specification for Panel Data: Monte Carlo Evidence and an Application to Employment Equations. *Review of Economic Studies* 58: 277–297.

Arellano, M., and O. Bover. 1995. Another Look at the Instrumental-Variable Estimation of Error Components Models. *Journal of Econometrics* 68: 29–52.

Barro, R. J. 2000. Inequality and Growth in a Panel of Countries. *Journal of Economic Growth* 5(1): 5–32.

Bjornskov, C. 2010. Do Elites Benefit from Democracy and Foreign Aid in Developing Countries? *Journal of Development Economics* 92: 115–124.

Blejer, M., and I. Guerrero. 1988. Stabilization Policies and Income Distribution in the Philippines. *Finance and Development* 25(4): 6.

Bourguignon, F. 2004. The Poverty–Growth–Inequality Triangle. *Poverty, Inequality and Growth* 69: 179–204.

Bourguignon, F., and C. Morrisson. 1990. Income Distribution, Development and Foreign Trade: A Cross-Sectional Analysis. *European Economic Review* 34(6): 1113–1132.

Breen, R., and C. Garcia-Peñalosa. 1999. *Income Inequality and Macroeconomic Volatility: An Empirical Investigation*. Florence, Italy: European University Institute.

Bruno, M., M. Ravallion, and L. Squire. 1996. Equity and Growth in Developing Countries: Old and New Perspectives on the Policy Issues. Vol. 1563. Washington, DC: The World Bank.

Bulíř, A., and A. M. Gulde. 1995. Inflation and Income Distribution: Further Evidence on Empirical Links. IMF Working Paper 95/86. Washington, DC: International Monetary Fund.

Calderón, C., and L. Servén. 2004. The Effects of Infrastructure Development on Growth and Income Distribution. No. 270. Washington, DC: The World Bank.

Chatterjee, S., and S. J. Turnovsky. 2012. Infrastructure and Inequality. *European Economic Review* 56(8): 1730–1745.

Cole, J., and C. Towe. 1996. Income Distribution and Macroeconomic Performance in the United States. IMF Working Paper 96/97. Washington, DC: International Monetary Fund.

De Gregorio, J., and J. W. Lee. 2000. Education and Income Inequality: New Evidence from Cross-Country Data. *Review of Income and Wealth* 48: 395–416.

Deininger, K., and L. Squire. 1997. Economic Growth and Income Inequality: Reexamining the Links. *Finance and Development* 34: 38–41.

Dollar, D., and A. Kraay. 2004. Trade, Growth, and Poverty. *The Economic Journal* 114(493): F22–F49.

Dreher, A., and N. Gaston. 2008. Has Globalization Increased Inequality? *Review of International Economics* 16: 516–536.

Fishlow, A. 1995. Inequality, Poverty and Growth, Where Do We Stand? In *OPS Document Reproduction Series* 65. Washington, DC: The World Bank.

Breen, R., and C. García-Peñalosa. 2005. Income inequality and Macroeconomic Volatility: An Empirical Investigation. *Review of Development Economics* 9(3): 380–398.

Gunatilaka, R., and D. Chotikapanich. 2006. Inequality Trends and Determinants in Sri Lanka 1980–2002: A Shapley Approach to Decomposition. Working Paper 6/06. Monash University, Department of Econometrics and Business Statistics.

Herzer, D., and P. Nunnenkamp. 2012. The Effect of Foreign Aid on Income Inequality: Evidence from Panel Cointegration. *Structural Change and Economic Dynamics* 23: 245–255.

Jantti, M., and S. P. Jenkins. 2001. Examining the Impact of Macro-Economic Conditions on Income Inequality. ISER Working Paper 2001-17. Colchester, United Kingdom: Institute for Social and Economic Research, University of Essex.

Kakwani, N. 1993. Poverty and Economic Growth with Applications to Cote d'Ivoire. *Review of Income and Wealth* 39(2): 121–139.

Kumhof, M., and R. Ranciere. 2010. Inequality, Leverage and Crises. IMF Working Paper 10/268. Washington, DC: International Monetary Fund.

Kuznets, S. 1955. Economic Growth and Income Inequality. *The American Economic Review* 45(1): 1–28.

Li, H., L. Squire, and H. Zou. 1998. Explaining International and Intertemporal Variations in Income Inequality. *The Economic Journal* 108: 26–43.

Maestri, V., and A. Roventini. 2012. Inequality and Macroeconomic Factors: A Time-series Analysis for a Set of OECD Countries. Available at: SSRN 2181399.

Marrewijk, C. V. 2007. *International Economics: Theory, Application and Policy*. Oxford University Press.

Milanovic, B. 2004. Is Inequality in Africa Really Different? Second draft. Washington, DC: The World Bank.

———. 2005. Can We Discern the Effect of Globalization on Income Distribution? Evidence from Household Surveys. *The World Bank Economic Review* 19(1): 21–44.

Nielsen, F., and A. S. Alderson. 1995. Income Inequality, Development, and Dualism: Results from an Unbalanced Cross-National Panel. *American Sociological Review* 60(5): 674–701.

Persson, T., and G. Tabellini. 1994. Is Inequality Harmful for Growth? *The American Economic Review* 84(3): 600–621.

Ravallion, M. 1995. Growth and Poverty: Evidence for Developing Countries in the 1980s. *Economics Letters* 48(3): 411–417.

Razin, A., and E. Sadka. 1996. A Pecking Order of Capital Inflows and International Tax Principles. *Journal of International Economics* 44(1): 45–68.

Rodrik, D. 1999. Democracies Pay Higher Wages. *The Quarterly Journal of Economics* 114: 707–738.

Sarel, M. M. 1997. How Macroeconomic Factors Affect Income Distribution: The Cross-Country Evidence. IMF Working Paper 97-152. Washington, DC: International Monetary Fund.

Stiglitz, J. 2011. Of the 1%, By the 1%, For the 1%. *Vanity Fair* 11.

UNU–WIDER. 2015. World Income Inequality Database, Version 3.3. May 2008. http://www.wider.unu.edu/research/Database/en GB/database/

You, J., and A. K. Dutt. 1996. Government Debt, Income Distribution, and Growth. *Cambridge Journal of Economics* 20(3): 335–351.

Zhuang, J., R. Kanbur, and C. Rhee. 2014. Rising Inequality in Asia and Policy Implications. ADBI Working Paper 463. Tokyo: Asian Development Bank Institute.

6

Education, Globalization, and Income Inequality in Asia

Kang H. Park

6.1 Introduction

Many studies have analyzed the relationship between income distribution and economic progress (e.g., Park 1996b; 1998). Some have further extended their analysis to the linkage of income inequality and political violence (see Park 1986). A pioneering study by Kuznets (1955) proposed that income inequality tends to initially increase, peak, and then fall as economies develop. The process involves structural changes that, along with dualism, cause this progression. Urbanization and population growth associated with the early stages of development initially exacerbate income inequality, but subsequent political factors and economic policies decelerate growth in the upper-income group, while simultaneously improving the situation of the lower-income group. The recent rise in national income inequality has prompted inquiry into the causes of the resurgence. Recent globalization and co-occurring outsourcing and wage compression may have fostered a reversal of the increasing trend of balanced income distribution.

This widely recognized inverted-U hypothesis of Kuznets has a contentious history. The academic world witnessed a surge of research on the Kuznets hypothesis in the 1970s, principally comparative empirical studies with cross-country data (Ahluwalia 1974; Robinson 1976; Stewart 1978; Winegarden 1979, to name a few). When updated data on income distribution became available in the 1990s and 2000s, there was a revival of cross-country empirical studies on the Kuznets hypothesis (Nielson and Alderson 1995; Checchi 2000; Wells 2006).

Most of the cross-country empirical research (Kuznets 1963; Ahluwalia 1974; Papanek and Kyn 1986; De Gregorio and Lee 2002) found evidence that supports the Kuznets hypothesis while a few studies disputed it (Saith 1983; Ravallion 2004). More recent studies have proposed the "great U-turn" hypothesis, implying that the trend again reverses further down the timeline of development for countries with very high income (Alderson and Nielsen 2002).

Due to the variety of its classifications, the concepts of income inequality that are used in the literature are clarified as follows. World income inequality (or global income inequality) ranks all individuals in all countries and territories from the richest to the poorest, not considering their country of origin. The citizen of the world is the unit of analysis instead of countries. The next concept is international income inequality (or between-countries income inequality), which measures income inequality existing between countries resulting from contradistinction of their per capita GDP or per capita income. In this second concept, countries are the units of analysis rather than individuals. The final, most commonly studied type is national, or within-country, income inequality. Yitzhaki (1994) indicated that global income inequality can be formulated as the sum of international income inequality, national income inequality, and the residual. The trends of these income inequalities for the period 1820 to 1992 are analyzed by Bourguignon and Morrisson (2002), relying on the copious data from 15 individual countries and 18 other regions composed of country clusters. Figure 6.1 shows the trends of the three different income inequalities. In our research, the focus is on national income inequality.

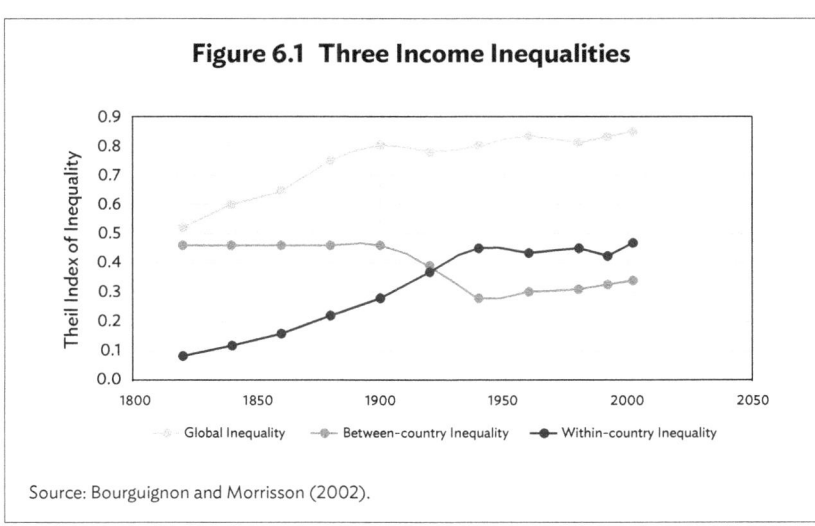

Figure 6.1 Three Income Inequalities

Source: Bourguignon and Morrisson (2002).

Although this study is an extension of abundant cross-country analyses previously performed on the Kuznets hypothesis, some particulars distinguish our research from past efforts. First, instead of focusing on the inverted-U hypothesis itself, the importance of education variables is emphasized. Second, the effect of globalization on income inequality is considered. Since the 1980s, many countries have enacted financial and trade liberalization policies and the level of globalization has generally been increasing with a few exceptions. Globalization affects income inequality both directly and indirectly by impacting education levels. Finally, the present study analyzes how globalization and education affect income inequality with a focus on the Asian and Pacific region.

The rest of the chapter is organized as follows. Section 6.2 reviews the relevant literature on the variables affecting income inequality, particularly education. The third section discusses educational attainment and educational inequality in the Asia and Pacific region while Section 6.4 discusses income inequality in Asia and the Pacific region. Section 6.5 presents models for estimating the influences of education and globalization on income inequality along with a description of the data and variables applied in the analysis. The regression results of the models are interpreted in Section 6.6. Conclusions and policy considerations are presented in the final section.

6.2 Literature Review

Subsequent to Becker's 1964 publication of human capital theory, several studies have considered education's influence on income distribution. As reported by Park (1996a), four different education variable categories are commonly presented in the literature on income distribution. First, a flow variable of schooling signified by institute enrollments at different education levels is used (e.g., primary and secondary education in Ahluwalia [1976]; secondary and tertiary education in Barro [2000] and Alderson and Nielsen [2002]); second, a stock variable of schooling characterized by the average or median years of schooling of the labor force or general population is utilized (Winegarden 1979; Ram 1984; De Gregorio and Lee 2002).

Many studies applied both the flow and stock variables, that is, enrollments at each level of schooling and the average years of education as the independent variables (e.g., Psacharopoulos and Tilak, 1991). The third and fourth types are inequality derived from educational attainment distribution (Checchi 2000) and the rate of return on education (Tilak 1989). There has been a substantial amount of research that considers both the average years of schooling and education inequality as main explanatory variables (Ram 1984; Park 1996a; De Gregorio and Lee 2002).

We limited our literature review to empirical research that analyzes the influence of both the level and inequality of education on income inequality. Numerous findings (Tinbergen 1972; Winegarden 1979; Park 1996a) indicate that more schooling and a more balanced dispersion of it throughout the population improve income distribution. However, Ram (1984) reported contrary empirical results, i.e., that more advanced education exerts a mild balancing influence on income distribution, which corresponds with most findings. However, his inference that a larger dispersion of schooling improves income distribution conflicts with many previous studies. Furthermore, the coefficients of the education inequality variable in his findings are not statistically significant.

Barro (2000) found different consequences of education level on income inequality: an inverse relationship between primary education enrollment and income inequality, but a direct relationship between tertiary education enrollment and income inequality. Alderson and Nielsen's 2002 findings indicate that income inequality has an inverse relationship with the average years of schooling in developed countries.

Other likely factors that influence income inequality have been studied by others. Li, Squire, and Zou (1998) concluded that no connection exists between political freedom and income inequality, while Li and Zou (2002) examined the effect of economic freedom on income inequality. Barro (2000) saw no evidence relating democracy to income inequality. Milanovic and Squire (2005) found the magnitude of liberal policies was inversely related to greater income equality in more impoverished countries and with less income equality in more affluent countries.

Some research concentrated on the link between globalization and income inequality. Alderson and Nielsen (2002) focused on the influences of three facets of globalization, that is, migration, North-South trade, and direct foreign investment. Heshmati (2003) found that the Kearney globalization index describes only 7%–11% of the variations in income inequality. Harjes (2007) suggested that general trends associated with globalization, such as technological changes and trade liberalization, may not be key drivers of income inequality. Ruffin (2009) suggested that globalization tends to improve global income inequality since poorer countries tend to benefit more from the exchange because of cheaper living costs. Because of the heterogeneity of these findings, our research redefines the connection between education and income inequality in the framework of an ever more globalized and integrated world economy, using expanded and updated data, with a focus on the Asian and Pacific region.

6. 3 Attainment and Inequality in Asian Education

Barro and Lee (2010) updated their existing panel dataset of 1993 and 2001 on educational attainment for 146 countries from 1950 to 2010. This new dataset includes 31 Asia and Pacific (hereafter Asian) countries. In 1950, the Asian population aged 15 and over had an average of 2.59 years of schooling, increasing steadily to 5.24 years in 1980, and reaching 8.29 years in 2010. Compared to the world population aged 15 and over, Asian countries started at a lower level than the world average of 3.2 years in 1950, but reached a higher level than the world average of 7.8 years in 2010. Figure 6.2 shows average years of schooling over time by attainment level, indicating steady growth in primary, secondary, and tertiary education.

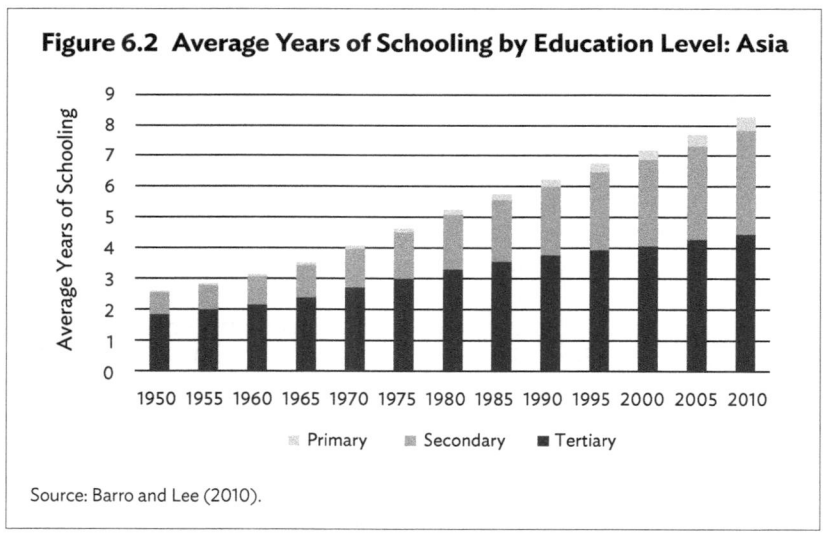

Figure 6.2 Average Years of Schooling by Education Level: Asia

Source: Barro and Lee (2010).

Educational inequality can be obtained by the following formula proposed by Thomas, Wang, and Fan (2003), with the mutually exclusive and collectively inclusive seven categories of Barro and Lee (2010). The seven categories are non-schooling, partial primary education, complete primary education, partial secondary education, complete secondary education, partial higher education, and complete higher education.

$$EDGini = 1/\mu \sum \sum p_i | y_i - y_j | p_j$$

where EDGini represents the education Gini index derived from the dispersion of educational attainment, μ is the mean years of education for the relevant population, p_i and p_j represent the proportions of population with specified levels of education, y_i and y_j are the years of education at different educational attainment levels, and n = 7 where it indicates the number of levels/categories in education attainment data. The cross-country pattern of the distribution of education in Figure 6.3 shows that education Gini coefficients decline continuously as the average years of schooling increase over time.

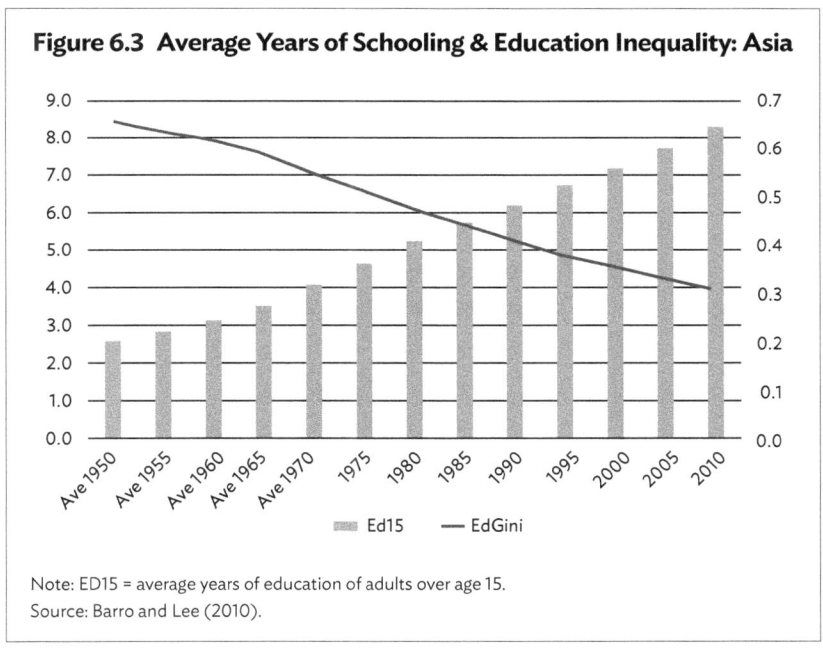

Figure 6.3 Average Years of Schooling & Education Inequality: Asia

Note: ED15 = average years of education of adults over age 15.
Source: Barro and Lee (2010).

This inverse relationship between educational attainment and educational inequality is confirmed not only over time (Figure 6.3), but also across countries in 2010 (Figure 6.4). The only outlier from this pattern is Cambodia.

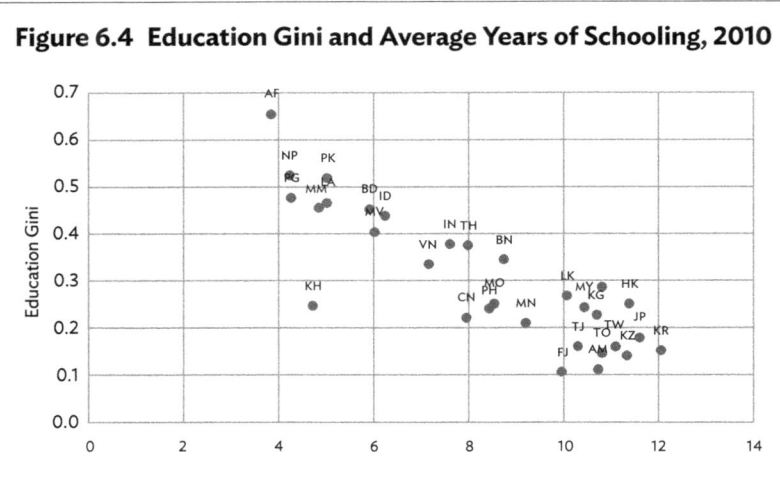

Figure 6.4 Education Gini and Average Years of Schooling, 2010

AF = Afghanistan; AM = Armenia; BD = Bangladesh; CN = China, People's Republic of; FJ = Fiji; HK = Hong Kong, China; ID = Indonesia; IN = India, JP = Japan; KG = Kyrgyz Republic; KH = Cambodia; KR = Republic of Korea; KZ = Kazakhstan; LA = Lao PDR; LK = Sri Lanka; MM = Myanmar; MN = Mongolia; MV = Maldives; MY = Malaysia; NP = Nepal; PH = Philippines; PK = Pakistan; TH = Thailand; TJ = Tajikistan; TW = Taipei,China; VN = Viet Nam.
Source: Barro and Lee (2010).

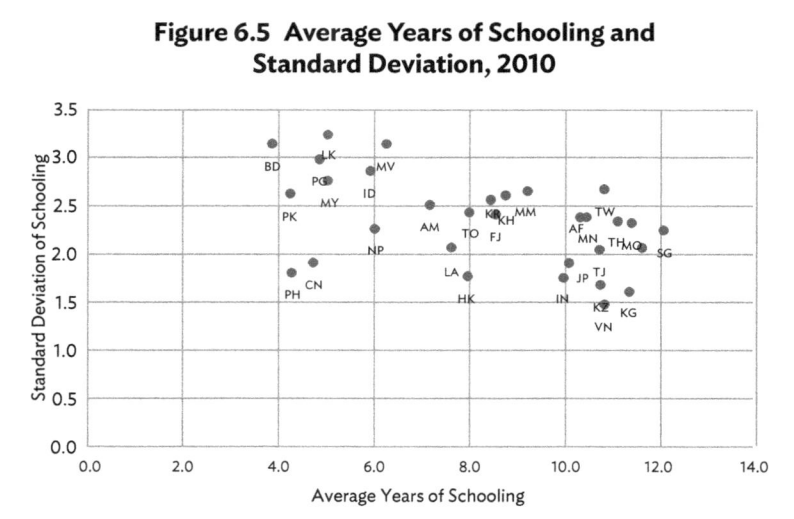

Figure 6.5 Average Years of Schooling and Standard Deviation, 2010

AF = Afghanistan; AM = Armenia; BD = Bangladesh; CN = China, People's Republic of; FJ = Fiji; HK = Hong Kong, China; ID = Indonesia; IN = India, JP = Japan; KG = Kyrgyz Republic; KH = Cambodia; KR = Republic of Korea; KZ = Kazakhstan; LA = Lao PDR; LK = Sri Lanka; MM = Myanmar; MN = Mongolia; MV = Maldives; MY = Malaysia; NP = Nepal; PH = Philippines; PK = Pakistan; TH = Thailand; TJ = Tajikistan; TW = Taipei,China; VN = Viet Nam.
Source: Barro and Lee (2010).

An alternative measure of educational inequality can be calculated by the standard deviation of schooling (EDSD) using the following formula:

$$EDSD = SQRT\left[\sum p_i (y_i - \mu)2\right]$$

In contrast to EDGini, EDSD does not show a clear relationship with educational attainment as shown in Figure 6.5. The standard deviation of schooling seems to have no consistent pattern. Therefore, education Gini is a more robust and better measure for educational inequality than the standard deviation.

6.4 Income Inequality in Asia

The World Income Inequality Database (WIID) (WIDER 2015) provides the most comprehensive set of income inequality statistics available for developed, developing, and transition countries. The WIID3.3, released in 2015, covers 175 countries for the period 1950 to 2012 for most countries. However, the dataset has missing years for many countries as well as many different observations for the same year. For example, in the case of the People's Republic of China (PRC), seven different Gini coefficients are reported for 2010, while no observations are reported for 1954–1963, 1965, 1969, 1971, and 1976.

Table 6.1 shows the trend of the Gini coefficient, as well as the bottom 20% income share and the top 20% income share in Asian countries between the mid-1990s and around 2010. Out of the 30 countries with available data for the mid-1990s, 14 showed high income inequality, with Gini coefficients greater than 40, the commonly known threshold for high inequality, while 10 out of the 32 countries around 2010 showed high income inequality. A decrease in the number of countries with high income inequality might give a spurious indication of improvement in income distribution, which would be misleading.

Table 6.1 Trends in Income Inequality in Asia

Economy	Code	Mid-1990s				Around 2010				
		Year	Δ Gini	Bottom 20%	Top 20%	Year	Gini	Bottom 20%	Top 20%	Δ Gini
Afghanistan	AF	--	--	--	--	2008	27.4	9.4	37.48	--
Armenia	AM	1996	48.2	4.56	55.3	2010	36.2	5.00	45.00	-12
Azerbaijan	AZ	1996	45.8	7.98	40.98	2008	33.7	7.99	42.08	-12.1

continued on next page

Table 6.1 continued

Economy	Code	Mid-1990s				Around 2010				
		Year	Δ Gini	Bottom 20%	Top 20%	Year	Gini	Bottom 20%	Top 20%	Δ Gini
Bangladesh	BD	1996	38.7	5.79	47.9	2010	45.8	5.22	51.79	7.1
Bhutan	BT	--	--	--	--	2012	36	7.10	43.70	--
Cambodia	KH	1997	44.7	5.96	54.16	2010	36	2.80	60.47	-8.7
China, People's Republic of	CN	1993	35.5	7.35	43.23	2010	48.1	6.44	39.24	12.6
Fiji	FJ	1991	46	5.1	50.1	2009	42.8	6.20	49.59	-3.2
Georgia	GE	1998	50.3	3.44	54.5	2010	43	5.38	46.90	-7.3
Hong Kong, China	HK	1996	52	3.7	56.3	2011	48.9	4.40	54.20	-3.1
India	IN	1992	32	8.8	41.1	2010	36.8	8.12	42.46	4.8
Indonesia	ID	1996	36.1	7.78	44.9	2010	38	7.15	45.47	1.9
Japan	JP	1993	24.9	10.58	35.65	2009	31.1	7.54	40.89	6.2
Kazakhstan	KZ	1996	39.4	6.68	42.33	2009	27.8	9.12	38.41	-11.6
Republic of Korea	KR	1996	32.8	5.99	38.8	2009	34.5	6.52	38.40	1.7
Kyrgyz Republic	KG	1996	48.5	3.08	54.1	2009	36.2	6.82	43.38	-12.3
Lao PDR	LA	1997	34.9	8.02	43.28	2008	36.7	7.64	44.84	1.8
Malaysia	MY	1995	48.5	4.21	55.26	2009	46.2	4.54	51.45	-2.3
Maldives	MV	1998	46.2	6.51	44.24	2010	37	7.00	43.00	-9.2
Mongolia	MN	1995	33.2	7.37	40.76	2008	36.5	7.10	44.04	3.3
Myanmar	MM	--	--	--	--	2010	30.3	11.98	31.97	--
Nepal	NP	1996	38.8	7.59	46.97	2010	32.8	8.27	41.46	-6
Pakistan	PK	1996	31.2	9.45	41.09	2011	30.6	9.40	40.10	-0.6
Philippines	PH	1997	42.7	6.01	48.91	2009	44.8	5.10	51.90	2.1
Singapore	SG	1997	44.4	3.6	48.2	2010	47.2	5.08	43.99	2.8
Sri Lanka	LK	1996	46.6	5.03	53.88	2007	40.3	6.94	47.79	-6.3
Taipei,China	TW	1996	31.7	7.23	38.39	2010	34.2	6.49	40.19	2.5
Tajikistan	TJ	1999	30.4	7.67	41.58	2009	30.8	8.29	39.37	0.4
Thailand	TH	1996	42.9	5.7	50.1	2009	40.8	6.10	48.70	-2.1
Turkmenistan	TM	1993	35.8	6.7	42.76	1999	35.8	6.70	42.76	0
Uzbekistan	UZ	1993	33.3	7.28	40.74	2003	36.7	7.14	44.19	3.4
Viet Nam	VN	1998	35.4	7.38	45.46	2008	35.6	7.42	43.41	0.2

Source: WIDER, World Income Inequality Database 3.3.

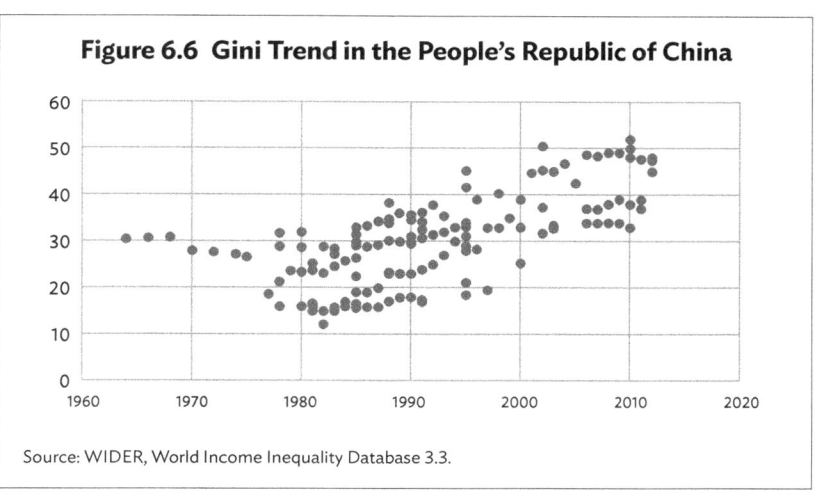

Source: WIDER, World Income Inequality Database 3.3.

From the last column of Table 6.1, 16 out of 32 Asian countries actually experienced worsening income distribution. In particular, the Gini coefficient of the PRC jumped by 12.6 points from 35.5 in 1993 to 48.1 in 2010 while Japan's Gini coefficient jumped by 6.2 points from 24.9 in 1993 to 31.1 in 2009. Figure 6.6 presents all Gini coefficient estimates for the PRC collected by WIID3.3 over the period 1964 to 2013, a total of 152 estimates. A rising income inequality in the PRC over time is clearly exhibited.

The countries that recorded an improvement in their Gini coefficients are mainly from Central Asia. They include Armenia, Azerbaijan, Georgia, Kazakhstan, and the Kyrgyz Republic. When they experienced drastic social and economic changes in the transition from a command economy to a market economy in the 1980s and 1990s, their Gini coefficients initially surged. As their economies have stabilized and more income opportunities have become available, their Gini coefficients have also steadily declined. For example, Armenia's Gini coefficient fluctuated from 26.9 in 1986 to 48.2 in 1996 to 36.2 in 2010. Other former Soviet Union countries such as Georgia, Kazakhstan, and the Kyrgyz Republic show a similar pattern. Cambodia also experienced a similar trend with its regime changes in 1975 and 1997. The trend of Gini coefficients in the Kyrgyz Republic is presented in Figure 6.7 with a total of 47 Gini coefficient estimates between 1981 and 2009; the graph clearly indicates the presence of the Kuznets Curve, an inverted U-curve.

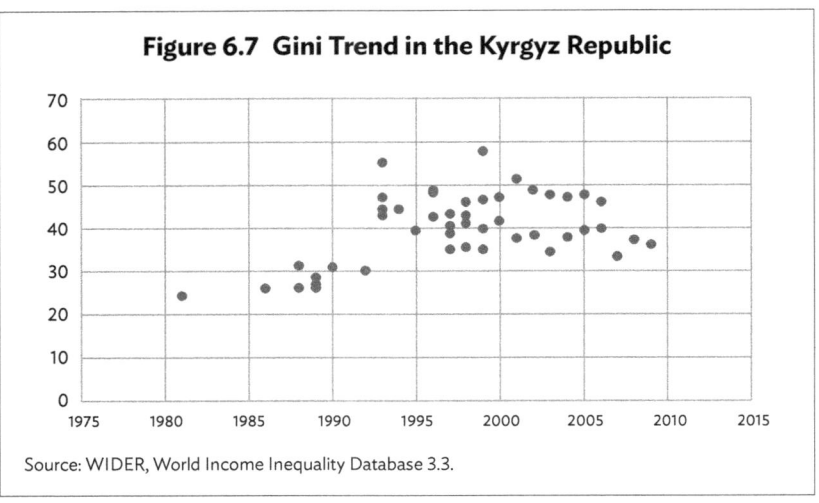

Figure 6.7 Gini Trend in the Kyrgyz Republic

Source: WIDER, World Income Inequality Database 3.3.

Most of Asia, except for some Central Asian countries, Cambodia, and a few small countries, experienced rising income inequality. Zhang, Kanbur, and Rhee (2014) pointed to technological progress, globalization, and market-oriented reform as the key driving factors. These factors helped the rapid growth of developing Asian countries in the last two decades. However, they also had negative effects on income distribution in the region. Technological progress combined with capital-intensive technology tends to favor skilled labor over unskilled labor, increasing skill premiums and causing income inequality. Globalization could favor particular regions (for example, the coastline over the interior in the PRC) or particular industries (industries with comparative advantage), thereby causing more income inequality. On the other hand, the Stopler-Samuelson theorem and "growth with equity" experiences in the Republic of Korea, Singapore, and Taipei,China suggest improvement in income distribution. Therefore, whether globalization has a positive or negative effect on income distribution in the Asia and Pacific region will be empirically tested in this study. Compared with Organisation for Economic Co-operation and Development (OECD) countries, Asia's income inequality is higher by 5.46 points on average. The average Gini coefficient of Asia's 32 countries around 2010 was 37.46, as shown in Figure 6.8, while the average Gini coefficient of 34 OECD countries was 32, as shown in Figure 6.9. While changes in the Gini coefficients in the OECD countries over time tend to be mild, many Asian countries experienced drastic surges or drops in their Gini coefficients between the 1990s and 2010.

Education, Globalization, and Income Inequality in Asia 143

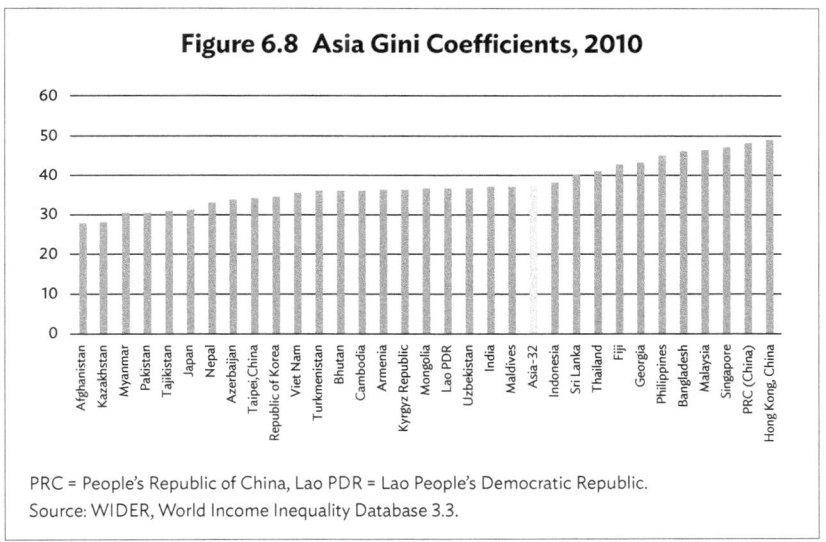

PRC = People's Republic of China, Lao PDR = Lao People's Democratic Republic.
Source: WIDER, World Income Inequality Database 3.3.

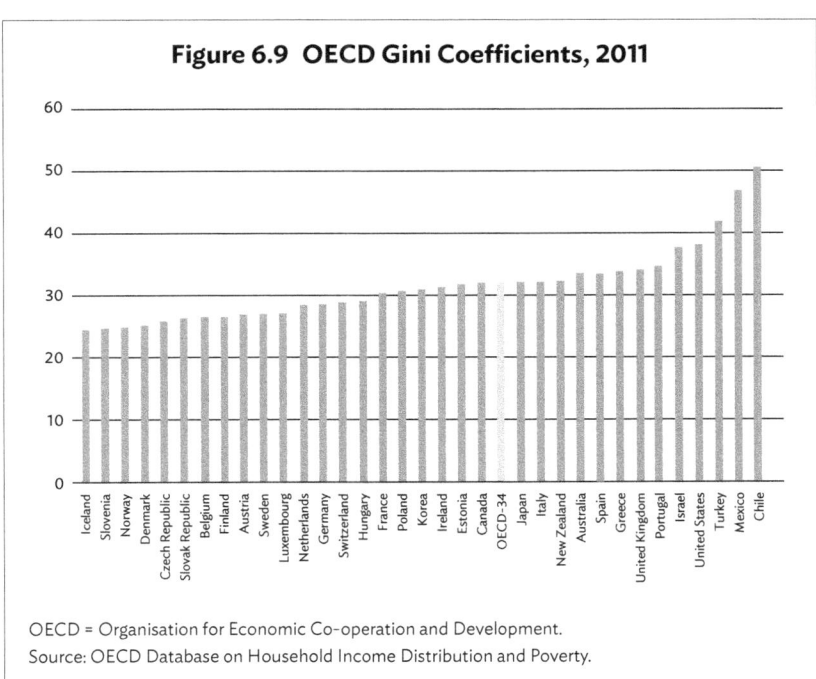

OECD = Organisation for Economic Co-operation and Development.
Source: OECD Database on Household Income Distribution and Poverty.

6.5 Model and Variables

There are different ways to structure models to formulate the Kuznets inverted-U hypothesis. A characteristic model that numerous authors (e.g., Park 1996a) have used may be presented as follows:

$$\text{Gini} = a_0 + a_1 \ln Y + a_2 (\ln Y)^2 + u \quad (1)$$

where Gini is the Gini index, an indication of income inequality, ln Y is shorthand for the logarithm of income of per capita GDP, which generally represents the level of economic development, and u is the residual. We expect a positive sign for a1 while a negative sign is predicted for a_2.

Several other independent variables that have been incorporated into cross-sectional studies are included along with the income variables. Two education variables are added to the model based on human capital theory as follows:

$$\text{Gini} = b_0 + b_1 \ln Y + b_2 (\ln Y)_2 + b_3 \text{ ED} + b_4 \text{ EDGini} + u \quad (2)$$

where ED represents the level of schooling or educational attainment and EDGini stands for its dispersion. The human capital theory proposes that the income level of an individual is determined by years of education and the rate of return to education. The human capital model as expressed by De Gregorio and Lee (2002) is given below:

$$\ln Y_s = \ln Y_0 + \Sigma \ln (1 + r_i) + \varepsilon \quad (3)$$

where Y_s is the income level with s years of schooling, r_i is the rate of return to the ith year of schooling, Σ is the summation from i = 1 to s years, and ε is the residual. Equation (3) can be approximated as $\ln Y_s = \ln Y_0 + r_s + \varepsilon$. After making variance transformation on both sides, the reformulated equation is shown below:

$$\text{Var} (\ln Y_s) = r^2 \text{Var} (S) + S_\mu^2 \text{Var} (r) + 2 r S_\mu \text{Cov} (r,S) + \text{Var} (\varepsilon) \quad (4)$$

where S_μ is the average schooling years.

This formula obviously indicates the existence of a direct correlation between inequality in education and income. However, the number of schooling years has an inconclusive influence on income inequality. If the level of education (s) and the rate of return (r) are independent, an increase in the years of schooling will make income inequality rise. However, if the covariance between the years of schooling (s) and the rate of return (r) is negative, a rise in the average years of schooling can reduce income inequality. So, the sign of b_3 is ambiguous, while a positive sign is predicted for b_4.

A country's globalization level and its degree of freedom, either political or economic, may influence the distribution of income, especially in the progressively integrated and globalized world. Relevant significant control variables are added to equation (2) as shown below:

$$\text{Gini} = c_0 + c_1 \ln Y + c_2 (\ln Y)^2 + c_3 \text{ ED} + c_4 \text{ EDGini} \quad (5)$$
$$+ c_5 \text{ FREEDOM} + c_6 \text{ GLOBAL} + u$$

where FREEDOM represents either a country's degree of economic freedom or degree of political freedom, and GLOBAL indicates the degree of globalization of a country.

There are various measures of income inequality and Park (1984) compared their similarities and differences. The best-known and most widely used measure of income inequality is the Gini coefficient. The WIID3.3 by UNU-WIDER (2015) has the most extensive data collection on the Gini coefficient, covering many countries for a long period of time. Additionally, the income share of the top 20% of the population (TOP20) and that of the bottom 40% (BOTTOM40) are used as alternative measures of the income inequality variable. As a proxy variable for the income level (or economic development), the logarithm of per capita GDP is used and the data are from the World Bank's World Development Indicators. One education variable, the mean years of schooling (ED), is acquired from the new dataset of educational attainment in the world 1950–2010 by Barro and Lee (2010), while the second education variable, the dispersion of schooling (EDGini), is calculated by the author according to the formula given in Section 3, using Barro and Lee's 2010 data. Two different measures of freedom are used to estimate the variable FREEDOM. First, the freedom of businesses and individuals from government restrictions constitutes economic freedom. How well legal and institutional systems preserve economic freedom is also considered. Since 1994, the Heritage Foundation rates countries annually based on 50 independent variables organized into 10 broad categories of economic freedom.

Second, a country's political freedom is rated by estimating the degree to which people are unrestricted in the areas of political and civil rights. Since 1978, Freedom House, a New York-based nonprofit organization, has annually ranked political rights and civil liberties in countries worldwide.

Among the various indices indicating the level of globalization of individual nations, the KOF index is used as a proxy variable. This index is available for 208 countries for the period 1970 to 2016 and suits our research as it covers many countries for a long period of time. The KOF globalization index is based on economic, political, and cultural integration of a country in the world and the degree of personal contact across national borders. The metrics for economic integration include convergence of domestic and international prices, movements of goods and services, and outward- and inward-directed foreign investment, as well as portfolio capital flows. On the other hand, the metrics for the degree of personal contact across national borders include international travel, memberships of international organizations, cross-border remittances, internet users and servers, and international phone calls.

6.6 Empirical Results

The data for income inequality are obtained from WIID3.3. Despite the improvements of WIID data over time, some observations of the Gini index are missing. In some instances, there are discrepancies in estimates for the same country in the same year. Therefore, an unbalanced panel data analysis, with 1990, 2000, and 2010 data, is carried out in this study. The sample size is inevitably reduced due to many missing Gini index observations.

To eliminate the possibility of reverse causality, we used lagged independent variables. While 1990, 2000, and 2010 data points are used for independent variables, the dependent variables, Gini, TOP20, and BOTTOM40, are from data of a few years later (at least 2–3 years) than 1990, 2000, and 2010, respectively.

Table 6.2 shows the regression results of estimating equation (1). The empirical results supported the Kuznets hypothesis. We observe an inverse U-shaped curve relationship for Gini and TOP20, while BOTTOM40 exhibits a U-shaped curve relationship. We obtained the predicted signs for all coefficients, and most of them are statistically significant at the 5% level, regardless of whether Gini, TOP20, or BOTTOM40 is used as the dependent variable. Due to the nature of the panel data, the sizes of the adjusted R^2 statistic tend to be small.

Table 6.3 shows the regression results of estimating equation (2) while adding the mean years of schooling and dispersion of schooling (or inequality in education). The mean years of schooling of the labor force (ED) is used as a proxy variable for the educational attainment level. As a proxy variable for the dispersion of educational attainment, EDGini is calculated by the author from Barro and Lee's 2010 data.

The regression results in Table 6.3, which include the additional ED and EDGini variables, are quite different from the results in Table 6.2. First, including the additional variables raised the adjusted R^2 statistic,

Table 6.2 Regression of Income Inequality on Income

	GINI	TOP 20%	BOTTOM 40%
Constant	-22.78	-11.57	32.49
	31.65	12.63	25.18
ln Y	23.29**	18.82**	-10.62**
	10.08	7.87	3.75
ln Y^2	-2.14**	-1.66**	1.19**
	0.81	0.74	0.57
N	78	78	78
Adj. R^2	.264	.329	.243

The first entry for each predictor is the coefficient estimate, and the second in parentheses is the standard error of the coefficient estimate. * indicates significance at the 10% level and ** at the 5% level.

Source: Author's calculation.

Table 6.3 Regression of Income Inequality on Income and Education Variables

	GINI	TOP 20%	BOTTOM 40%
Constant	14.85	4.36	22.73
	22.75	7.27	30.34
ln Y	14.68*	13.90*	-6.14
	8.02	7.71	4.68
ln Y^2	-1.32	-1.05	0.64
	1.67	0.81	0.42
ED	-2.39**	-1.47**	1.02**
	0.67	0.59	0.43
EDGini	6.18**	5.97**	-3.92**
	1.98	2.17	1.64.
N	72	72	72
Adj. R^2	.397	.425	.353

The first entry for each predictor is the coefficient estimate, and the second in parentheses is the standard error of the coefficient estimate. * indicates significance at the 10% level and ** at the 5% .level.

Source: Author's calculation.

thereby contributing to improvement in the explanatory power of the model. Second, both education variables have significant effects on income inequality, while the magnitude and significance of the income variables declined, as can be seen from the smaller and less significant coefficients of both ln Y and (ln Y)^2. A negative and significant coefficient of ED on Gini and TOP20 indicates that a higher level of schooling reduces overall income inequality (lower Gini index and lower TOP 20% income share), while a positive and significant coefficient of ED on BOTTOM40 indicates that a higher level of schooling improves the income share of the poor (higher BOTTOM 40% income share). On the other hand, a positive effect of EDGini on GINI and TOP20 and a negative effect of EDGini on BOTTOM40 indicate that the larger the dispersion of schooling, the more unequal the distribution of income.

Table 6.4 shows the regression results of estimating equation (5), which, in addition to two income variables and two education variables, includes the Heritage Foundation economic freedom index, the Freedom House political freedom index, and the KOF globalization index as control variables. A moderate improvement in the adjusted R^2 statistic is obtained. The significance of the two education variables remains unchanged while the two income variables become less significant, though they exhibit predicted signs.

Table 6.4 Regression of Income Inequality on Income, Education, and Globalization

	GINI	TOP 20%	BOTTOM 40%
Constant	10.56	3.28	16.34
	12.84	5.26	10.74
ln Y	13.21	12.63*	-4.26
	7.68	7.14	2.94
ln Y^2	-1.55	-1.13	0.73
	1.17	0.72	0.58.
ED	-1.72*	-2.17**	0.98**
	0.96	0.66	0.44.
EDGini	5.94**	6.94**	-4.76**
	2.37	1.13	1.91
ln ECONOMIC FREEDOM INDEX	1.73	2.184	-1.31*
	2.05	2.12	0.71
POLITICAL FREEDOM RATING	-0.15	0.28	-0.09
	0.29	0.63	0.11
ln GLOBALIZATION INDEX	2.95**	3.01**	-1.01*
	1.13	0.97	0.54
N	69	69	69
Adj. R^2	.445	.489	.394

The first entry for each predictor is the coefficient estimate, and the second in parentheses is the standard error of the coefficient estimate. * indicates significance at the 10% level and ** at the 5% level.

Source: Author's calculation.

Economic freedom, though not significant, is positively related to income inequality. Our results do not indicate a meaningful association between political freedom and income inequality. This study also confirms that some variations in income inequality can be explained by globalization, thereby sustaining the great U-turn hypothesis proposed by Alderson and Nielsen (2002). So, the longitudinal tendency toward rising income inequality may be partially explained by globalization trends. Globalization may influence income inequality through technical changes favoring highly educated and skilled workers with bias against unskilled workers, causing wider wage differentials.

6.7 Conclusion and Implications

Education has been a crucial factor in economic and social policies because of its potential to promote progress for the individual as well as the country as a whole. Historically, education as a human capital investment and its effect on economic growth have been major subjects of concern for scholars as well as policymakers. Lately, the importance of establishing the relationship between education and income and between education and income distribution has gained prominence.

In our chapter, we show how education level and education inequality influence income inequality in the Asian and Pacific region, based on the panel data of 1990, 2000, and 2010. Results from the panel data analysis indicate that a higher level of schooling of the population has reduced income inequality while a greater dispersion of schooling has increased income inequality. We support the presence of the inverted-U curve when only the income variables are included in the model as independent variables. Then again, the effect of the income variables becomes weaker and statistically less significant when the average years of schooling and the dispersion of schooling are incorporated into the model.

We also studied the effects of freedom and globalization on income distribution. Our analysis demonstrates that an increasing degree of globalization results in increasing inequality in income distribution. However, freedom, either political or economic, has only limited impacts on income distribution. With the adjusted R2 ranging between 0.4 and 0.5, a substantial proportion of the changes in income inequality across countries remain unexplained. To identify additional determinants of income inequality, further study is warranted.

This study offers policy implications on how to improve income distribution. The chief finding of this study is that education plays a significant role in reducing income inequality. If a government plans to improve the distribution of income, it is suggested that government policymakers focus on education policies that promote educational expansion while affording individuals equal and greater access to educational opportunities. Educational expansion with less dispersion of schooling is also identified by Park (1998) as a major factor contributing to economic growth. Government policymakers need to monitor the dispersion of educational attainment because education expansion under certain circumstances may increase education inequality.

At the same time, as changes in educational attainment and dispersion of schooling take longer, this indirect and long-term education policy needs to be supplemented by a more direct and short-term government policy focusing on a progressive income tax structure and transferring benefits to the poor. Some argue that redistributive policies tend to have a negative impact on economic growth. However, equitable distribution may not necessarily be detrimental as Japan; Taipei,China; and Republic of Korea represent a few cases of achieving both equity and economic growth with their emphasis on education in their economic development. Equity and growth can be achieved through an optimal mix of long-term education policies and short-term redistributive government policies.

This study also confirms the important role played by globalization in determining income inequality. The difficulty in establishing relationships comes from the complexity of globalization measurements. The globalization index comprises numerous elements, such as movements of goods and services, inward and outward foreign direct investment as well as portfolio capital flows, convergence of domestic and international prices, and international travel. To discover which elements play important roles in determining income inequality, further research on different components of globalization would be required.

References

Ahluwalia, M. 1974. Income Inequality, Some Dimensions of the Problem. In *Redistribution with Growth*, edited by H. Chenery et al. New York: Oxford University Press.

Ahluwalia, M. 1976. Inequality, Poverty and Development. *Journal of Development Economics* 3: 307–342.

Alderson, A., and F. Nielsen. 2002. Globalization and the Great U-turn: Income Inequality Trends in 16 OECD Countries. *American Journal of Sociology* 107: 1244–1299.

Barro, R. 2000. Inequality and Growth in a Panel of Countries. *Journal of Economic Growth* 5: 5–32.

Barro, R., and J. Lee. 2010. *A New Data Set of Educational Attainment in the World, 1950–2010*, Working Paper No.15902. Cambridge, MA: National Bureau of Economic Research.

Becker, G. 1964. *Human Capital: A Theoretical and Empirical Analysis, with Special Reference to Education*. New York: Columbia Univ. Press.

Bourguignon, F., and C. Morrisson. 2002. Inequality among World Citizens: 1820–1992. *American Economic Review* 92: 727–744.

Checchi, D. 2000. *Does Educational Achievement Help to Explain Income Inequality?* Working Paper No. 208. Helsinki: United Nations University, World Institute for Development Economics Research.

De Gregorio, J., and J. Lee. 2002. Education and Income Inequality: New Evidence from Cross-country Data. *The Review of Income and Wealth* 48: 395–416.

Harjes, T. 2007. *Globalization and Income Inequality: A European Perspective*. IMF Working Paper. Washington, DC: IMF.

Heshmati, A. 2003. *The Relationship between Income Inequality and Globalization*. WIDER Working Paper. Helsinki: The United Nations University.

Kravis, I. G. 1960. International Differences in the Distribution of Income. *Review of Economics and Statistics* 42: 408–416.

Kuznets, S. 1955. Economic Growth and Income Inequality. *American Economic Review* 45: 1–28.

Kuznets, S. 1963. Quantitative Aspects of the Economic Growth of Nations VIII: Distribution of Income by Size. *Economic Development and Cultural Change* 11: 1–80.

Li, H., Squire, L., and H. Zou. 1998. Explaining International and Intertemporal Variations in Income Inequality. *Economic Journal* 108: 26–43.

Li, H., and H. Zou. 2002. Inflation, Growth, and Income Distribution: A Cross-country Study. *Annals of Economics and Finance* 3: 85–101.

Milanovic, B., and L. Squire. 2005. Does Tariff Liberalization Increase Wage Inequality? Some Empirical Evidence. World Bank Policy Research Working Paper No. 3571. Washington DC: World Bank.

Nielsen, F., and A. Alderson. 1995. Income Inequality, Development, and Dualism: Results from an Unbalanced Cross-national Panel. *American Sociological Review* 60: 674–701.

Papanek, G., and O. Kyn. 1986. The Effect on Income Distribution of Development, the Growth Rate and Economic Strategy. *Journal of Development Economics* 23: 55–65.

Park, K. 1984. Comparison of Income Inequality Measures. *Studies in Economics and Finance* 8: 35–58.

Park, K. 1986. Re-examination of the Linkage between Income Inequality and Political Violence. *Journal of Political and Military Sociology* 14: 185–197.

Park, K. 1996a. Educational Expansion and Educational Inequality on Income Distribution. *Economics of Education Review* 15: 51–58.

Park, K. 1996b. Income Inequality and Economic Progress. *American Journal of Economics and Sociology* 55: 87–96.

Park, K. 1998. Distribution and Growth: Cross-country Evidence. *Applied Economics* 30: 943–949.

Psacharopoulos, G., and J. B. G. Tilak. 1991. Schooling and Equity. In *Essays on Poverty, Equity and Growth*, edited by G. Psacharopoulos. Oxford: Pergamon Press.

Ram, R. 1984. Population Increase, Economic Growth, Educational Inequality and Income Distribution. *Journal of Development Economics* 14: 419–428.

Ravallion, M. 2004. Competing Concepts of Inequality in the Globalization Debate. World Bank Policy Research Working Paper No. 3038. Washington DC: World Bank.

Robinson, S. 1976. A Note on the U-hypothesis Relating Income Inequality and Economic Development. *American Economic Review* 66: 437–440.

Ruffin, R. 2009. Globalization and Income Inequality. *Trade and Development Review* 2: 56–69.

Saith, A. 1983. Development and Distribution: A Critique of the Cross-country U-hypothesis. *Journal of Development Economics* 13: 367–382.

Stewart, F. 1978. Inequality, Technology and Payment System. *World Development* 6: 275–293.

Thomas, V., Y. Wang, and X. Fan. 2003. Measuring Education Inequality: Gini Coefficients of Education for 140 countries, 1960–2000. *Journal of Education Planning and Administration* 17: 5–33.

Tilak, J. B. G. 1989. Rates of Return to Education and Income Distribution. *De Economist* 137: 454–465.

Tinbergen, J. 1972. The Impact of Education and Income Distribution. *Review of Income and Wealth* 19: 255–265.

Wells, R. 2006. Education's Effect on Income Inequality: an Economic Globalisation Perspective. *Globalisation, Societies and Education* 4: 371–391.

Winegarden, C. R. 1979. Schooling and Income Distribution: Evidence from International Data. *Economica* 46: 83–87.

World Institute for Development Economics Research WIDER. 2015. World Income Inequality Database 3.3. United Nations University.

Yitzhaki, S. 1994. Economic Distance and Overlapping of Distributions. *Journal of Econometrics* 61: 147–159.

Zhang, J., R. Kanbur, and C. Rhee, 2014. What Drives Asia's Rising Inequality. In *Inequality in Asia and the Pacific: Trends, Drivers and Policy Implications*, edited by J. Zhang, R. Kanbur, and C. Rhee. Manila: Asian Development Bank.

7

Economic Growth and Income Distribution in Transition Economies of Central Asia: A Pure Empirical Study of the Post-Communist Development Era

Odiljon Komolov

7.1 Introduction

Central Asian economies have chosen a long and gradual path of economic transition instead of the "great leap" policy preferred by several post-communist counterparts in Eastern Europe and the Caucasus to minimize risk of problems related to tax evasion, transition to private ownership, and employment. However, a prolonged economic transition policy led to a long-term income poverty period in the first decade of independence, as governments implemented key economic reforms to adopt market principles. Economy-wide privatization of Soviet-inherited completely state-owned assets and freely determined pricing with supply and demand forces widened the already existing poverty gap and stimulated uneven distribution of income among population classes.

The new millennium was marked by sparks of significant economic growth with diversified economic orientation in Central Asia. Economies started recovering from the implications of a decade of extreme economic tightening, supply chain crises, closedowns of structurally important and too-big-to-fail enterprises, and consequent absolute unemployment. Ownership reform and the collapse of the communist economic structure in all post-Soviet economies affected the prosperity of all income groups of the population in different aspects. The growing business sector and economy-wide promotion of private ownership had mixed results and consequences in terms of income levels.

This chapter presents the findings of more than 10 years of ongoing research with a historical overview and fact-based analysis but without any econometric calculations and hypotheses to deliver the message with a true understanding of the income inequality and economic growth trends in Central Asia.

7.2 Literature Review

Although the relationship between economic growth and income inequality in transition economies has been sufficiently studied, this interrelation has been a hot research topic since the publication of the pioneering research paper by Simon Kuznets (1955). Kuznets' findings have attracted the research interest of many researchers and experts and inspired new theories and approaches. His theory implies that income inequality worsens during the early stages of economic development as resources are reallocated from low-productivity sectors such as agriculture to high-productivity sectors such as manufacturing. But new trends in global economic development led to new research and new hypotheses emerged. The concepts of Kuznets were contradicted by Piketty and Saez (2003), who concluded that advanced economies are more prone to rising income inequality, which they showed using the case of the United States economy. Further, the Organisation for Economic Co-operation and Development, in its working papers, suggested similar and more seriously contradictory evidence that income inequality is in an upward trend. This trend is even over the Kuznets curve, and market forces are not able to regulate it in a growing economy.

Some literature rejects the relationship between economic growth and income inequality. For example, in his empirical studies, Ravallion (2004) found that there is zero correlation between shifts in inequality and economic growth. Ravallion and Chen (1997), Ravallion (2004), and the World Bank (2005) provided evidence that the relationship may be neutral, as factors and actions that boost economic growth may influence income inequality both negatively and positively.

Furthermore, several studies explain different effects of economic growth on equality. In his research, Fields (1987) used an assumption of an economy that has only two sectors with different productivity and wages. Economic growth is rooted in these sectors through employment and productivity growth. Fields' analysis proved that when both sectors have the same rate of employment and productivity growth, income equality does not shift despite economic growth.

7.3 Income Inequality and Economic Growth in Central Asia

The 20th century witnessed unequalled success in improving the living standard of people in most parts of the world (Tabassum 2008). Polarization of economic development across the planet led to the coining of a new term: "poor and rich nations." The social status of nations is often marked by the income they earn. Central Asian economies, which were an integral part of the former Soviet Union, as a low-cost resource provider for the sake of membership of a strictly and poorly administered union, were commonly seen as poor nations with a high level of poverty and illiteracy, as well as a low lifespan and living standards. All Central Asian economies were key suppliers of particular products or raw materials to the central body. Their economies were specialized for respective sectors appointed by the Soviet government, which made them monosectoral. In that harsh period, the living standards of Central Asian people worsened, and income stability went backwards (Figure 7.1). In Uzbekistan alone, nearly half of the population lived below the poverty line, 97% of the population earned less than 75 rubles per month, and more than 10 million people were officially recognized as poor in 1989. Other economies, especially those of the Kyrgyz Republic and Tajikistan, were purely monosectoral economies that produced per capita output several times less than the Soviet Union average.

In the Soviet era, during communist propaganda campaigns, extremely odd economic concepts were wrongly promoted. The economy was built on a very fragile and vulnerable principle—absolute income equality and zero income gap. The acme of the Soviet economic system was a supreme socialist economy in which people met their needs for free depending on their performance and societal contribution. This utopian socialist mind contradicted the fundamental principles of economic systems. Consequently, corruption and bribery bred across all income groups of society. After the dissolution of the Soviet Union, Central Asian economies faced a long-term supply chain and unemployment crisis that lasted nearly a decade in some economies. Large-scale privatization and early steps toward a market economy widened the income inequality gap and increased the number of people who needed public support to be eked out. The early transition strategies of all Central Asian economies

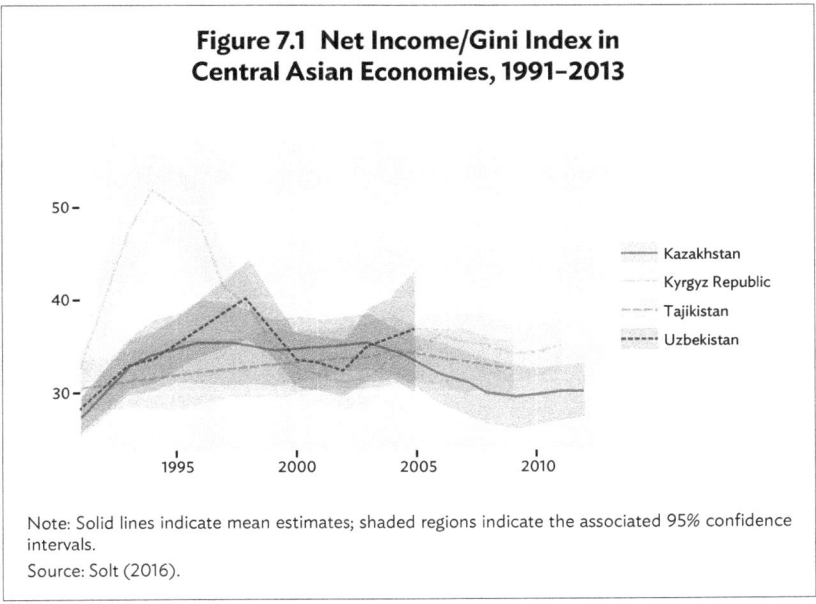

Figure 7.1 Net Income/Gini Index in Central Asian Economies, 1991–2013

Note: Solid lines indicate mean estimates; shaded regions indicate the associated 95% confidence intervals.
Source: Solt (2016).

differentiated in orientation, actions, and principles. Although the priority goal was unique for all, the paths chosen to reach it were different. Privatization was the driving force behind income inequality and distribution in newly independent economies. In the early stages of privatization, many enterprises went to private hands, which fixed strict requirements for labor to boost productivity and profit. Private ownership stimulated the existence of new labor relations and created a new competitive and quality-oriented labor market by removing outdated favoritism-based traditional labor relations. In this recovery period, income inequality began normalizing.

The introduction of private ownership and business relations, which were strictly prohibited and prosecuted in the former Soviet era, potentially increases income inequality in line with Piketty and Saez (2003). We assume that their hypothesis coincides with the economic growth history of the Central Asian economies. All economies in the region experienced a relentless growth and the private sector had already become the backbone of the domestic economy. This suggests that the number of top earners was increasing and that of low earners was decreasing. Though it is a positive trend, as the economy grows and society gets richer, the difference/ratio between the top and lowest earners is a progressive trend (Figure 7.2).

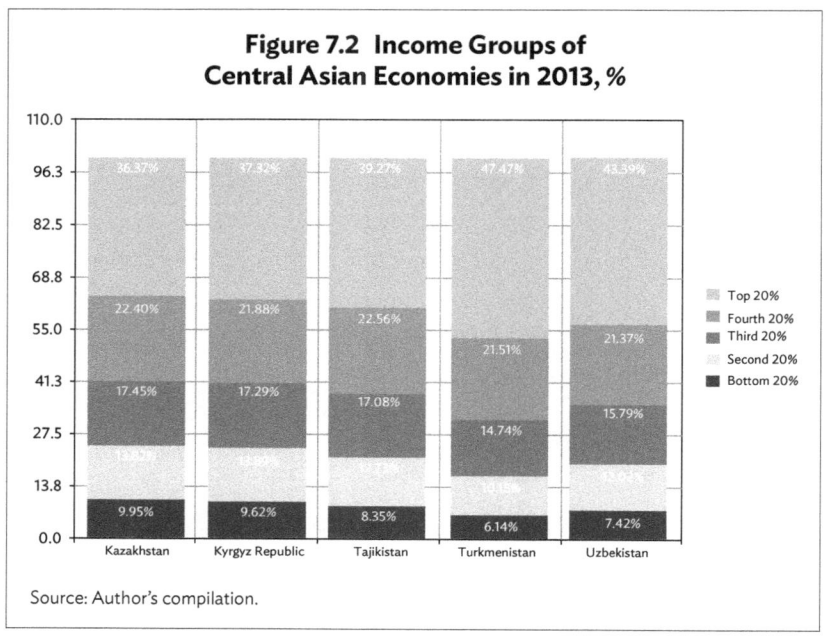

Figure 7.2 Income Groups of Central Asian Economies in 2013, %

Source: Author's compilation.

7.4 Why Income Distribution is Different in Transition Economies: The Case of Central Asia

Income distribution—and poverty in general—is determined by a broad set of factors including economic growth, the skills distribution of the workforce, the changing demand for labor with different skills, demographic developments (aging, family formation, etc.), the dynamics of domestic policy (electoral cycles, different social and economic policies), and a number of (residual) country-specific factors (Medgyesi and Tóth 2009). However, income distribution differs hugely in economic groups of countries in terms of factors and measures. Country-specific features of economic development level and structure often create significant and visible differences in income, which stimulates the cross-border movement of labor. In advanced economies, the gap in income distribution has a growing trend, as top earners have gained a large share of overall income, while the gain of other income groups has risen insignificantly. Sophisticated business relations, a powerful private sector, and a highly competitive labor market in advanced economies redistribute the income among all income groups through different channels. The scenario is very different in developing economies: The comparatively higher level of poverty and the transforming economy widen the income gap in parallel with economic growth. Economies in transition stick to a high social orientation. Despite different transition paths and policies, all transition economies maintain income equality as a key element of systemic transformation. In Central Asian transition economies in particular, cancellation of communist economic views and adoption of market principles made the socioeconomic condition vulnerable to any collateral shocks. The Soviet-inherited philosophy of absolute social equality contradicted market economy principles. People suffered from privatization and dissolution of absolute public ownership, as enterprises went to private hands and new market-based employment conditions came into force. As a result, a growing need to support the balance between the top and lowest earners through welfare and other tools emerged in all Central Asian economies. Transferring from the public budget to support poor families and retired people, postponing the defined contribution pension system, and free primary and secondary education and medical services are the main tools to maintain social equality and to narrow the margin of income levels.

In all respects, the stance of income distribution and economic growth relationships in transition economies is strongly linked with economic structure. A transitional character brings particular elements that are unique to transition and some developing economies. A new economic policy, financial interactions, labor relations, and a private and corporate sector under formation are inherent only to economies in transition.

7.5 Conclusions

This historically rooted study has presented only a glimpse of the income inequality and economic growth in Central Asia by avoiding econometric calculations and hypothetical assumptions. We attempted to study the real case with retrospective analysis to reveal the untouched scene in terms of equality and growth in transition economies through the sample of these five economies, which have been on the path of transition for more than 2 decades.

Our retrospective analysis is not limited to presenting a historical view. We have been investigating the topic for nearly a decade and over this period we identified several areas to be improved toward a smooth transition to a market economy in terms of supporting sustainable economic growth and optimal income distribution in the region.

(1) Labor market policy should keep pace with economic development and the global labor market environment. Employment procedures should be simplified and special margins for the lowest salary should be fixed (this practice is in use in Uzbekistan). Moreover, employee rights and responsibilities should be revised in accordance with corporate social responsibility principles, which are new to Central Asian economies.
(2) Education is the central tool to ensure economic growth and the future income stability of the population, as all five countries provide guaranteed free primary and secondary education. Free education is guaranteed, but quality of education is not at an adequate level to have a better job opportunity in some countries, especially in Tajikistan and the Kyrgyz Republic. Therefore, the education policy should be strongly supported in some economies of Central Asia. Reducing tuition payments at private and public primary, secondary, and tertiary education institutions ensures accessibility and inclusion.
(3) In all economies, tax evasion mainly refers to taxes and other compulsory payments. Ensuring income equality, in some respects, is linked with labor income tax. Creating a tax-friendly environment for labor relations may result in more favorable conditions for productivity, which should lead to higher economic growth.

References

Kuznets, S. 1955. Economic Growth and Income Inequality. *The American Economic Review* 45: 1–28.

Fields, G. 1987. Measuring Inequality Change in an Economy with Income Growth. *Journal of Development Economics* 26(2): 357–374.

Medgyesi, M., and I. G. Toth. 2009. Economic Growth and Income Inequalities. In *European Inequalities: Social Inclusion and Income Distribution in the European Union*, edited by T. Ward, O. Lelkes, H. Sutherland, and I. Toth. Budapest: Tarki Social Research Institute.

Piketty, T., and E. Saez. 2003. Income Inequality in the United States, 1913–1998. *Quarterly Journal of Economics* 118(1): 1–39.

Ravallion, M. 2004. Pro-Poor Growth: A Primer. Policy Research Working Paper 3242. Washington, DC: World Bank.

Ravallion, M., and S. Chen. 1997. What Can New Survey Data Tell Us About Recent Changes in Distribution and Poverty? *World Bank Economic Review* 11(2): 357–382.

Solt, F. 2016. The Standardized World Income Inequality Database. *Social Science Quarterly* 97(2): 1–28.

Tabassum, A. 2008. Economic Growth and Income Inequality Relationship: Role of Credit Market Imperfection. *Pakistan Development Review* 47(4): 727–743.

Appendix

Figure A7.1 Economic Growth Statistics of Central Asian Countries

(a) Economic Growth of Turkmenistan in 1994–2014, %

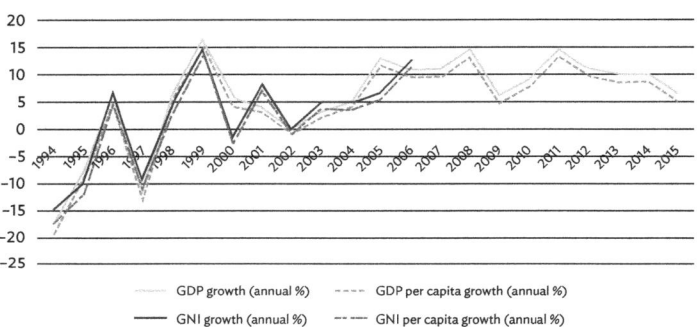

GDP = gross domestic product, GNI = gross national income.
Source: The World Bank Group (2016).

(b) Economic Growth of Tajikistan in 1994–2013, %

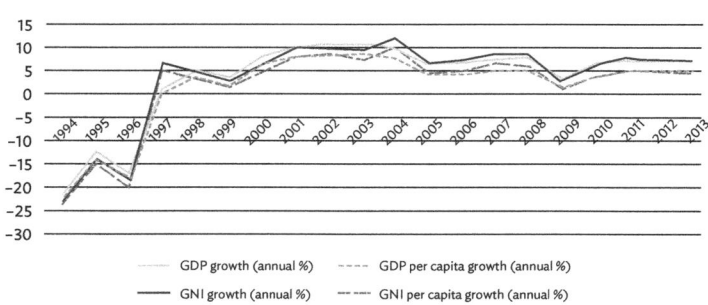

GDP = gross domestic product, GNI = gross national income.
Source: The World Bank Group (2016).

(c) Economic Growth of Kyrgyz Republic in 1994–2014, %

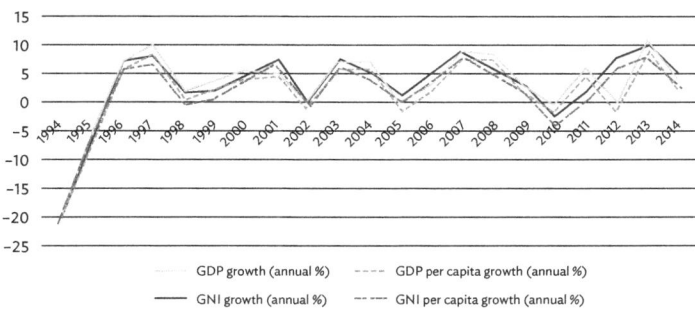

GDP = gross domestic product, GNI = gross national income.
Source: The World Bank Group (2016).

(d) Economic Growth of Kazakhstan in 1994–2014, %

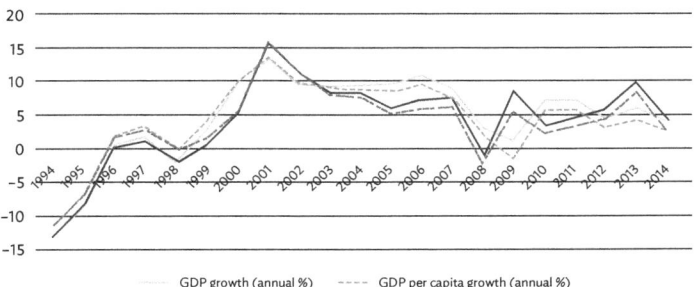

GDP = gross domestic product, GNI = gross national income.
Source: The World Bank Group (2016).

(e) Economic Growth of Uzbekistan in 1996–2015, %

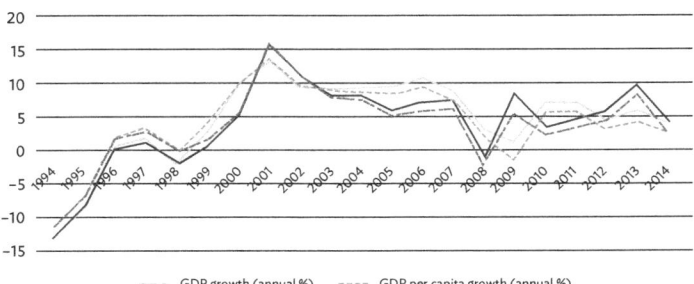

GDP = gross domestic product, GNI = gross national income.
Source: The World Bank Group (2016).

Figure A7.2 Income Distribution Statistics of Central Asian Countries

(a) Income Distribution in Kazakhstan in 2001–2013, %

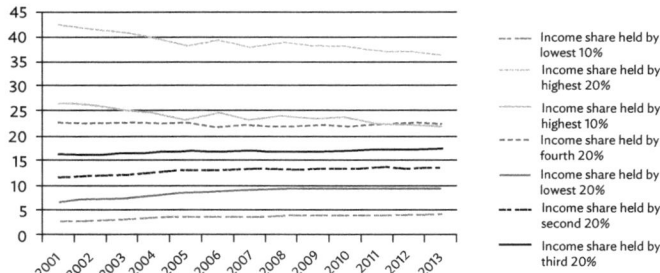

Source: The World Bank Group (2016).

(b) Income Distribution in Kyrgyz Republic in 2001–2012, %

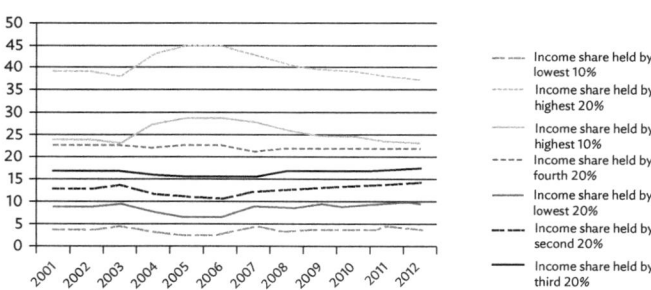

Source: The World Bank Group (2016).

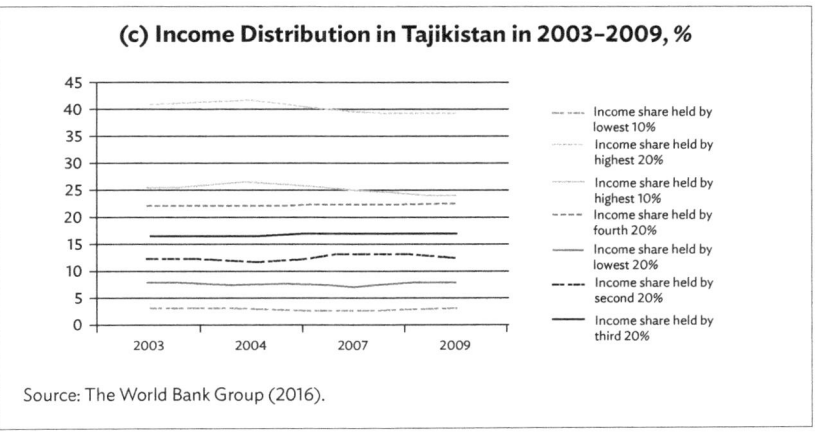

(c) Income Distribution in Tajikistan in 2003–2009, %

Source: The World Bank Group (2016).

8
Middle-Class Composition and Growth in Middle-Income Countries

Riana Razafimandimby Andrianjaka

8.1 Introduction

By focusing on two social groups—the high- and low-income groups—political economy has long tended to neglect the socioeconomic role that such intermediate groups as middle-classes can play in economic development. The huge expansion of this income group over the last decade has brought to light new issues and challenges attached to this distributional change. Ravallion (2010) estimated that the middle-class grew from 1.4 billion to 2.6 billion individuals between 1990 and 2005, representing 48.5% of the world population in 2005 against 32.7% in 1990. Obviously, the economic weight of this group has increased accordingly, with many emerging economies and international development banks attaching great importance to it.

Although the rise of the middle-class in developing countries has been described and commented on by a number of recent studies (Banerjee and Duflo 2008; Birdsall 2000; Chun 2010; Kharas 2010; Ravallion 2010), empirical analyses of the macroeconomic impact of this change in income distribution remain scant. Whilst various analyses have been conducted by private or public institutions or regional development banks, they generally are mainly descriptive and lack sound econometric analysis (see for instance AFDB 2011; Brandi and Büge 2014). One reason for this gap in the literature may be found in the lack of reliable, complete, and comparable panel data on the distribution of income, which has limited research to one single dimension of the middle-class—its size in terms of population and/or consumption (Kaufmann et al. 2013).

Yet, limiting the analysis to one dimension of the middle-class—its demographic size—may miss the point since other dimensions of the distribution of income within the middle class reflecting the internal heterogeneity and asymmetry of this income group may well explain gross domestic product (GDP) growth or differences across time and space. Although an increase in the size of the middle-class has often been related to overall inequality in the recent literature,[1] the size of the middle class has never been connected to the inequality within this income group. Strong inequality potentially prevails within the middle-class group, especially when the income range used to identify it is broad, like, for instance, the $0 to $100 range used by Kharas (2010) and Kaufmann et al. (2013). Income inequality within the middle-class may dampen or magnify the impact of the size.

In addition, the size indicators adopted by the various studies do not necessarily converge, the middle-class being itself a complex concept, hugely context-dependent, which cannot be easily measured. Basically, a country's middle-class is composed of people who are neither poor nor rich. Numerous empirical studies therefore measure the middle class in terms of income, either through an absolute, relative, or mixed approach (Banerjee and Duflo 2008; Kharas 2010; Ravallion 2010; Easterly 2001; Birdsall 2010, 2014). Various other studies have attempted to identify more specific and detailed decompositions of the middle-class income group on the basis of socioeconomic criteria fitted to the context of the study (Bonnefond et al. 2015; Nallet 2014; Handley 2015). Yet, since these analyses generally use national household surveys' micro-economic data they cannot investigate the impact of different attributes of the middle class on such macroeconomic features as economic growth.

Despite its limitation, notably in terms of the choice of thresholds and the number of middle class subgroups, this paper is the first attempt, to the best of our knowledge, to fill the gap in the literature highlighted above. Using an unbalanced panel dataset of 120 middle-income countries from 1985 to 2012, we first describe various statistical features of the middle-class income group (size, economic weight, heterogeneity, and configuration) by using grouped data drawn from the World Bank Povcal database. Then, we analyze econometrically the impact of these various statistical features on GDP growth for the panel of countries

---

[1] Easterly (2001) used the size of middle class as a proxy for income equality as well as other concentration or disparity measures. In the same vein, Van de Walle (2011) showed that the correlation between the middle-class size and global inequality is negative: a society in which middle-class is large enough is more likely to be less unequal. Conversely, Birdsall (2010) argued that the increase of the share of national income held by the middle-class is not always associated with a decline of income inequality at the country level. In the People's Republic of China, Brazil, or India, the growth of their middle-classes' economic power has even been associated with a considerable increase of overall inequality.

investigated. What we are interested in is to determine if what matters for growth is the single size of the middle class, or if other aspects of the middle-class income distribution need also to be considered and accounted for.

Addressing the growth impacts of rising middle-classes in developing countries in the way we do in this chapter is unprecedented in the literature. Nevertheless, our underlying hypothesis—that when the middle-class becomes numerically large enough with respect to total population, its household members tend to adopt behavior whose aggregation might have aggregate impact on economic dynamics—relies largely on previous work. In a nutshell, the main characteristic of these middle-classes indeed lies in their capacity to prompt macroeconomic changes through the aggregation of micro-economic changes with regard to consumption, labor supply, or investment. Such mechanisms have been frequently mentioned in the literature (Clément and Rougier 2014; Handley 2015) without being systematically empirically investigated. The issue is complex since the implication of the emergence of the middle-class on macroeconomic dynamics can be analyzed from several angles, like growth or structural change, and by looking at several channels of transmission, like investment in human capital, entrepreneurship, or political participation. Moreover, the relation is not necessarily unidirectional: the growth dynamics prompted by middle-classes may also favor the promotion of this middle-class behavior, for example when increased productivity or industrialization raises the skill premium and educational returns. There are good reasons to think that, at some stage, a virtuous circle may appear by which middle class expansion may spur economic transformation, while being, in turn, triggered by this economic and political change. In this chapter, we are primarily interested in the first linkage—the impact of middle class expansion on economic growth.

Various authors have emphasized that the size of the middle-class might have a strong positive impact on economic growth through different channels like mass consumption, productivity increase arising from scale effects (Murphy et al. 1989; Easterly 2001), or learning spillovers (Desdoigt and Jaramillo 2014). Also considering that the large middle class of England in the early 19th century is a key explanatory determinant of this country's early industrialization; Landes (1998) depicted how a society endowed with a wide middle-class becomes increasingly capable of reaching global prosperity. For Adelman and Moris (1967), the middle-class has been the engine of economic development in industrialized countries and will be the key driver of growth in low-income countries. Birdsall (2010) went further by arguing that the increasing size and economic command of the middle-class may well be the signal that the underlying growth regime is based on genuine productivity gains and wealth creation by a modern private sector. This relationship between middle-class and economic growth is not necessarily unidirectional, though. Ravallion (2010) has provided convincing evidence that the faster the economic growth, the faster the expansion of the middle-class and that growth tends to be more pro-poor in the developing countries exhibiting a larger initial middle class. Birdsall (2010) went a step further by contending that the emergence of a middle-class—partially driven by more people escaping from poverty—may be an outcome of growth rather than one of its determinants.

The chapter is organized as follows. Section 8.1 describes our data and methodology for identifying the middle-class. Section 8.2 presents our preliminary descriptive analyses. Section 8.3 presents our econometric models and Section 8.4 presents our results.

8.2 Data and Methodological Choices

Since we aim to analyze specific patterns concerning the middle classes in lower- and middle-income countries, we need to first of all identify them. We have used grouped data collected from Povcal (PPP^2 2005) that provide headcounts (corresponding to our five thresholds), consumption/income distribution by deciles, as well as monthly consumption/income per capita and the overall population Gini index for each survey year. For the years located between two surveys, we calculate the mean of years before and after for each aggregate. In addition, we have excluded the countries with populations of less than 1 million, because they may have specific productive structures and dynamics that potentially generate biases.[3] We have also excluded the countries with less than one survey available. The number of surveys differs between countries, so that we end up with an unbalanced panel of 120 middle-income countries, with the maximum years available for each of them from 1985 to 2012.[4] For the empirical investigation, we limit the dataset to a sample of 52 middle-income countries.

To classify countries according to their development level, some authors use an arbitrary threshold based on countries' convergence achievement or on quantiles (middle countries are usually those left when the poorest and the richest have been identified): Eichengreen

---

[2] PPP = purchasing power parity.

[3] Those countries are for the most those with less than seven observations.

[4] See Table 8.9 for the list of countries.

(2011, 2013) set a superior threshold at $10,000; Ozturk (2016), for example, considered as middle-income countries those with 20% to 55% of United States GDP per capita. Among the existing country classifications, those of the United Nations Development Program (UNDP) (providing their Human Development Index [HDI] levels) and the World Bank are the most used. The latter provides a threshold that can be applied to a long-run dataset of gross national income (GNI). Since such data are not available before the 1990s for the majority of countries, researchers (Felipe 2012, Van der Hout 2014) have calculated GDP per capita corresponding thresholds.[5] We will use Van der Hout's (2014) classification based on Penn World Table GDP in constant 2005 purchasing power parity (PPP) dollars. So, a country is classified as low-income if its GDP per capita is less than $2,250, as lower- middle-income if it is between $2,250 and $7,500, as upper middle-income if it is between $7,500 and $14,500, and as high-income if it is $14,500 or higher. Countries' classification is determined based on their income level in 2012.

Constructing a comparable and comprehensive long-run dataset on global middle-class including as many countries as possible requires choosing sufficiently large intervals. In the case of the United States, for example, Birdsall (2010) has found a high level of middle class inequality making her assume that there may be at least two sub-categories of middle-class in the country. In the same vein, Ravallion (2010) could identify two subcategories of middle class households in developing, one ranging from $2 to $9 and another from $9 to $13. Rather than a unique middle-class whose identification by using income thresholds is debatable, the mixed approach used by Ravallion (2010) seems more relevant to our purpose. Accordingly, we will consider in this chapter four subcategories of middle-class, composed of the three bottom categories identified by AFDB (2011) to which we add a higher interval.

As we want to identify each middle-class potential configuration according to three dimensions (incidence, consumption level, and heterogeneity), we need to set a threshold for each dimension measure. For now, we will set the threshold for each indicator at its median value for the sample. To begin with, we calculate each indicator distinguishing between (i) developed and developing countries; and (ii) income classification. In this section, middle-class is composed of those with consumption per day between $2 and $100.

---

[5] Of course, there is no perfect match with the World Bank's classification, resulting in some differences in the repartition of countries.

8.3 Preliminary Evidence

To highlight the potential differences amongst countries' income levels in terms of middle-class composition, we first use an extended panel dataset composed of 120 countries including all income levels[6] from 1985 to 2012.

8.3.1 Middle-Class Incidence: Size and Economic Weight

Middle-class size refers to the share of the population that belongs to the middle class and its economic weight is the middle-class total consumption share. For the developing world, the mean and median sizes are 72.52% and 81%, respectively, while those for developed countries are both 98%. In terms of economic weight, developed countries' mean and median are 95.7% and 97.9%, respectively, while those for developing ones are 86.44% and 95.44%, respectively.

Secondly, Table 8.1 displays the indicators for each income category and shows that the size and weight of the middle-class increases with development level. Following Birdsall's (2010) methodology, the size and economic weight of the middle-class will be included separately, as they are two different but complementary indicators of inclusive growth.

Table 8.1 Minimum, Mean, and Median Size and Economic Weight by Income Category

	Low Income		Lower Middle		Upper Middle		High Income		Sample	
	Size	Weight	Size	Weight	Size	Weight	Size	Weight	Size	Weight
Mean	42.30	62.83	59.24	79.56	84.14	94.74	96.85	96.73	77.67	88.36
Median	37.93	63.65	63.15	87.66	87.26	96.54	98	98.53	87.73	95.97
Min	1.02	3.24	8.91	21.93	15.04	32.40	71.76	66.56	1.02	3.24

Source: Author's calculation.

---

[6] This dataset includes countries from Eastern Europe and Central Asian countries (17), Latin America and Caribbean (19), Middle East and North (9), South Asia (5), East Asia (9), Sub-Saharan Africa (33), Western Europe and North America (28). See Table A.2 of the Appendix for the detailed list of countries.

8.3.2 Four Subcategories of Middle-Class

Beyond the distinction between developing and developed countries, which is standard in the literature (AFDB 2011; Ravalion 2010; Gertz and Kharas 2010), we will need to identify different middle-class subgroups and their relative size. Indeed, since middle class corresponds to people that are not poor but are not rich, it corresponds to a wide range of income. Instead of fixing a wide and unique interval that does not reflect all features of middle class or consensual either, we distinguish four subgroups of middle class whose thresholds are based on previous work:[7] 1) the floating class in the interval ($2–$4) comprises no longer poor but still vulnerable households (Birdsall 2010; Clément and Rougier 2014); 2) the lower middle-class corresponds to households earning between $4 and $10; 3) the upper middle-class ($10–$20), and 4) the higher middle-class ($20–$100). In addition, we have calculated the ratio (in terms of population share) as a proxy of how rich a country's middle-class is: the higher this ratio, the better for a country. Indeed, an increase in this ratio can be associated with an upward mobility from bottom to top middle-class of a number of households. It means an improvement of their well-being, and a change in their consumption habits and their behavior, that will in turn have positive outcomes in terms of growth through different channels.

Although the four aforementioned categories can be identified for most countries, throughout the whole period some low-income countries only have the three lowest categories[8] and some high-

---

[7] Millanovic and Yitzhaki (2002) and Bussolo et al. (2008) considered all the households with per capita income situated between the average per capita incomes of Brazil and Mexico or between $10 and $20 a day in PPP 2005. ADB (2010), Ravallion (2010), and Banerjee and Duflo (2008) adopted as lower border the international threshold of $2, considering that middle-class begins where poverty ends. This threshold is often criticized because the households with an income between $2 and $4 dollars are still vulnerable (Clément and Rougier 2014) and it does not correspond to middle-class on numerous criteria (Birdsall 2010), for example, in terms of their economic interest and political weight. For that reason, other authors choose higher lower borders, for example Clément and Rougier (2014) who fix it at $4, and Birdsall (2010) and Kharas (2010) at $10. This threshold constitutes the superior border of the interval retained by Banerjee and Duflo (2008). Ravallion (2010) took the poverty line of the United States $13; ADB (2010) and Clément and Rougier (2014) $20; Kharas (2010) $100.

[8] Those countries are Albania, Azerbaijan, Bangladesh, People's Republic of China, Ethiopia, Ghana, Guinea, Indonesia, Kyrgyz Republic, Lao PDR, Madagascar, Mauritania, Mozambique, Nigeria, Romania, Senegal, Sri Lanka, Tajikistan, Tanzania, Uganda, Viet Nam, and Zambia.

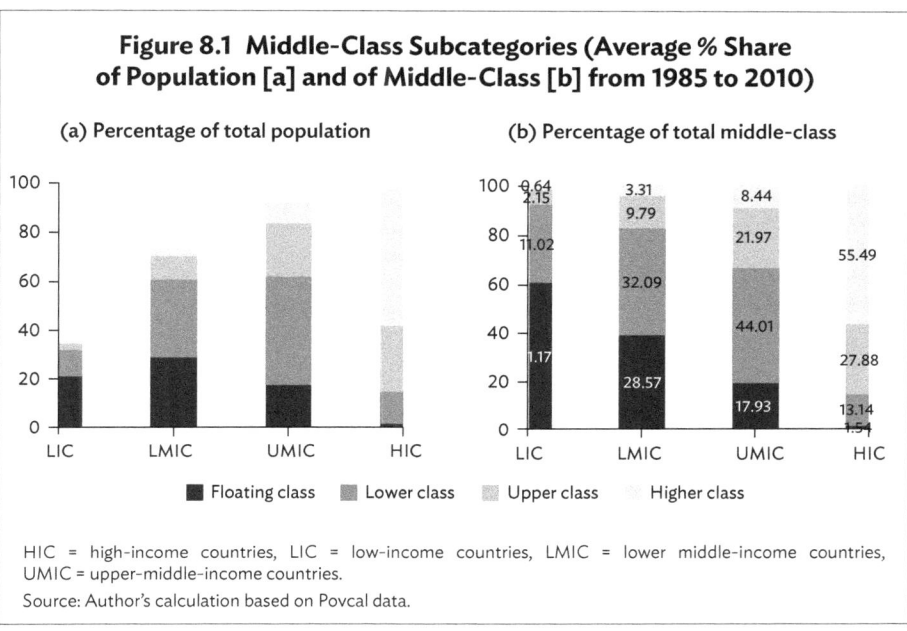

Figure 8.1 Middle-Class Subcategories (Average % Share of Population [a] and of Middle-Class [b] from 1985 to 2010)

HIC = high-income countries, LIC = low-income countries, LMIC = lower middle-income countries, UMIC = upper-middle-income countries.
Source: Author's calculation based on Povcal data.

income countries[9] only have the three upper ones. Depending on the countries' income level, each sub-class's share of total population may be different. As we can see in Figure 8.1, the middle-class is mostly located in the lowest range of income in poorer countries and progressively moves to the highest range of income when income per capita increases.

When we look at each subgroup's economic weight in panel (b) of Figure 8.1, the pattern is similar, with an interesting variation for low-income countries in which, on average, 42% of total population accounts for 62% of total consumption; and each one of the three top subgroups' share in total consumption is worth two times its share in population. Figure 8.1 also illustrates the dynamics of middle-class expansion. Indeed, as a country develops, more and more people escape from poverty to the floating class, and then move from the floating class to the lower middle-class, and so on.

Table 8.2 confirms the huge gap between developing—including upper-middle-income—and developed countries' middle-classes:

---

[9] Those countries are Austria, Belgium, Canada, Denmark, Finland, France, Germany, Italy, Netherlands, Norway, Sweden, and Switzerland.

Table 8.2 Ratio of the Upper and Higher Subgroups on the Floating and Lower Subgroups

	Low Income	Lower Middle	Upper Middle	High Income
Mean	0.06	0.22	0.56	31.71
Median	0.03	0.15	0.46	12.32
Min	0	0.001	0	0.19
Max	0.34	2.7	6.12	297.97

Source: Author's calculation.

on average the middle-classes in developing countries are less wealthy than those of developed ones. Yet, a large "poor" middle class is likely to have different impacts on socioeconomic aggregates than a large "rich" middle-class. Those statistics highlight the limitation of the use of absolute thresholds to identify a unique global middle-class: its structure matters and makes a huge difference depending on the development level. Furthermore, we can say that besides the need to reduce poverty, another challenge for developing countries is to prompt the transition of bottom middle-class households to higher categories.

8.3.3 Middle-Class Living Standards: Using the Average Annual Consumption per Capita

Middle-class living standard indicates how rich a country's middle-class is on average. As a measure of the living standards, we will use the average annual consumption per capita of the middle class. As we recall, the distribution data from Povcal are based either on consumption or income. For income-based data, we calculate the consumption per capita using the World Development Indicators (WDI) consumption share of GDP. For the developing world, the mean and median are respectively $2,727.24 and $2,735.80, while those of developed countries are $10,107.80 and $10,148.21, respectively.

Table 8.3, reporting computations of the average consumption per capita for each income category, shows a polarized global middle-class, with a striking difference between developed and developing countries. Even in upper-middle income countries, where the size of the middle-class is on average 91%, their average consumption is three times smaller than for the higher-income countries.

Table 8.3 Middle-Class Average Consumption per Capita by Income Category ($)

	Low	Lower-middle	Upper-middle	Higher	Developing	Developed	All Sample
Mean	1,702	2,102	3,249	7,456	2,660	8,503	4,152
Median	1,469	1,777	3,286	5,466	2,589	8,145	3,119
Min	530	1,032	974	1,668[1]	530	1,791	530
Max	3,222	4,403	6,263	18,481	6,263[2]	18,481	18,481

Notes: Values are expressed in United States dollars.(1) This is the average consumption per capita of Kazakhstan in 2010, which has been classified as a high-income country since that year according to Hout's thresholds classification. (2) This is the average consumption per capita of Bosnia and Herzegovina in 2007.
Source: Author's calculation.

8.3.4 Middle-Class Heterogeneity: Dispersion and Concentration

To apprehend the heterogeneity of the middle-class, four aspects will be considered. The first one—the distinction between four subcategories of middle-class—is presented in section 15.3.2. Second, indicators of statistical concentration and dispersion provide two complementary descriptions of inequality within the middle-class of each country throughout the period.

The middle-class statistical dispersion may give an approximation of what Birdsall (2010, 2014) and Handley (2015) called "class identity." Without being a perfect indicator, it could be a good statistical proxy of the identity dimension of a social class since high-income dispersion within the middle-class would suggest that the different groups of the latter will find it more difficult to share a common identity. Many other socioeconomic features must obviously be taken into consideration when talking about a social class. Nevertheless, people with similar living standards—imperfectly measured by their consumption level—may share common consumption behavior that reflects their needs and aspirations. Thus, the more heterogeneous those behaviors, that reflect a heterogeneous consumption level, the more miscellaneous their impacts on socioeconomic aggregates.

Skewness and Kurtosis characteristics indicate where the density of consumption is concentrated within the middle-class. Using Fisher coefficients of Skewness and Kurtosis, we identify four distribution forms: 1) positively skewed and flat; 2) negatively skewed and flat; 3) positively skewed and thin; 4) negatively skewed and thin. In our sample, we find that most developing countries' consumption distributions exhibit the third form—positively skewed and thin—meaning that consumption is concentrated in the low middle-classes, with a small number of extreme values. High-income countries featuring the first form are those with a significant proportion of their middle-class in the upper middle level. Those with the third form are mostly countries of the ex-Soviet Union that still have a significant proportion of their population in the lower middle-class.

We now compute[10] a Gini index on the middle-class distribution to get an indication whether middle-class consumption is driven by a small percentage of its population. For the developing world, the mean and median Gini of the middle-class are 18.61 and 20.05, respectively, while those of the developed countries are 20.97 and 20.57, respectively. The overall middle-class—including both developed and developing countries'—mean and median are 19.10 and 20.14, respectively.

Table 8.4 reports the computations of the Gini statistics for each middle-class subgroup of income. The very low levels of the Gini index in the developing world are explained by the fact that in some countries, one subcategory of middle-class encompasses more than 70% of the middle-class population and of middle-class consumption. For instance, in Guinea 98% of the middle -class population belongs to the floating class and their share in middle-class consumption is 98%. At first sight, it seems that the relationship between middle-class inequality and

Table 8.4 Middle-Class Gini Indicator by Income Category

	Low Income	Lower Middle	Upper Middle	High Income
Mean	13.22	13.99	20.63	24.99
Median	12.18	13.69	20.76	24.07
Min	0	1.40	2.96	13.31
Max	23.69	26.18	37.31	43.58

Note: Gini coefficient varies from 0 to 100 with 0 meaning no inequality/no concentration/perfect equity and 100 very strong inequalities.
Source: Author's calculation.

---

[10] Since we use Stata 12, we compute the Gini index using the command ineqdeco. It is worth noting that grouping leads to a downward bias of the Gini. Following Van Ourti and Clarke (2011), we use a first-order correction term to deal with those biaises by treating grouping as a form of measurment error. It consists of multiplying the Gini by K2/ (K2 − 1).

development level is positive: on average, inequality within the middle-class tends to increase with development level.

To graphically check the relationship between inequality and development, we have plotted both the Gini coefficient of the middle-class and the overall population against GDP per capita and adjusted it by using a nonparametric approach. Figures 8.2 and 8.3 show the adjustment by a local polynomial smoothing of degree 3 using the Epanechnikov kernel with a bandwidth determined by rule-of-thumb by default.[11]

First, although we cannot draw a strong conclusion about the shape of the relationship, it appears to be non-linear. Middle-class income inequality seems to increase until almost $30,000 and past this income level, corresponding to high-income countries, it tends to decrease. Secondly, Figure 8.2 supports what we have seen in Tables 8.2 and 8.3: the higher the development level, the larger and more economically

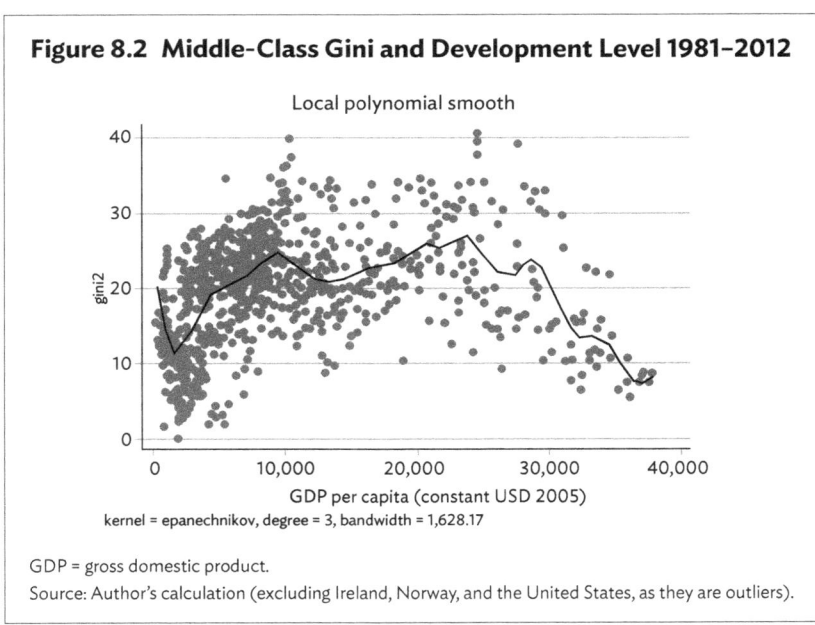

Figure 8.2 Middle-Class Gini and Development Level 1981–2012

GDP = gross domestic product.
Source: Author's calculation (excluding Ireland, Norway, and the United States, as they are outliers).

---

[11] Some authors have shown that the quadratic function does not fit the relationship between inequality and development but polynomials of three degrees for Organization for Economic Co-operation and Development (OECD) and four degrees for non-OECD (Li and Zhou 2011). Gallup (2012) found that the former increases the confidence interval.

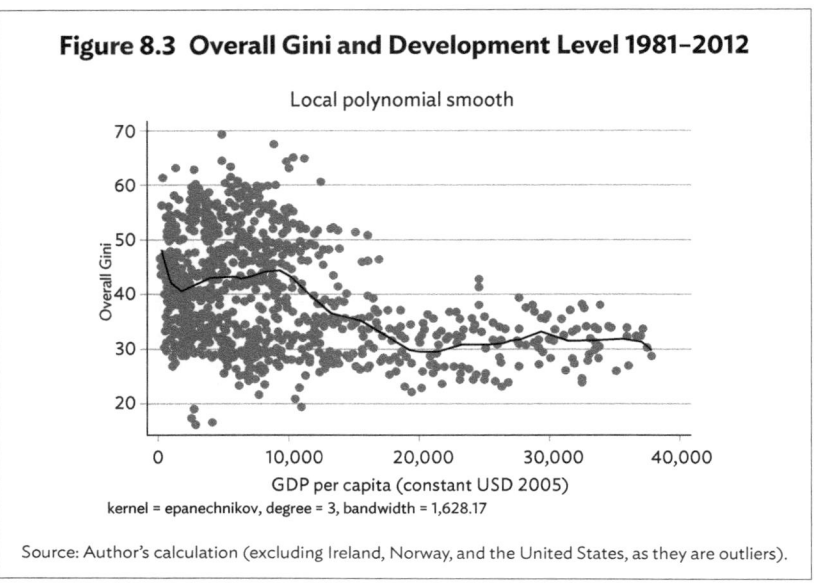

Figure 8.3 Overall Gini and Development Level 1981–2012

Source: Author's calculation (excluding Ireland, Norway, and the United States, as they are outliers).

empowered the middle-class, but a large middle-class does not necessarily imply lesser overall inequality. We remain cautious in the interpretation of the inequality since we are aware of potential data and measure issues, among which the limits of using grouped data (following Knowles 2001; Deninger and Square 1999, to cite just a few studies) even if Povcal is probably the most reliable source for distribution data. To improve the reliability of our results, we will calculate alternate measures of inequality in further work, as far as our data allows us to do so. Nonetheless, its particular pattern supports the fact that economic transformations are closely linked to what happened specifically at intermediate levels of income. It is confirmed when we look at the evolution of the middle-class' structure, meaning an inversion of the subcategory representation among the population in high- compared with low-income countries.

8.3.5 Eight Configurations of Middle-Classes

Finally, we construct an ordinal variable with eight modalities corresponding to all possible combinations[12] of the three dimensions of middle-class: size, the average consumption per year, and

---

12    $C_3^0 + C_3^1 + C_3^2 + C_3^3 = 8$

concentration. To begin with, we shall set thresholds above which a middle-class is considered large, deep, or egalitarian. For this purpose, we chose the median value of each indicator. We could have chosen the mean but using the median has the advantage of excluding potential biases linked to extreme values. Thus, a country's middle class is considered large when it represents more than 87.73% of total population and more than 95.97% of total consumption. Secondly, we have seen in the previous section that there is a huge gap between the higher-income countries and the others in terms of average consumption level. To account for this difference, two thresholds will be set. For developing countries, middle-class is considered as deep when its average annual consumption per capita is above $2,735.80, whereas for developed countries annual consumption should be above $10,148.21. Finally, a middle-class is relatively egalitarian when its Gini index is lower than 20.14.

By combining information on average consumption, concentration, and size, we will identify eight middle-class configurations. The first set of configurations refers to middle-classes that display only one of the three characteristics—1) large but neither deep nor egalitarian; 2) deep but neither large nor egalitarian; and 3) egalitarian but neither large nor deep. The second set is composed of middle-classes that combine two of these three characteristics: 4) large and deep but not egalitarian; 5) large and egalitarian but not deep; and 6) deep and egalitarian but not large. Finally, the ideal configuration would be a 7) large, deep, and egalitarian middle-class, and the worst would be a middle-class that is 8) neither large, nor deep, nor egalitarian.

Table 8.5 Middle-Class Configurations by Country Income Level[a]

	Low Income	Lower Middle	Upper Middle	High Income
1) Large but neither deep nor egalitarian		5.64	11.36	24.26
2) Deep but neither large nor egalitarian	16.67	10.53	21.75	0.89
3) Egalitarian but neither large nor deep	76.47	62.42	14.29	1.18
4) Large and deep but not egalitarian	2.94	1.50	14.94	20.71
5) Large and egalitarian but not deep			2.27	8.88
6) Deep and egalitarian but not large		14.29	11.69	
7) Large, deep, and egalitarian		3.01	19.48	43.20
8) Neither large, nor deep and egalitarian	3.92	2.63	4.22	

[a] We only show the statistics and configurations with more than two observations.
Source: Author's calculation.

First, during the period of study, whilst the worst configuration (neither large nor deep nor egalitarian) can be observed only in the developing world, the shares of countries that display the first or the ideal configurations increases with higher development levels. In high-income countries, almost half of the countries' middle-classes are indeed large, deep, and relatively egalitarian. Besides, the other most frequently observed configurations for this income level have in common the large size of the middle-class. We can also see a huge difference between the developed and developing countries for which the second configuration (a middle-class that is relatively wealthy but small and unequal) has frequently been observed. It is quite interesting, since most middle classes in both low- and lower-middle income countries are only either deep or egalitarian and only very few of them are large or combine two of the criteria. Nevertheless, the middle-class configurations seem to be improving with higher development levels. Indeed, more than 50% of the observations for low-income and middle-income countries correspond to the third configuration: middle-classes that are egalitarian, but neither rich nor large. As we have seen in Figure 8.1, those countries' middle-classes tend to be mostly concentrated in the floating class or/and lower-middle class and account for almost the same proportion of total consumption, which may be the reason why their consumption levels are low in value but relatively homogeneous. But, 14% of lower-middle income middle classes combine two criteria: a higher consumption share and low inequality. And for the upper-middle-income level, the diversity of configuration observed amongst the countries over the study period suggests a modification of the middle-class that is more country- or region-specific.

Table 8.6 indeed shows that the third configuration is mostly observable in the developing world but less in Latin America and Caribbean countries. For those countries, the middle-class seems to be a smaller (34%) or larger (18%) group with a higher level of consumption on average but with a higher level of inequality. Middle-classes configurations for Central Europe and Asia and the Middle-East and North Africa are close, with the exception that the ideal configuration is also frequently observed for the former countries. For the period of study, South Asia's middle-classes have been quite homogenous but not wealthy or large enough, which has also been the case for most of Sub-Saharan Africa's countries' middle-classes.

Not surprisingly, the middle-class structure, composition, and configuration are quite different according to the development level. On average, the gap between developing and developed countries is huge, notably in terms of average consumption levels and configurations. Nevertheless, middle-class features seem to improve as a country develops. Whilst the enlargement of this intermediate category has often

Table 8.6 Middle-Class Configurations by Region[a]

	Central Europe and Asia	Latin America and Caribbean	Middle-East and North Africa	South Asia	East Asia	Sub-Saharan Africa	Western Advanced Countries[b]
1) Large but neither deep nor egalitarian	21.57	1.27	29.41		8.16		23.79
2) Deep but neither large nor egalitarian		34.08				6.93	
3) Egalitarian but neither large nor deep	32.34	9.24	44.12	100	78.57	85.15	
4) Large and deep but not egalitarian	5.99	17.83	8.82		6.12		17.10
5) Large and egalitarian but not deep	5.39						10.4
6) Deep and egalitarian but not large		21.97				3.96	
7) Large, deep and egalitarian	27.54	11.78			2.04		47.96
8) Neither large, nor deed and egalitarian		3.82	14.71		5.10		

[a] We only show the statistics and configurations with more than two observations.
[b] In this category, we include Australia and Israel.
Source: Author's calculation.

been shown to prompt growth, it seems more interesting to investigate if the other dimensions of middle-class, independent of each other or combined, have different impacts on this aggregate. From this descriptive analysis, we draw our hypothesis for the empirical investigation: 1) the size of the middle-class is an important characteristic, but the consumption and inequality level may dampen or catalyze its impact on growth; 2) instead of a homogenous positive impact of a singular middle-class, each subcategory of middle-class is likely to have slightly different impacts on growth.

8.4 Estimating the Impact of Middle-Class on Income Growth

We now turn to the empirical estimation of the relationship between middle-class and growth.

8.4.1 Estimation Issues

As we recall, our panel dataset is unbalanced. Besides, as we have seen in the literature review, without having all been tested, the relationships between middle-class and those economic aggregates may be bidirectional. Endogeneity biases also pertain to reverse causality or measurement errors of the other variables that will be used as explanatory variables. Omitted variables can also be sources of endogeneity bias. Whilst a fixed-effect model could be used, Nickell (1981) showed that the within estimator produces estimations of parameters that are inconsistent and biased downward in the presence of endogeneity. The first-difference generalized method of moments (GMM) estimator may provide biased results for a finite sample size. Besides, the lagged levels of variables are not reliable instruments when dependent and independent variables are continuous.

For those reasons, the appropriate method for us seems to be the two-step system GMM estimator proposed by Blundell and Bond (1998), which can also properly manage an unbalanced dataset as well as address the problem of heteroscedasticity. This system estimator encompasses a regression equation in both differences and levels with their own specific set of internal instrumental variables—1) a set of equations in first-differences, and with adequately lagged levels as instruments; 2) a set of equations in levels and variables, with adequately lagged first-differences as instruments. Since the two-step estimation may produce downward biased results when using finite samples, Windmeijer (2005) proposed a correction for the variance–covariance matrix.

Two crucial assumptions must be met to ensure the validity of GMM. First, the instruments are exogenous, i.e., not correlated with the error terms. Since we will adjust our estimations for heteroscedasticity, this hypothesis is tested using the Hansen test of overidentifying restrictions. Secondly, if a negative first-order autocorrelation (AR1) in residuals may be acceptable, the absence of second-order autocorrelation (AR2) must be verified. We test it using the Arellano–Bond test for AR1 and AR2. Time dummies will be included to make this assumption hold well by preventing contemporaneous correlation.

Finally, as Rodman (2009) stated, a 1-year lag is only consistent for predetermined but not very endogenous variables for which corrections will be minor, but it is not recommended to use too many estimators. We then limit the numbers of lags for our explanatory variables to two.

Our variables of interests are introduced as explanatory variables in different models: dummy variables for each identified configuration (*model 1*), the one we use as reference is the eighth: neither large, nor deep and equal; floating and lower middle-classes' share successively in percentage of population and total consumption (*model 2*); upper and higher middle-classes' share successively in percentage of population and total consumption (*model 3*); the ratio of top subclasses—upper and higher middle-class to bottom ones—floating and lower middle-class (*model 4*); size, annual average consumption, and Gini both in level and in quadratics terms (*model 5*).

In addition to our specific focus on middle-class indicators, we are specifically interested in what happens at the middle-income level. So, the estimations will be run on identified middle-income countries over the period of study (1985 to 2012). Our control variables are introduced gradually to check for the stability of our results. There are no great changes for our variables of interest except lower coefficients. The results presented in Table 8.7 are then the full specification. The Hansen test shows that we cannot reject the null hypothesis of the absence of correlation between instruments and error terms for all our models. In addition to that, the Arellano–Bond test for absence of second-order autocorrelation (AR2) is verified for all of our models.

8.4.2 Estimating the Impact of the Middle-Class on GDP Growth

Primarily, we want to check if the different configurations and subcategories of middle-class have significant and specific impacts on development. Our explained variable is the real GDP per capita of country *i* at time *t*. The growth equation we are going to estimate is the following:

$$y_{i,t} = \alpha X_{i,t} + \beta Z_{i,t} + \varepsilon_{i,t} \qquad (3)$$

Where X represents our aforementioned variables of interest, Z represents the determinants of growth in the literature, and is the error term.

The first set is composed of: i) gross fixed capital formation as a percentage of GDP as a proxy for investment, both public and private, which is supposed to have a positive impact; ii) a demographic determinant—we calculate demographic growth, which is the sum: n + g + δ. n, population growth, is a proxy of fertility, *g* the technical progress growth rate, and δ the capital deterioration rate. Following Mankiw, Romer, and Weil (1992), we suppose that g + δ is invariant through time and countries and is equal to 0.05. This aggregate is expected to have negative impact on growth. Then, following Mankiw Romer, and Weil we add secondary and tertiary education achievement rate as a proxy for human capital accumulation. According to the economic level, those variables are not supposed to have the same impacts. While secondary education provides imitators, innovators emerge from tertiary education and for the specific transformations and challenges at play in middle-income countries; the former may have negative outcomes, whereas the latter may have positive outcomes. Thirdly, public expenditure has been shown to be necessary for development (Barro 1996), and even more so if the middle-class is to be considered as an engine of growth (Birdsall 2010; Handley 2015). This is why we introduce government final expenditure as a percentage of GDP. However, another effect may imply a negative sign of this variable since public expenditures are mostly funded by taxation, which may be detrimental to growth. Foreign direct investment—which we introduce as a percentage of GDP—has also been shown to be a determinant of growth, but depending on its sign, it is either complementary to (Grossman and Helpman 1991) or substitutable for (Luiz and De Mello 1999) domestic investment. Finally, although the idea that institutions are key determinants of growth is widely spread (See for instance Rodrik and Subramanian 2003; Acemoglu et al. 2005), available data and measures are quite tricky. For this purpose, we choose to use a polity2 indicator of democracy. In addition, we control for poverty incidence in model 2 and for rich population share in models 3 and 4.

Concerning our control variables, investments (in model 4), tertiary education (in model 3), public expenditures (in model 2 and 3), and polity2 in the three models are, as expected, significant and positive.

As for middle-class configurations, the coefficients are not significant for model 3 and 5. In the other estimations, we can see that 2) deep; 4) large and deep; and 7) large, deep, and egalitarian middle-classes have positive impacts on economic growth. The coefficients are higher for the last two configurations. This result suggests that, for middle-income countries, the income level of the middle-class is a crucial condition to ensure economic growth. The coefficient for the seventh configuration is even lower than for the fourth, suggesting that a middle-class that is large and with higher consumption capacity even if it is quite unequal is more likely to have a positive impact in terms of growth. The fact that middle-class income level matters is again confirmed in model 4. Indeed, the expansion of upper middle-class' consumption share, relatively to floating and lower middle-class, has positive and strongly significant effects on growth. When the share of rich people in the total population is introduced, it is positive, whereas the share of top middle-class in the population is insignificant.

Those findings are consistent with the argument of Birdsall et al. (2000). They pointed out that the public discourse tends to ignore average households thereby contributing to the vulnerability of this middle-class. According to the authors, during the last decade, public spending has been allocated more and more to specific social programs for the poor. Middle-class households are not concerned since they

Table 8.7 Estimates of GDP per Capita (Constant 2005 $) on Middle-Class Indicators using FEGMM Estimator

	Model 1			Model 2			Model 4		
Configuration 1	4,907								
	(3,127)								
Configuration 2	4,132**								
	(2,108)								
Configuration 3	886.8								
	(2,214)								
Configuration 4	6,617***								
	(2,223)								
Configuration 5	3,682								
	(2,792)								
Configuration 6	3,486								
	(2,301)								
Configuration 7	5,391**								
	(2,493)								
Floating MC (% population)		−94.09**	−108.9*						
		(36.74)	(66.45)						
Lower MC (% population)		−19.64	−67.97						
		(45.71)	(111.6)						
Poverty headcount ratio			−48.94						
			(101.0)						
Floating MC (% consumption)					−39.98	−64.19*			
					(48.34)	(36.77)			
Lower MC (% consumption)					−89.25***	−85.22			
					(33.22)	(66.25)			
Poor (% consumption)						−51.87			
						(79.59)			
Ratio (% population)									30.25
									(64.33)
Ratio (% consumption)								1,177***	
								(387.4)	
Rich (% consumption)									4,195**
									(1,807)
Controls	Yes	Yes	Yes	Yes	Yes	Yes	Yes	Yes	Yes
Time-fixed effects	Yes	Yes	Yes	Yes	Yes	Yes	Yes	Yes	Yes

continued on next page

Table 8.7 continued

	Model 1		Model 2			Model 4	
Constant	3,662	5,544**	9,163	5,786**	11,183*	3.579**	3,902
	(4,039)	(2,379)	(10,635)	(2,825)	(6,349)	(1,699)	(3,029)
Observations	441	453	453	444	444	444	453
Number of country2	41	41	41	41	41	41	41
Hansen test of over identification	2.92	2.41	3.02	4.66	10.14	5.36	7.13
	0.405	0.878	0.883	0.588	0.181	0.373	0.309
Arellano–Bond test for AR(1)	−1.61	1.77	1.87	1.04	2	2.229	0.32
	0.108	0.077	0.061	0.296	0.046	0.022	0.748
Arellano–Bond test for AR(2)	−1.37	−0.89	−043	−0.32	0.26	−0.64	−0.78
	0.169	0.375	0.665	0.752	0.792	0.521	0.435

AR = autocorrelation, FEGMM = fixed effect generalized method of moment, GDP = gross domestic product, MC = middle-class.
Notes: We report estimates in which our interest variables are significant. Standard errors in parentheses. *** p<0.01, ** p<0.05, * p<0.1.
Source: Author's calculation.

seem "too rich" to benefit from social programs. Yet, they are not rich enough to be able to constitute consequent savings that are necessary to ensure their resilience. In many countries, politics have favored pro-poor programs to the detriment of services aimed at the middle-classes, which have seen the quality of their public services deteriorate as a result of lack of public financing (this is the case, for example, in the Czech Republic, Egypt, Mexico, and Brazil). With regard to our results on floating and lower middle class, and the lack of significance of the top middle-class categories, this statement seems to be especially true for middle-income countries. Indeed, compared to low-income countries, the latter face different challenges and need other growth drivers, among which the differentiation of production through innovation that can be prompted by middle-class consumers (Matsuyama 2012). In another work, we found that the expansion of the top middle-class is a driver of productive change since it supports manufacturing and its modernization (diversification and sophistication) and reduces the share of non-modern activities. Reducing poverty is obviously a priority, but for middle-income countries to catch up with the high-income ones, the challenges are both to reduce poverty and to improve the well-being of the households that have successfully escaped from poverty. Thus, policies aimed at improving the well-being, capabilities, and opportunities for those households are necessary to avoid a "stuck in the middle" phenomenon—meaning a floating and lower middle-class bulge with slow transition to superior categories—that is detrimental to growth.

8.5 Conclusion

The objective of this chapter is to contribute to the literature on the middle-class at the macroeconomic level by taking into account dimensions other than its size, and reverse causality, which is a possible source of endogeneity. Using data from Povcal, we construct an unbalanced panel dataset of 120 countries from 1985 to 2012. First, we identify eight types of middle-class based on three criteria: size, inequality, and average consumption level. Then, instead of considering the middle-class as a single entity, we identify four sub-categories of a country's middle-class according to their consumption/income level: a floating class (from $2 to $4); a lower middle-class (from $4 to $10); an upper middle-class (from $10 to $20); and a higher middle-class (from $20 to $100). This chapter investigates if such internal features of the middle-class as living standards or heterogeneity impact economic development. The existence of reverse causality between the former economic aggregates and middle-class has been pointed out in the previously existing literature and cannot be ignored in an empirical model. Besides, the traditional determinants of growth are endogenous. To answer our specific question, we address the endogeneity issue using a two-step system GMM estimator (Blundell and Bond 1998) with Windmeijer's (2005) finite sample correction for the variance-covariance matrix. We run estimates specifically on a reduced sample of 52 countries at middle-income level.

In a preliminary analysis, we look at the specificity of each development level when considering growth from the middle-class perspective. We found that whilst most countries, even low-income ones, have all four subcategories of middle-class and that they account for more than two thirds of total consumption, there is a huge gap between developed and developing countries (including upper middle-income countries) whose average consumption is at least three times lower than that of developed countries. Our empirical results are consistent with our hypothesis and descriptive statistics: for middle-income countries, the size of a middle-class alone is not what matters the most for growth. A wealthier middle-class is what positively impacts growth and the impact is more important when it is combined with the size. Given the low share of higher middle-class in middle-income countries in particular, upward mobility between subcategories of middle-classes seems rather difficult in middle-income countries. There is also the possibility of downward transition. Besides, an increase of the floating-class size, which is composed with vulnerable middle-class households that barely escaped from poverty, has negative impacts on growth. This suggests that, to take full advantage of the dynamics behind the expansion of this intermediate class, middle-income countries should design policies that are consistent with the needs of middle-class households and increase their resilience.

References

Acemoglu, D., S. Johnson, and J. Robinson. 2005. Institutions as a Fundamental Cause of Long-run Growth. In *Handbook of Economic Growth, Volume I A*, edited by P. Aghion and S. N. Durlauf. Amsterdam: Elsevier.

Asian Development Bank (ADB). 2010. The Rise of Asia's Middle-class. In *Key Indicators for Asia and the Pacific*. Manila: Asian Development Bank.

Adelman, M. C. 1967. *Society, Politics and Economic Development— A Quantitative Approach*. Baltimore, MD: Johns Hopkins University Press.

African Development Bank (AFDB). 2011. The Middle of the Pyramid: Dynamics of the Middle-class in Africa. In *The Economics of Growth*, edited by P. Aghion and P. Howit. Cambridge, MA: MIT Press.

Aristole. 1986. *The Politics, Book IV*, Chapter XI. Buffalo, NY: Prometheus Books.

Banerjee, A., and E. Duflo. 2008. What is Middle-class about the Middle-Classes around the World? *Journal of Economic Perspectives* 22(2): 3–28.

Barro, R. (1996). Determinants of Economic Growth: A Cross-country Empirical Study. NBER Working Paper 5698. Cambridge, MA: National Bureau of Economic Research.

Barro, R., and J. W. Lee. 2013. A New Data Set of Educational Attainment in the World, 1950–2010. *Journal of Development Economics* 104: 184–198.

Berliner, T., K. Thanh, and A. Mccarty. 2013. Inequality, Poverty Reduction and the Middle-Income Trap in Vietnam. *World Development Report* (July): 1–20.

Birdsall, N. 2010. *The (Indispensable) Middle-Class in Developing Countries; or, The Rich and the Rest, Not the Poor and the Rest*. Washington, DC: World Bank.

Birdsall, N., C. Graham, and S. Pettinato. 2000. Stuck in the Tunnel: Is Globalization Muddling the Middle-class? Center On Social and Economic Dynamics Working Paper 14. Washington, DC: Brookings Institution.

Blundell, R., and S. Bond 1998. Initial Conditions and Moment Restrictions in Dynamic Panel Data Models. *Journal of Econometrics* 87: 115–143.

Bonnefond, C., M. Clément, and F. Combarnous. 2015. In Search of the Elusive Chinese Urban Middle-class: An Exploratory Analysis. *Post-Communist Economies* 27(1): 41–59.

Chimhanzi, J., and A. Gounden. 2012. Deloitte on Africa: The Rise and Rise of the African Middle-class. In *Deloitte on Africa Collection: Issue 1*. Johannesburg: Deloitte and Touche.

Brandi, C. et al. 2014. A Cartography of the New Middle-classes in Developing and Emerging Countries. Discussion Paper Deutsches Institut für Entwicklungspolitik 35/14. Bonn, Germany: Deutsches Institut für Entwicklungspolitik.

Castellani, F., and G. Parent. 2011. Being Middle-Class in Latin America. OECD Development Centre Working Paper 305. Paris: Organisation for Economic Co-operation and Development.

Chenery, H. B., S. Robinson, and M. Syrquin. 1986. Development Patterns among Countries and Over Time. *Review of Economics and Statistics* 50(November): 391–416.

Chun, N. 2010. Middle-class Size in the Past, Present, and Future: A Description of Trends in Asia. ADB Economics Working Paper 217. Manila: Asian Development Bank.

Chunling, L. 2010. Characterizing China's Middle-class: Heterogeneous Composition and Multiple Identities. In *China's Emerging Middle-class: Beyond Economic Transformation*, edited by C. Li. Washington, DC: Brooking Institution Press.

Clément, M., and E. Rougier. 2014. Classes Moyennes et Émergence en Asie de l'Est: Mesures et Enjeux. *Mondes en Développement* 43(2015/1/No.169): 31–45.

Dahan, M., and D. Tsiddon. 2000. *Income Distribution and Economic Growth. Journal of Economic Growth* 3(1): 29–52.

Darbon, D. 2012. Classes(s) Moyenne(s): Une Revue de la Littérature. Un Concept Utile pour Suivre les Dynamiques de l'Afrique. *Afrique Contemporaine* 244(4): 33–51.

Desdoigt, A., and F. Jaramillo. 2009. Trade, Demand Spillovers, and Industrialization: The Emerging Global Middle class in Perspective. *Journal of International Economics* 79(2): 248–258.

Easterly, W. 2001, The Middle-Class Consensus and Economic Development. *Journal of Economic Growth* 6(4): 317–335.

Eichengreen, B., D. Park, and K. Shin. 2013. Growth Slowdowns Redux: New Evidence on the Middle-income Trap. NBER Working Paper 18673. Cambridge, MA: National Bureau of Economic Research.

Ehrhart, C. 2009. The Effects of Inequality on Growth: A Survey of the Theoretical and Empirical Literature. ECINEQ Working Paper 107. Verona, Italy: Society for the Study of Economic Inequality.

Felipe, J. 2012. Tracking the Middle-Income Trap: What is It, Who is in It, and Why? Part 1. ADB Economics Working Paper 306. Manila: Asian Development Bank.

Funatsu, T., and K. Kagoya. 2003. The Middle-classes in Thailand: The Rise of the Urban Intellectual Elite and their Social Consciousness. *The Developing Economies* (Special issue) 41: 243–263.

Galor, O., and O. Moav. 2004. From Physical to Capital the Accumulation: Inequality and the Process of Development. *Review of Economic Studies* 71: 1001–1026.

Grossman, G. M., and E. Helpman. 1991. *Innovation and Growth in Global Economy*. Cambridge, MA: The MIT Press.

Handley, A. 2015. Varieties of Capitalists? The Middle-Class, Private Sector and Economic Outcomes in Africa. *Journal of International Development* 27(5).

Hugon P., D. Nicet–chenaf, and E. Rougier. 2013. La Crise qui Révéla L'émergence: 2008–2009. In Émergencescapitalistes aux *Suds*, edited by A. Piveteau, E. Rougier, and D. Nicet–Chenaf. Paris: Karthala.

Kongsamut, P., A. Rebelo, and D. Xie. 2001. Beyond Balanced Growth. *Review of Economic Studies* 68: 869–882.

Kharas, H., and G. Gertz. 2010. The New Global Middle-class: A Crossover from West to East. Wolfensohn Center for Development at Brookings. Draft version. Washington, DC: Brookings Institution Press.

Kharas, H. 2010. The Emerging Middle-class in Developing Countries. OECD Development Centre Working Paper 285. Paris: Organisation for Economic Co-operation and Development.

Landes, D. S. 1998. *The Wealth and Poverty of Nations: Why Some are So Rich and Some So Poor*. London: W. W. Norton & Company.

de Mello, L. R. Jr. 1999. Foreign Direct Investment-led Growth: Evidence from Time Series and Panel Data. *Oxford Economic Papers* 51: 133–151.

Lundvall, B. 2007. Higher Education, Innovation and Economic Development. Department of Business Studies, Aalborg University, Denmark.

Mankiw, N. G., D. Romer, and D. N. Weil. 1992. A Contribution to the Empirics of Economic Growth. *The Quarterly Journal of Economics* 107(2): 407–437.

Matsuyama, K. 2002. The Rise of Mass Consumption Societies. *Journal of Political Economy* 110: 1035–1070.

Milanovic, B., and S. Yitzhaki. 2002. Decomposing the World Income Distribution: Does the World have a Middle-class? *Review of Income and Wealth* 48(2): 155–178.

Nallet, C. 2014. Classes Moyennes Éthiopiennes: Étude Empirique d'une Assignation Catégorielle Incertaine. Science Politique, Université de Bordeaux.

Ngai, L. R., and C. A. Pissarides. 2006. Structural Change in a Multi-Sector Model of Growth. Revised Version of May 2006 (forthcoming in the *American Economic Review*).

Ozturk, A. 2016. Examining the Economic Growth and the Middle-income Trap from the Perspective of the Middle-class. *International Business Review* 1208.

Ravallion, M. 2010. The Developing World's Bulging (But Vulnerable) Middle-class. *World Development* 38: 445–454.

Rodman, D. 2009. A Note on the Theme of Too Many Instruments. *Oxford Bulletin of Economic and Statistics* 71(1): 135–158.

Rodrik, D., and A. Subramanian. 2003. The Primacy of Institutions. *Finance and Development* June: 31–34.

Rodrik, D. 2013. Structural Change, Fundamentals and Growth: An Overview. Institute for Advanced Study. Mimeo. Available online at: http://drodrik.scholar.harvard.

Salama, P. 2014. Les Classes Moyennes Peuvent-elles Dynamiser la Croissance du PIB dans les Économies Émergentes Latino-américaines et Asiatiques? *Revue Tiers Monde* 219: 141–157.

Van der Hout, A. 2014. Escaping the Middle-income Trap: The Importance of Inclusiveness for Further Growth. Unpublished Masters Thesis. Rotterdam, The Netherlands: Erasmus University.

Van de Walle, N. 2011. Democracy, the State and the African Middle-class. Mimeo. Ithaca, NY: Cornell University.

Van Ourti, T., and P. Clarke. 2011. A Simple Correction to Remove the Bias of the Gini Coefficient due to Grouping. *The Review of Econometrics and Statistics* 93(3): 982–994.

Williamson, J., and K. H. O'Rourke. 1999. *Globalization and History: The Evolution of a 19th Century Atlantic Economy*. Cambridge, MA: MIT Press.

Appendix

Table A8.1 Data and Sources

Variables	Source	Period
Headcount ratios Consumption/Income share by decile Mean household consumption/income	PovcalNet (PPP 2005)[a]	Survey years during the period 1985–2010 2010 being the year with most observations (62 countries)
GDP per capita ($ constant 2005)	Penn World Table; World Development Indicators (PWT 8.1)	1985–2012
Gross fixed capital formation (% GDP)	UNCTAD	1985–2012
Population (growth rate in %)	World Development Indicators	1985–2012
Secondary and tertiary education achievement (%)	Barro and Lee 2013	1985–2012
Government final expenditure (% GDP)	World Development Indicators	1985–2012
Foreign Direct Investment (% GDP)[b]	UNCTAD	1985–2012
Sectoral share of value added (% total value added)	UNCTAD	1985–2012
Economic complexity index	Atlas of economic complexity	1985–2012
Labor force (total and agriculture share)	UNCTAD	1985–2012
Urban population (% total population)	World Development Indicators	1985–2012
Trade openness (exports + imports in % of GDP)	UNCTAD	1985–2012
Domestic credit to private sectors (% GDP)	World Development Indicators	1985–2012

GDP = gross domestic product, PPP = purchasing power parity, UNCTAD = United Nations Conference on Trade and Development, US = United States.

[a] For the PRC, India, and Indonesia, we complete national data with the weighted mean of urban and rural data.
 When there is more than one survey for a year, we calculate the mean when the types of data (consumption or income) are the same, and use the consumption data as they are when they are different.

[b] Yemen: FDI data are that of the democratic republic of Yemen (1980–1990) because of the lack of information from UNCTAD.

Source: Author.

Table A8.2 Countries by Region

Eastern Europe and Central Asia	Latin America and Caribbean	Middle-East and North Africa	South Asia
Albania	Bolivia	Algeria	Bangladesh
Armenia	Brazil	Egypt, Arab Rep.	India
Azerbaijan	Chile	Iran, Islamic Rep.	Nepal
Belarus	Colombia	Jordan	Pakistan
Bosnia and Herzegovina	Costa Rica	Morocco	Sri Lanka
Bulgaria	Dominican Republic	Tunisia	
Georgia	Ecuador	West Bank and Gaza	
Kazakhstan	El Salvador	Yemen, Rep.	
Kyrgyz Republic	Guatemala	Israel	
Macedonia, FYR	Honduras		
Moldova	Jamaica		
Romania	Mexico		
Serbia	Nicaragua		
Tajikistan	Panama		
Turkey	Paraguay		
Turkmenistan	Peru		
Ukraine	Trinidad and Tobago		
	Uruguay		
	Venezuela, RB		

continued on next page

Table A8.2 *continued*

Sub-Saharan Africa		East Asia	Western Europe and North America	
Benin	Mauritania	Cambodia	Australia	Poland
Botswana	Mauritius	PRC	Austria	Russian Federation
Burkina Faso	Mozambique	Indonesia	Belgium	Slovakia
Burundi	Niger	Lao PDR	Canada	Slovenia
Cameroon	Nigeria	Malaysia	Croatia	Spain
Central African Republic	Rwanda	Philippines	Czech Republic	Sweden
Chad	Senegal	Thailand	Denmark	Switzerland
Congo, Rep.	Sierra Leone	Timor-Leste	Estonia	United Kingdom
Cote d'Ivoire	South Africa	Viet Nam	Finland	United States
Ethiopia	Swaziland		France	
Gambia, The	Tanzania		Germany	
Ghana	Togo		Greece	
Guinea	Uganda		Hungary	
Guinea-Bissau	Zambia		Ireland	
Kenya			Italy	
Lesotho			Latvia	
Madagascar			Lithuania	
Malawi			Netherlands	
Mali			Norway	

PRC = People's Republic of China.
Source: Author.

PART III
Country Case Studies

9

Growth Pro-poorness from an Intertemporal Perspective with an Application to Indonesia, 1997–2007

Florent Bresson, Jean-Yves Duclos, and Flaviana Palmisano

9.1 Introduction

The dynamic relationship between economic growth and distribution changes is a long-lasting subject of investigations from both the micro- and macroeconomic perspectives. In particular, a specific and micro-oriented branch of the literature, known as "pro-poor growth," is generating sustained scrutiny from both the scientific and policy spheres, with the prime objective of assessing how growth is associated with poverty changes. This literature resulted in the development of numerous analytical tools for that purpose (see notably, Ravallion and Chen 2003; Son 2004; Essama-Nssah 2005; Essama-Nssah and Lambert 2009; Duclos 2009; Berenger and Bresson 2012).

In line with the traditional focus on cross-sectional poverty, a crucial role is played in these tools by the "anonymity" assumption that the identity of the growth beneficiaries shall not be regarded as relevant in the analysis. This is an often uncontroversial hypothesis, in particular if the aim is to identify the purely cross-sectional impact of growth. However, postulating anonymity means that income dynamics are then disregarded, namely that mobility observed during the growth process is not of measurement and normative interest. To illustrate that point, consider the following two separate income transformations A and B undergone by a four-person distribution of income from period t to $t + 1$:

$$(40,60,90,90) \rightarrow (90,90,40,60), \quad (1)$$
$$A$$
$$(40, 60, 90, 90) \rightarrow (40, 60, 90, 90) \quad (2)$$
$$B$$

Let us assume that in both periods the poverty line is equal to 70. In both cases, traditional indexes used to assess the pro-poorness of such growth processes like the rate of pro-poor growth (RPPG) (Ravallion and Chen 2003) would return zero values as the final marginal distribution of income is strictly identical to the initial marginal distribution.[1] Yet, the two income dynamics are quite different: considerable mobility is implied by A whereas B leaves everyone's income unchanged. We may therefore wish a pro-poorness index to behave differently when considering the two growth patterns. To circumvent these limitations, it is argued that a "non-anonymous" perspective should be endorsed for growth pro-poorness assessments (see notably Grimm 2007; Jenkins and Van Kerm 2011; Bourguignon 2011; Palmisano and Peragine 2015; Palmisano and Van de Gaer 2016). Proponents of this position emphasize the crucial role of mobility in the distributional effects associated with growth. While measurement aspects of growth pro-poorness and of mobility are both quite developed, the analysis of the impact of mobility on growth pro-poorness is a promising field that has yet to be developed to our knowledge.[2]

Bringing together these two issues means considering the individual poverty trajectories over time, hence considering an intertemporal evaluation of poverty. Mobility will then have converse effects on intertemporal poverty. On the one hand, consistent with Friedman (1962), mobility generally implies some equalization of permanent incomes across individuals. On the other hand, mobility induces variability costs, since risk-averse individuals may experience welfare losses with time variability. In the present study, the pro-poor or anti-poor nature of growth is determined by comparing observed intertemporal poverty with a counterfactual situation consisting of the absence of any kind of distributional change.

Various pro-poorness features of growth are also explored in this chapter through a set of additive decompositions. The first one

---

[1] See also Kakwani and Pernia (2000), Kakwani and Son (2003), and Kakwani and Son (2008) for alternative grow pro-poorness indexes.

[2] See for instance the reviews on mobility measurement in Fields and Ok (1999), Fields (2008), or J¨antti and Jenkins (2015).

disentangles the measurement of anonymous growth from that of its non-anonymous component. The second decomposition isolates the snapshot effects of income changes from multitemporal ones. The third decomposition separates the contribution of reranking, inequality changes, and pure growth in explaining growth pro-poorness. Finally, a fourth decomposition makes it possible to estimate the contribution of each subperiod to intertemporal poverty changes.

The approach suggested in the present chapter differs both methodologically and conceptually from past contributions on this topic. For instance, the individual RPPG introduced by Grimm (2007), defined as the average income growth of the initially poor individuals, specifically focuses on the impact of growth on the initially poor and does not take into account the negative income effects of those who experience deprivation after growth. Foster and Rothbaum (2012) proposed using cutoff-based mobility measures to identify variations of poverty over time, but, their method restricts poverty measurement to two specific snapshot poverty indexes, namely the headcount index and the mean poverty gap whose limitations are widely acknowledged (Sen 1976).

This chapter's contribution to the literature is twofold. The first contribution is to account for the impact of a growth process on intertemporal poverty, hence making it possible to disentangle the anonymous impact of growth from its mobility impact (the non-anonymous growth). The second contribution is an extension of the "mobility as equalizer" framework to take into account the effect of horizontal mobility on poverty, corrected for poverty transiency costs as well as for social welfare losses due to inequality in the distribution of intertemporal poverty among the population.

The rest of the chapter is organized as follows. Section 9.2 introduces a family of intertemporal indexes that can be interpreted as a representative income shortfall, that is the welfare loss, expressed as a share of the poverty line, due to the existence of poverty over the whole period. Section 9.3 describes our conceptual framework for assessing intertemporal growth pro-poorness and describes its properties when used with the suggested intertemporal poverty indexes. Section 9.4 suggests various decompositions of the proposed indexes that help to understand the pro-poor or anti-poor nature of observed growth processes. An empirical illustration of this framework is contained in Section 9.5 considering Indonesia during the period 1997–2007. It is notably shown that, unless variability aversion is large relative to inter-individual inequality aversion, growth can be deemed intertemporally pro-poor in Indonesia during this period. Section 9.6 concludes.

9.2 Intertemporal Poverty Assessment

The analysis focuses on the dynamics of a distribution of living standards (incomes, without loss of generality) for a population of n persons, with individuals denoted $i = 1, ..., n$ over $T > 1$ time periods (annual or monthly for instance) of their life. Each generic period is denoted by $t = 1, ..., T$ and the duration T is supposed to be the same for the whole population—we are comparing people's living conditions over the same spell.

Periodic income $y_{(i,t)}$ is supposed to be non-negative. Let $y_{(i)} \equiv (y_{i,1}, ..., y_{i,t}, ..., y_{i,T})$ then be the vector of individual i's incomes across the T periods and y_t be a cross-sectional vector of incomes at time t. The income profile $y_{(i)}$ is the ith row of the $n \times T$ matrix Y. For the sake of simplicity, we normalize incomes at time t by the corresponding poverty line $z_t > 0$. Poverty lines can either be absolute (constant in real terms) or relative (to income norms that are likely to vary across time). Censoring incomes at the corresponding poverty line yields $\tilde{y}_{i,t} \equiv \min\{y_{i,t}, 1\}$. Then poverty can be measured over an individual's lifetime by $p(y_{(i)})$ with $p(y_{(i)}) \geq 0$ whenever $\exists t \in \{1, ..., T\}$ such that $y_{(i,t)} < 1$ and $p(y_{(i)}) = 0$ otherwise. Intertemporal poverty at the population level is measured by the index $P(Y)$.

9.2.1 Individual illfare

Let the (normalized) poverty gap for person i at period t be defined by $g_{i,t} \equiv 1 - \tilde{y}_{i,t}$. Then vector $g_{(i)} \equiv (g_{i,1}, ..., g_{i,t}, ..., g_{i,T})$ describes the sequence of poverty gaps for this person i across T periods, and G is the $n \times T$ matrix of normalized poverty gaps for the whole population. Finally, the vector $g_t \equiv (g_{i,t}, ..., g_{n,t})$ gives the cross-sectional distribution of gaps at time t. In the literature, the income gap $g_{i,t} \in [0,1]$ is a standard measure of individual poverty for both snapshot and intertemporal poverty measurement. For instance, the widely used FGT class (Foster, Greer, and Thorbecke 1984) of additive poverty indexes relies on the aggregation of simple transformations of poverty gaps.[3] Using an FGT-like formulation, the poverty of each individual i over the T periods can be measured by:

---

[3] It also serves as a basis for the intertemporal generalizations of FGT indexes proposed in Foster (2009); Canto, Gradín, and del Rio (2012); or Busetta and Mendola (2012), not to mention specific members of the family of indexes introduced by Hoy and Zheng (2011); Bossert, Chakravarty, and d'Ambrosio (2012); and Dutta, Roope, and Zank (2013).

$$p_\gamma(y_{(i)}) \equiv \sum_{t=1}^{T} \omega_t g_{i,t}^\gamma, \quad \text{with } \gamma \geq 0, \tag{3}$$

where the $\omega_t > 0$, $t \in \{1, \ldots, T\}$ and $\sum_{t=1}^{T} \omega_t = 1$, define a weighing scheme that indicates the sensitivity of poverty to the sequence of experienced deprivations. With decreasing weights, priority is given to eradicating poverty experienced earlier in life, for instance in childhood; with weights increasing through time, more importance is on the contrary given later deprivations.[4]

The parameter γ measures the social evaluator aversion to inequality and variability in a person's poverty gaps. A larger value for γ means higher weight is given to income losses for severe deprivations when compared with light deprivations. For $\gamma = 1$, the index (3) is the simple weighted average of i's poverty gaps across time. For $\gamma > 1$, a sequence of income increments and decrements that leaves the weighted mean of income gaps unchanged but shrinks intertemporal variability reduces $p_\gamma(g_{(i)})$. It is worth stressing that the index relies on a "union" definition of the poverty domain since individuals are regarded as poor, from an intertemporal perspective, whenever they experience at least one deprivation during the whole period.[5]

So as to account explicitly for the cost of time variability, we suggest using the poverty counterpart of the "equally distributed equivalent income" introduced by Atkinson (1970) for the assessment of inequality and social welfare. This equally distributed equivalent (EDE) poverty gap for person i, $\pi_\gamma(g_{(i)})$, is defined by:

$$\pi_\gamma(g_{(i)}) \equiv p_\gamma^{-1}\left(p_\gamma(y_{(i)})\right) = \left(\sum_{t=1}^{T} \omega_t g_{i,t}^\gamma\right)^{\frac{1}{\gamma}}. \tag{4}$$

The EDE gap $\pi_\gamma(g_{(i)})$ is the gap level that, if experienced at each period of i's lifetime, would result in the same level of poverty for i over time as that generated by its observed sequence of relative deprivations.

---

[4] The index (3) is a specific version of the lifetime individual poverty measure introduced by Hoy and Zheng (2011). See also Bresson and Duclos (2015).

[5] A generalization with other definitions of the poverty domain using a counting approach 'a la Alkire and Foster (2011) can easily be performed by censoring vectors $g_{(i)}$ whose (weighted) number of deprivations is less than a given threshold $\in]1,T]$.

For $\gamma = 1$, $\pi_\gamma(g_{(i)})$, then corresponds to the simple weighted average gap over time, i.e $\pi_1(g_{(i)}) = \sum_{t=1}^{T} \omega_t g_{i,t}$. For $\gamma \geq 1$, $\pi_\gamma(g_{(i)})$ is never lower than $\pi_1(g_{(i)})$ because variability is regarded as a social bad. The difference between these two values can be interpreted as the cost of individual i's deprivation variability:

$$c_\gamma(g_{(i)}) \equiv \pi_\gamma(g_{(i)}) - \pi_1(g_{(i)}) \quad (5)$$

Hence, intertemporal poverty for i can be expressed as:

$$\pi_\gamma(g_{(i)}) = \pi_1(g_{(i)}) + c_\gamma(g_{(i)}). \quad (6)$$

Consequently, $c_\gamma(g_{(i)})$ is the sum of the (weighted) average intertemporal income gap and of the intertemporal cost of mobility.

9.2.2 Social illfare

Here, we consider the aggregation of these individual EDE gaps so as to obtain a comparable value for the whole population. As in the case of traditional snapshot poverty, many functional forms can be proposed to perform this social aggregation. Here, we also make use of the FGT formulation for aggregation:[6]

$$P_{\alpha,\gamma}(Y) \equiv \frac{1}{n}\sum_{i=1}^{n} \left(\pi_{\gamma(g_{(i)})}\right)^\alpha, \quad (7)$$

where parameter $\alpha \geq 1$ measures aversion to poverty inequality across individuals. A socially representative EDE gap for the population, $\Pi_{\alpha,\gamma}(G)$, is then given by:

$$\Pi_{\alpha,\gamma}(G) \equiv \left(\frac{1}{n}\sum_{i=1}^{n} \left(\pi_{\gamma(g_{(i)})}\right)^\alpha\right)^{\frac{1}{\alpha}}. \quad (8)$$

---

[6] The resulting index Pα is the one proposed by Bourguignon and Chakravarty (2003) in the context of multidimensional poverty measurement. It also generalizes Duclos, Araar, and Giles (2010), where $\alpha = \gamma$ and $\omega_t = \frac{1}{T} \forall t \in \{1,\ldots,T\}$

In general, individual dynamics are taken into account with this intertemporal index, but an anonymous evaluation of intertemporal poverty can be performed using $\Pi_\alpha \equiv \Pi_{\alpha,\alpha}$. Switching two poor persons' income at any t will then not impact the social evaluation of intertemporal poverty, whatever the income streams of the two individuals in the other periods.[7]

Indices $P_{\alpha,\gamma}$ and $\Pi_{\alpha,\gamma}$ are ordinally equivalent and so can be used equally for comparing any pair of distributions. However, $\Pi_{\alpha,\gamma}(G)$ can be usefully interpreted as the relative gap level which, if assigned uniformly to all individuals at every time period, would yield the same poverty level as that observed with the intertemporal distribution G. It is thus a representative gap that indicates the social cost, expressed as a fraction of the poverty line, of observed poverty.

The poverty ranking of two distributions showing the same marginal income distributions but different joint distributions will depend on the preferences of the social evaluator with respect to poverty variability and poverty inequality. Note that, in that case, the cross-sectional distributions of poverty gaps are the same under the two processes. If aversion toward inequality and variability is the same (i.e. $\alpha = \gamma$), the two distributions will then be judged equivalent in terms of poverty. Let $\tilde{G}$ be a permutation of G so that individual ranks are kept unchanged during the whole growth process. Distribution $\tilde{G}$ is regarded as no worse than G with indifference toward variability ($\gamma = 1$), while insensitivity toward inequality ($\alpha = 1$) makes distribution G no worse than $\tilde{G}$. Hence, whether poverty is more severe in G or $\tilde{G}$ will crucially depend on the chosen values for α and γ.

As with individual illfare, useful decompositions can be performed for the poverty index Π_α. Let

$$c_{\alpha,\gamma}(G) \equiv \Pi_{\alpha,\gamma}(G) - \Pi_{1,\gamma}(G) \qquad (10)$$

be the cost of inequality of intertemporal poverty across individuals. It shall not be confused with:

$$\frac{1}{n}\sum_{i=1}^{n} c_\gamma(g_{(i)}) \equiv \Pi_{1,\gamma}(G) - \Pi_{1,1}(G), \qquad (11)$$

---

[7] This can be more easily seen if we express $\Pi_\alpha(G)$ as:

$$\Pi_{\alpha(G)} = \left(\sum_{t=1}^{T} \omega_t \frac{1}{n}\sum_{i=1}^{n} g_{i,t}^\alpha\right)^{\frac{1}{\alpha}} = \left(\sum_{t=1}^{T} \omega_t\, P_{\_\alpha}(g_t)\right)^{\frac{1}{\alpha}} \qquad (9)$$

that is the average cost of deprivation variability at the aggregate level. Associating (11) with (10) and solving for $\Pi_{\alpha,\gamma}(G)$ we obtain:

$$\Pi_{\alpha,\gamma}(G) = \Pi_{1,1}(G) + \frac{1}{n}\sum_{i=1}^{n} c_\gamma\big(g_{(i)}\big) + c_{\alpha,\gamma}(G). \quad (12)$$

Equation (12) additively decomposes aggregate intertemporal poverty into three components: the average individual intertemporal poverty gap, the average cost of deprivation variability, and the cost of inequality in intertemporal poverty.

9.3 Measurement of Pro-poorness in an Intertemporal Setting

9.3.1 General framework

Usually, that is in the context of cross-sectional analyses of poverty, assessing the pro-poor nature of a given growth process implies comparing the observed poverty level at the end of the period with the level that would have been observed under some given benchmark. This benchmark could be either a targeted poverty level or a counterfactual one. Let $\hat{Y}$ denote that reference distribution.

The suggested measurement of pro-poor growth is anchored to an intertemporal pro-poorness (IPP) evaluation function $IPP\big(P(\hat{Y}), P(Y)\big)$ that takes the simple linear form in the present chapter for expositional simplicity:

$$IPP\big(P(\hat{Y}), P(Y)\big) \equiv P(\hat{Y}) - P(Y), \quad (13)$$

that satisfies standard appealing properties. For instance, $IPP\big(P(\hat{Y}), P(Y)\big) = 0$ if observed poverty is identical to benchmark poverty. Moreover, the measure will be deemed pro-poor (anti-poor) if estimated intertemporal poverty is lower (larger) than the chosen counterfactual poverty level. Finally, values of the index can be compared, a larger (lower) value for one given growth spell being qualified as more pro-poor (anti-poor).[8]

---

[8] Fields (2010) uses similar properties for the measurement of mobility.

The definition of the counterfactual situation is crucial as different benchmark distributions will naturally result in different evaluations of growth pro-poorness. A crucial element is whether an absolute or a relative definition of growth pro-poorness is chosen—the former view considers that growth is pro-poor when poverty decreases absolutely speaking while the latter states that growth is pro-poor when the incomes of the poor rise faster than some norm (often proportional to mean income). For the sake of simplicity, this chapter follows an absolute approach. However, it is worth pointing out that generalizing to a relative approach simply means dividing incomes by the chosen norm.

Similarly, "mobility means different things to different people," in the words of Fields (2008: 1), and some agreement is necessary with respect to that concept. In this chapter, mobility is interpreted as any temporal change in individual income. A natural candidate for the counterfactual scenario is then the status quo, namely the absence of distributional changes. The benchmark Y_1 is then a counterfactual distribution in which every person would receive exactly the same income as the one he or she got initially.[9] The IPP index is consequently the difference between poverty in a counterfactual situation in which the first period deprivation is extended over the T-period growth spell and observed intertemporal poverty.[10]

Of course, as known in the growth pro-poorness literature (Duclos 2009), rival versions can be proposed for the counterfactual distribution. For instance, the counterfactual distribution could only refer to the absence of exchange mobility, hence resulting in a counterfactual distribution showing the same marginal distributions as the observed distribution but without reranking from year to year. Another possibility is to take a relative view on, that is to consider a "neutral" growth process (in terms of snapshot inequality) over the studied period.[11] However it is

---

[9] A similar approach is used by Chakravarty, Dutta, and Weymark (1985) and Fields (2010), although the benchmark in the former study is based on relative immobility, that is the share of each person in total income is assumed to be constant across time.

[10] This property relates to the normalization axiom proposed by Hoy and Zheng (2011) that requires a person's lifetime poverty to be represented by snapshot poverty if this person gets the same income level every period.

[11] As stressed by an anonymous referee, a possible issue is that year $t = 1$ was an abnormal year during the period of interest, hence resulting in large values of the IPP, in particular if T is relatively large. We acknowledge this possible issue but note that the same problem is likely to hold with usual growth "pro-poorness" tools. A possible solution to fix that issue could be to test the sensitivity of the results by considering a contiguous year as the reference or averaging individual incomes for the very first years of the growth spell. However, one can simply argue that no interpretation of the IPP should be given without any ex ante description of the studied growth spell.

worth stressing that some of the decompositions proposed in Section 4 make it possible to obtain quite easily the corresponding values of the IPP as components or sum of components of our preferred version of the IPP.

9.3.2 Intertemporal pro-poorness indexes

Using the benchmark deprivation matrix G_1 referring to Y_1, we have $\Pi_{\alpha,\gamma}(G_1) = \Pi_\alpha(g_1)$, that is:

$$\Pi_\alpha(g_1) = \left(\frac{1}{n}\sum_{i=1}^{n} g_{i,1}^\alpha\right)^{\frac{1}{\alpha}}, \qquad (14)$$

This is then the EDE income gap corresponding to the value of the FGT index at year $t = 1$. Using the family of poverty indexes introduced in the previous section, we obtain an operational expression for (13):

$$IPP_{\alpha,\gamma} = \Pi_\alpha(g_1) - \Pi_{\alpha,\gamma}(G). \qquad (15)$$

The index equals 0 when everyone's deprivation level is left unchanged during the whole growth spell. It takes a positive value if intertemporal poverty is less severe than initial cross-sectional poverty, and negative in the opposite case. If growth is associated with the eradication of poverty at the subsequent periods, then $IPP_{\alpha,\gamma}$ will be equal to $(1 - \omega_1)\Pi_\alpha(g_1) > 0$. This is an upper bound for the IPP index and is equal to the amount of intertemporal poverty that is eliminated through growth, which corresponds to discounted value of poverty experienced in the first period.

The cost of individual variability as well as the benefits of a potential reduction of intertemporal inequalities, both resulting from mobility, are incorporated in the $IPP_{\alpha,\gamma}$ index.[12] $IPP_{\alpha,\gamma}$ satisfies the usual

---

[12] It is worth underlining that the family of indexes proposed in Equation (18) are normative in nature.

Such normatively grounded indexes are derived from explicit social illfare functions and are measures of the change in intertemporal social illfare resulting from mobility. Such measures contrast with indexes of mobility that aim at describing some aspects of mobility. Hence our framework is not meant to provide statistical measures of income changes but to assess the impact of such changes on intertemporal illfare. By using a welfare function to perform this comparison, our pro-poorness indexes allow us to determine whether the observed changes were desirable in terms of poverty or social illfare reduction.

properties of anonymity (in the identity of individual gap vectors), scale invariance, continuity, population invariance, and subgroup consistency required for social evaluations. $IPP_{\alpha,\gamma}$ increases with initial poverty and decreases with intertemporal poverty. Nevertheless, changes in first-period gaps have ambiguous effects since both poverty levels are affected.

To illustrate the behavior of the index, consider the example (1) used in the introduction. As the average income gap is left unchanged during this growth process, the sign of $IPP_{\alpha,\gamma}$ will uniquely depend on the chosen values for the aversion to poverty variability and aversion to intertemporal poverty parameters—assigned values for the weighing scheme do not determine the sign of the index here. In particular, for $\gamma > \alpha$ variability aversion dominates aversion to poverty inequality and the other way around for $\gamma < \alpha$. Let us consider the case of $\omega_1 = \omega_2$. With more emphasis given to variability aversion, for instance $\alpha = 3$ and $\gamma = 4$, the index becomes negative (e.g. $IPP_{3,4} = -0.016$). Because of the cost of temporal variability the growth process is not regarded as pro-poor. With $\alpha = 3$ and $\gamma = 2$ the index takes a positive value (e.g. $IPP_{3,2} = 0.029$) and the transformation can be deemed pro-poor because of the poverty equalization effect of mobility.

9.4 Decompositions

In this section, we suggest four decompositions of the $IPP_{\alpha,\gamma}$ index that show the respective contributions of mean income growth, mobility, inequality, and subperiod changes. For the sake of simplicity, we set $t = 2$ for the first three decompositions.[13] The first decomposition disentangles the anonymous and the mobility components of growth:

$$IPP_{\alpha,\gamma} = \underbrace{\Pi_\alpha(g_1, g_1) - \Pi_\alpha(g_1, g_2)}_{AG} + \underbrace{\Pi_\alpha(g_1, g_2) - \Pi_{\alpha,\gamma}(g_1, g_2)}_{M}. \quad (16)$$

The index $\Pi_\alpha(g_1, g_2)$ returns an anonymous evaluation of intertemporal poverty. Consequently, it does not account for the social evaluation of the benefits and costs of mobility: AG accordingly assesses the poverty effect of an anonymous growth process, while M captures the non-anonymous effects of observed mobility during the growth spell. The component AG is positive if we observe both a decrease in the mean poverty gap and a contraction in the periodic distribution of

---

[13] A generalization to larger values of T is provided in the appendix.

poverty gaps. The component M is positive if inter-individual inequality aversion is stronger than temporal variability aversion ($\alpha > \gamma$), zero for $\alpha = \gamma$, and otherwise negative. The sign of the two effects is not determined by the weights ω_t. With example (1), we obtain $AG = 0$ and $M = 0.029$ with $\alpha = 3$ and $\gamma = 2$. As the anonymous growth impact is nil, the beneficial impact of the whole growth process on intertemporal poverty can exclusively be attributed to a (pro-poor) effect of observed mobility.

The distinction between standard anonymous pro-poorness and our intertemporal approach is further highlighted with the second decomposition. For that purpose, it is worth noting that the poverty cost of inter-person inequality in $\Pi_\alpha(g_1)$ is the poverty cost of initial inequality, that is, $c_\alpha(g_1)$. Using (10), a decomposition of the benchmark poverty level is:

$$\Pi_\alpha(g_1) = \Pi_1(g_1) + c_\alpha(g_1). \tag{17}$$

that is the sum of the average poverty gap in the first period and the cost of inequality in the initial distribution of individual poverty gaps. In a two-period setting, equation (12) can then be rewritten as:

$$\Pi_{\alpha,\gamma}(g_1 g_2) = \omega_1 P_1(g_1) + \omega_2 P_1(g_2)$$
$$+ \frac{1}{n}\sum_{i=1}^{n} c_\gamma(g_{(i)}) + c_{\alpha,\gamma}(g_1, g_2). \tag{18}$$

The following decomposition of the *IPP* index can then be proposed:

$$IPP_{\alpha,\gamma} = \underbrace{\omega_2[P_1(g_1) - P_1(g_2)]}_{\Delta P^c} + \underbrace{\omega_2[c_\alpha(g_1) - c_\alpha(g_2)]}_{\Delta c^c}$$
$$+ \underbrace{\omega_1 c_\alpha(g_1) + \omega_2 c_\alpha(g_2) - c_{\alpha,\gamma}(G)}_{M^c} - \underbrace{\frac{1}{n}\sum_{i=1}^{n} c_\gamma(g_{(i)})}_{CV}. \tag{19}$$

The interpretation for those four components is the following:

ΔP^c captures changes in the average cross-sectional gaps, $P_1(g_1)$ and $P_1(g_2)$, and so does not depend on variability and intertemporal inequalities.

Δc^c is, up to a multiplicative term, the difference between the cost of inequality in the initial and in the final periods. Δc^c can be both positive or negative, depending on whether inequality in cross-sectional poverty has fallen or has increased between the two periods.

M^c is the difference between the weighted sum of the cost of cross-sectional inequalities and the cost of intertemporal inequality, which is mobility's ability to decrease inequality between individuals, taking the cost of variability into account.

CV eflects the cost of the longitudinal variability induced by mobility. CV is always negative when $\gamma > 1$ since variability aversion then systematically assigns a social cost to the variability associated with mobility.

Disregarding the weighing term ω_2, the first two components ΔP^c and Δc^c capture the usual components of anonymous pro-poor growth in the spirit of Ravallion and Chen (2003).[14] Conversely, the two components M^c and CV reflect the social evaluator's trade-off between the costs and benefits of mobility, that is the intertemporal pro-poorness effects. It can be noted that $\Delta c^c = 0$ and $M^c = 0$ with $\alpha = 1$, while $CV = 0$ when $\gamma = 0$. In the specific case of $\alpha = \gamma = 1$, $\Delta c^c = M^c = CV = 0$ and consequently $IPP_{\alpha,\gamma} = \Delta P^c$, the difference in the average poverty gap.

Turning back again to example (1), the first two components, ΔP^c and Δc^c, are nil as the (anonymous) cross-sectional income distribution is the same in both periods. For $\alpha = 3$, $\gamma = 2$, $M^c = 0.089$ shows a positive value indicating that growth has shrunk deprivation inequalities from an intertemporal point of view. Income inequalities are the same in both periods, but considering a larger two period time-horizon, they have decreased in comparison with the benchmark case. Lastly, $CV = -0.059$.

With the third decomposition, the emphasis is put on the reranking effect of growth.

---

[14] It deserves to be noted that $AG = 0$ and the sum $\Delta P^c + \Delta c^c$ generally differ, since we have:

$$AG = \left(P_\alpha(g_1)\right)^{\frac{1}{\alpha}} - \left(\omega_1 P_\alpha(g_1) + \omega_2 P_\alpha(g_2)\right)^{\frac{1}{\alpha}}, \quad (20)$$

$$\Delta P^c + \Delta c^c = \omega_2 \left(\left(P_\alpha(g_1)\right)^{\frac{1}{\alpha}} - \left(P_\alpha(g_2)\right)^{\frac{1}{\alpha}}\right). \quad (21)$$

Note that $AG = \Delta P^c + \Delta c^c$ when $\alpha = 1$; when $\alpha > 3$, we have instead $AG \leq \Delta P^c + \Delta c^c$.

It is obtained by making use of two counterfactual distributions g_1^I and g_1^{IR}. The counterfactual distribution g_1^I is obtained starting from the distribution of individuals' poverty gaps at the final period but scaling them to obtain the average poverty gap of the first period and ordering them on the basis of their rank in the first period, that is $g_1^I \equiv \tilde{g}_2 \frac{\Pi_1(g_1)}{\Pi_1(g_2)}$ with $\tilde{g}_2 \equiv r(g_2, g_1)$ where $r(a,b)$ orders elements from a according to observed ranks in b.[15] It is clear that the only feature that differs between g_1 and g_1^I is inequality. The counterfactual distribution g_1^{IR} is obtained starting from the previous counterfactual distribution g^I, but ordering individuals on the basis of their rank at the end of the growth spell, that is $g_1^{IR} \equiv g_2 \frac{\Pi_1(g_1)}{\Pi_1(g_2)}$.[16] So, the unique difference between g_1^I and g_1^{IR} is reranking. As a consequence, g_1^{IR} and g_2 only differ with respect to their average poverty gap. Note that the counterfactual distributions g_1^{IR} and g_1^I are computed by considering the inequality structure and the ranks of the poverty gaps distribution and not of the income distribution. Although this choice may seem debatable, it is in line with considering an index showing sensitivity to deprivations variability across time (through γ) and to inequalities of intertemporal poverty across persons (through α).

Noting that $\Pi_\alpha(g_1) = \Pi_{\alpha,\gamma}(g_1, g_1)$, the third decomposition is then:[17]

$$IPP_{\alpha,\gamma} = \underbrace{\Pi_{\alpha,\gamma}(g_1, g_1) - \Pi_{\alpha,\gamma}(g_1, g_1^I)}_{I} + \underbrace{\Pi_{\alpha,\gamma}(g_1, g_1^I) - \Pi_{\alpha,\gamma}(g_1, g_1^{IR})}_{R}$$

$$+ \underbrace{\Pi_{\alpha,\gamma}(g_1, g_1^{IR}) - \Pi_{\alpha,\gamma}(g_1, g_2)}_{PG}. \qquad (22)$$

The interpretation of each component is the following:

I captures the intertemporal effects of inequality and variability in poverty (g^I and g_1^I share the same arithmetic mean and they rank individuals in the same manner). More specifically, I assesses the effects of inequality across time

---

[15] Consider a situation in which the distribution of income is the initial distribution from example (1) and (10, 6, 5, 8) at $T = 2$. Given the poverty line $z = 7$, g_2 is then (0.29, 0.14, 0, 0). Since $\tilde{g}_2 = (0, 0.14, 0.29, 0)$, $\Pi_1(g_1) = 0.143$ and $\Pi_1(g_2) = 0.108$, we consequently have $g_1^I = (0, 0.14, 0.29, 0) \times \frac{0.143}{0.108}$.

[16] Considering the example proposed in footnote 15, g_1^{IR} will then be $(0.29, 0.14, 0, 0) \times \frac{0.108}{0.143}$.

[17] Ruiz–Castillo (2004) proposed a similar decomposition of the ethical index of mobility introduced by Chakravarty et al. (1985).

and individuals when initial ranks are preserved. Increasing inequalities will systematically result in a negative value for I, no matter the chosen values for the aversion parameters α and γ. With $\alpha = \gamma = 1$, I will be null as the index becomes neutral with respect to intertemporal variability and inequality in poverty.

R measures the effect of reranking on intertemporal poverty (g_1^{IR} and g_1^{I} show the same mean and the same degree of cross-sectional inequality, but differ with respect to the way individuals are ranked). Naturally, if reranking is observed during the growth spell, then $R = 0$. When individual ranks change, the values of the aversion parameters determines the sign of the R component. In case $\alpha < \gamma$, R is strictly negative because reranking induces deprivation variability at the individual level and the costs of variability are deemed larger than the benefits of inequality associated with reranking. Alternatively, in case $\alpha > \gamma$, R is strictly positive since reranking has an equalizing effect on poverty over time and this beneficial effect is valued more than the costs of variability. Finally, $\alpha = \gamma = 1$ implies $R = 0$.

PG assesses a "pure" growth effect on intertemporal poverty (g_2 and g_1^{IR} only differ with respect to their average value). This component is positive (negative) if "pure" growth is associated with a reduction in individuals' intertemporal poverty. Its sign is not determined by the values of α and γ, though the higher γ is with respect to α, the higher the absolute value of the effect tends to be.

When $\alpha = \gamma = 1$, $IPP_{\alpha,\gamma} = PG$; the pro-poor nature of any growth process is solely determined by the "pure" growth effect. It can be noted that, contrary to PG, the component AG from the first decomposition is not purged from the inequality and reranking effects.[18]

With the example in (1), $I = 0$ given that inequality is identical in both periods; $R = -0.016$ for $\alpha = 3$, $\gamma = 4$, since there is a reshuffling of

---

[18] As indicated above, this decomposition is characterized by path dependency. The value of the components would differ with alternative "paths" for the decomposition. For instance, we could have considered capturing first the growth effect, then the impact of reranking, and lastly, the inequality effect. No sequence can be regarded as necessarily more appropriate than another (see e.g. DiNardo, Fortin, and Lemieux 1996). A possible way of dealing with that issue is to apply a Shapley–Shorrocks decomposition, consisting of computing the Shapley value of each effect across all possible sequences (see Shorrocks 2013).

individuals in the distributions (the two initially poor individuals become the two richest), but the variability costs are higher than the benefits. Finally, $PG = 0$ given that the average gap is unchanged.

Finally, the studied growth spell is likely to last over a relatively long period and it may be desirable to isolate the contribution of a specific subperiod, provided the available data make it possible to perform a multi-period analysis ($T > 2$).

Let the intertemporal poverty measure $\Pi_{\alpha,\gamma}(G)$ be denoted by $\Pi_{\alpha,\gamma}(g_1, \ldots, g_T)$ and benchmark poverty, $\Pi_\alpha(g_1)$, by $\Pi_\alpha(g_1, \ldots, g_1)$. Assuming $T = 3$ and noting C^t the contribution of growth to $IPP_{\alpha,\gamma}$ from t to $t + 1$, we then have the following decomposition of $IPP_{\alpha,\gamma}$:

$$IPP_{\alpha,\gamma} = \underbrace{\Pi_\alpha(g_1, g_1, g_1) - \Pi_{\alpha,\gamma}(g_1, g_2, g_2)}_{C^1}$$
$$+ \underbrace{\Pi_{\alpha,\gamma}(g_1, g_2, g_2) - \Pi_{\alpha,\gamma}(g_1, g_2, g_3)}_{C^2}. \qquad (23)$$

As the result of the decomposition is likely to be path dependent, it may be worth considering a Shapley decomposition (Shorrocks 2013).[19]

9.5 Empirical Illustration

Data are from the second, third, and fourth rounds of the Indonesian Family Life Survey (IFLS) conducted by the RAND Corporation, the

---

[19] The two components can then be computed as:

$$C^1 = \frac{1}{2}\big(\Pi_\alpha(g_1, g_1, g_1) - \Pi_{\alpha,\gamma}(g_1, f_{1,2}(g_1), f_{1,2}(g_1))\big)$$
$$+ \frac{1}{2}\big(\Pi_{\alpha,\gamma}(g_1, g_1, f_{2,3}(g_1)) - \Pi_{\alpha,\gamma}(g_1, f_{1,2}(g_1), f_{2,3}(f_{1,2}(g_1)))\big), \qquad (24)$$
$$= \frac{1}{2}\big(\Pi_\alpha(g_1, g_1, g_1) - \Pi_{\alpha,\gamma}(g_1, g_2, g_2)\big)$$
$$+ \frac{1}{2}\big(\Pi_{\alpha,\gamma}(g_1, g_1, f_{2,3}(g_1)) - \Pi_{\alpha,\gamma}(g_1, g_2, g_3)\big), \qquad (25)$$
$$C^2 = \frac{1}{2}\big(\Pi_\alpha(g_1, g_1, g_1) - \Pi_{\alpha,\gamma}(g_1, g_1, f_{2,3}(g_1))\big)$$
$$+ \frac{1}{2}\big(\Pi_{\alpha,\gamma}(g_1, f_{1,2}(g_1), f_{1,2}(g_1)) - \Pi_{\alpha,\gamma}(g_1, f_{1,2}(g_1), f_{2,3}(f_{1,2}(g_1)))\big), \qquad (26)$$
$$= \frac{1}{2}\big(\Pi_\alpha(g_1, g_1, g_1) - \Pi_{\alpha,\gamma}(g_1, g_1, f_{2,3}(g_1))\big)$$
$$+ \frac{1}{2}\big(\Pi_{\alpha,\gamma}(g_1, g_2, g_2) - \Pi_{\alpha,\gamma}(g_1, g_2, g_3)\big), \qquad (27)$$

where $f_{t,t+1}(g_k) \equiv 1 - \delta_{t,t+1}(1 - g_k)$ with $\delta_{t,t+1} \equiv \left(\frac{\bar{y}_{1,t}}{\bar{y}_{1,t+1}}, \ldots, \frac{\bar{y}_{n,t}}{\bar{y}_{n,t+1}}\right)$.

University of California, Los Angeles, and the Demographic Institute of the University of Indonesia. The IFLS is an ongoing longitudinal socioeconomic and health survey, that contains over 30,000 individuals representing 83% of the Indonesian population living in 13 (out of 26) provinces, mostly on Sumatra and Java. Data are collected on individual respondents, their families, their households, the communities in which they live, and the health and education facilities they use (Strauss, et al. 2009). For the present study, we rely on expenditure estimates provided for the years 1997, 2000, and 2007. More specifically, our estimates are computed using per capita expenditures adjusted for inflation, using the official consumer price index, and for regional price level differences, using regional poverty lines provided with the IFLS. Using Jakarta in 2007 as a reference for price levels, the poverty line is set at Rp264,383. It is worth noting that, though the time span of the growth spell is relatively large, we only have three observations for each household over the period. As a consequence, our results will mostly emphasize long-term dynamics. Short-term dynamics are then not taken into account, hence resulting in an underestimation of the social cost or benefits (depending on $\alpha \gtreqless \gamma$ of income variability at the individual level).

For the present study, each period is given the same weight for the estimation of the IPP index and its components.

Table 9.1 shows both snapshot and intertemporal poverty estimates for values of α and γ within the set {1, 2, 3}. First, it can be seen that during the whole period, cross-sectional poverty has decreased. More specifically, poverty did not significantly change between 1997 and 2000, but decreased substantially during the later subperiod whatever the value for α. These results are robust, i.e. do

Table 9.1 Cross-sectional and Intertemporal EDE Gaps for Indonesia, 1997–2007

	Snapshot poverty			Intertemporal poverty		
	1997	2000	2007	$\gamma=1$	$\gamma=2$	$\gamma=3$
$\alpha=1$	0.0419	0.0403	0.0162	0.0328	0.0476	0.0548
	(0.00201)	(0.00175)	(0.00107)	(0.00111)	(0.00155)	(0.0017)
$\alpha=2$	0.13	0.123	0.073	0.0822	0.112	0.127
	(0.00373)	(0.00333)	(0.00311)	(0.00204)	(0.00235)	(0.00275)
$\alpha=3$	0.202	0.191	0.13	0.123	0.159	0.18
	(0.00503)	(0.005)	(0.0048)	(0.0031)	(0.00288)	(0.00302)

EDE = equally distributed equivalent.
Note: Bootstrapped standard errors in parentheses (200 replications).
Source: The authors.

not depend on the specific value for the poverty line or the chosen poverty index within the set of monotone subgroup-consistent indexes.[20] The Asian crisis explains the deceiving results for the earliest subperiod, the per capita income representing in 2000 only 85% of its level in 1997.[21] The recovery and the sustained growth (about 4% per year between 2000 and 2007) have later been associated with poverty alleviation. It is worth noting that the pace of poverty alleviation over the period shrinks with the chosen value for α. This means that the growth process was less successful in lowering extreme poverty than moderate poverty.

The decreasing values for cross-sectional EDE gaps can be directly compared with the reported values for the intertemporal EDE gap as the same metric is used in both cases. Disregarding the welfare costs of income variability ($\gamma = 1$) the value for the intertemporal EDE gap is a simple average of snapshot EDE gaps. Raising the value of the income variability sensitivity parameter γ increases the EDE gap and thus offsets the observed improvement in cross-sectional poverty. When inequality aversion dominates variability aversion, the compensation is partial and the intertemporal EDE gap is lower than the corresponding value for 1997. But in the opposite situation, the social cost of income variability is regarded as so important that it fully cancels the observed improvement after 2000.

The values of $IPP_{\alpha,\gamma}$ reported in Table 9.2 reflect these opposite effects, but nevertheless show that, unless variability aversion is large relatively to inequality aversion (see Figure 9.1), growth can be deemed intertemporally pro-poor in Indonesia during the period 1997–2007. The beneficial effect may even be regarded as substantial for some values of the parameters α and γ. For instance, with $\alpha = 3$ and $\gamma = 1$, we observe that the overall well-being shift and the mobility-as-equalizer effect have contributed to a decrease of 7.9 percentage points in the initial corresponding EDE gap. Compared with the maximum theoretical values of the $IPP_{\alpha,\gamma}$, our results underline significant progress with respect to poverty alleviation in Indonesia if we only consider the equalizing effects of mobility.

Table 9.3 shows that, taking an anonymous perspective, growth in Indonesia was unambiguously pro-poor during the whole period since the anonymous growth component AG is significantly positive.

---

[20] Cdf curves (not reported here but available upon request) are crossing and look very close for the years 1997 and 2000. The curve for the year 2007 is always lower for all income values.

[21] The same figures are reported for gross domestic product per capita in 2011 purchasing power parity by the World Bank.

Table 9.2 Values of the IPP Index for Indonesia, 1997–2007

	$\gamma = 1$	$\gamma = 2$	$\gamma = 3$	Max
$\alpha = 1$	0.00911	−0.00563	−0.0129	0.0279
	(0.00119)	(0.00119)	(0.0012)	(0.0008)
$\alpha = 2$	0.0479	0.0184	0.00286	0.0867
	(0.00282)	(0.00234)	(0.00245)	(0.0017)
$\alpha = 3$	0.0792	0.043	0.0225	0.134
	(0.00396)	(0.00326)	(0.0035)	(0.0022)

IPP = intertemporal pro-poorness.
Note: Bootstrapped standard errors in parentheses (200 replications).
Source: The authors.

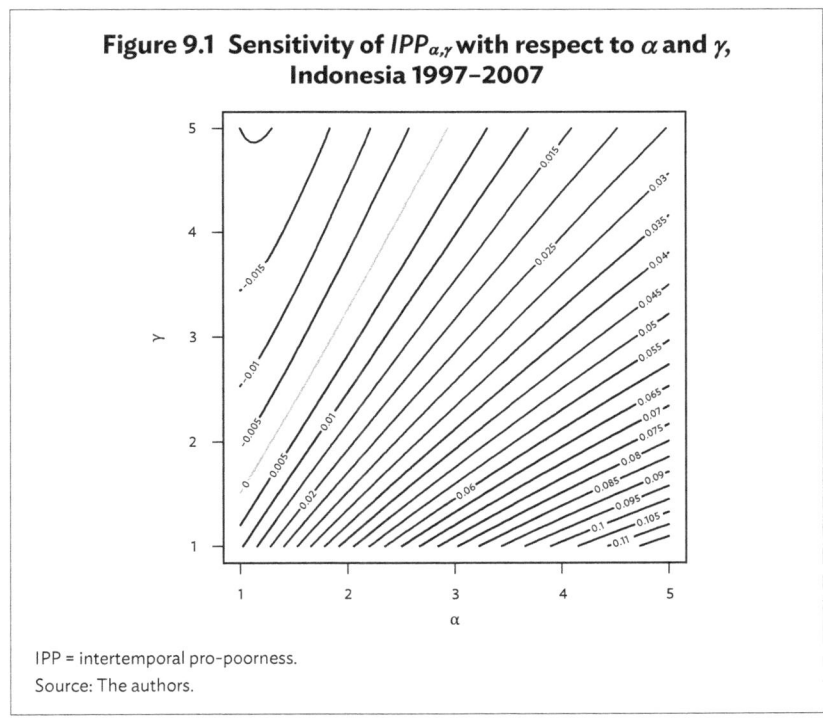

Figure 9.1 Sensitivity of $IPP_{\alpha,\gamma}$ with respect to α and γ, Indonesia 1997–2007

IPP = intertemporal pro-poorness.
Source: The authors.

However, that anonymous effect is rather small over a 10-year period. Once the effects of mobility on intertemporal poverty are taken into account (i.e. $\gamma \neq \alpha$), mobility plays a decisive role in determining the

Table 9.3 Decomposition into Anonymous (AG) and Non-anonymous (M) for Indonesia, 1997–2007

	AG	M		
		$\gamma=1$	$\gamma=2$	$\gamma=3$
$\alpha=1$	0.00911	0	−0.0147	−0.022
	(0.00122)	..	(0.000464)	(0.000686)
$\alpha=2$	0.0184	0.0295	0	−0.0155
	(0.00243)	(0.000842)	..	(0.00037)
$\alpha=3$	0.0225	0.0567	0.0206	0
	(0.00307)	(0.00181)	(0.000563)	..

Note: Bootstrapped standard errors in parentheses (200 replications).
Source: The authors.

sign of our intertemporal pro-poorness index. Indeed, the magnitude of the mobility sensitivity effect is relatively large in comparison with the anonymous growth component. This can be explained by the relatively low correlation between individual incomes in 1997 and 2000—Pearson's correlation coefficient is only 0.12 and becomes not significantly different from zero considering only those identified as poor from an intertemporal point of view—hence showing that mobility was high in the aftermath of the Asian crisis.[22]

This relatively high mobility associated with the first subperiod growth process explains why its contribution is relatively large (Table 9.4) though the cross-sectional income distributions are almost identical. With a marked aversion for extreme poverty ($\alpha=3$, for instance), the mobility-as-equalizer effect during the period 1997–2000 was a large contributor to observed intertemporal growth pro-poorness between 1997 and 2007.

Regarding the pattern of growth during the subperiod 2000–2007, the contribution has generally been positive, but it can be stressed that the magnitude of the contribution was relatively low compared with the first subperiod growth pattern. The results of a further decomposition into anonymous changes and mobility effects are presented in Table 9.5. It can be seen that changes in the average poverty gap have contributed little to growth pro-poorness. Consequently, the anonymous component

---

[22] Considering the subperiod 2000–2007, the two values for this correlation coefficient were respectively 0.43 and 0.04, both significantly different from zero.

Table 9.4 Subperiod Contributions to the IPP Index for Indonesia, 1997–2007

	$\gamma=1$		$\gamma=2$		$\gamma=3$	
	C^1	C^2	C^1	C^2	C^1	C^2
$\alpha=1$	0.00489	0.00423	−0.00573	0.000099	−0.0108	−0.00202
	(0.00127)	(0.00044)	(0.00125)	(0.00044)	(0.00118)	(0.00052)
$\alpha=2$	0.0325	0.0154	0.0109	0.00746	−0.000263	0.00312
	(0.00315)	(0.00091)	(0.00267)	(0.00075)	(0.00255)	(0.00083)
$\alpha=3$	0.0564	0.0228	0.0297	0.0134	0.0146	0.00794
	(0.00445)	(0.00142)	(0.00404)	(0.00107)	(0.00362)	(0.00094)

IPP = intertemporal pro-poorness.
Note: Bootstrapped standard errors in parentheses (200 replications).
Source: The authors.

of the IPP index is mostly explained by changes in cross-sectional gap inequalities between the poor. The relative size of the mobility-as-equalizer effect M^C with respect to the cost of individual income variability CV depends primarily on the chosen values for the parameters α and γ.

Rank mobility was effective during the considered period in Indonesia and our results (Table 9.6) show its significant influence on intertemporal pro-poorness when income variability sensitivity is low ($\gamma=1$). Our estimates finally show that changes in the cross-sectional relative distributions of gaps, net of the reranking effect, were significantly anti-poor from an intertemporal perspective and have been offset by the pro-poor effect of pure growth.

Table 9.5 Decomposition into Average Poverty Gap (ΔP^c), Cross-sectional Inequality (Δc^c), Difference between Intertemporal and Unitemporal Inequality (M^c), and Variability (CV) for Indonesia, 1997–2007

	$\gamma=1$				$\gamma=2$				$\gamma=3$			
	ΔP^c	Δc^c	M^c	CV	ΔP^c	Δc^c	M^c	CV	ΔP^c	Δc^c	M^c	CV
$\alpha=1$	0.00911	0	0	0	0.00911	0	0	-0.0147	0.00911	0	0	-0.022
	(0.00128)	..	..	..	(0.00123)	..	..	(0.00048)	(0.00115)	..	..	(0.00071)
$\alpha=2$	0.00911	0.0122	0.0266	0	0.00911	0.0122	0.0118	-0.0147	0.00911	0.0122	0.00353	-0.022
	(0.00116)	(0.00161)	(0.00073)	..	(0.00118)	(0.00151)	(0.00051)	(0.00044)	(0.00115)	(0.00158)	(0.00053)	(0.00067)
$\alpha=3$	0.00911	0.0187	0.0513	0	0.00911	0.0187	0.0299	-0.0147	0.00911	0.0187	0.0166	-0.022
	(0.00128)	(0.00332)	(0.00163)	..	(0.00123)	(0.00304)	(0.00111)	(0.00051)	(0.00123)	(0.00297)	(0.00094)	(0.00077)

Note: Bootstrapped standard errors in parentheses (200 replications).
Source: The authors.

Table 9.6 Decomposition into Inequality Change (I), Reranking (R), and Pure Growth (PG) for Indonesia, 1997–2007

	$\gamma=1$			$\gamma=2$			$\gamma=3$		
	I	R	PG	I	R	PG	I	R	PG
$\alpha=1$	0	0	0.0092	-0.00261	-0.0164	0.0135	-0.0042	-0.0243	0.0157
	..	..	(0.000481)	(0.000135)	(0.000289)	(0.000752)	(0.000209)	(0.00042)	(0.000821)
$\alpha=2$	-0.0156	0.0349	0.0287	-0.0218	0	0.0403	-0.0273	-0.0168	0.0471
	(0.000975)	(0.000601)	(0.00138)	(0.00148)	..	(0.0023)	(0.00165)	(0.000283)	(0.00231)
$\alpha=3$	-0.0393	0.0679	0.0507	-0.0502	0.0226	0.0708	-0.0608	0	0.0835
	(0.00242)	(0.00136)	(0.00252)	(0.0033)	(0.000403)	(0.0039)	(0.0037)	..	(0.00415)

Note: Bootstrapped standard errors in parentheses (200 replications).
Source: The authors.

9.6 Conclusion

Many studies have challenged the issue of testing the pro-poor nature of growth, but focusing on snapshot evaluations of poverty. In the present chapter, we argue that a comprehensive assessment of the pro-poor nature of a growth spell may require a shift from the traditional cross-sectional perspective to a longitudinal one, so as to account fully for the dynamics of individual deprivations over time.

For that purpose, a family of aggregate indexes of intertemporal pro-poorness is introduced. While previous studies are essentially based on the comparison of the initial and final income distributions, we suggest here performing an evaluation of growth pro-poorness using the joint distribution of income, hence considering more information than usually provided by marginal or conditional income distributions. The proposed family of intertemporal pro-poorness indexes aggregates "equally distributed equivalent" measures of the sequence of poverty gaps experienced by each individual in the population. An appealing feature of these indexes is their ability to capture both the cost of deprivation variability and the benefit of intertemporal equalization associated with mobility. Different decomposition procedures are also introduced to disentangle the different contributions of pure growth, cross-sectional and intertemporal inequalities, exchange mobility, and temporal variability in explaining the intertemporal pro-poorness of any growth process.

This measurement framework is illustrated using panel data for Indonesia between 1997 and 2007. Although the Indonesian population was severely hit by the Asian crisis in the late 1990s, we show that growth could be deemed pro-poor from an intertemporal perspective unless we assumed marked aversion with respect to individual income variability. Changes in cross-sectional poverty have positively contributed to these beneficial changes, but mobility was also substantial during the period of analysis and had noticeable effects on intertemporal poverty.

References

Alkire, S., and J. Foster. 2011. Understandings and Misunderstandings of Multidimensional Poverty Measurement. *Journal of Economic Inequality* 9: 289–314.

Atkinson, A. 1970. On the Measurement of Inequality. *Journal of Economic Theory* 2: 244–263.

Béranger, V., and F. Bresson. 2012. On the "Pro-poorness" of Growth in a Multidimensional Context. *Review of Income and Wealth* 58: 457–480.

Bossert, W., S. Chakravarty, and C. d'Ambrosio. 2012. Poverty and Time. *Journal of Economic Inequality* 10: 145–162.

Bourguignon, F. 2011. Non-anonymous Growth Incidence Curves, Income Mobility and Social Welfare Dominance. *Journal of Economic Inequality* 9: 605–627.

Bourguignon, F., and S. Chakravarty. 2003. The Measurement of Multidimensional Poverty. *Journal of Economic Inequality* 1: 25–49.

Bresson, F., and J.-Y. Duclos. 2015. Intertemporal Poverty Comparisons. *Social Choice and Welfare* 44: 567–616.

Busetta, A., and D. Mendola. 2012. The Importance of Consecutive Spells of Poverty: A Path-Dependent Index of Longitudinal Poverty. *Review of Income and Wealth* 58: 355–374.

Canto, O., C. Gradín, and C. del Rio. 2012. Measuring Poverty Accounting for Time. *Review of Income and Wealth* 58: 330–354.

Chakravarty, S., B. Dutta, and J. Weymark. 1985. Ethical Indices of Income Mobility. *Social Choice and Welfare* 2: 1–21.

DiNardo, J., N. Fortin, and T. Lemieux. 1996. Labors Market Institutions and the Distribution of Wages, 1973-1992: A Semiparametric Approach. *Econometrica* 64: 1001–1044.

Duclos, J.-Y. 2009. What is "Pro-poor"? *Social Choice and Welfare* 32: 37–58.

Duclos, J.-Y., A. Araar, and J. Giles. 2010. Chronic and Transient Poverty: Measurement and Estimation, with Evidence from China. *Journal of Development Economics* 91: 266–277.

Dutta, I., L. Roope, and H. Zank. 2013. On Intertemporal Poverty Measures: The Role of Affluence and Want. *Social Choice and Welfare* 41: 741–762.

Essama-Nssah, B. 2005. A Unified Framework for Pro-Poor Growth Analysis. *Economic Letters* 89: 216–221.

Essama-Nssah, B., and P. J. Lambert. 2009. Measuring Pro-Poorness: A Unifying Approach With New Results. *Review of Income and Wealth* 55: 752–778.

Fields, G. 2008. Income Mobility. In *The New Palgrave*, edited by L. Blume and S. Durlauf. Basingstoke, United Kingdom: Palgrave Macmillan.

Fields, G., and E. Ok. 1999. The Measurement of Income Mobility: An Introduction to the Literature. In *Handbook of Income Inequality Measurement*, edited by J. Silber. Dordrecht, The Netherlands: Kluwer Academic Publishers.

Fields, G. S. 2010. Does Income Mobility Equalize Longer-term Incomes? New Measures of an Old Concept. *The Journal of Economic Inequality* 8: 409–427.

Foster, J., J. Greer, and E. Thorbecke. 1984. A Class of Decomposable Poverty Measures. *Econometrica* 52: 761–766.

Foster, J., and J. Rothbaum. 2012. Mobility Curves: Using Cutoffs to Measure Absolute Mobility. Mimeo. Washington, DC: George Washington University.

Foster, J. E. 2009. A Class of Chronic Poverty Measures. In *Poverty Dynamics: Interdisciplinary Perspectives*, edited by T. Addison, D. Hulme, and R. Kanbur. Oxford, United Kingdom: Oxford University Press.

Friedman, M. 1962: *Capitalism and Freedom*. Chicago, IL: University of Chicago Press.

Grimm, M. 2007. Removing the Anonymity Asiom in Assessing Pro-Poor Growth. *Journal of Economic Inequality* 5: 179–197.

Hoy, M., and B. Zheng. 2011. Measuring Lifetime Poverty. *Journal of Economic Theory* 146: 2544–2562.

Jantti, M., and S. Jenkins. 2015. Income Mobility. In *Handbook of Income Distribution, Volume 2*, edited by A. Atkinson and F. Bourguignon. Duivendrecht, The Netherlands: Elsevier–North Holland.

Jenkins, S., and P. van Kerm. 2011. Trends in Individual Income Growth: Measurement Methods and British Evidence. IZA Discussion Paper 5510. Bonn, Germany: IZA Institute of Labor Economics.

Kakwani, N., and E. Pernia. 2000. What is Pro-Poor Growth? *Asian Development Review* 18: 1–16.

Kakwani, N., and H. Son. 2003. Pro-Poor Growth: Concepts and Measurement with Country Case Studies. *The Pakistan Development Review* 42: 417–444.

———. 2008. Global Estimates of Pro-Poor Growth. *World Development* 36: 1048–1066.

Palmisano, F., and V. Peragine. 2015. The Distributional Incidence of Growth: A Non-anonymous and Rank Dependent Approach. *Review of Income and Wealth* 61: 440–464.

Palmisano, F., and D. van de Gaer. 2016. History Dependent Growth Incidence: A Characterisation and an Application to the Economic Crisis in Italy. *Oxford Economic Papers* 68: 585–603.

Ravallion, M., and S. Chen. 2003. Measuring Pro-poor Growth. *Economics Letters* 78: 93–99.

Ruiz–Castillo, J. 2004. The Measurement of Structural and Exchange Mobility. *Journal of Economic Inequality* 2: 219–228.

Sen, A. 1976. Poverty: An Ordinal Approach to Measurement. *Econometrica* 44: 219–231.

Shorrocks, A. 2013. Decomposition Procedures for Distributional Analysis: A Unified Framework Based on the Shapley Value. *The Journal of Economic Inequality* 11: 99–126.

Son, H. H. 2004. A Note on Pro-Poor Growth. *Economic Letters* 82: 307–314.

Strauss, J., J. Witoelar, B. Sikoki, and A. Wattie 2009. The Fourth Wave of the Indonesian Family Life Survey (IFLS4): Overview and Field Report. RAND Labor and Population Working Paper WR-675/1-NIA/NICHD. Santa Monica, CA: RAND Corporation.

Appendix

Generalization to T periods

As mentioned in the main text, the decompositions provided in this chapter can be generalized to time horizons of $T > 2$ periods.

The first decomposition is obtained by adding and subtracting in (15) the EDE of periodic individual poverty as follows:

$$\underbrace{\Pi_\alpha(g_1) - \Pi_\alpha(G)}_{AG} + \underbrace{\Pi_\alpha(G) - \Pi_{\alpha,\gamma}(G)}_{M}.$$

To generalize the second decomposition, observe that (12) can be rewritten as:

$$\Pi_{\alpha,\gamma}(G) = \omega_1 P_1(g_1) + \omega_2 P_1(g_2) + \cdots + \omega_T P_1(g_T) + c_{\alpha,\gamma}(G) + \frac{1}{n}\sum_{i=1}^{n} c(g_{(i)}).$$

$\Pi_{\alpha,\gamma}$ can then be decomposed as:

$$\underbrace{\omega_2[P_1(g_1) - P_1(g_2)] + \omega_3[P_1(g_1) - P_1(g_3)] + \cdots + \omega_T[P_1(g_1) - P_1(g_T)]}_{\Delta P^c}$$

$$+ \underbrace{\omega_2[c_\alpha(g_1) - c_\alpha(g_2)] + \omega_3[c_\alpha(g_1) - c_\alpha(g_3)] + \cdots + \omega_T[c_\alpha(g_1) - c_\alpha(g_T)]}_{\Delta c^c}$$

$$+ \underbrace{\omega_1 c_\alpha(g_1) + \omega_2 c_\alpha(g_2) + \cdots + \omega_T c_\alpha(g_T) - c_{\alpha,\gamma}(G)}_{M^c}$$

$$+ \underbrace{\frac{1}{n}\sum_{i=1}^{n} c_{-\gamma}(g_{(i)})}_{CV}.$$

Lastly, when $T > 2$, the third decomposition can be obtained as:

$$\underbrace{\Pi_{\alpha,\gamma}(g_1) - \Pi_{\alpha,\gamma}(g^I)}_{I} + \underbrace{\Pi_{\alpha,\gamma}(g^I) - \Pi_{\alpha,\gamma}(g^{IR})}_{R} + \underbrace{\Pi_{\alpha,\gamma}(g^{IR}) - \Pi_{\alpha,\gamma}(G)}_{PG}.$$

Here, $g^I = (g_1, g_2^I, \ldots, g_T^I)$, where g_t^I denotes the counterfactual distribution of poverty gaps at time t obtained by preserving the same average poverty gaps and ranks as observed in the first period distribution. Similarly, $g^{IR} = (g_1, g_2^{IR}, \ldots, g_T^{IR})$, where g_t^{IR} denotes the counterfactual time-specific distribution of poverty gaps obtained by keeping the same average poverty gap as that of the first period distribution.

10

Spatial Dimensions of Expenditure Inequality in a Decentralizing Indonesia

Takahiro Akita and Sachiko Miyata*

10.1 Introduction

A number of studies have been conducted to analyze regional development dynamics and the evolution of interregional income inequalities in Indonesia as large differences in socioeconomic indicators persist among its regions and provinces due largely to unequal distributions of resource endowments, public infrastructure, and economic activities. The capital province of Jakarta, for example, has the largest per capita gross domestic product (GDP), followed by the resource-rich provinces of East Kalimantan, Riau, and Papua. Conflict-ridden North Maluku registers the smallest and the ratio of the largest to smallest per capita GDP is 18. With respect to the incidence of poverty, West Nusa Tenggara is the poorest province with a poverty headcount ratio of 20%, which is more than six times larger than the smallest headcount ratio.

To mitigate interregional inequalities and cope with periodic secessionist movements (e.g., the Free Aceh Movement and the Free Papua Movement), Indonesia embarked on its so-called "Big Bang" decentralization in 2001 (World Bank 2003; Fitrani, Hofman, and Kaiser 2005).[1] Under decentralization, the central government is responsible

---

* The authors are grateful to the Japan Society for the Promotion of Science for its financial support (Grant-in-Aid for Scientific Research 15K03458, 15K03473 and 18K01589).

[1] Two decentralization laws, Law 22 in 1999 on Regional Government and Law 25 in 1999 on the Fiscal Balance between the Central Government and the Regions, were promulgated in 1999 in the aftermath of the 1997/1998 financial crisis and the subsequent fall of the Suharto regime. They were implemented in 2001. Under Law 22/1999, the hierarchical governance system linking district (kabupaten and kota) governments to the central government was replaced by the system where district governments are granted considerably greater autonomy (Brodjonegoro and

for religious affairs, national defense and security, the judicial system, fiscal and monetary policy, foreign affairs, and other specially designated functions such as macroeconomic planning and national standards, while authority over and responsibilities for most other functions, including education, health management, and public works, are devolved to regional governments, particularly district (kabupaten and kota) governments (Brodjonegoro and Asanuma 2000; Alm, Aten, and Bahl 2001). Decentralization is expected to bring the government closer to the people, thereby ensuring an effective and efficient provision of public services in line with local needs and costs (Oates 1999). However, its effects on interregional inequalities remain uncertain. As the world's largest archipelagic country consisting of more than 13,000 islands with approximately 350 ethnic groups, whether administrative and fiscal decentralization increases or decreases interregional inequalities is one of the most important policy issues, which has attracted many researchers.

Most previous studies on interregional inequalities in Indonesia were based on regional accounts data, such as gross regional domestic product (GRDP) and gross regional domestic expenditure (GRDE), either at the provincial or district level.[2] However, even under fiscal decentralization, much of the revenues generated from oil and natural gas and certain proportions of revenues from other natural resources have still accrued to the central government, and thus GRDP and GRDE are not good indicators of regional welfare levels. The main objective of our study is to analyze spatial dimensions of inequality under decentralization in Indonesia from 1996 to 2010. Unlike most previous studies, however, our study employs household expenditure data rather than regional accounts data. By applying the hierarchical inequality decomposition method of the Theil indexes, developed by Akita (2003) and extended by Akita and Miyata (2013), to household expenditure data

---

Asanuma 2000; Silver, Azis, and Schroeder 2001). Under Law 25/1999, autonomous region subsidy (SDO: Subsidi Daerah Otonom) and presidential instruction development grants (Inpres: Instruksi Presiden) were abolished and replaced by intergovernment transfers including general allocation grants (DAU: Dana Alokasi Umum), special allocation grants (DAK: Dana Alokasi Khusus), and shared revenues from natural resources and taxes (DBH: Dana Bagi Hasil) (Lewis 2001; Silver, Azis, and Schroeder 2001). Currently, revenues of regional governments consist mainly of these intergovernment transfers, own source revenues (PAD: Pendapatan Asli Daerah), and regional government borrowings.

[2] See, for example, Esmara (1975), Uppal and Budiono (1986), Akita (1988), Hill (1992), Akita and Lukman (1995), Garcia–Garcia and Soelistianingsih (1998), Tadjoeddin, Suharyo, and Mishra (2001), Akita and Alisjahbana (2002), Akita (2003), Resosudarmo and Vidyattama (2006), Hill (2008), Hill, Resosudarmo, and Vidyattama (2008), Akita, Kurniawan, and Miyata (2011), Vidyattama (2013), and Hill and Vidyattama (2014).

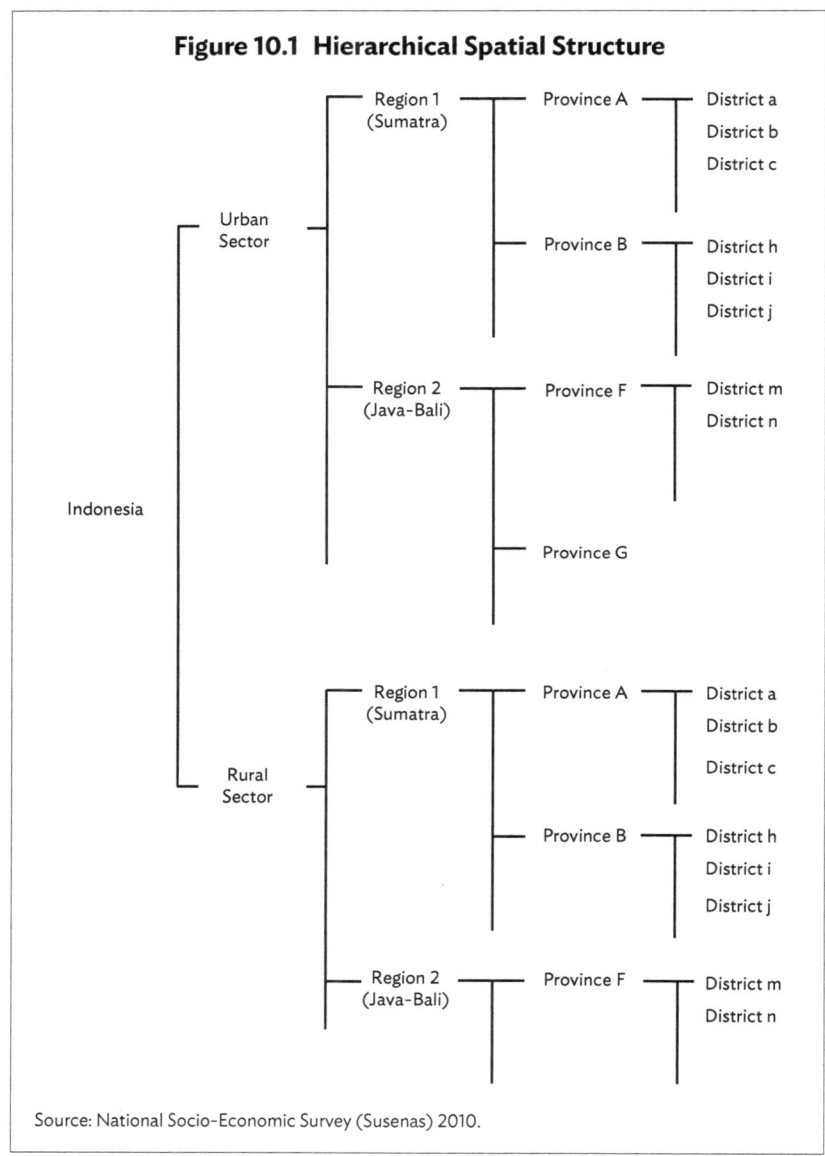

Figure 10.1 Hierarchical Spatial Structure

Source: National Socio-Economic Survey (Susenas) 2010.

from the National Socio-Economic Survey (Susenas), it examines the contributions of inequalities between spatial units to overall expenditure inequality among households in two hierarchical spatial frameworks, i.e., urban or rural sector–district and region–province–district frameworks (Figure 10.1).³ It does not explore the cause-and-effect relationship between decentralization and spatial inequalities; it tries to investigate the magnitudes and patterns of spatial inequalities under decentralization.

Among the questions that are addressed in this study are the following. First, to what extent is urban–rural disparity responsible for overall expenditure inequality? Have there been any changes in its contribution to overall inequality in the 1996–2010 period? Second, is there any difference between the urban and rural sectors in the magnitude of inequality among districts (*kabupatens* and *kotas*)? To what extent does inequality among districts contribute to overall expenditure inequality, after controlling for the urban–rural difference? Have there been any changes in its contribution to overall expenditure inequality? Third, what are possible factors of the changes in overall expenditure inequality? Fourth, among interregional, interprovincial and interdistrict inequalities, which spatial inequality contributes most to urban and rural expenditure inequalities? Here, interprovincial and interdistrict inequalities are defined, respectively, as a weighted average of interprovincial inequalities within regions and a weighted average of interdistrict inequalities within provinces.

10.2 Literature Review

When measuring spatial inequality, we should distinguish three approaches (Kanbur and Venables 2005; Milanovic 2005). The first approach concerns unweighted variation in per capita GDP across regions. It compares regions in terms of their per capita GDP, but ignores their population sizes. Regional convergence analysis advanced by Barro and Sala-i-Martin (1992, 1995), which examines regional differences in per capita GDP (sigma-convergence) and per capita GDP growth rates (beta-convergence), is an example of the first approach. In Indonesia, Garcia-Garcia and Soelistianingsih (1998), Shankar and Shah (2003), Resosudarmo and Vidyattama (2006), Hill, Resosudarmo, and Vidyattama (2008), and Vidyattama (2010, 2013) conducted a regional convergence analysis using provincial and/or district-level per capita GDP data and thus belong to this category. In contrast, the

---

³   In this study, Indonesia is divided into five regions: Sumatra, Java–Bali, Kalimantan, Sulawesi, and Eastern Indonesia, where Eastern Indonesia includes the provinces of East Nusa Tenggara, West Nusa Tenggara, Maluku, North Maluku, Papua, and West Papua. Provinces in each of these five regions are made up of districts (*kabupatens* and *kotas*). Provinces and districts have their own local governments and parliamentary bodies.

second approach concerns population-weighted variation in per capita GDP across regions. An analysis based on the population-weighted coefficient of variation introduced by Williamson (1965) is an example of the second approach. In Indonesia, studies using the population-weighted coefficient of variation include Esmara (1975), Uppal and Budiono (1986), Akita (1988), Akita and Lukman (1995), Tadjoeddin, Suharyo, and Mishra (2001), Shankar and Shah (2003), Akita, Pudji, and Miyata (2011), Vidyattama (2013), and Hill and Vidyattama (2014).

The third approach uses individuals or households as the unit of analysis. By using additively decomposable inequality measures, it assesses the contribution of income variation across spatial units, such as urban and rural locations, regions, provinces and districts, to income variation among all individuals or households. It is usually referred to as spatial decomposition of income inequality, where overall inequality is decomposed additively into the between-group and within-group inequality components. Shorrocks and Wan (2005) presented basic theoretical properties of spatial decomposition of income inequality. It also provided a review of empirical literature on spatial decomposition. One of the major findings from their study is that the magnitude of the between-group component tends to increase with the number of identified spatial units; however, it is very sensitive to how spatial units are defined; an urban–rural division, for example, appears to be more significant than an east–west or north–south division.

Our study follows the third approach, but it extends the approach and analyzes spatial dimensions of expenditure inequality in the two hierarchical spatial frameworks mentioned above. Some of the studies that employed the third approach in Indonesia are Akita and Lukman (1999), Skoufias (2001), Tadjoeddin, Suharyo, and Mishra (2001), Akita and Miyata (2008), Yusuf, Sumner, and Rum (2014), and Hayashi, Kataoka, and Akita (2014). Akita and Lukman (1999) used household expenditure data for 1987–1993 from *Susenas* to assess the contribution of interprovincial inequality to overall expenditure inequality among households as measured by the Theil indexes. Tadjoeddin, Suharyo, and Mishra (2001) conducted similar research based on updated *Susenas* data. According to these studies, interprovincial inequality accounted for around 15%–20% of overall expenditure inequality in the 1990s.

Akita and Lukman (1999) also conducted an inequality decomposition analysis by urban and rural areas and found that the contribution of urban and rural disparity to overall expenditure inequality was around 20%–25% for 1987–1993. Akita and Miyata (2008) and Hayashi, Kataoka, and Akita (2014) did an updated analysis, respectively, for 1996–2002 and 2008–2010. Using the Theil T index, these studies observed that the disparity between urban and rural areas accounted for 15%–20%

of overall expenditure inequality.[4] Hayashi, Kataoka, and Akita (2014) also conducted a decomposition analysis by five regions: Sumatra, Java–Bali, Kalimantan, Sulawesi, and Eastern Indonesia. They found that the between-region inequality was insignificant as it constituted merely 1% of overall inequality. This implies that much of the inequality among households is due to within-region inequalities. However, with its high within-region inequality and large population share, Java–Bali's within-region inequality was responsible for 65% of overall expenditure inequality. According to Yusuf, Sumner, and Rum (2014), the contributions of interprovincial inequality and urban–rural disparity to overall expenditure inequality appear to have been declining over the last 2 decades, though there are some fluctuations.

It should be noted that Akita (2003) and Akita and Alisjahbana (2002) conducted a hierarchical inequality decomposition analysis using the Theil indexes. However, these studies were based on district-level GDP data and assessed the contributions of interregional and interprovincial inequalities to inequality among districts in per capita GDP. Our study, on the other hand, uses household expenditure data to analyze the contributions of inequalities between spatial units, such as urban and rural locations, regions, provinces, and districts, to overall expenditure inequality among households.

10.3 Method and the Data

10.3.1 Method: Hierarchical Decomposition of Expenditure Inequality by the Theil Index L

To investigate spatial dimensions of expenditure inequality in Indonesia, we perform hierarchical inequality decomposition analyses based on household expenditure data from *Susenas*. The analyses are done using the Theil index L (i.e., the mean logarithmic deviation) in two hierarchical spatial frameworks: urban or rural sector–district and region–province–district frameworks.[5] The Theil index L belongs to the generalized

---

[4]   We should note that according to an alternative approach introduced by Elbers and others (2008), the disparity between urban and rural areas becomes more significant where the disparity is assessed against the maximum between-group inequality attainable given the number and relative sizes of the groups rather than overall inequality that is used in the conventional approach (Hayashi, Kataoka, and Akita 2014).

[5]   A decomposition analysis is conducted also using the Theil index T. But the results are similar to the ones by the Theil index L qualitatively, thus only the Theil L results are presented and discussed in this paper.

entropy class of inequality measures and satisfies several desirable properties as an inequality measure, such as anonymity, population homogeneity, income homogeneity, and the Pigue–Dalton principle (Anand 1983). In addition, it is additively decomposable by population subgroups as described below (Bourguignon 1979; Shorrocks 1980).

Hierarchical Inequality Decomposition Analysis: Urban or Rural Sector–District Framework

We consider a population of N households. In a hierarchical inequality decomposition analysis performed in the urban or rural sector–district framework, all households are first classified into the urban and rural sectors (sectors 1 and 2, respectively), where there are, respectively, N_1 and N_2 households. Households in each of the urban and rural sectors are then grouped into collectively exhaustive districts (*kabupatens* and *kotas*) according to their residential locations, where there are, respectively, m_1 and m_2 districts. We should note that m_1 is not equal to m_2, since in some districts there are no rural households (e.g., districts in Jakarta) and in some other districts there are no urban households. In 2010, there were 451 and 438 districts in the urban and rural sectors, respectively, while in Indonesia as a whole, there were 474 districts.

To obtain the hierarchical inequality decomposition equation, we let y_{sdh} and Y denote, respectively, the per capita expenditure of household h in district d in sector s and the total per capita expenditure of all households. Overall inequality in per capita expenditure (hereafter, referred to as expenditure inequality) is then measured by the Theil index L as follows:

$$L = \sum_s \sum_d \sum_h \left(\frac{1}{N}\right) \log\left(\frac{1/N}{y_{sdh}/Y}\right) \tag{1}$$

The Theil index L in Equation (1) can be decomposed hierarchically into the between-sector inequality component (L_{BS}) the within-sector between-district inequality component (L_{WSBD}) and the within-sector within-district inequality component (L_{WSWD}) as follows (for details, see Akita and Miyata 2013):

$$\begin{aligned} L &= L_{BS} + \sum_s \left(\frac{N_s}{N}\right) L_s \\ &= L_{BS} + \sum_s \left(\frac{N_s}{N}\right) L_{BDs} + \sum_s \sum_d \left(\frac{N_{sd}}{N}\right) L_{sd} \\ &= L_{BS} + L_{WSBD} + L_{WSWD}. \end{aligned} \tag{2}$$

where (N_{sd}), (L_s), (L_{BDs}) and (L_{sd}) are, respectively, the number of households in district d in sector s, expenditure inequality within sector s, expenditure inequality among districts in sector s, and expenditure inequality within district d in sector s. Equation (2) presents the hierarchical inequality decomposition equation in the urban or rural sector–district framework.

In this decomposition framework, the order of decomposition can be reversed, i.e., first by districts and then by urban and rural sectors. In other words, overall inequality can be decomposed hierarchically into the between-district component (L_{BD}), the within-district between-sector component (L_{WDBS}), and the within-district within-sector component (L_{WDWS}) as follows:

$$\begin{aligned} L &= L_{BD} + \sum_d \left(\frac{N_d}{N}\right) L_d \\ &= L_{BD} + \sum_d \left(\frac{N_d}{N}\right) L_{BSd} + \sum_d \sum_s \left(\frac{N_{ds}}{N}\right) L_{ds} \\ &= L_{BD} + L_{WDBS} + L_{WDWS} \end{aligned} \quad (3)$$

where N_d, L_d, L_{BSd} and L_{ds} are, respectively, the number of households in district d, expenditure inequality within district d, expenditure inequality between sectors in district d, and expenditure inequality within sector s in district d. It should be noted that L_{WDWS} in Equation (3) is the same as L_{WSWD} in Equation (2).

In connection with this multivariate decomposition method, Tang and Petrie (2009) suggested an alternative multivariate decomposition framework, called the non-hierarchical decomposition method, which, in the context of urban or rural sector and district, is given by:

$$L = L_{BS} + L_{BD} + L_{ISD} + L_{WSWD} \quad (4)$$

where L_{ISD} is the sector–district interaction term. Since $L_{WSBD} = L_{BD} + L_{ISD}$ from equations (2) and (4), the interaction term is given by $L_{ISD} = L_{WSBD} - L_{BD}$, which could be negative if expenditure inequality among districts is due in part to the disparity between the urban and rural sectors. The non-hierarchical method is, however, unable to examine the difference between the urban and rural sectors in the magnitude of inequality among districts, even though it could indicate the extent of the sector–district interaction. In contrast, the hierarchical decomposition method is able to analyze this urban–rural difference by conducting a one-stage decomposition analysis by district for each sector.

Hierarchical Inequality Decomposition Analysis: Region–Province–District Framework

Indonesia, as the world's largest archipelagic country, can be divided into the following five regions in accordance with its main islands: Sumatra, Java–Bali, Kalimantan, Sulawesi, and Eastern Indonesia. In a hierarchical decomposition analysis in the region–province–district framework, households in each of these five regions are grouped hierarchically into provinces and then districts (*kabupatens* and *kotas*) according to their residential locations. In contrast to the urban or rural sector–district decomposition framework, there is a natural hierarchical order, i.e., each region includes a distinct set of provinces and each province contains a distinct set of districts; thus, the order of decomposition cannot be reversed. Since there are differences in expenditure inequality between the urban and rural sectors, we perform this hierarchical decomposition analysis for the urban and rural sectors separately.[6] This enables us to analyze the structural differences between these two sectors with respect to the spatial dimensions of expenditure inequality.

We let y_{rpdh} denote the per capita expenditure of household h in district d in province p of region r. Overall expenditure inequality is then measured by the Theil index L as follows:

$$L = \sum_r \sum_p \sum_d \sum_h \left(\frac{1}{N}\right) \log\left(\frac{1/N}{y_{rpdh}/Y}\right) \qquad (5)$$

The Theil index L in Equation (5) can be decomposed hierarchically into the four inequality components: the between-region (L_{BR}), between-province (L_{BP}), between-district (L_{BD}), and within-district (L_{WD}) components as follows (for details, see Akita 2003 and Paredes, Iturra, and Marcelo 2016):

---

[6] Urban inequality is usually higher than rural inequality since the urban sector offers a much wider variety of jobs than the rural sector (see Eastwood and Lipton 2004). In Indonesia, urban expenditure inequality has been much larger than rural inequality.

$$L = L_{BR} + \sum_r \left(\frac{N_r}{N}\right) L_r$$

$$= L_{BR} + \sum_r \left(\frac{N_r}{N}\right) L_{B\Pr} + \sum_r \sum_p \left(\frac{N_{rp}}{N}\right) L_{rp} \quad (6)$$

$$= L_{BR} + \sum_r \left(\frac{N_r}{N}\right) L_{B\Pr} + \sum_r \sum_p \left(\frac{N_{rp}}{N}\right) L_{BDrp} + \sum_r \sum_p \sum_d \left(\frac{N_{rpd}}{N}\right) L_{rpd}$$

$$= L_{BR} + L_{BP} + L_{BD} + L_{WD}$$

where L_r, L_{rp}, L_{rpd}, $L_{B\Pr}$ and L_{BDrp} are, respectively, inequality within region r, inequality within province p of region r, inequality within district d in province p of region r, inequality between provinces in region r, and inequality among districts in province p of region r. Equation (6) presents the three-stage hierarchical decomposition equation in the region–province–district framework. It should be noted that the between-province (L_{BP}) and between-district (L_{BD}) components should be called, more precisely, the "within-region between-province" and "within-province between-district" components, respectively. But, for simplicity, the terms "between-province" and "between-district" components are used hereafter.

10.3.2 The Data

To investigate the spatial dimensions of expenditure inequality, this study employs monthly household expenditure data from 1996 to 2010, which are obtained from the National Socio-Economic Survey (*Susenas*) conducted by the Central Bureau of Statistics. Since 2011, *Susenas* has been conducted quarterly; therefore, our study does not include data from 2011 to avoid the comparability problem. We should note that *Susenas* has covered the whole country in the study period, but the province of Aceh is excluded from our data set due to missing data in some years.[7]

When Aceh is excluded, *Susenas* had 194,997 households in 1996, of which 62,426 and 132,571 were, respectively, in urban and rural areas. The sample size has increased since then, and in 2010, *Susenas* included 282,321 households, of which 126,785 and 155,536 were, respectively, in urban and rural areas. However, the *Susenas* sample

---

[7] *Susenas* was not conducted in Aceh due to political and security reasons for some years.

constitutes a constant proportion of the population of all households in Indonesia. According to the estimated number of households obtained using household sampling weights, urbanization has proceeded rapidly over the study period; in 1996, the urban sector constituted 36% of all households, but its share has risen prominently and in 2010 reached 50%. On the other hand, the shares of the five regions, i.e., Sumatra, Java–Bali, Kalimantan, Sulawesi, and Eastern Indonesia, have remained almost constant over the study period; Java–Bali has the largest share at 63%–65%, followed by Sumatra (17%–19%), Sulawesi (6%–7%), Eastern Indonesia (5%–6%), and Kalimantan (5%–6%).

Before 1999, Indonesia had 26 provinces including Aceh, but the number of provinces has increased gradually since the two decentralization laws were promulgated in 1999. In 1999, North Maluku was established by splitting Maluku. Subsequently in 2000, Bangka-Belitung Islands, Banten, and Gorontalo were created, respectively, by splitting South Sumatra, West Java, and North Sulawesi. Furthermore, between 2002 and 2004, Riau Islands, West Papua, and West Sulawesi were established by partitioning Riau, Papua, and South Sulawesi, respectively.[8] Finally, in 2012, North Kalimantan was established by splitting East Kalimantan. As a result, Indonesia now has 34 provinces. In this study, however, these new provinces are merged back into the provinces that they used to belong to; thus, a hierarchical inequality decomposition analysis based on Equation (6) is performed with 25 provinces excluding Aceh.

When Aceh is excluded, *Susenas* provided expenditure data for 283 districts (*kabupatens* and *kotas*) before 1999. However, the number of districts has risen significantly since the two decentralization laws were promulgated in 1999. In 2010 there were 474 in the dataset (Figure 10.2).[9] Before 1999, the Java–Bali region had the largest number of districts at 116, which was followed by Sumatra, Sulawesi, Eastern Indonesia, and Kalimantan, respectively, at 63, 40, 35, and 29 districts. Between 1999 and 2010, 191 districts were newly established by splitting existing districts, but much of the increase has occurred in non-Java–Bali regions. Particularly in Sumatra and Eastern Indonesia, the number of districts has increased substantially, and in 2010, Sumatra had the largest number of districts at 128, followed by Java–Bali, Eastern Indonesia, Sulawesi,

---

[8] Papua was formerly called Irian Jaya.

[9] In 2000 and 2002, the number of districts in the *Susenas* dataset fell slightly from the preceding year, but this is due mainly to missing observations for some districts in Maluku, North Maluku, and Papua.

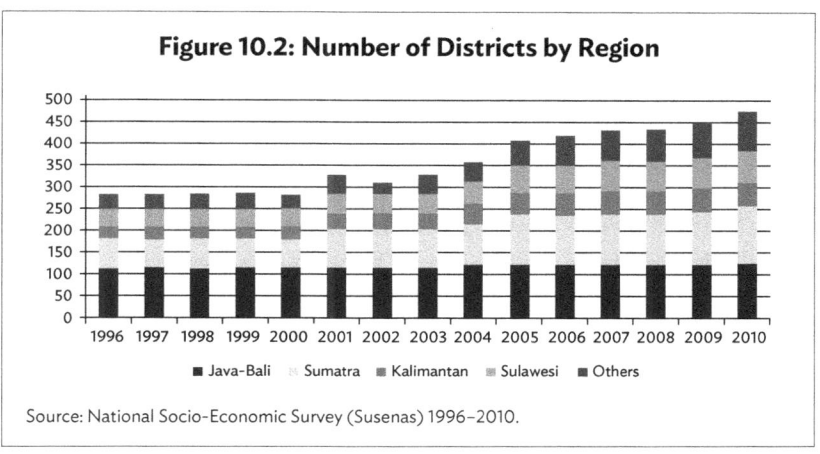

Figure 10.2: Number of Districts by Region

Source: National Socio-Economic Survey (Susenas) 1996–2010.

and Kalimantan, respectively, at 127, 91, 73, and 55 districts.[10] We should note that only 11 new districts were established in Java–Bali between 1999 and 2010, while the other four regions created 180 in total.[11] This suggests that the decentralization has had much larger effects on non-Java–Bali regions in terms of the establishment of new districts.[12]

In this study, newly established districts are not merged back into the districts from which they were separated. Therefore, some care should be taken in interpreting the result for the between-district inequality component in Equation (6). Given the distribution of household expenditures, the between-district inequality component, as measured by the Theil index L, depends on both the number of districts and differences in district expenditure means (Shorrocks and Wan 2005). It rises monotonically with the number of districts if new districts are created by dividing existing districts. However, the increment would get smaller and smaller as the number of districts increases. Since the total

---

[10] In Eastern Indonesia, much of the increase had occurred in Papua.

[11] According to Firman (2009, 2013), actually 164 *kabupatens* and 34 *kotas* had been newly established between 1999 and 2009 including the special province of Aceh, while general allocation funds (DAU) for districts had increased by 12% per year between 2001 and 2009. He argued that territorial splits have not only reinforced spatial fragmentation and local selfishness but also exerted an additional burden on the national budget and suggested a need to make mergers a more attractive option for the better provision of public services.

[12] Based on a district-level dataset for 1998–2004, Fitrani, Hofman, and Kaise (2005) found that new districts are mostly concentrated in off-Java provinces and typically those with low population densities and limited formal human capital.

number of districts is quite large at 300–500 after 2001, the effect of the increase on the between-district component would be small given the spatial distribution of household expenditures.

10.4 Empirical Results

10.4.1 Hierarchical Inequality Decomposition Analysis: Urban or Rural Sector–District Framework

Figure 10.3 shows the evolution of overall, urban, and rural inequalities and the disparity between the urban and rural sectors (i.e., the between-sector inequality) from 1996–2010, as measured by the Theil index L (for details, see Table A10.1 in the Appendix). Like most other Asian countries, rural inequality was much smaller than urban inequality (Eastwood and Lipton 2004), but except for a few years, its rising and declining trends were very similar to those of urban inequality. As discussed above, urbanization proceeded very rapidly over this period. Due mainly to this rising urbanization and relatively high urban inequality, the levels and trends of overall inequality very closely resemble those of urban inequality. Though much smaller in magnitude, the disparity between the urban and rural sectors had a similar trend pattern to overall inequality, and its contribution to overall inequality was around 15%–25%. And there was a large difference between the

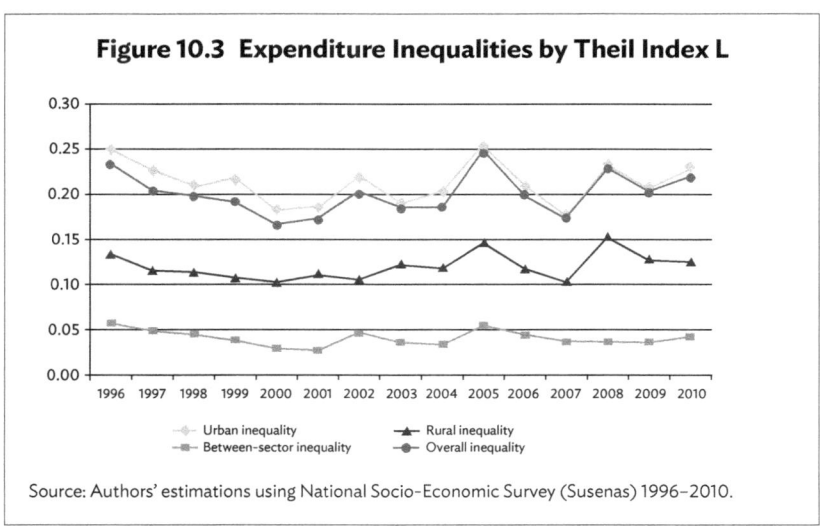

Figure 10.3 Expenditure Inequalities by Theil Index L

Source: Authors' estimations using National Socio-Economic Survey (Susenas) 1996–2010.

urban and rural sectors in the magnitude of inequality among districts (see Table A10.1 in the Appendix). After controlling for the urban–rural difference, inequality among districts accounted for 15%–25% of overall inequality (see Tables A10.1 and A10.2 in the Appendix).

Before the two decentralization laws were implemented, overall expenditure inequality showed a declining trend. But after reaching the bottom in 2000 at 0.17, it started to rise and peaked at 0.25 in 2005. After it had decreased to 0.17 in 2007, it started to increase again.[13] According to the result of the hierarchical decomposition analysis in the urban or rural sector–district framework (Figure 10.4), the main determinant of the decline in overall expenditure inequality until 2000 appears to have been the decrease in the urban–rural expenditure disparity (for details, see Tables A10.1 and A10.2 in the Appendix). Its contribution amounted to more than 40% of the decline, despite the fact that the urban–rural expenditure disparity accounted for around 20%–25% of overall inequality in the period. In passing, the urban–rural ratio in mean per capita expenditure was 2.0 in 1996, but fell to 1.6 in 2000. We should note that this period included the 1997–1998 financial crisis. As pointed out by Akita and Alisjahbana (2002), the financial crisis appears to have narrowed the disparity between the urban and rural sectors, particularly between major urban areas and other areas in Sumatra and Java–Bali.

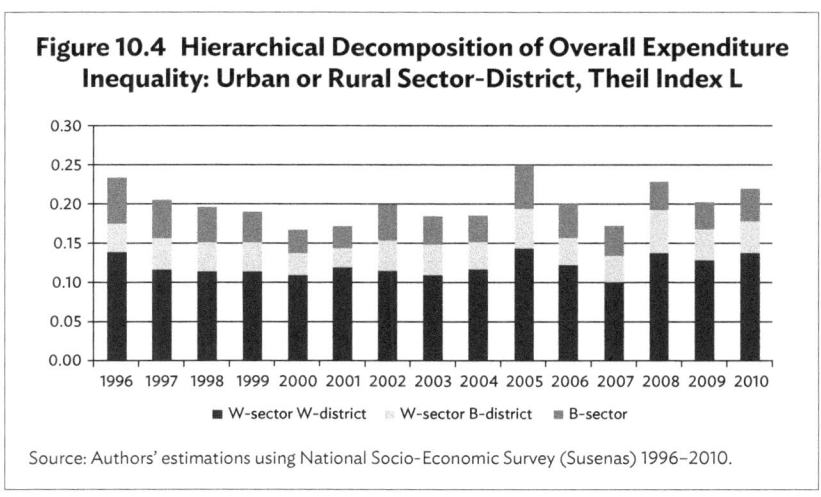

Figure 10.4 Hierarchical Decomposition of Overall Expenditure Inequality: Urban or Rural Sector-District, Theil Index L

Source: Authors' estimations using National Socio-Economic Survey (Susenas) 1996–2010.

---

[13] According to standard errors estimated by bootstrapping, the changes in expenditure inequality are all statistically significant.

This is because the effect of the crisis was borne disproportionately by these major urban areas due to their high reliance on the financial, non-oil and gas manufacturing, and construction sectors, which were hit hardest by the crisis.

On the other hand, the main determinant of the rise in overall expenditure inequality between 2000 and 2005 seems to have been the increase in the between-district inequality component in both the urban and rural sectors in addition to the rise in the urban–rural disparity (Table A10.1). Since the two decentralization laws were implemented in 2001, the number of districts has increased conspicuously, particularly in non-Java–Bali regions (Figure 10.2): while Java–Bali increased its districts from 117 to 124 between 2000 and 2005, the other four regions increased their districts notably from 167 to 283. This has raised, to some extent, the between-district inequality component, since, as discussed above, the between-district inequality component increases with the number of districts if new districts were established by splitting existing districts. While it is not possible to confirm the causal relationship in our study, one of the possible factors for the rise in inequality among districts would be fiscal decentralization, since the natural resources revenue sharing scheme has made natural-resource-abundant districts richer as compared with resource-poor districts.[14]

It should be noted that besides fiscal decentralization, rising domestic rice prices would be another factor behind the rapid rise in overall inequality, particularly from 2004 to 2005, since the price increase would have exerted a more detrimental effect on the poor than the rich (McCulloch 2008; Yusuf, Sumner, and Rum 2014). This is, in fact, indicated by the rise in the within-sector within-district inequality component, i.e., non-spatial component, since the hike in domestic rice prices is less likely to have spatial effects. From 2004 to

---

[14] Under the natural resources revenue sharing scheme introduced by Law 25/1999, regions (provinces and districts) receive 15% and 30% of oil and gas revenues, respectively, and 80% of the revenue from other natural resources (i.e., forestry, fishery, and general mining); with a few exceptions, of the amount allocated to the producing regions, 20% goes to the province, 40% goes to the producing districts, and the other 40% is shared equally among the nonproducing districts in the province (Brodjonegoro and Asanuma 2000; Brodjonegoro and Martinez–Vazquez 2004; Bahl and Tumennasan 2004). It should be noted that the special autonomous provinces of Aceh, West Papua, and Papua receive much higher shares of their oil and gas revenues (Agustina, Schulze, and Fengler 2012). On the other hand, under the tax revenue sharing scheme introduced also by Law 25/1999, regions (provinces and districts) receive 20% of the revenue from personal income tax, while they receive 90% and 80%, respectively, of the revenues from property tax and tax on the transfers of land and building ownership (Brodjonegoro and Asanuma 2000; Brodjonegoro and Martinez–Vazquez 2004).

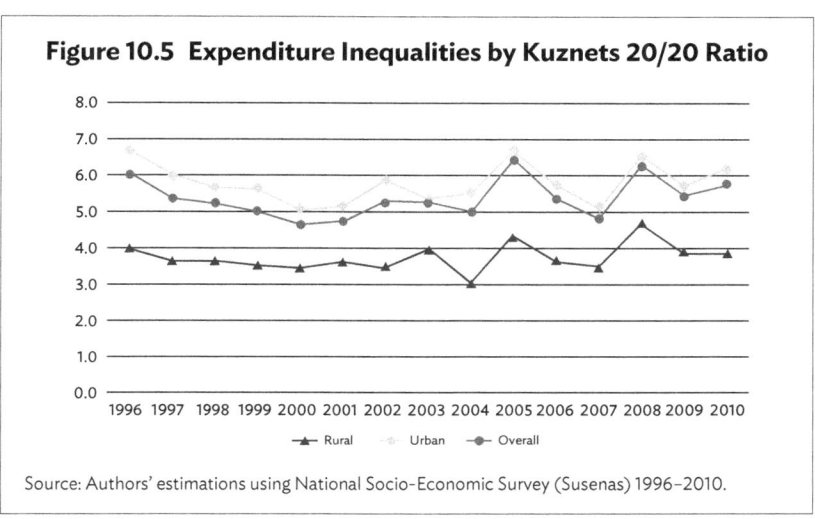

Figure 10.5 Expenditure Inequalities by Kuznets 20/20 Ratio

Source: Authors' estimations using National Socio-Economic Survey (Susenas) 1996–2010.

2005, the expenditure share of the richest 20% of households increased significantly, while the share of the poorest 20% decreased in both sectors. Thus, the ratio of the expenditure share of the richest 20% to that of the poorest 20% (Kuznets 20/20 ratio) rose notably, from 3.0 to 4.3 in the rural sector and from 5.5 to 6.7 in the urban sector (Figure 10.5).

Overall expenditure inequality declined substantially between 2005 and 2007. It seems that three inequality components in Equation (2), i.e., the between-sector, within-sector between-district, and within-sector within-district components, are equally responsible for the decrease, since their contributions to overall inequality remained almost constant over the period (Tables A10.1 and A9.2). This period corresponds to the period after the enactment of the two revised decentralization laws (i.e., Law 32/2004 and Law 33/2004).[15] Though

---

[15] In 2004, the two revised decentralization laws, i.e., Law 32/2004 on Regional Government and Law 33/2004 on the Fiscal Balance between the Central Government and the Regions, were enacted and replaced Law 22/1999 and Law 25/1999, respectively. Under Law 32/2004, the roles of provincial governments were strengthened: provincial governors, who are now elected by popular vote, not only guide and supervise the governance of their district governments but also coordinate the implementation of central government affairs in their provinces, while under Law 33/2004, which was fully implemented in 2008, the revenue shares of oil- and gas-producing regions (provinces and districts) increased slightly, to 15.5% and 30.5%, respectively, for oil and gas, and geothermal energy has been added in other natural resources (Soesastro and Atje 2005).

the effects of Law 32/2004, which redesigned the intergovernmental governance framework and strengthened the roles of provincial governments, is uncertain, the law might have exerted some effects on the decline in expenditure inequality.[16]

In 2005, the government reduced fuel subsidies and more than doubled domestic fuel prices.[17] The intention was not only to narrow the gap between domestic and international prices but also to reduce the burden on the national budget as fuel subsidies constituted a substantial portion of the budget (Mcleod 2008; Agustina, Schulze, and Fengler 2012; Howes and Davies 2014). At the same time, the government provided massive unconditional cash transfers to the poor (BLT) to compensate for the damage caused by the domestic fuel price increase (Sumarto and Suryahadi 2010).[18] While the gap between domestic and international fuel prices still existed, this policy package seems to have mitigated expenditure inequality in both the urban and rural sectors from 2005 to 2007.

After 2007, overall inequality started to rise again. Unlike the previous periods, however, the within-sector within-district inequality component, i.e., non-spatial component, was mostly responsible for the change, as it accounted for 80% of the increase. Its contribution to overall inequality rose from 59% to 64% over 2007–2010. Yusuf, Sumner, and Rum (2014) argued that large fuel subsidies would have increased inequality, since their impact on expenditures is known to have been regressive and thus they have had a dis-equalizing effect on household expenditures. They also argued that changes in formal labor market regulations, such as increasing minimum wages, rising retirement benefits, and the strengthening of labor unions, would have increased inequality, as the changes are likely to have benefited the rich disproportionately more than the poor. Since these factors were less

---

[16] From 2005 to 2007, the share of general and special allocation grants (DAU and DAK) in the total district government budget increased significantly, from 59% to 67%, while the proportion of the shared revenues from natural resources and taxes (DBH) declined from 24% to 17% (Lewis and Smoke forthcoming). DAU is widely referred to as an equalization grant and thought to have inequality-reducing effects, as opposed to DBH (Lewis 2001).

[17] The government raised the price of premium gasoline from Rp1,810 to Rp4,500 per liter. It also raised the price of kerosene from Rp700 to Rp2,000 per liter.

[18] An unconditional cash transfer program, known as BLT (Bantuan Langsung Tunai), was launched in October 2005. The government allocated more than half of the savings generated by the fuel subsidy cut to this cash transfer program. The BLT program provided poor households (more than a quarter of all households) with Rp300,000 per household every 3 months from the fourth quarter of 2005 to the third quarter of 2006 (Sumarto and Suryahadi 2010).

likely to have spatial effects, they might have had some bearing on the increase in the within-sector within-district component.

From 2007–2008, both rural and urban inequalities rose sharply (Figures 10.3 and 10.5) and this rapid rise was found to be uniform across districts as most districts recorded an increase in their within-district inequalities in both sectors. This suggests that non-spatial factors were mainly responsible for the rise. In this period, the world oil price rose sharply from around $60 per barrel to more than $90 per barrel, and this was accompanied by a rapid increase in the consumer price index inflation rate, from 6% in mid-2007 to more than 10% (McLeod 2008). Meanwhile, domestic fuel prices remained low owing to large fuel subsidies, and the gap between domestic and international fuel prices widened This has made domestic fuels much less expensive than other commodities. Since the rich consume much more energy, this has benefited the rich more than the poor. As mentioned above, the effect of fuel subsidies on expenditures was regressive, particularly under the situation where the difference between domestic and international fuel prices is large. Large fuel subsidies in this period thus appear to have raised expenditure inequality substantially. In October 2008, the government cut fuel subsidies again and raised fuel prices by 33% (Howes and Davies 2014).[19] At the same time, it introduced a social protection program, including unconditional cash transfers (BLT) and rice subsidies to the poor, to compensate for the domestic fuel price increase. This policy package would have lowered expenditure inequalities slightly between 2008 and 2009, particularly in the rural sector. However, a large gap has still existed between domestic and international fuel prices, and it was not until July 2013 that the government raised domestic fuel prices (Howes and Davies 2014).

10.4.2 Hierarchical Inequality Decomposition Analysis in the Urban and Rural Sectors: Region–Province–District Framework

According to Table .A10.2 in the Appendix, which provides the result of a non-hierarchical decomposition analysis, the sector–district interaction term has a large negative value (see Equation [4]). This indicates that expenditure inequality among districts is due in part to the expenditure disparity between the urban and rural sectors. Therefore, an inequality

---

[19] The government increased the price of premium gasoline from Rp4,500 to Rp6,000 per liter and kerosene from Rp2,000 to Rp2,500 per liter. However, this fuel price increase did not last owing to an oil price decrease.

decomposition analysis needs to be conducted for each sector separately, not only to examine the urban–rural difference in the magnitude of inequality among districts but also to analyze the contributions of interregional and interprovincial inequalities in each of the urban and rural sectors. In this section, we perform a hierarchical decomposition analysis in the region–province–district framework to investigate the spatial dimensions of expenditure inequality for each sector (see Equation [6]).

Figures 10.6a and 10.6b present the results of the region–province–district hierarchical decomposition analysis in the rural and urban sectors, respectively. Several observations emerge from the analysis. While there were some fluctuations over the study period, around 25%–30% of urban inequality and around 15%–25% of rural inequality are explained by inequality among districts, i.e., the sum of the between-region, between-province, and between-district inequality components.[20] In other words, inequality among districts constitutes a significant portion of expenditure inequality in both the urban and rural sectors. However, the contribution of the disparity between the five regions (the between-region component) is very small. Particularly in the urban sector, it is almost negligible as it amounts to merely

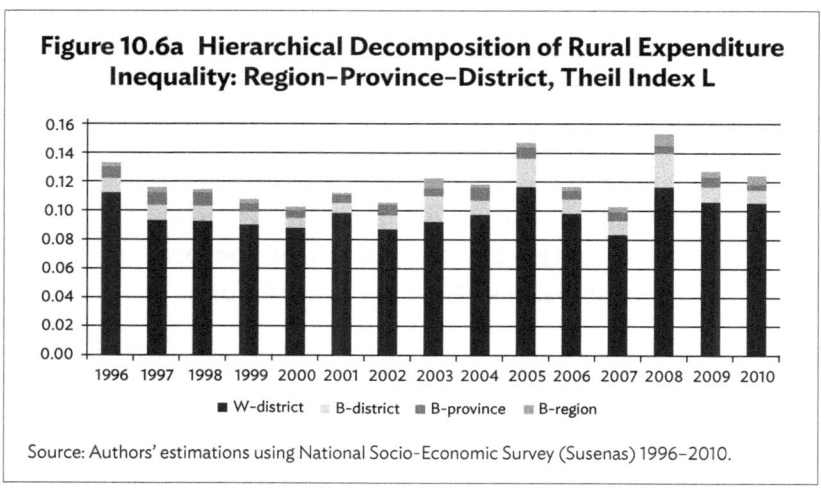

Figure 10.6a Hierarchical Decomposition of Rural Expenditure Inequality: Region–Province–District, Theil Index L

Source: Authors' estimations using National Socio-Economic Survey (Susenas) 1996–2010.

---

[20] As mentioned in the methodology section, the between-province and between-district inequality components refer, respectively, to the within-region between-province and within-province between-district components.

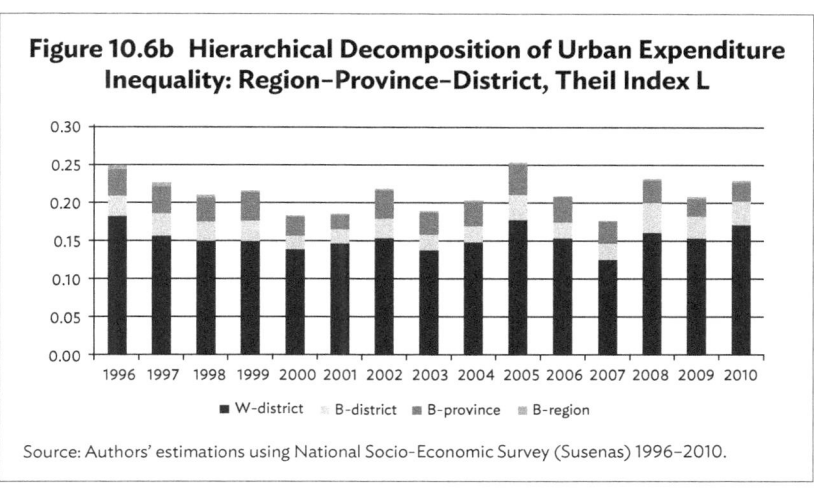

Figure 10.6b Hierarchical Decomposition of Urban Expenditure Inequality: Region–Province–District, Theil Index L

Source: Authors' estimations using National Socio-Economic Survey (Susenas) 1996–2010.

0%–2% of urban inequality; for the five regions, the ratio of the largest to smallest mean per capita expenditure is only around 1.2–1.4. On the other hand, the disparity between the five regions constitutes 1%–5% of rural inequality, and it appears to have been increasing over the study period.

On the other hand, the between-province and between-district inequality components have much larger contributions in both the urban and rural sectors. Their combined contribution is 25%–30% to urban inequality and 10%–20% to rural inequality. If a comparison is made between these two components, the between-district component has played a more important role in the rural sector. Its contribution amounts to 5%–15% of rural inequality. In contrast, the between-province component had played a more important role in urban inequality, though this was up until 2007 and the between-district component overtook the between-province component in 2008. We should note, however, that much of the urban sector's between-province inequality component is due to interprovincial inequality in the Java–Bali region, particularly the disparity between Jakarta and the other Java–Bali provinces, as Java–Bali's interprovincial inequality accounts for more than 80% of the between-province component in the urban sector. Jakarta, the largest metropolitan area, has the largest mean per capita expenditure among 26 provinces in Indonesia; its mean per capita expenditure has been more than twice as large as the smallest (registered by Central Java) in the Java–Bali region. If Jakarta and its adjacent province (West Java) were merged and treated as one province, Java–Bali would have a much smaller disparity between provinces, making the between-province inequality component smaller than the between-district component.[21]

While spatial inequality constitutes a significant portion of expenditure inequality among households, the contribution of the within-district inequality component is much larger, amounting to 70%–75% of urban inequality and 75%–85% of rural inequality. Figures 10.7a and 10.7b present, respectively, frequency distributions of districts in the rural and urban sectors with respect to within-district inequality in 2010, where districts are classified into the Western and Eastern regions. The Western region includes Sumatra and Java–Bali, while the Eastern region includes Kalimantan, Sulawesi, and Eastern Indonesia.[22] The Eastern region has a higher mean within-district inequality than the Western region in both rural and urban areas. The Eastern region also has a larger variation than the Western region. In Eastern rural areas, most of the high-inequality districts (inequality above 0.20) are concentrated in Eastern Indonesia, particularly in the province of Papua (11 out of 15 high-inequality districts), while in Eastern urban areas, 47 high-inequality districts are scattered over Eastern provinces. On the other hand, more than 90% of Western rural districts have inequalities smaller than 0.15 and only two Western rural districts are high-inequality districts (inequality above 0.20). In Western urban areas, three-quarters of the districts have inequality in the range of 0.10–0.20 and half of high-inequality districts are concentrated in the provinces of Jakarta, West Java, and Central Java.

Though it is not the task of our study to explore factors determining expenditure inequalities within urban and rural areas, education and occupation of household head appear to have been the main factors. According to randomly selected urban and rural districts from the 2010 *Susenas* sample, educational and occupational differences constitute 20%–30% of inequalities within urban and rural districts. However, there are large variations in the contributions of these factors among districts, due perhaps to social, economic, and cultural differences.

---

[21] Akita and Lukman (1995) indicated this point, though they employed the provincial GDP data to measure interprovincial inequalities.

[22] In the Western region, there are 221 districts in the rural sector and 254 districts in the urban sector; in the Eastern region, the rural sector has 217 districts and the urban sector 197 districts.

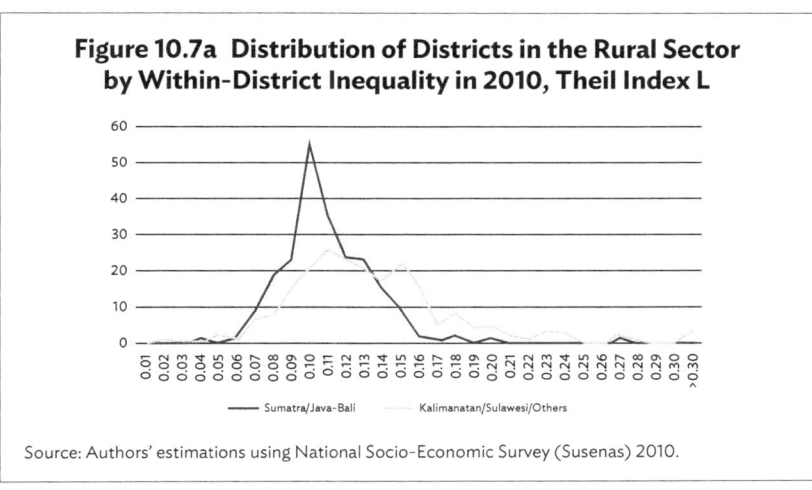

Figure 10.7a Distribution of Districts in the Rural Sector by Within-District Inequality in 2010, Theil Index L

Source: Authors' estimations using National Socio-Economic Survey (Susenas) 2010.

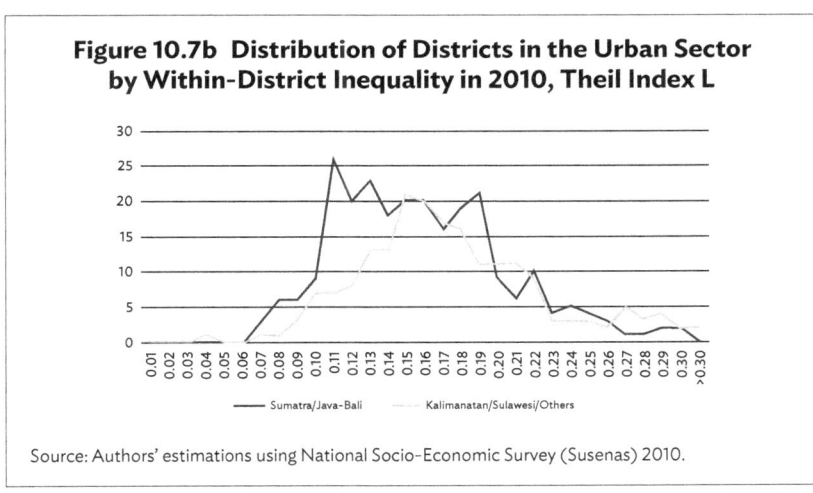

Figure 10.7b Distribution of Districts in the Urban Sector by Within-District Inequality in 2010, Theil Index L

Source: Authors' estimations using National Socio-Economic Survey (Susenas) 2010.

10.5 Conclusions

Based on the National Socio-Economic Survey (*Susenas*) from 1996 to 2010, this study analyzed spatial dimensions of inequality under decentralization in Indonesia using the hierarchical decomposition method of the Theil index. Unlike most previous studies, it used household expenditure data rather than regional accounts data to measure spatial inequalities as the former is considered a better indicator of regional welfare levels. The following summarizes the major findings. First, due mainly to rising urbanization and relatively high urban inequality, the levels and trends of overall expenditure inequality resemble very closely those of urban inequality. Urban–rural disparity has a similar trend pattern, and its contribution to overall inequality is around 15%–25%. Second, a large difference exists between urban and rural areas in the magnitude of inequality among districts (*kabupatens* and *kotas*). After controlling for the urban–rural difference, the inequality accounts for 15%–25% of overall expenditure inequality.

Third, the main determinant of the decline in overall expenditure inequality until 2000 appears to have been the decrease in urban–rural disparity. The 1997–1998 financial crisis seems to have narrowed the disparity, as the effect was borne disproportionately by major urban areas. Fourth, rising overall inequality from 2000 to 2005 seems to have been due to the increase in inequality among districts in both urban and rural areas. While the increasing number of districts under the "Big-Bang" decentralization has raised the inequality to some extent, one of the possible factors would be fiscal decentralization, since the natural resources revenue sharing scheme has made natural-resource-abundant districts richer as compared with resource-poor districts.

Fifth, all inequality components seem to be equally responsible for the decrease in overall inequality from 2005 to 2007. While the effects of the 2004 revised decentralization laws remain ambiguous, the revision might have exerted some effects on the decline. Meanwhile, a drastic reduction of fuel subsidies in 2005 accompanied by a compensation package may have reduced expenditure inequality in both urban and rural areas. Though we do not claim a direct causal relationship of a fuel subsidy reduction since there are various other potential factors that could be behind the decline of inequality during this period, we believe the effect of policy change in fuel subsidy was not negligible. Sixth, the non-spatial component (i.e., within-district inequality component) is mostly responsible for the rise in overall inequality from 2007 to 2010, as it accounts for 80% of the increase. Among others, changes in formal labor market regulations would have increased inequality as the changes are likely to have benefited the rich disproportionately more than the poor. Low domestic fuel prices owing to sustained large fuel subsidies may also have raised inequality since they have benefited the rich, who consume much more energy. While a cut in fuel subsidies accompanied by a compensation package in 2008 would have lowered inequality slightly, the increasing trend seems to have persisted. Finally, in both urban and rural areas, inequality among districts constitutes a significant portion of expenditure inequality as it accounts for 25%–30% of urban inequality and 15%–

25% of rural inequality. However, disparity between Sumatra, Java–Bali, Kalimantan, Sulawesi, and Eastern Indonesia is almost negligible. Meanwhile, inequalities between districts within provinces seem to have been playing an increasingly important role in both urban and rural inequalities.

To mitigate spatial inequalities and to cope with periodic secessionist movements, the government embarked on "Big-Bang" decentralization in the aftermath of the 1997/1998 financial crisis and the subsequent fall of the Suharto regime. However, the effects of the decentralization remain uncertain and large inequalities still exist between provinces and districts. According to district-level data from *Susenas*, the ratio of the largest to smallest mean per capita expenditure was 6.8 in 2010, compared with 6.3 in 1996. If nominal expenditure data are adjusted for price differentials across districts, the inequalities will be reduced to some extent, but not substantially.

As Akita, Kurniawan, and Miyata (2011) suggested, there are three major factors of spatial inequalities in Indonesia. The first is the uneven spatial distribution of immobile natural resources. Though this has become less prominent due to the declining role of mining activities in the national economy, the resource-rich provinces of Riau, East Kalimantan, and West Papua still have relatively high mean per capita expenditure. The second is the primacy of Jakarta and its adjacent districts, i.e., Bogor, Depok, Tangerang, and Bekasi (usually abbreviated as Jabodetapek). Under globalization and economic liberalization, Jabodetapek has nurtured agglomeration economies as the center of politics and economy. Its mean per capita expenditure is more than twice as large as the national average. As pointed out by Hill, Resosudarmo, and Vidyattama (2008), the regions that have easier access to the global economy, such as Jabodetapek, appear to have performed much better than those that have poor access. The third factor is related to the industry structure of Indonesia: the uneven spatial distribution of resource-based manufacturing industries such as wood processing and plantation- and mineral-based industries in Sumatra, Kalimantan, and Eastern Indonesia, as these industries tend to be located closer to areas where raw materials are available. There are other factors that could be responsible for spatial inequality such as migration. For example, given the increase in economic agglomeration in urban areas observed, such as in the Jabodetapek area, a substantial number of people migrated to urban areas seeking jobs.[23] Though gradual structural transformation away from the primary sector has been observed overall at the national

---

[23] Internal migration versus spatial inequality is an important issue in itself. However, it is beyond the scope of this study.

level, the spatial inequalities still continue to persist in Indonesia due to these possible factors.

Given uneven spatial distributions of resource endowments, public infrastructure, and economic activities, some spatial inequalities are inevitable from the efficiency point of view. Nevertheless, sustained efforts are necessary to reduce spatial inequalities to facilitate national unity, cohesion, and stability. In a geographically and culturally diverse archipelagic country where natural resources and economic activities are unevenly distributed, the government needs to accelerate infrastructure development, particularly development of transportation networks.

Indonesia is facing a major infrastructure deficit (Ray and Ing 2016). In the road transport sector, the number of motor vehicles increased conspicuously by 12% per year between 1970 and 2013 owing to rapid motorization, while the total length of roads (national, provincial, and district) grew by only 4% per year in the same period (McCawley 2015). Furthermore, due to poor construction quality, overloading, and poor maintenance, roads tend to have short asset lives (Ray and Ing 2016). In the rail transport sector, on the other hand, the total number of passengers grew by 3.5% per year between 1970 and 2013, but Java accommodates much of the railway system and many of its main railway lines remain single-track (McCawley 2015). Poor transport connectivity would not only weaken the competitiveness of the national economy but also facilitate disparities among regions. Recently, infrastructure policy has been a major concern among economic policy makers in Indonesia. Fortunately, in 2015, the world oil price declined notably, from above $100 to less than $50 per barrel; this enabled the government to shift its budget from fuel subsidies to infrastructure spending. Given the limited amounts of financial resources, however, coordinated efforts are imperative among public and private sectors based on a strategic long-term plan to promote infrastructure development.

This study is not without its limitations. First, it employed nominal expenditure data from *Susenas*. But as there are price differentials across regions, it is preferable that nominal expenditures are adjusted for price differentials to examine real disparities across spatial units. One of our future studies will be to estimate spatial inequalities using price adjusted expenditure data. Second, it is not possible for our study to analyze the causal relationship between decentralization and spatial inequalities. Further empirical research, perhaps using regional panel data, is necessary to explore the causal relationship. Third, our study did not include the period after 2010. According to Yusuf, Sumner, and Rum (2014) and Yusuf and Sumner (2015), expenditure inequality has increased further, and in 2013 the Gini coefficient had risen to

0.41, from 0.33 in 2001. This is an alarming level considering the fact that inequality is measured by expenditure rather than income data. Although the Gini coefficient stabilized at around 0.41 between 2013 and 2015, due perhaps to the end of the commodity boom (Yusuf and Sumner 2015), it is still very high by international standards. It would be interesting, therefore, to examine spatial dimensions of expenditure inequality after 2010.

References

Agustina, C., W. Fengler, and G. Schulze. 2012. The Regional Effects of Indonesia's Oil and Gas Policy: Options for Reform. *Bulletin of Indonesian Economic Studies* 48(3): 369–397.

Akita, T. 1988. Regional Development and Income Disparities in Indonesia. *Asian Economic Journal* 2(2): 165–191.

———. 2003. Decomposing Regional Income Inequality in China and Indonesia using Two-stage Nested Theil Decomposition Method. *The Annals of Regional Science* 37(1): 55–77.

Akita, T., and A. Alisjahbana. 2002. Regional Income Inequality in Indonesia and the Initial Impact of the Economic Crisis. *Bulletin of Indonesian Economic Studies* 38(2): 201–222.

Akita, T., and R. Lukman. 1995. Interregional Inequalities in Indonesia: A Sectoral Decomposition Analysis for 1975–92. *Bulletin of Indonesian Economic Studies* 31: 61–81.

———. 1999. Spatial Patterns of Expenditure Inequalities in Indonesia: 1987, 1990, and 1993. *Bulletin of Indonesian Economic Studies* 35(2): 65–88.

Akita, T., and S. Miyata. 2008. Urbanization, Educational Expansion, and Expenditure Inequality in Indonesia in 1996, 1999, and 2002. *Journal of the Asia Pacific Economy* 13(2): 147–167.

———. 2013. The Roles of Location and Education in the Distribution of Economic Wellbeing in Indonesia: Hierarchical and Non-hierarchical Decomposition Analyses. *Letters in Spatial and Resource Sciences* 6(3): 137–150.

Akita, T., P. Kurniawan, and S. Miyata. 2011. Structural Changes and Regional Income Inequality in Indonesia: A Bi-dimensional Decomposition Analysis. *Asian Economic Journal* 25(1): 55–77.

Alm, J., R. Aten, and R. Bahl. 2001. Can Indonesia Decentralize Successfully? Plans, Problems and Prospects. *Bulletin of Indonesian Economic Studies* 37(1): 83–102.

Anand, S. 1983. *Inequality and Poverty in Malaysia: Measurement and Decomposition*. New York, NY: Oxford University Press.

Bahl, R., and B. Tumennasan. 2004. How Should Revenues from Natural Resources be Shared in Indonesia? In *Reforming Intergovernmental Fiscal Relations and the Rebuilding of Indonesia*, edited by J. Alm, J. Martinez-Vazquez, and S. Mulyani Indrawati. Cheltenham, United Kingdom: Edward Elgar.

Barro, R., and X. Sala-i-Martin. 1992. Convergence. *Journal of Political Economy* 100(2): 223–251.

———. 1995. *Economic Growth*. New York, NY: McGraw Hill.

Bourguignon, F. 1979. Decomposable Income Inequality Measures. *Econometrica* 47(4): 901–920.
Brodjonegoro, B., and J. Martinez-Vazquez. 2004. An Analysis of Indonesia's Transfer System: Recent Performance and Future Prospects. In *Reforming Intergovernmental Fiscal Relations and the Rebuilding of Indonesia*, edited by J. Alm, J. Martinez-Vazquez, and S. Mulyani Indrawati. Cheltenham, United Kingdom: Edward Elgar.
Brodjonegoro, B., and S. Asanuma. 2000. Regional Autonomy and Fiscal Decentralization in Democratic Indonesia. *Hitotsubashi Journal of Economics* 41(2): 111–122.
Eastwood, R., and M. Lipton. 2004. Rural and Urban Income Inequality and Poverty: Does Convergence Between Sectors Offset Divergence Within Them? In *Inequality, Growth, and Poverty in an Era of Liberalization and Globalization*, edited by G. A. Cornia. Oxford, United Kingdom: Oxford University Press.
Elbers, C., P. Lanjouw, J. Mistiaen, and B. Ozler. 2008. Reinterpreting Between-group Inequality. *Journal of Economic Inequality* 6(3): 231–245.
Esmara, H. 1975. Regional Income Disparities. *Bulletin of Indonesian Economic Studies* 11: 41–57.
Firman, T. 2009. Decentralization Reform and Local-government Proliferation in Indonesia. *Review of Urban and Regional Development Studies* 21(2/3): 143–157.
_____. 2013. Territorial splits (*Pemekaran Daerah*) in decentralizing Indonesia, 2000–2012: Local Development Drivers or Hindrance? *Space and Polity* 17(2): 180–196.
Fitrani, F., B. Hofman, and K. Kaiser. 2005. Unity in Diversity? The Creation of New Local Governments in a Decentralizing Indonesia. *Bulletin of Indonesian Economic Studies* 41(1): 57–79.
Garcia-Garcia, J., and L. Soelistianingsih. 1998. Why do Differences in Provincial Incomes Persist in Indonesia? *Bulletin of Indonesian Economic Studies* 34(1): 95–120.
Hayashi, M., M. Kataoka, and T. Akita. 2014. Expenditure Inequality in Indonesia, 2008–2010: A Spatial Decomposition Analysis and the Role of Education. *Asian Economic Journal* 28(4): 389–411.
Hill, H. 1992. Regional Development in a Boom and Bust Petroleum Economy: Indonesia since 1970. *Economic Development and Cultural Change* 40(2): 351–380.
_____. 2008. Globalization, Inequality, and Local-level Dynamics: Indonesia and the Philippines. *Asian Economic Policy Review* 3(1): 2–61.
Hill, H., and Y. Vidyattama. 2014. Hares and Tortoises: Regional Development Dynamics in Indonesia. In *Regional Dynamics in a*

Decentralized Indonesia, edited by H. Hill. Singapore: Institute of South East Asian Studies.

Hill, H., B. Resosudarmo, and Y. Vidyattama. 2008. Indonesia's Changing Economic Geography. *Bulletin of Indonesian Economic Studies* 44(3): 407–435.

Howes, S., and R. Davies. 2014. Survey of Recent Developments. *Bulletin of Indonesian Economic Studies* 50(2): 157–183.

Kanbur, R., and A. Venables. 2005. Spatial Inequality and Development. In *Spatial Inequality and Development*, edited by R. Kanbur and A. Venables. New York, NY: Oxford University Press.

Lewis, B. 2001. The New Indonesian Equalization Transfer. *Bulletin of Indonesian Economic Studies* 37(3): 325–343.

Lewis, B., and P. Smoke. Forthcoming. Intergovernmental Fiscal Transfers and Local Incentives and Responses: The Case of Indonesia. *Fiscal Studies*. DOI: 10.1111/1475-5890.12080.

McCawley, P. 2015. Infrastructure Policy in Indonesia, 1965–2015: A Survey. *Bulletin of Indonesian Economic Studies* 51(2): 263–285.

McCulloch, N. 2008. Rice Prices and Poverty in Indonesia. *Bulletin of Indonesian Economic Studies* 44(1): 45–63.

Mcleod, R. 2008. Survey of Recent Developments. *Bulletin of Indonesian Economic Studies* 44(2): 183–208.

Milanovic, B. 2005. Half a World: Regional Inequality in Five Great Federations. *Journal of the Asia Pacific Economy* 10(4): 408–445.

Oates, W. 1999. An Essay on Fiscal Federalism. *Journal of Economic Literatures* 37(3): 1120–1149.

Paredes, D., V. Iturra, and M. Lufin. 2016. A Spatial Decomposition of Income Inequality in Chili. *Regional Studies* 50(5): 771–789.

Ray, D., and L. Ing. 2016. Survey of Recent Developments: Addressing Indonesia's Infrastructure Deficit. *Bulletin of Indonesian Economic Studies* 52(1): 1–25.

Resosudarmo, B., and Y. Vidyattama. 2006. Regional Income Disparity in Indonesia: A Panel Data Analysis. *ASEAN Economic Bulletin* 23(1): 31–44.

Shankar, R., and A. Shah. 2003. Bridging the Economic Divide within Countries: A Scorecard on the Performance of Regional Policies in Reducing Regional Income Disparities. *World Development* 31(8): 1421–1441.

Shorrocks, A. 1980. The Class of Additively Decomposable Inequality Measures. *Econometrica* 48(3): 613–625.

Shorrocks, A., and G. Wan. 2005. Spatial Decomposition of Inequality. *Journal of Economic Geography* 5(1): 59–81.

Silver, C., I. Azis, and L. Schroeder. 2001. Intergovernmental Transfers and Decentralization in Indonesia. *Bulletin of Indonesian Economic Studies* 37(3): 345–362.

Skoufias, E. 2001. Changes in Regional Inequality and Social Welfare in Indonesia from 1996 to 1999. *Journal of International Development* 13(1): 73–91.

Soesastro, H., and R. Atje. 2005. Survey of Recent Developments. *Bulletin of Indonesian Economic Studies* 41(1): 5–34.

Sumarto, S., and A. Suryahadi. 2010. Post-crisis Social Protection Programs in Indonesia. In *Poverty and Social Protection in Indonesia*, edited by J. Hardjono, N. Akhmadi, and S. Sumarto. Singapore: Institute of Southeast Asian Studies.

Tadjoeddin, M., W. Suharyo, and S. Mishra. 2001. Regional Disparity and Vertical Conflict in Indonesia. *Journal of the Asia Pacific Economy* 6(3): 283–304.

Uppal, J., and S. Budiono. 1986. Regional Income Disparities in Indonesia. *Ekonomi dan Keuangan Indonesia* 34: 286–304.

Vidyattama, Y. 2010. A Search for Indonesia's Regional Growth Determinants. *ASEAN Economic Bulletin* 27(3): 281–294.

———. 2013. Regional Convergence and the Role of the Neighborhood Effect in Decentralised Indonesia. *Bulletin of Indonesian Economic Studies* 49(2): 193–211.

Williamson, J. 1965. Regional Inequality and the Process of National Development: A Description of the Patterns. *Economic Development and Cultural Change* 13: 3–45.

World Bank. 2003. *Decentralizing Indonesia: A Regional Public Expenditure Overview Report*. Report No. 26191-IND. Washington, DC: World Bank East Asia Poverty Reduction and Economic Management Unit.

Yusuf, A., and A. Sumner. 2015. Survey of Recent Developments: Growth, Poverty, and Inequality under Jokowi. *Bulletin of Indonesian Economic Studies* 51(3): 323–348.

Yusuf, A., A. Sumner, and I. Rum. 2014. Twenty Years of Expenditure Inequality in Indonesia, 1993–2013. *Bulletin of Indonesian Economic Studies* 50(2): 243–254.

Appendix

Table A10.1 Decomposition of Expenditure Inequality by Urban and Rural Sectors and by District in Each Sector, Theil Index L

	Inequality	Contrib. (%)	Pop. Share (%)		Inequality	Contrib. (%)	Pop. Share (%)
1996							
Total	0.233	100.0					
B-sector	0.058	25.0					
W-sector	0.175	75.0					
Urban	0.249	38.6	36.2	Rural	0.133	36.4	63.8
B-district	0.066	10.2		B-district	0.020	5.6	
W-district	0.183	28.4		W-district	0.112	30.8	
2000							
Total	0.166	100.0					
B-sector	0.030	17.8					
W-sector	0.137	82.2					
Urban	0.183	46.5	42.2	Rural	0.103	35.7	57.8
B-district	0.043	11.0		B-district	0.015	5.1	
W-district	0.140	35.5		W-district	0.088	30.7	
2005							
Total	0.248	100.0					
B-sector	0.055	22.1					
W-sector	0.193	77.9					
Urban	0.254	44.2	43.2	Rural	0.147	33.7	56.8
B-district	0.075	13.0		B-district	0.030	6.9	
W-district	0.179	31.2		W-district	0.117	26.8	
2007							
Total	0.172	100.0					
B-sector	0.038	21.9					
W-sector	0.134	78.1					
Urban	0.177	43.9	42.7	Rural	0.103	34.2	57.3
B-district	0.051	12.6		B-district	0.018	6.1	
W-district	0.126	31.3		W-district	0.084	28.1	

continued on next page

Table A10.1 continued

	Inequality	Contrib. (%)	Pop. Share (%)		Inequality	Contrib. (%)	Pop. Share (%)
2008							
Total	0.228	100.0					
B-sector	0.037	16.0					
W-sector	0.192	84.0					
Urban	0.233	49.2	48.3	Rural	0.153	34.7	51.7
B-district	0.071	15.1		B-district	0.036	8.2	
W-district	0.161	34.2		W-district	0.117	26.6	
2010							
Total	0.218	100.0					
B-sector	0.041	18.9					
W-sector	0.177	81.1					
Urban	0.229	52.5	50.1	Rural	0.125	28.6	49.9
B-district	0.056	12.9		B-district	0.019	4.4	
W-district	0.173	39.6		W-district	0.106	24.1	

Source: Authors' estimations using National Socio-Economic Survey (Susenas) 1996–2010.

Table A10.2 Hierarchical vs Non-Hierarchical Decomposition of Expenditure Inequality, Theil Index L

	Hierarchical Decomposition		Non-Hierarchical Decomposition	
	Inequality	Contribution (%)	Inequality	Contribution (%)
1996				
B-sector	0.058	25.0	0.058	25.0
B-district			0.082	35.1
Interaction term			−0.045	−19.3
W-sector B-district	0.037	15.8		
W-sector W-district	0.138	59.2	0.138	59.2
Total	0.233	100.0	0.233	100.0
2000				
B-sector	0.030	17.8	0.030	17.8
B-district			0.049	29.7
Interaction term			−0.023	−13.6
W-sector B-district	0.027	16.1		
W-sector W-district	0.110	66.1	0.110	66.1
Total	0.166	100.0	0.166	100.0
2005				
B-sector	0.055	22.1	0.055	22.1
B-district			0.091	36.7
Interaction term			−0.042	−16.8
W-sector B-district	0.050	20.0		
W-sector W-district	0.144	57.9	0.144	57.9
Total	0.248	100.0	0.248	100.0

continued on next page

Table A10.1 continued

	Hierarchical Decomposition		Non-Hierarchical Decomposition	
	Inequality	Contribution (%)	Inequality	Contribution (%)
2007				
B-sector	0.038	21.9	0.038	21.9
B-district			0.063	36.8
Interaction term			−0.031	−18.1
W-sector B-district	0.032	18.7		
W-sector W-district	0.102	59.4	0.102	59.4
Total	0.172	100.0	0.172	100.0
2008				
B-sector	0.037	16.0	0.037	16.0
B-district			0.080	35.1
Interaction term			−0.027	−11.9
W-sector B-district	0.053	23.3		
W-sector W-district	0.139	60.7	0.139	60.7
Total	0.228	100.0	0.228	100.0
2010				
B-sector	0.041	18.9	0.041	18.9
B-district			0.070	32.1
Interaction term			−0.032	−14.7
W-sector B-district	0.038	17.3		
W-sector W-district	0.139	63.8	0.139	63.8
Total	0.218	100.0	0.218	100.0

Source: Authors' estimations using National Socio-Economic Survey (Susenas) 1996–2010.

11

The Sources of Income Inequality in Indonesia: A Regression-Based Decomposition

Eko Wicaksono, Hidayat Amir, and Anda Nugroho*

11.1 Background

Given its abundant natural resources, as well as its large labor force, Indonesia has prospered in recent decades, having become a Group of Twenty (G20) member in 2008, and having a high likelihood of being among the top seven global economies by 2030 (McKinsey Global Institute 2012). Furthermore, the country has been able to address its high poverty rate. Nevertheless, inequality has increased sharply in the last decade. Figure 11.1 shows how the associated economic indicators have evolved. In 1978, almost one-third of the Indonesian population lived below the poverty line. Two decades later, as the per capita gross domestic product (GDP) grew moderately, the poverty rate decreased to around 15% right before the currency crisis hit the Southeast Asian region.

Indonesia managed to recover quickly from the crisis, as shown by the higher growth period in GDP per capita after 2000, with concomitant improvements in the poverty rate. On the other hand, higher growth seems to have negatively impacted income distribution, as shown by the Gini index, which reached 0.41 in 2014. The 10-percentage point Gini increase over 10 years was high compared to other developing countries. It was also the highest increase for a South Asian country.

---

* The authors are very grateful for useful feedback from Professor Erbiao Dai (Asian Growth Institute) and the participants of the Income Inequality Workshop, which was held by ADBI–World Economy on 26–27 July 2016 in Tokyo, Japan. The views expressed in this chapter are those of the authors and do not necessarily represent those of the Ministry of Finance of the Republic of Indonesia or ministry policy.

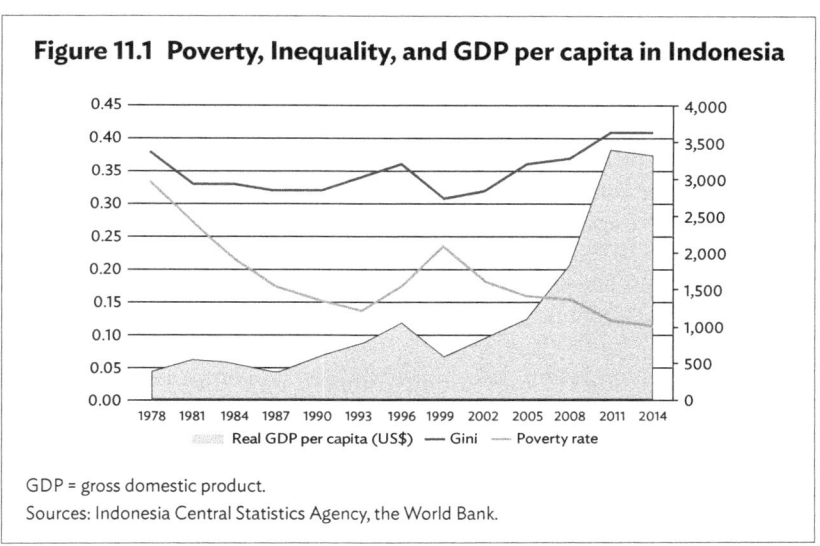

Figure 11.1 Poverty, Inequality, and GDP per capita in Indonesia

GDP = gross domestic product.
Sources: Indonesia Central Statistics Agency, the World Bank.

At some point, inequality is necessary to spur the economy. However, persistent gaps in income distribution will eventually affect economic performance (Stiglitz 2016) and become a concern for the government. A medium-term government target is to reduce the Gini Index by 2019.

Two of the most interesting income inequality studies used household-level data in the PRC (Morduch and Sicular 2002; Wan and Zhou 2004); and it is possible to conduct the same study in Indonesia using microdata. Moreover, household-level data allow us to decompose the inequality measures into contributing factors.

Of the several methods of income inequality decomposition, population sub-groups and factor components are the most popular (Shorrocks 1980, 1982, 1984; Bourguignon 1979). Population sub-group decomposition includes gender, age, and race differences, while a factor components decomposition can attribute income inequality by its source, such as wages and investments. Regression-based decomposition, initiated by Oaxaca (1973) and Blinder (1973), and subsequently developed by Juhn et al. (1998), and Wan and Zhou (2004), overcomes both methods' inability to explain certain fundamental factors, including education, experience, wealth, and other personal or family characteristics.

In this study, we use a regression-based decomposition of the Gini index. The Shapley value decomposition framework proposed by Shorrocks (1999) and the method employed by Wan (2002) are used to decompose the source of income inequality.

11.2 Literature Review

Most previous income inequality studies found education as the most important factor (Chongvilaivan and Kim 2016; Contreras et al. 2009; De Silva and Sumarto 2013; Dos Santos and da Cruz Vieira 2013; Morduch and Sicular 2002; Sapelli 2011). Some also found that access to finance also explains income inequality (Wan and Zhou 2004; Bae, Han, and Son 2012). According to a World Bank study (2016), there are several main causes of income inequality in Indonesia: (i) unequal opportunity; (ii) unequal jobs; (iii) high wealth concentration; and (iv) low resiliency.

Previous population subgroup studies decomposed them into between-group and within-group components of inequality. According to Morduch and Sicular (2002), this method can only explain the decomposition based on discrete variables, and the inclusion of multiple factors would constitute a constraint since the number of groups would increase in line with the number of categories. Furthermore, Shorrocks and Wan (2004) noted that this approach is limited, since it cannot control the contribution of other variables, as well as fundamental determinants.

More recent studies using regression-based decomposition determined the source of income inequality in rural People's Republic of China (PRC) (Morduch and Sicular 2002; Wan and Zhou 2004). In Indonesia, the same approach was employed by de Silva and Sumarto (2013). Despite using the same approach, these studies differed in terms of their treatment of contributing factors other than the proposed variables, i.e., constants and residuals. In particular, Morduch and Sicular (2002) determined the contribution of each factor as the inequality measured over the income prediction. The main flaw of this method was the non-trivial contribution made by the constant, as well as residuals. Wan (2002) noticed this pitfall and proposed a new method of decomposing contributions using Shapley value decomposition, as was discussed in Shorrocks (1999). Under this method, we can disentangle the contribution made by the constant and residuals and focus on that made by the factors under examination.

The following explanation illustrates this method. Suppose that the measured inequality, determined by, for example, the Gini index, is $I(Y)$. This index can be decomposed using the income generation function obtained from the regression of income (Y) on the explaining variables such as age, education, wealth, etc. The fitted value of income ($\hat{Y}$) can be used to measure the inequality contributed by the factors plus constant and residuals ($I(\hat{Y})$). The contribution of residuals (CO_e) can be measured as $I(Y) - I(\hat{Y})$. Furthermore, the constant contribution can be netted out by measuring the inequality given the constant (C) equal to zero. Therefore, we get $Y^* = (\hat{Y}|\ C = 0)$ to measure the net contribution of factors under examination. Finally, the inequality measure associated with contributing factors is $I(Y^*)$, which is subject to further decomposition.

11.3 Data and Methodology

This study draws on data obtained from the Indonesia Family Life Survey (IFLS), a household and community longitudinal survey conducted by RAND Corporation, the first wave of which was conducted in 1993. Currently, five waves of IFLS data are available, including the surveys conducted in 1993, 1997, 2000, 2007, and 2014. IFLS is a rich dataset consisting of a wide array of household and community characteristics, i.e., household structure, education, income, health, etc. Despite the survey covering only 13 of 34 provinces, it represents 83% of the Indonesian population, with at least 7,000 households and around 30,000 individuals surveyed.

Decomposition initially determines the inequality measure, $I(Y)$, based on household income. Second, a regression function obtains the equation that can predict income based on each household characteristic. A semi-log income-generating function is applied in this study. Third, the exponential of fitted value of income determines the new inequality measure, $I(\hat{Y})$, with which the residuals contribution (CO_e) can be netted out from $I(Y)$. Finally, the Shapley value decomposition method determines the net contribution of each factor.

The income equation employed in this study is as follows:

$$\ln(y_i) = x_i \beta + \varepsilon_i \qquad (1)$$

$\ln(y_i)$ is the natural log of per capita annual household income, while x_i is vector of the independent variables explaining household income. The variables included are:
1. Head of Household gender
2. Household size
3. Head of household age
4. Head of household age squared
5. Head of household years of education
6. Head of household years of education squared
7. Household wealth per capita
8. Proportion of household members who are wage earners
9. Dummy variable for rural

10. Dummy variable for eastern Indonesia

Gender is included in the income equation to account for discrimination in labor participation between males and females. Age and education are included since these covariates can represent productivity and knowledge, which can be correlated with income. Furthermore, household wealth is included in the income-generating function since it can influence inequality both directly and indirectly. The proportion of wage-earners to household members accounts for the impact of labor markets. To account for regional disparity, dummy variables for rural and eastern Indonesia are also included.

The summary statistics are presented in Table 11.1. This study includes only the three latest waves of IFLS, that is, IFLS 3 (2000), IFLS 4 (2007), and IFLS 5 (2014). Based on the summary statistics, it can be inferred that the average amount of education in Indonesia is still low (around 6 to 8 years); nevertheless, this increases over time.

Table 11.1 Summary Statistics of the Variables

Variable	2000		2007		2014	
	Mean	Std. Dev.	Mean	Std. Dev.	Mean	Std. Dev.
Log of per capita income (in rupiah)	13.69	1.26	14.56	1.23	15.33	1.29
Male-headed	0.85	0.36	0.86	0.35	0.86	0.35
Household size (in persons)	4.55	1.97	4.22	1.81	4.02	1.71
Age (in years)	48.57	12.95	49.75	12.62	47.73	12.57
Age-squared	2,526.50	1,327.76	2,634.31	1,315.21	2,436.22	1,275.79
Education (in years)	6.11	4.63	6.84	4.77	7.97	4.70
Education-squared	58.82	69.94	69.51	76.17	85.62	79.02
Wealth (in rupiah)	10,200,000	28,200,000	22,300,000	47,000,000	49,500,000	95,700,000
Proportion of Wage-earners per household	0.21	0.24	0.17	0.23	0.20	0.25
Rural	0.55	0.50	0.50	0.50	0.42	0.49
Eastern Indonesia	0.11	0.31	0.11	0.31	0.12	0.32
Observations	6,407		6,720		8,337	

Source: Authors' calculation.

The average accumulation of wealth also shows a significant increase over time, which is in line with high growth between 2000 and 2014. The average wage-earner proportion is one-fifth of household members and is quite stable over time. The proportion of households living in urban areas shows an increasing trend, which, in 2014, was only around 42% of those living in rural areas. The mean of other explanatory variables is quite stable over time.

After the fitted value of income per capita is predicted and the contribution of residuals has been netted out, the Shapley value decomposition determines the contribution of each income source. Suppose that there are k factors of variable in the income generation function so that:

$$Y = F(X) + e \qquad (2)$$

$$Y = \hat{Y} + e \qquad (3)$$

Therefore, we can decompose inequality and disentangle the contribution of residuals as follows:

$$I(Y) = I(\hat{Y}|X_1, X_2, ... X_k) + CO_e \qquad (4)$$

where $I(Y)$ is income inequality measured on actual income, $I(\hat{Y}|X_1, X_2, ... X)$ is income inequality measured on predicted income, and CO_e is the contribution of residuals. Since we employ a semi-log equation, we can ignore the contribution of the constant on income inequality.

The contribution of each factor is then described as follows:

$$I(\hat{Y}|X_1, X_2, ..., X_k) = C_1 + C_2 + ... + C_k \qquad (5)$$

where C_1 is the contribution of X_1 in income inequality. The contribution of each factor is determined as the impact on income inequality if a factor is removed by replacing it either with its means value or zero. In this method, we use the means value as the replacement. The contribution of each factor is then determined as follows:

$$C_j = \frac{1}{k!} \Sigma_{\pi \in \Pi_k} \left[I(\hat{Y})|B(\pi, Xj) \cup \{X_J\})) - I(\hat{Y}|B(\pi, X_J)) \right] \qquad (6)$$

where $I(\hat{Y}|X)$ is the inequality measured on predicted income, and Π_k is the set of all possible permutations of the k variables. $B(\pi, X_j)$ is the set of variables ahead of X_j in the ordering π.

The share of each factor contribution in income inequality (S_j) then can be determined as follows:

$$S_j = C_j/(I(Y)) \qquad (7)$$

This method requires extensive calculation since the possible permutations from the set of variables increases as more factors are included in the income equation.

11.4 Results and Discussions

The obtained income generation function is presented in Table 11.2. The sign of the coefficients is as expected, with most significant at the 1% level. Male household heads positively correlate with per capita income, which suggests that different gender participation patterns exist in the Indonesian labor market. Age negatively correlates with per capita income, which implies that productivity may decrease as age goes up, thus leading to lower per capita income. Household size also has a negative relationship with per capita income. This finding is consistent since more household members will lower per capita income. Meanwhile, education, wealth, and the proportion of wage-earners positively correlate with income per capita. Regional disparity also matters in determining per capita income. Households in rural areas tend to have lower per capita income compared to those in urban areas. Moreover, households in eastern Indonesia generate less per capita income compared to those in western Indonesia.

Table 11.2 The Estimated Income–Generating Function

Variables	2000 Coeff.	2007 Coeff.	2014 Coeff.
Male-headed	0.2122***	0.2635***	0.2737***
	(0.040)	(0.038)	(0.036)
Household size	−0.0507***	−0.0683***	−0.0220***
	(0.007)	(0.007)	(0.007)
Age	0.0591***	0.0512***	0.0472***
	(0.008)	(0.007)	(0.007)
Age-squared	−0.0006***	−0.0005***	−0.0005***
	(0.000)	(0.000)	(0.000)

continued on next page

Table 11.2 continued

Variables	2000 Coeff.	2007 Coeff.	2014 Coeff.
Education	0.0401***	0.0338***	−0.0032
	(0.009)	(0.009)	(0.009)
Education-squared	0.0023***	0.0018***	0.0035***
	(0.001)	(0.001)	(0.001)
Wealth	0.0000***	0.0000***	0.0000***
	(0.000)	(0.000)	(0.000)
Wage-earner	0.9346***	1.3448***	1.4010***
	(0.059)	(0.060)	(0.052)
Rural	−0.2811***	−0.1923***	−0.1964***
	(0.030)	(0.028)	(0.026)
Eastern Indonesia	−0.1708***	−0.2105***	−0.1511***
	(0.044)	(0.041)	(0.038)
Constant	11.9547***	12.8603***	13.5750***
	(0.192)	(0.186)	(0.176)
Observations	6,407	6,720	8,337
R-squared	0.261	0.295	0.253

Standard errors in parentheses
*** p<0.01, ** p<0.05, * p<0.1
Source: Authors' calculation.

After the income generation is specified, a Shapley value decomposition determines each factor contributing to income inequality. The result of the decomposition is presented in Table 11.3.

In this decomposition, the Gini index is the main measure of inequality. In 2000, education was the most significant contributor to income inequality, accounting for one-fifth of the total. This is also in line with previous income inequality studies (Chongvilaivan and Kim 2016; De Silva and Sumarto 2013), and implies that more equal access to education can increase human capital. Duflo (2000) also found that greater access to education significantly improved wages in Indonesia.

Wealth was second to education in determining income inequality, implying that asset accumulation can give better access to education, as well as health services, either through inheritance or more income generated from asset ownership. The contribution of wealth to income inequality is also found in Manna and Regoli (2012).

Table 11.3 Shapley Value Decomposition Results, 2000

No.	Variables	Gini %	Theil L %	Atkinson %
1	Male-headed	1.02	0.47	0.53
2	Household size	2.95	1.88	1.97
3	Age	15.48	1.11	5.97
4	Education	20.99	15.34	16.65
5	Wealth	19.07	19.40	21.92
6	Wage-earner	8.29	4.22	4.84
7	Rural	5.89	3.98	4.30
8	Eastern Indonesia	0.89	0.53	0.57
	All variables	74.63	46.93	56.75
	Residuals	25.37	53.07	43.25
	Total	100.00	100.00	100.00

Source: Authors' calculation.

Age comes in third in explaining income inequality, suggesting that individual qualifications, especially experience, matter in determining income. Being a wage-earner explains about 8% of income inequality, with regional disparity accounting for about 6%. Interestingly, being located in eastern Indonesia accounted for less than 1% of income inequality. In terms of geography, the difference between rural and urban is associated with unequal development, especially regarding infrastructure.

As shown in Table 11.4, there was no significant change in the contribution of each factor to income inequality in 2007, except for wage-earners. Wealth and education still were responsible for about 40% of income inequality. One noticeable change was the contribution of wage-earners, which increased from 4% in 2000 to 21% in 2007. This can be attributed to skill difference as a result of unequal access to education. Moreover, the strength of labor unions in Indonesia also contributed to inequality since they can negotiate on regional minimum wages every year. Regional difference contributions to income inequality were also found to be lower in 2007. This can be associated with the progress on decentralization that started in Indonesia in early 2000.

In 2014, as shown in Table 11.5, wage-earners and wealth were the largest contributors to income inequality, with each being responsible for one-fifth of the total. The contribution of education decreased moderately, showing the government's progress on improving

Table 11.4 Shapley Value Decomposition Results, 2007

No.	Variables	Gini %	Theil L %	Atkinson %
1	Male-headed	0.37	−0.72	−0.58
2	Household size	4.51	3.43	3.47
3	Age	16.04	2.50	6.53
4	Education	19.24	15.62	16.04
5	Wealth	19.70	20.70	22.28
6	Wage-earner	21.27	17.72	18.90
7	Rural	4.03	2.90	2.96
8	Eastern Indonesia	1.18	0.77	0.80
	All variables	86.35	62.93	70.40
	Residuals	13.65	37.07	29.60
	Total	100.00	100.00	100.00

Source: Authors' calculation.

Table 11.5 Shapley Value Decomposition Results, 2014

No.	Variables	Gini %	Theil L %	Atkinson %
1	Male-headed	0.87	−0.03	0.04
2	Household size	1.32	0.88	0.91
3	Age	14.68	3.60	4.74
4	Education	16.70	11.63	12.84
5	Wealth	19.20	18.02	20.33
6	Wage-earner	20.22	13.47	15.11
7	Rural	3.74	2.31	2.48
8	Eastern Indonesia	0.61	0.15	0.18
	All variables	77.32	48.04	57.82
	Residuals	22.68	51.96	42.18
	Total	100.00	100.00	100.00

Source: Authors' calculation.

access. Meanwhile, regional disparity's contribution decreased by a negligible amount.

As an alternative to Gini Index, Theil L as well as the Atkinson Index were used and similar patterns were found. So far, the decomposition results using both measures are consistent with the above explanation. The noticeable difference is the higher contribution of residuals, which is also found in Wan and Zhou (2004), as well as Dos Santos and da Cruz Vieira (2013).

Our findings show that the sources of income inequality in Indonesia resemble those of other developing countries. The problem of unequal access to education persists since those with higher income can provide better education for their children, while children who live in low-income families will be less educated, making inequality worse for the next generation.

The Indonesian government has had a significant education budget since 2009. Given the impact of education on income inequality, the large amount spent on education should go into effective improvement programs that increase school participation rates.

The contribution of wealth to income inequality in Indonesia is quite stable over time. Since efficient credit can broaden access to finance for the poor, basic problems in credit markets (asymmetric information) must be addressed (de Aghion and Morduch 2004).

Employment status is also found to have significant impact on the widening gap in income distribution. The contribution of wage-earners rose significantly during the first two periods of observation before becoming stable during the last two observations. Again, this finding can be attributed to unequal access to education in early life. Finally, infrastructure development is important to spur economic growth in regions that were considered left behind.

11.5 Conclusion

This study employs the Shapley value decomposition framework and regression-based inequality decomposition approach to determine the main sources of inequality in Indonesia. Three waves of household survey data were utilized in this study, which represent those for 2000, 2007, and 2014. Education, wealth, and employment status rates are the main determinants of income inequality. The combination of those factors can explain almost 60% of income inequality. Furthermore, the connection between these factors can explain why inequality grew significantly in the last decade. These findings suggest that in order to decrease inequality, more efforts should be aimed at reducing unequal access to education as well as finance. Lastly, equal development between rural and urban areas is also important in reducing income inequality in Indonesia.

References

Bae, K., D. Han, and H. Sohn. 2012. Importance of Access to Finance in Reducing Income Inequality and Poverty Level. *International Review of Public Administration* 17(1): 55–77.

Blinder, A. S. 1973. Wage Discrimination: Reduced Form and Structural Estimates. *Journal of Human Resources* 8: 436–55.

Bourguignon, F. 1979. Decomposable Income Inequality Measures. *Econometrica* 47(4): 901–920.

Chongvilaivan, A., and J. Kim. 2016. Individual Income Inequality and Its Drivers in Indonesia: A Theil Decomposition Reassessment. *Social Indicators Research* 126(1): 79–98.

Contreras, D., O. Larrañaga, E. Puentes, and T. Rau. 2009. Evidence for Inequality of Opportunities: A Cohort Analysis for Chile. Facultad Economía y Negocias, Paper SDT 298. Santiago: Universidad de Chile.

de Aghion, B. A., and J. Morduch. 2004. *The Economics of Microfinance*. Cambridge: MIT Press.

de Silva, I., and S. Sumarto. 2013. Poverty-Growth Inequality Triangle: The Case of Indonesia. TNP2K Working Paper. Retrieved from: http://www.tnp2k.go.id/images/uploads/downloads/WP4-PovertyTriangle(1).pdf

Duflo, E. 2000. *Schooling and Labor Market Consequences of School Construction in Indonesia: Evidence from an Unusual Policy Experiment (No. w7860)*. National Bureau of Economic Research.

Juhn, C., K. M. Murphy, and B. Pierce. 1993. Wage Inequality and the Rise in Returns to Skill. *Journal of Political Economy* 101: 410–442.

Manna, R., and A. Regoli. 2012. Regression-Based Approaches for the Decomposition of Income Inequality in Italy 1998–2008. *Rivista di Statistica Ufficiale* 1.

McKinsey Global Institute. 2012. *The Archipelago Economy: Unleashing Indonesia's Potential*. McKinsey and Company. http://www.mckinsey.com/insights/asia-pacific/the_archipelago_economy

Morduch, J., and T. Sicular. 2002. Rethinking Inequality Decomposition, With Evidence from Rural China. *The Economic Journal* 112(476): 93–106.

Oaxaca, R. 1973. Male–Female Wage Differences in Urban Labour Markets. *International Economic Review* 14: 693–709.

Santos, V. F. D., and W. D. C. Vieira. 2013. Effects of Growth and Reduction of Income Inequality on Poverty in Northeastern Brazil 2003-2008. *Economia Aplicada* 17(4): 647–666.

Sapelli, C. 2011. A Cohort Analysis of the Income Distribution in Chile. *Estudios de Economía* 38(1): 223–242.

Shorrocks, A. F. 1980. The Class of Additively Decomposable Inequality Measures. *Econometrica* 48: 613–25.

———. 1982. Inequality Decomposition by Factor Components. *Econometrica* 50:193–211.

———. 1984. Inequality Decomposition by Population Subgroups. *Econometrica* 52:1369–85.

———. 1999. *Decomposition Procedures for Distributional Analysis: A Unified Framework Based on the Shapley Value* (Unpublished manuscript). University of Essex, Colchester.

Shorrocks, A. F., and G. H. Wan. 2005. *Spatial Decomposition of Inequality* (No. 2004/01). WIDER Discussion Papers/World Institute for Development Economics (UNU-WIDER).

Stiglitz, J. E. 2016. Inequality and Economic Growth. In *Rethinking Capitalism: Economics and Policy for Sustainable and Inclusive Growth,* edited by M. Jacobs and M. Mazzucato. Oxford: John Wiley and Sons.

Wan, G. H. 2002. *Regression-Based Inequality Decomposition: Pitfalls and a Solution Procedure* (No. 2002/101). WIDER Discussion Papers/World Institute for Development Economics (UNU-WIDER).

Wan, G., and Z. Zhou. 2004. *Income Inequality in Rural China: Regression-based Decomposition Using Household Data* (No. 2004/51). WIDER Discussion Papers/World Institute for Development Economics (UNU-WIDER).

World Bank. 2016. Indonesia's Rising Divide. Washington, DC: World Bank Group. http://documents.worldbank.org/curated/en/267671467991932516/Indonesias-rising-divide

12

Intragenerational and Intergenerational Mobility in Viet Nam

Nguyen Tran Lam and Nguyen Viet Cuong

12.1 Introduction

There are different definitions of social mobility (e.g., Behrman 2000; Torche 2015). Social mobility can refer to movement of individuals and households across different social positions. Social mobility includes intergenerational mobility and intragenerational mobility. Intergenerational mobility is the change in position of a person or a household as compared with previous generations, while intragenerational mobility is the change in position of a person or a household over time. Social mobility can be measured in terms of education, employment, and income. The movement can be downward or upward.

There is an association between social mobility and inequality. In a society with high-income inequality, there are very rich as well as very poor households, and family background can be an important factor in determining income of children (Corak 2013a). For example, being born in a rich family can result in better health and education for children. Family resources and networks also affect children's networks and employment (Corak 2013a). Children born in rich families are more likely to have good jobs and high earnings. As a result, high inequality can result in low social mobility including both intragenerational and intergenerational mobility. The invert association between intergenerational mobility and inequality is described by the Great Gatsby curve (Corak 2013b). Countries with high-income inequality tend to have higher intergenerational elasticity or low-income mobility across the generations.

Viet Nam has achieved high economic growth during the recent decades. Poverty has significantly decreased over time. The proportion of people below the expenditure poverty line decreased from 58.1% in 1993 to 14.5% in 2008 and 10% in 2012. The poverty rate has declined in all population groups and in all geographic regions (World Bank 2013).[1] However, the poverty rate remains very high in remote and mountainous areas where there are high proportions of ethnic minorities. In some remote areas, more than 80% of people still live below the poverty line (Nguyen 2011; Lanjouw, Marra, and Ngyuen 2013). There is a large gap in the living standards of ethnic minorities and the Kinh people. The absolute income gap between the top income quintile and the bottom income quintile also tends to increase over time.

There is an influential view that equality in opportunity can moderate income equality. Poor as well as rich children should have the same opportunities for education and better employment (Black and Devereux 2010). Understanding social mobility is very important to improve equality in opportunities and welfare in Viet Nam. Thus, this study provides a descriptive analysis of the situation and trend of social mobility in Viet Nam, and subsequently examines factors associated with social mobility. More specifically, this study has three objectives. The first is to present the descriptive analysis of intragenerational mobility of income and employment mobility in Viet Nam. The second is to analyze the intergenerational mobility of employment and earnings. The third is to analyze the association of different factors, especially education, with intragenerational and intergenerational mobility. Data used for this analysis are from the Viet Nam Household Living Standard Surveys (VHLSS) in 2004, 2008, 2010, and 2014.

There is a large number of studies on intergenerational mobility (for review e.g., see Black and Devereux 2010; Solon 2013; and Torche 2015). Most studies focus on the United States (US) and other developed countries. There is little empirical evidence on intergenerational mobility in developing countries, possibly because of the lower availability of data sets in these countries. In Viet Nam, two studies estimate intergenerational elasticity. Using the VHLSS 1998, Hertz et al. (2008) estimated the elasticity of education between parents and children at 0.58. Emran and Shilpi (2011) found a high correlation of intergenerational occupation in Viet Nam using the VHLSS 1993. Most recently, Brand-Weiner, Francavilla, and Olivari (2015) examined the intragenerational mobility of income and occupation using VHLSS in 2004 and 2008, showing rather high-income mobility in Viet Nam. However, the mobility of employment across sectors (agriculture, services, and industry) is small. Several studies looked at poverty

---

[1] For poverty measurement in Viet Nam, see for example Nguyen (2011) and Nguyen and Tran (2014).

transition of households over time (e.g., Nguyen 2012; Baulch and Vu 2010; Nguyen, Phung, and Westbrook 2015). Overall, these studies found that ethnic minority and low education households tend to be more chronically poor than the Kinh majority and high education households.

Compared with previous studies on social mobility in Viet Nam, this study differs in several ways. First, it examines not only intragenerational mobility but also intergenerational mobility in both occupational and earning outcomes. Previous studies look at either intragenerational mobility or intergenerational mobility. Second, we use most of the recent VHLSS (from 2004 to 2014) to examine the change in social mobility over time. Finally, using regressions, we are able to investigate the association between several socioeconomic factors and social mobility.

This chapter is structured into five sections. After the Introduction, Section 12.2 introduces the VHLSS data set. Section 12.3 presents income inequality and intragenerational income mobility of households in Viet Nam. Section 12.4 analyzes the intragenerational occupational mobility of individuals over time. Section 12.5 presents the analysis of intergenerational mobility. Finally, Section 12.6 concludes.

12.2 Data Sets

This study uses sets of VHLSS in 2004, 2008, 2010, and 2014. These surveys were conducted by the General Statistics Office (GSO) of Viet Nam with technical assistance from the World Bank. VHLSSs are conducted every 2 years. The latest survey was released in 2014. In this study, we use the four VHLSSs mainly to analyze the changes in 2004–2008 and in 2010–2014. The surveys contain household-level and individual-level data. Data include basic demography, employment and labor force participation, education, health, income, expenditure, housing, fixed assets and durable goods, and participation of households in poverty alleviation programs.

The number of households sampled in VHLSS 2004, 2008, 2010, and 2014 is 9,188, 9,189, 9,399, and 9,398, respectively. There were 40,437 individuals from the sampled households for VHLSS 2004, 38,253 for VHLSS 2008, 36,999 for VHLSS 2010, and 35,520 for 2014. The VHLSSs are representative at the urban/rural and regional levels. There were 1,817 panel households during the VHLSS 2004 and the VHLSS 2008, 1,817 households for VHLSS 2010, and 1,813 households for VHLSS 2014. However, there are no panel data between the VHLSS 2008 and the VHLSS 2010. The VHLSSs for 2010 and 2012 used the new sample frame (from the 2009 Population and Housing Census). As a result, there is no link between the VHLSS 2010 and the earlier VHLSSs.

12.3 Household Income Mobility

12.3.1 Income Inequality

Inequality in Viet Nam, which is measured by the Gini index, has been quite stable over time. Inequality increased lightly in 2008 and 2010 and decreased in 2012 and 2014. Figure 12.1 presents the income and expenditure Gini indexes from 2004–2014. Income inequality is higher than expenditure inequality, but the difference is small. In 2014, the income and expenditure Gini indexes were 0.39 and 0.35, respectively. It should be noted that household surveys can underestimate income inequality since they do not capture the richest people of the country.

Although the Gini coefficient did not increase over time, the gap in income between groups increased over time. The absolute per capita income gap between urban and rural households increased from VND4,754 ($213) in 2004 to VND6,344 ($288) in 2014 (Figure 12.2). The gap between the Kinh/Hoa and ethnic minorities is larger—not only the absolute income gap but also the relative income gap increased over time. The ratio of per capita income of the Kinh/Hoa to that of ethnic minorities increased from 2.1 in 2004 to 2.3 in 2014.[2]

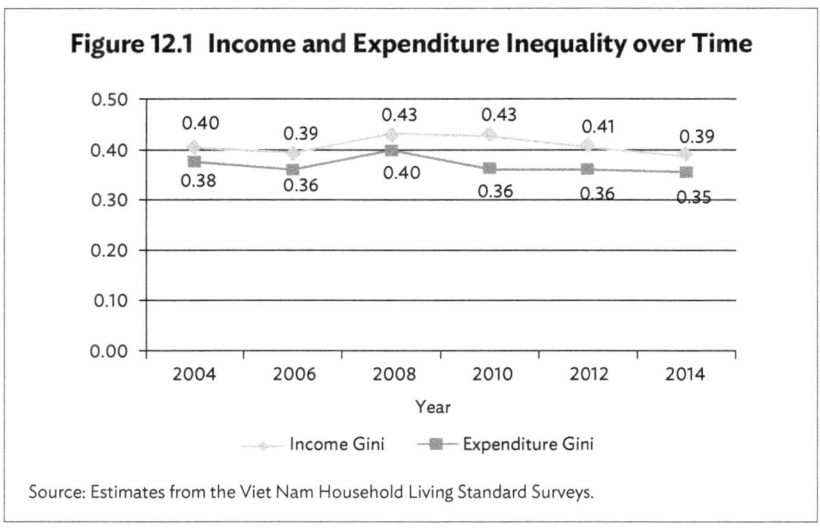

Figure 12.1 Income and Expenditure Inequality over Time

Source: Estimates from the Viet Nam Household Living Standard Surveys.

---

[2] There are 54 ethnic groups in Viet Nam, in which the Kinh majority accounts for 85% of the population. The Kinh tend to live in delta areas and have higher living standards than other ethnic minorities. The Hoa (Chinese) is a rich group and also lives in delta areas. Thus, the Hoa is often grouped with the Kinh in studies on household welfare in Viet Nam.

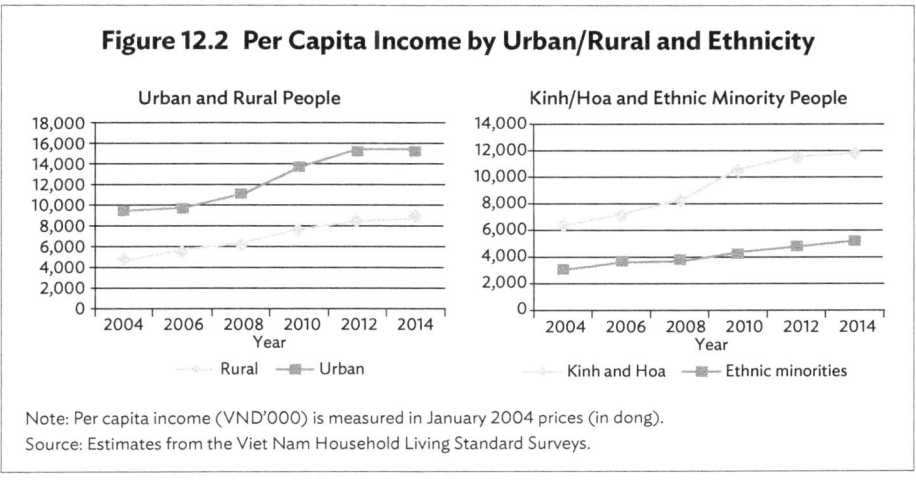

Figure 12.2 Per Capita Income by Urban/Rural and Ethnicity

Note: Per capita income (VND'000) is measured in January 2004 prices (in dong).
Source: Estimates from the Viet Nam Household Living Standard Surveys.

The left panel of Figure 12.3 presents the per capita income of all households and the 40% lowest income households. The Sustainable Development Goal on inequality is to "by 2030, progressively achieve and sustain income growth of the bottom 40% per cent of the population at a rate higher than the national average." From 2004 to 2014, the average annual growth rate of real per capita income of the bottom 40% of the population was 5.4% per year, while the corresponding rate of the national average was 5.5% per year. To achieve the Sustainable Development Goal target, households in lower income quintiles should have a higher growth rate of income.

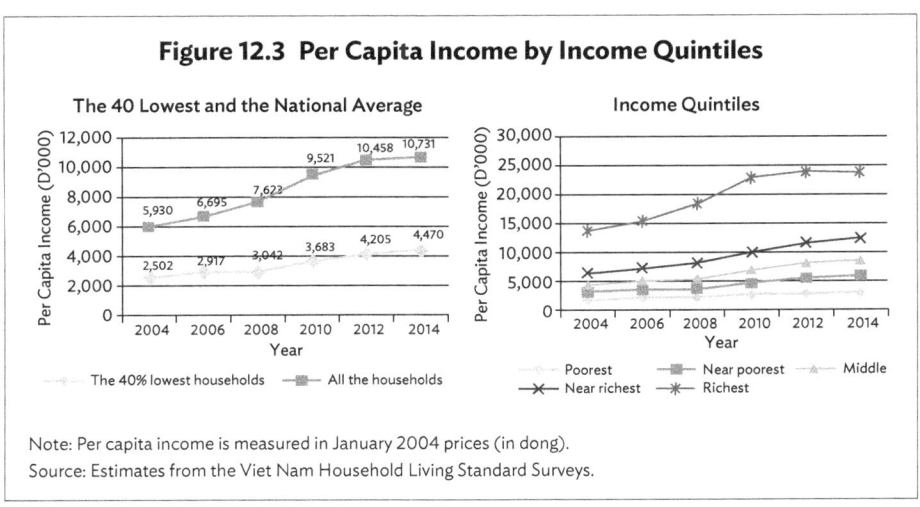

Figure 12.3 Per Capita Income by Income Quintiles

Note: Per capita income is measured in January 2004 prices (in dong).
Source: Estimates from the Viet Nam Household Living Standard Surveys.

The right panel of Figure 12.3 shows an important point of income inequality in Viet Nam. There are no large gaps in per capita income among those in the bottom quintile to the nearest richest quintile. However, there is a large jump in per capita income from the near richest to the richest quintile. It implies that there are very rich households in the richest quintile, and it would be very difficult to move to the richest quintile from a lower quintile.

12.3.2 Income Mobility

To examine income mobility, we use panel household data from VHLSS 2004 and VHLSS 2008, and from VHLSS 2010 and VHLSS 2014. Households are grouped into income quintiles. Figure 12.4 presents the percentage of households that improved their income level from the bottom income quintile (the 20% lowest income) to a higher income quintile over time by characteristics of household heads. It shows that 45% of households in the bottom quintile in 2004 had moved to a higher income quintile in 2008; for 2010–2014 it was 37%. It implies that the mobility of the lowest quintile households tended to decrease over time.

Urban households are more likely to move up than rural households. The gap in income mobility is large between the Kinh/Hoa and ethnic minorities. From 2010–2014, around 19% of ethnic minorities in the bottom quintile moved to a higher income quintile, whereas it was 49% for the Kinh and Hoa.

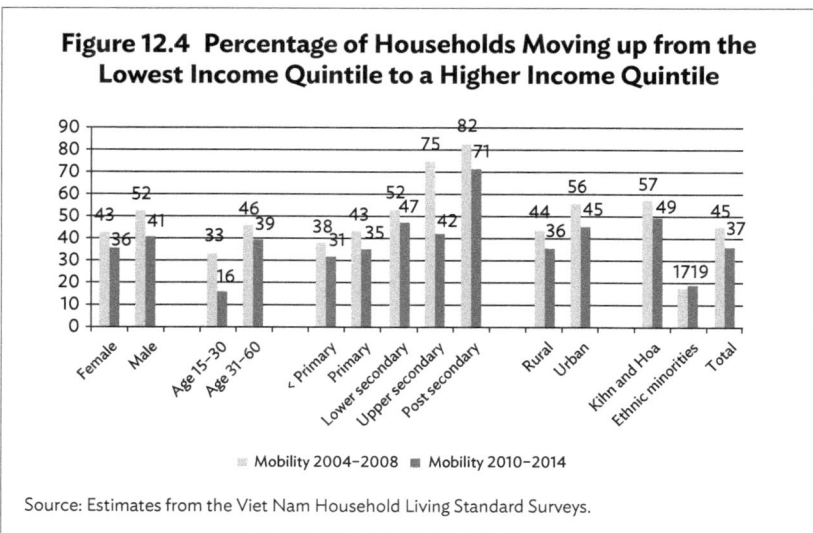

Figure 12.4 Percentage of Households Moving up from the Lowest Income Quintile to a Higher Income Quintile

Source: Estimates from the Viet Nam Household Living Standard Surveys.

Income mobility of households is also correlated with characteristics of household heads. In the VHLSSs, household heads are defined as those who have the most power in households. Around 22% of households have female heads. However, around two-thirds of female heads are either single or divorced, which means that female-headed households tend to be smaller and have more difficulties than male-headed households. Mobility rates differ between households with male heads and those with female heads, though the difference is not very large. From 2010 to 2014, 35% of female-headed households and 41% of male-headed households escaped from the bottom income quintile.

Income mobility is also correlated with the age of the household head. Households with young heads are substantially less likely to be mobile than those with older heads. From 2010–2014, 39% of households with heads aged 31–60 moved from the bottom quintile to a higher quintile, while only 16% of households with heads aged below 31 moved from the bottom quintile to a higher quintile. Interviews also show that young people have less experience and find it more difficult to move upward.

Education plays an important role in achieving better employment and earnings. The returns to education have consistently been found to be high in both developed and developing countries (Psacharopoulos and Partinos 2004; Schultz 1997, 2002). Figure 12.4 shows the important role of education in Viet Nam, especially post-secondary education (college and above) in income mobility. In 2010–2014, 71% of households with post-secondary heads moved from the bottom to a higher income quintile. For households with low-education heads (below primary and primary), the rates are only 31% and 35%, respectively.

Table 12.1 presents a more detailed analysis of income mobility from 2010–2014. In Table A12.1 in the Appendix, we present the analysis of mobility from 2004 to 2008 for comparison. Overall, the mobility trend does not change significantly over time. To avoid repetition, we use the results of income mobility in 2010–2014 for interpretation.

In addition to income mobility from the 20% lowest income quintile to a higher income quintile, Table 12.1 presents the mobility from the 40% lowest income quintiles to a higher income quintile. The trend of mobility from the 40% lowest income quintiles is similar to the trend of mobility from the 20% lowest income quintile. Households with female, young, and low education heads are less likely to move up than households with male, older, and high education heads. Rural and ethnic minority households are also less likely to move up. It should be noted that the proportion of mobility in the higher income quintiles is lower. This means that it is more difficult to move up when households have high income or belong to a high-income quintile.

We also look at the downward mobility from a higher income quintile to lower income quintiles. Households with young heads are more likely to fall down. Education plays an important role in reducing the downward mobility of households. Kinh/Hoa and urban households are less likely to have downward mobility than ethnic minority and rural households.

In the last two columns of these tables, we estimate the absolute and relative income mobility indexes (Fields and Ok 1996, 1999). The absolute change index is equal to the average of the absolute difference between 2010 income and 2014 income. The relative change index is equal to the average of the absolute change divided by per capita income in the base year (i.e., 2010 in Table 12.1).[3] Table 12.1 shows that female-headed households have lower mobility than male-headed households. Households with young heads are less likely to be mobile than those with older heads. Households with high education heads have a higher absolute mobility than those with low education. However, since the base income of households with high education heads is higher, their relative mobility is lower.

Table 12.1 Income Mobility of Households from 2010–2014

	% Moving Up from the 20% Bottom in 2010 to a Higher Quintile in 2014	% Moving up from the 40% Bottom in 2010 to a Higher Quintile in 2014	% Moving Down from the 40% Top in 2010 to a Lower Quintile in 2014
Sex of household head			
Male	40.5	17.8	11.9
Female	35.1	11.0	11.9
Age of household head			
Age 15–30	15.6	2.4	16.6
Age 31–60	39.2	13.2	11.6
Education of household head			
< Primary	31.4	8.1	19.4
Primary	34.7	8.5	12.6

continued on next page

---

[3] More specifically, the average absolute income change is computed as follows: $I = \frac{1}{n}\sum_{j=1}^{n}|Y_j^f - Y_j^i|$, and the relative absolute income change is computed as follows: $I = \sum_{j=1}^{n}|Y_j^f - Y_j^i| / \sum_{j=1}^{n} Y_j^i$, where $Y_j^{i,f}$ is the income level of individual or household j in the initial (i) or final (f) period. n is the number of individuals or households in the data set.

Table 12.1 *continued*

	% Moving Up from the 20% Bottom in 2010 to a Higher Quintile in 2014	% Moving up from the 40% Bottom in 2010 to a Higher Quintile in 2014	% Moving Down from the 40% Top in 2010 to a Lower Quintile in 2014
Lower-secondary	46.9	11.9	12.1
Upper-secondary	42.1	19.7	4.7
Post-secondary	71.3	22.7	3.8
Rural/Urban			
Rural	35.8	10.9	15.0
Urban	45.2	17.0	3.3
Ethnicity of household head			
Kinh and Hoa	48.7	13.4	9.3
Ethnic minorities	18.7	5.0	35.7
Total	**36.5**	**12.6**	**11.9**

	% Moving Down from the 20% Top in 2010 to a Lower Quintile in 2014	Absolute Change in per Capita Income 2010–2014 (Fields and Ok Index)	Relative Change in per Capita Income 2010–2014
Sex of household head			
Male	43.0	5,652.4	61.9
Female	36.6	4,257.6	47.8
Age of household head			
Age 15–30	53.0	3,440.5	45.5
Age 31–60	37.5	4,683.6	51.7
Education of household head			
< Primary	48.2	3,355.8	55.6
Primary	58.4	4,489.3	60.4
Lower-secondary	38.2	4,314.8	50.2
Upper-secondary	31.8	5,544.7	54.1
Post-secondary	30.9	6,348.2	43.3
Rural/Urban			
Rural	44.7	4,198.6	54.5
Urban	32.0	5,656.3	46.0
Ethnicity of household head			
Kinh and Hoa	37.9	4,964.0	51.2
Ethnic minorities	47.8	2,479.9	52.7
Total	**38.4**	**4,597.0**	**51.3**

Source: Estimates from the Viet Nam Household Living Standard Surveys 2004 and 2008.

Table 12.2 presents ordinary least squares (OLS) regression of the probability of upward and downward income mobility from 2010–2014. The regression analysis for 2004–2008 is presented in Table A12.2 in the Appendix. Unlike the descriptive analysis in Table 12.1, an estimated coefficient of an explanatory variable in regression reflects the partial correlation between this variable and the dependent variable once other explanatory variables in the regression are controlled for. It shows that sex and age of household heads are not strongly correlated with income mobility after other explanatory variables are controlled for.

Compared with the Kinh and Hoa, ethnic minorities are more likely to move down but less likely to move up in income mobility. Households with higher-education heads are more likely to move up and less likely to move down. They are also more mobile than households with lower-education heads. However, for households in the bottom quintile and the top quintile, the education of household heads is not significant in regression of income mobility. This might be because of the small sample size of the bottom and top quintiles used in the regressions.

Table 12.2 Regression of Income Mobility of Households from 2010–2014

Explanatory Variables	Moving Up from the 20% Bottom in 2010 to a Higher Quintile in 2014	Moving Up from the 40% Bottom in 2010 to a Higher Quintile in 2014	Moving Down from the 40% Top in 2010 to a Lower Quintile in 2014
Gender of household head (male = 1, female = 0)	0.0744	−0.0818**	0.0102
	(0.0712)	(0.0323)	(0.0242)
Age of household head	0.0027	0.0005	−0.0003
	(0.0024)	(0.0011)	(0.0011)
Ethnicity of head (Kinh, Hoa = 0; ethnic minorities = 1)	−0.1904***	−0.0452	0.2439***
	(0.0701)	(0.0312)	(0.0488)
Household head with primary education	0.0011	0.0125	−0.0321
	(0.0638)	(0.0287)	(0.0316)
Household head with lower-secondary degree	0.1078	0.0609*	−0.0175
	(0.0735)	(0.0352)	(0.0325)
Household head with upper-secondary degree	0.1060	0.1182**	−0.0770**
	(0.1436)	(0.0596)	(0.0371)

continued on next page

Table 12.2 *continued*

Explanatory Variables	Moving Up from the 20% Bottom in 2010 to a Higher Quintile in 2014	Moving Up from the 40% Bottom in 2010 to a Higher Quintile in 2014	Moving Down from the 40% Top in 2010 to a Lower Quintile in 2014
Household head with college, university	0.2276	0.1639***	−0.1086***
	(0.1546)	(0.0420)	(0.0314)
Household size	−0.0193	0.0201**	−0.0191**
	(0.0170)	(0.0097)	(0.0076)
Proportion of children below 15	−0.1223	−0.1418**	0.0367
	(0.1389)	(0.0676)	(0.0554)
Proportion of members above 60	−0.3701***	−0.0862	0.1863***
	(0.1381)	(0.0539)	(0.0627)
Log of annual crop land	−0.0044	−0.0043	−0.0002
	(0.0117)	(0.0040)	(0.0032)
Log of perennial crop land	0.0124	−0.0033	−0.0015
	(0.0085)	(0.0037)	(0.0040)
Urban (urban = 1, rural = 0)	0.0265	−0.0269	−0.0665***
	(0.1174)	(0.0360)	(0.0238)
Northeast	−0.2212**	0.0209	0.0213
	(0.1051)	(0.0364)	(0.0347)
Northwest	−0.1416	−0.0612	0.0629
	(0.1257)	(0.0384)	(0.0762)
North Central Coast	−0.1529	−0.0013	0.1188***
	(0.1117)	(0.0359)	(0.0381)
South Central Coast	−0.2003*	−0.0098	0.0748*
	(0.1148)	(0.0352)	(0.0430)
Central Highlands	−0.3150***	0.0560	0.0791*
	(0.1154)	(0.0563)	(0.0462)
Southeast	−0.1365	0.1366***	−0.0157
	(0.1414)	(0.0478)	(0.0244)
Mekong River Delta	0.0163	0.0310	0.0328
	(0.1114)	(0.0366)	(0.0278)
Constant	0.5351***	0.0683	0.1709**
	(0.1784)	(0.0814)	(0.0756)
Observations	403	1,084	1,084
R-squared	0.177	0.078	0.136

continued on next page

Table 12.2 continued

Explanatory Variables	Moving Down from the 20% Top in 2010 to a Lower Quintile in 2014	Absolute Change in per Capita Income 2010–2014 (Fields and Ok Index)	Relative Change in per Capita Income 2010–2014
Gender of household head (male = 1, female = 0)	−0.0923	−1,190.39	−0.1685**
	(0.0690)	(727.91)	(0.0719)
Age of household head	−0.0039	−4.90	−0.0013
	(0.0034)	(14.56)	(0.0022)
Ethnicity of head (Kinh, Hoa = 0; ethnic minorities = 1)	−0.0783	−1,440.9***	−0.0895
	(0.1512)	(427.65)	(0.0913)
Household head with primary education	0.0916	950.32	0.0295
	(0.1267)	(770.97)	(0.0756)
Household head with lower-secondary degree	−0.1144	705.57	−0.0358
	(0.1081)	(447.25)	(0.0646)
Household head with upper-secondary degree	−0.1894	1,497.65**	−0.0780
	(0.1225)	(629.51)	(0.0715)
Household head with college, university	−0.1684	2,558.29***	−0.1484**
	(0.1023)	(572.05)	(0.0721)
Household size	0.0170	−162.43	0.0205
	(0.0209)	(118.18)	(0.0140)
Proportion of children below 15	0.0892	−2,749.3***	−0.1860
	(0.1932)	(898.67)	(0.1365)
Proportion of members above 60	0.2111	−2,783.0***	−0.1559*
	(0.1498)	(887.03)	(0.0943)
Log of annual crop land	0.0313***	−59.18	−0.0025
	(0.0107)	(80.53)	(0.0072)
Log of perennial crop land	−0.0129	−28.50	0.0004
	(0.0107)	(78.35)	(0.0087)
Urban (urban = 1, rural = 0)	0.0101	−353.33	−0.0589
	(0.0712)	(984.89)	(0.0723)
Northeast	0.1452	425.61	0.1483
	(0.0946)	(567.30)	(0.1032)
Northwest	0.1588	−479.45	0.1337
	(0.2708)	(557.96)	(0.1380)

continued on next page

Table 12.2 *continued*

Explanatory Variables	Moving Down from the 20% Top in 2010 to a Lower Quintile in 2014	Absolute Change in per Capita Income 2010–2014 (Fields and Ok Index)	Relative Change in per Capita Income 2010–2014
North Central Coast	0.2134*	−492.96	0.0729
	(0.1225)	(488.69)	(0.0748)
South Central Coast	0.1144	−343.29	−0.0795
	(0.1129)	(543.75)	(0.0592)
Central Highlands	−0.0199	886.50	0.0036
	(0.0970)	(727.88)	(0.0903)
Southeast	0.0340	2,717.99**	0.0998
	(0.0817)	(1,151.56)	(0.0811)
Mekong River Delta	−0.0482	559.60	0.0117
	(0.0811)	(602.11)	(0.0652)
Constant	0.5565**	6,403.48***	0.8131***
	(0.2259)	(1,515.47)	(0.1667)
Observations	326	1,813	1,813
R-squared	0.120	0.045	0.018

Notes: Robust standard errors in parentheses; *** $p<0.01$, ** $p<0.05$, * $p<0.1$.
Source: Estimates from the Viet Nam Household Living Standard Surveys 2004 and 2008.

Interestingly, household composition is also correlated with income mobility. Households with more children and more elderly tend to have lower income mobility. They are less likely to move up to a higher quintile, but more likely to move down to a lower income quintile. Clearly, more dependents create more pressure for households to increase their income. Agricultural land is not important for income mobility. Having more land might restrict households to agricultural production, and they are less likely to move.

There are no large differences in income mobility between urban and rural households. Regarding the regional variables, households in the Southeast—the richest region in Viet Nam—have the highest income mobility. Compared with households in the Red River Delta (the reference group), households in the Northeast, South Central Coast, and Central Highlands are less likely to move up from the lowest quintile. Households in the Southeast are more likely to move up from the bottom

40%. Regarding downward mobility, households in the North Central Coast and Central Highlands are more likely to move down from the high-income quintiles.

12.4 Intragenerational Employment Mobility

12.4.1 Employment Structure

In this section, we examine the intragenerational mobility of individuals in terms of employment. Table 12.3 shows the share of individuals aged 15–60 by occupation from 2004 to 2014. The definition of employment is similar to Brand-Weiner, Francavilla, and Olivari (2015). The categories are unskilled manual, skilled manual (e.g., craft and related trades workers, machine operators), and nonmanual (e.g., service and sales workers, technicians, managers). The nonmanual occupation is considered highly skilled. The share of unskilled workers decreased notably over time. The proportion of individuals aged 15–60 with unskilled employment was 72.3% in 2004 and 45.9% in 2014.

We also analyze employment status mobility, which defines workers by wage employment and self-employment. It shows that the share of self-employed workers decreased from 66.5% in 2004 to 57.8% in 2014. The share of wage workers increased over time, an indication of the expansion of the formal sector.

Employment is classified by sectors including agriculture, industry, and services. Laborers in the agriculture sector tend to have lower skills and income than laborers in the other two sectors. From 2004 to 2014, the number of agricultural laborers decreased, and they moved to the service and industry sectors. However, from 2010 to 2014, the share of agricultural workers did not decrease, possibly due to the economic slowdown in Viet Nam in recent years.

Table 12.4 presents the employment structure of workers by different characteristics in 2014. Men are more likely to have skilled, and nonfarm jobs with wage than women. There is no difference in occupation by skills between young and older people. Young people are more likely to have wage jobs in the industrial sector than older people. There is a strong correlation between education and employment. People with high education, especially post-secondary school, have a substantially higher proportion of skilled and nonmanual occupation, wage, and nonfarm jobs than those with low education.

There is also a large gap in skilled occupation between urban and rural people, and between the Kinh/Hoa and ethnic minority people. The share of self-employed and farm workers is also higher in rural and ethnic minority people.

Table 12.3 Employment of Individuals Aged 15–60 over Time

	Occupation			Employment		Sector		
Year	Unskilled Manual	Skilled Manual	Nonmanual	Self-employed	Wage Earner	Agriculture	Industry	Service
2004	72.3	15.2	12.5	66.5	33.5	52.7	19.8	27.6
2008	64.6	20.1	15.3	63.5	36.5	49.4	22.1	28.6
2010	48.1	26.8	25.1	60.5	39.5	42.9	25.5	31.6
2014	45.9	28.7	25.3	57.8	42.2	44.5	24.3	31.2

Source: Estimates from the Viet Nam Household Living Standard Surveys 2004, 2008, 2010, and 2014.

Table 12.4 Employment of Individuals Aged 15–60 in 2014

	Occupation			Employment		Sector		
Group	Unskilled Manual	Skilled Manual	Nonmanual	Self-employed	Wage Earner	Agriculture	Industry	Service
Sex								
Male	43.3	35.8	20.9	51.6	48.4	42.4	28.8	28.8
Female	48.6	21.4	29.9	64.1	35.9	46.5	19.7	33.7
Age								
Age 15–30	46.9	28.8	24.3	46.9	53.1	41.5	29.6	29.0
Age 31–60	45.5	28.7	25.8	62.6	37.4	45.8	22.0	32.2
Education								
Less primary	69.4	21.8	8.8	70.7	29.3	69.5	14.4	16.2
Primary	56.4	30.1	13.4	66.7	33.3	55.3	24.5	20.2
Lower-secondary	53.4	31.5	15.1	68.4	31.6	50.1	27.7	22.2
Upper-secondary	37.3	32.2	30.5	56.8	43.2	33.1	29.5	37.4
Post-secondary	10.2	26.2	63.5	22.7	77.3	11.3	23.7	65.0
Rural/urban								
Rural	54.8	29.2	16.1	63.8	36.2	55.3	23.4	21.3
Urban	22.9	27.6	49.4	42.1	57.9	16.3	26.7	57.0
Ethnicity								
Kinh and Hoa	38.7	32.3	28.9	53.3	46.7	36.8	27.6	35.6
Ethnic minorities	82.1	10.8	7.2	80.3	19.7	82.6	8.0	9.3
Total	**45.9**	**28.7**	**25.3**	**57.8**	**42.2**	**44.5**	**24.3**	**31.2**

Source: Estimates from the Viet Nam Household Living Standard Survey 2014.

12.4.2 Mobility of Employment

Figure 12.5 presents the occupation mobility from unskilled to skilled and manual occupation over time using panel data from the VHLSSs. Among the unskilled workers in 2004, 17% became skilled or nonmanual workers in 2008. The upward mobility of occupation increased from 2010 to 2014. Of unskilled workers in 2010, 24% had a skilled manual or nonmanual job in 2014. The occupation mobility increased for all groups of workers including ethnic minorities and the Kinh/Hoa, urban and rural people, male and female, young and older, and people with different education levels. However, there is a large gap in occupation mobility between urban and rural people, between the Kinh/Hoa and ethnic minority people, and between people with different education levels. Having a high education plays an important role in changing from unskilled to skilled jobs.

In Table 12.5, we analyze employment mobility from 2010 to 2014 in more detail. The analysis of employment mobility from 2004 to 2008 is presented in Table A12.3 in the Appendix. It shows that 23.6% of unskilled workers in 2010 found skilled or nonmanual jobs in 2014. However, there was also downward mobility—19.7% of skilled and nonmanual workers in 2010 had unskilled jobs in 2014. The movement between self-employed workers and wage workers and movement between the farm and nonfarm sectors were quite low.

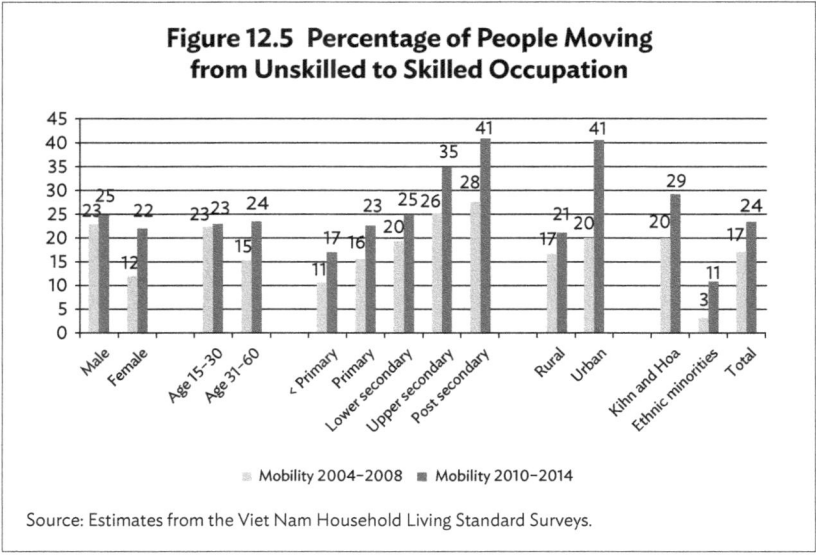

Source: Estimates from the Viet Nam Household Living Standard Surveys.

Table 12.5 Employment Mobility of Individuals from 2010–2014

	Moving Up from Unskilled to Skilled and Nonmanual	Moving Down from Skilled and Nonmanual to Unskilled	Moving from Self-employed to Wage Jobs
Sex			
Male	25.20	17.01	21.06
Female	22.11	22.97	12.71
Age			
Age 15–30	23.18	15.08	30.64
Age 31–60	23.72	21.15	12.97
Education			
Less primary	17.08	34.24	14.28
Primary	23.04	29.90	17.11
Lower secondary	25.03	24.28	17.84
Upper secondary	35.22	16.33	14.99
Post secondary	41.18	5.45	12.82
Rural/urban			
Rural	21.34	25.95	17.63
Urban	40.82	9.74	10.51
Ethnicity			
Kinh and Hoa	29.38	18.75	15.20
Ethnic minorities	10.84	37.12	19.92
Total	**23.58**	**19.69**	**16.23**

	Moving from Wage Jobs to Self-employed	Moving from Agricultural to Nonagricultural	Moving from Nonagricultural to Agricultural
Sex			
Male	19.30	14.65	15.73
Female	22.32	14.35	17.53
Age			
Age 15–30	13.54	16.85	13.28
Age 31–60	23.86	13.82	17.80
Education			
Less primary	24.43	9.03	32.52
Primary	28.89	12.38	20.71

continued on next page

Table 12.5 continued

	Moving from Wage Jobs to Self-employed	Moving from Agricultural to Nonagricultural	Moving from Nonagricultural to Agricultural
Lower secondary	24.41	19.83	22.97
Upper secondary	18.58	22.44	8.51
Post secondary	9.75	16.26	4.61
Rural/urban			
Rural	23.94	13.89	24.55
Urban	12.94	21.72	4.76
Ethnicity			
Kinh and Hoa	18.77	17.25	13.21
Ethnic minorities	31.10	8.09	57.29
Total	**20.43**	**14.49**	**16.55**

Source: Estimates from the Viet Nam Household Living Standard Surveys 2010 and 2014.

There are only small differences in employment mobility between men and women. Regarding age, young people had higher movement from self-employed to employed employment, and lower movement from employed to self-employed employment than older people. Having a high education helps people find a skilled or nonmanual job and reduce the downward change from a skilled to an unskilled job. Rural people and ethnic minority people are less likely to move up but more likely to move down in employment than urban and Kinh/Hoa people.

12.4.3 Regression of Employment Mobility

Table 12.6 presents the regressions of mobility of occupation from 2010–2014. The dependent variables include the change in occupation, employment status, and working sectors. The analysis for 2004–2008 is presented in Table A12.4 of the Appendix. It shows that men are less likely to move down from skilled and nonmanual occupation to unskilled occupation than women and that they are more likely to move from self-employed to employed (wage) work than women.

Age is not correlated with the occupation movement. However, there is a negative relationship between age and the probability of moving from self-employed to wage jobs. As age increases, the probability to move from self-employed to wage jobs decreases at a decreasing rate.

Table 12.6 Regression of Employment Mobility of Individuals from 2010–2014

Explanatory Variables	Dependent Variables		
	Moving Up from Unskilled to Skilled and Nonmanual	Moving Down from Skilled and Nonmanual to Unskilled	Moving from Self-employed to Wage Jobs
Male = 1, female = 0	0.0214	−0.0625***	0.0842***
	(0.0227)	(0.0192)	(0.0198)
Age	−0.0021	−0.0086	−0.0183***
	(0.0066)	(0.0086)	(0.0064)
Age squared	0.0000	0.0001	0.0001*
	(0.0001)	(0.0001)	(0.0001)
Ethnic minorities (yes = 1; Kinh, Hoa = 0)	−0.0624	0.1356**	0.0386
	(0.0457)	(0.0602)	(0.0412)
Having primary education	0.0207	−0.0072	0.0002
	(0.0272)	(0.0534)	(0.0275)
Having lower-secondary degree	0.0553*	−0.0896*	0.0066
	(0.0324)	(0.0536)	(0.0296)
Having upper-secondary degree	0.1331**	−0.1322**	−0.0558
	(0.0558)	(0.0605)	(0.0366)
Having college, university	0.1919***	−0.2303***	−0.0340
	(0.0672)	(0.0512)	(0.0368)
Household size	−0.0076	0.0003	−0.0196***
	(0.0084)	(0.0105)	(0.0069)
Proportion of children below 15	0.0622	0.0441	−0.0685
	(0.0661)	(0.0687)	(0.0562)
Proportion of members above 60	−0.0170	0.0027	−0.1122
	(0.1017)	(0.0978)	(0.0770)
Log of annual crop land	−0.0056	0.0170***	0.0017
	(0.0057)	(0.0046)	(0.0038)
Log of perennial crop land	0.0014	0.0147**	−0.0037
	(0.0042)	(0.0062)	(0.0034)
Urban (urban = 1, rural = 0)	0.1252*	−0.0023	−0.0564*
	(0.0661)	(0.0318)	(0.0339)

continued on next page

Table 12.6 *continued*

	Dependent Variables		
Explanatory Variables	Moving Up from Unskilled to Skilled and Nonmanual	Moving Down from Skilled and Nonmanual to Unskilled	Moving from Self-employed to Wage Jobs
Northeast	−0.0801	−0.0370	−0.0746*
	(0.0489)	(0.0365)	(0.0415)
Northwest	−0.0840	−0.1252***	−0.1495**
	(0.0560)	(0.0464)	(0.0592)
North Central Coast	0.0934*	−0.0223	−0.0186
	(0.0512)	(0.0512)	(0.0423)
South Central Coast	0.1258*	−0.0746**	0.0256
	(0.0654)	(0.0376)	(0.0451)
Central Highlands	−0.0654	0.0264	−0.0123
	(0.0623)	(0.0637)	(0.0521)
Southeast	0.1997***	−0.0638	0.0079
	(0.0722)	(0.0388)	(0.0450)
Mekong River Delta	0.0488	−0.0505	−0.0353
	(0.0562)	(0.0424)	(0.0369)
Constant	0.2806**	0.4035**	0.7811***
	(0.1401)	(0.1628)	(0.1448)
Observations	1,618	1,434	1,721
R-squared	0.105	0.134	0.086

	Dependent Variables		
Explanatory Variables	Moving from Wage Jobs to Self-employed	Moving from Agricultural to Nonagricultural	Moving from Nonagricultural to Agricultural
Male = 1, female = 0	−0.0554**	0.0111	−0.0247
	(0.0239)	(0.0190)	(0.0165)
Age	−0.0124	0.0050	−0.0159**
	(0.0094)	(0.0057)	(0.0076)

continued on next page

Table 12.6 continued

Explanatory Variables	Dependent Variables		
	Moving from Wage Jobs to Self-employed	Moving from Agricultural to Nonagricultural	Moving from Nonagricultural to Agricultural
Age squared	0.0003**	−0.0001*	0.0003**
	(0.0001)	(0.0001)	(0.0001)
Ethnic minorities (yes = 1; Kinh, Hoa = 0)	0.0223	−0.0249	0.2369***
	(0.0415)	(0.0324)	(0.0582)
Having primary education	0.0640	0.0009	−0.0655*
	(0.0429)	(0.0218)	(0.0379)
Having lower-secondary degree	0.0012	0.0427	−0.0646
	(0.0419)	(0.0270)	(0.0410)
Having upper-secondary degree	−0.0217	0.0523	−0.1508***
	(0.0531)	(0.0429)	(0.0433)
Having college, university	−0.1145***	0.0212	−0.1960***
	(0.0410)	(0.0508)	(0.0410)
Household size	0.0063	−0.0030	−0.0161**
	(0.0087)	(0.0062)	(0.0076)
Proportion of children below 15	−0.0070	−0.0790	0.0582
	(0.0663)	(0.0527)	(0.0575)
Proportion of members above 60	0.1649	0.0005	0.1431
	(0.1034)	(0.0954)	(0.0882)
Log of annual crop land	0.0092**	−0.0115***	0.0196***
	(0.0045)	(0.0036)	(0.0039)
Log of perennial crop land	0.0129***	0.0008	0.0165**
	(0.0049)	(0.0030)	(0.0064)
Urban (urban = 1, rural = 0)	−0.0033	0.0047	−0.0232
	(0.0335)	(0.0550)	(0.0245)
Northeast	0.0612	−0.1994***	0.0112
	(0.0471)	(0.0469)	(0.0343)
Northwest	0.0316	−0.2548***	0.2584***
	(0.0562)	(0.0476)	(0.0755)
North Central Coast	0.0455	−0.1237**	−0.0286
	(0.0424)	(0.0478)	(0.0377)

continued on next page

Table 12.6 continued

Explanatory Variables	Dependent Variables		
	Moving from Wage Jobs to Self-employed	Moving from Agricultural to Nonagricultural	Moving from Nonagricultural to Agricultural
South Central Coast	−0.0545	−0.1248**	−0.0625**
	(0.0371)	(0.0547)	(0.0265)
Central Highlands	0.1496**	−0.2627***	0.0687
	(0.0593)	(0.0504)	(0.0454)
Southeast	−0.0109	−0.1802***	−0.0322
	(0.0397)	(0.0551)	(0.0281)
Mekong River Delta	−0.0567	−0.1844***	−0.0334
	(0.0431)	(0.0435)	(0.0365)
Constant	0.2440	0.4182***	0.4624***
	(0.1809)	(0.1315)	(0.1446)
Observations	1,331	1,512	1,540
R-squared	0.123	0.083	0.246

Notes: Robust standard errors in parentheses; *** $p<0.01$, ** $p<0.05$, * $p<0.1$.
Source: Estimates from the Viet Nam Household Living Standard Surveys 2010–2014.

Education plays an important role in labor mobility from unskilled to skilled employment. Compared with people with no education, having a post-secondary degree increases the probability of moving up from unskilled to skilled or nonmanual occupation by 0.19. It also reduces the probability of moving down from skilled and manual occupation to unskilled occupation by 0.23.

Education is less correlated with the employment and sector movement. The regression results show that education is neither correlated with the movement from self-employed to employed work nor the movement from agricultural to nonagricultural work. However, higher education reduces the movement from employed to self-employed work and from nonagricultural to agricultural work.

Overall, household composition such as household size and age structure is not correlated with employment mobility of household members. However, having more agricultural land increases the movement from employed to self-employed work and the movement from nonagricultural to agricultural work. Urban and regional variables also matter to mobility of employment, especially the mobility between agriculture and nonagriculture sectors. Urban people tend to move up from unskilled to skilled and nonmanual occupation more than rural people. Compared with workers in the Red River Delta (the reference group), workers in the North Central Coast, South Central Coast, and Southeast are more likely to move up from unskilled to skilled and nonmanual. Workers in the northern mountains including the Northeast and Northwest are less likely to move from self-employed to wage jobs as well as move from agricultural to nonagricultural employment. Workers in the Central Highlands are more likely to transit from wage jobs to self-employment, but less likely to move from agricultural to nonagricultural employment.

12.5 Intergenerational Mobility

12.5.1 Intergenerational Employment Mobility

In this section, we analyze the intergenerational mobility of employment —that is, a correlation between parents' employment and children's employment. We use the sample of children and parents who are still working, and children aged from 15 to 60. We define parent as the one with higher wages—that is, if the mother has higher wages than the father, the mother is defined as the parent and vice versa.

Figure 12.6 shows that, in 2004, among children who had a parent with unskilled occupation, 19% were able to find skilled or nonmanual jobs. In other words, 81% of children had unskilled occupations like their parents. Occupation mobility greatly improved in 2014—38% of children with unskilled parents found skilled or nonmanual occupation. One reason for this upward mobility is the increase in skilled and nonmanual employment from 2004–2014.

The improvement in occupation mobility is higher for females and older people than males and young people. Education plays an important role for improvement in intergenerational mobility of occupational skills. With post-secondary degree holders, 80% of people whose parents are unskilled have skilled or nonmanual occupation. Urban and Kinh/Hoa people are more likely to have skilled and nonmanual occupation than rural and ethnic minorities.

Table 12.7 presents the intergenerational mobility of employment in 2014 by different types of employment and different characteristics of individuals. This table presents not only upward but also downward intergenerational mobility of employment. The analysis of intergenerational employment mobility in 2004 is presented in Table A12.5 of the Appendix.

296　Demystifying Rising Inequality in Asia

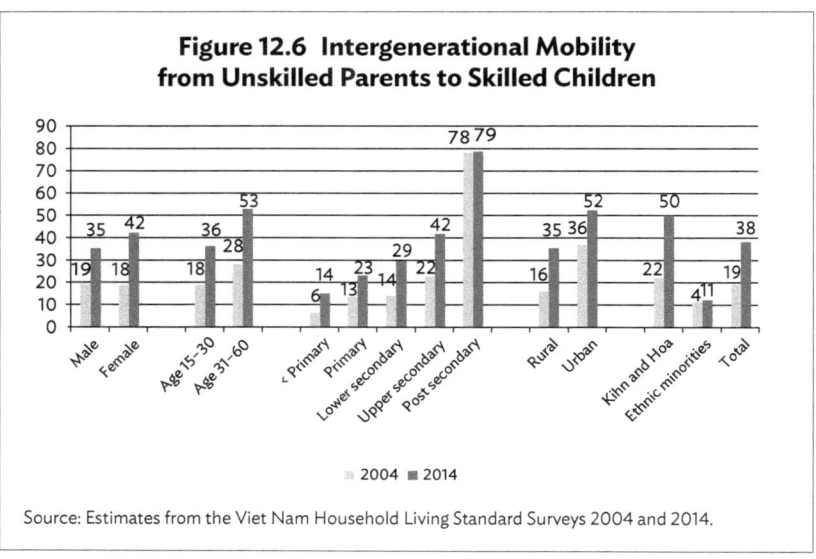

Figure 12.6 Intergenerational Mobility from Unskilled Parents to Skilled Children

Source: Estimates from the Viet Nam Household Living Standard Surveys 2004 and 2014.

It shows that of children whose parents have skilled or nonmanual occupation, 27.7% had unskilled occupation. This is regarded as downward intergenerational mobility. This downward rate is very high for ethnic minorities—67% of ethnic minority children had unskilled occupations even though their parents had skilled or nonmanual occupations. The Kinh/Hoa and urban people, especially those with high education, have a remarkably lower downward rate of intergenerational skills.

Table 12.7 Intergenerational Mobility of Employment in 2014

Characteristics of Children	Skill Upward: Skilled Children and Unskilled Parents	Skill Downward: Unskilled Children and Skilled Parents	Employment Upward: Wage Children and Self-employed Parents
Sex			
Male	35.02	30.14	44.12
Female	42.02	23.97	46.13
Age			
Age 15–30	35.92	28.84	43.66
Age 31–60	52.81	17.69	55.11
Education			
Less primary	14.43	41.38	30.38

continued on next page

Table 12.7 *continued*

Characteristics of Children	Skill Upward: Skilled Children and Unskilled Parents	Skill Downward: Unskilled Children and Skilled Parents	Employment Upward: Wage Children and Self-employed Parents
Primary	22.51	44.71	37.08
Lower secondary	29.22	43.71	30.74
Upper secondary	41.71	29.06	43.64
Post secondary	78.58	8.42	73.57
Rural/urban			
Rural	34.94	36.17	41.03
Urban	51.99	12.22	59.63
Ethnicity			
Kinh and Hoa	49.91	23.47	54.52
Ethnic minorities	10.86	67.47	17.77
Total	**37.62**	**27.68**	**44.89**

Characteristics of Children	Employment Downward: Self-employed Children and Wage Parents	Sector Upward: Nonagricultural Children and Agricultural Parents	Sector Downward: Agricultural Children and Nonagricultural Parents
Sex			
Male	20.27	40.05	13.84
Female	24.84	45.44	13.76
Age			
Age 15–30	22.60	40.39	14.32
Age 31–60	16.13	57.81	9.82
Education			
Less primary	21.18	19.76	17.88
Primary	17.04	29.25	14.80
Lower secondary	39.71	31.56	25.86
Upper secondary	25.20	50.51	16.78
Post secondary	10.16	76.91	4.82
Rural/urban			
Rural	26.20	40.52	21.52
Urban	14.17	53.24	3.87
Ethnicity			
Kinh and Hoa	19.54	54.87	11.95
Ethnic minorities	45.43	14.82	45.33
Total	**22.02**	**42.02**	**13.80**

Source: Estimates from the Viet Nam Household Living Standard Surveys 2014.

Over time, there has been an expansion in the formal sector as well as the nonfarm sector. The proportion of wage workers and nonagricultural workers tends to increase over time. As a result, 44.9% of children with self-employed parents found wage jobs. On the other hand, around 22% of children with wage parents had self-employed work. The intergenerational movement from agriculture to nonagriculture sectors is higher than the intergenerational movement from nonagriculture to agriculture sectors.

12.5.2 Intergenerational Correlations of Earnings

An important issue in intergenerational mobility is the estimate of intergenerational correlations of earnings or the intergenerational elasticity. In this study, we use OLS regression to estimate intergenerational elasticity. More specifically, we regress log of annual wages of children on log of annual wages of parents as follows:

$$Log(wage_{children}) = \alpha + \beta Log(wage_{parent}) + Age_{children} + Age^2_{children} + \varepsilon.$$

The coefficient of log of annual wages of parents is the estimate of intergenerational elasticity. The above model is widely used to estimate the intergenerational elasticity of earning in empirical studies (Black and Devereux 2010). Since we do not have data on permanent income in the VHLSSs, we have to use income in the year of surveys. To correct for this life-cycle problem, in which income varies across age, we control age of children in regression. We estimate intergenerational elasticity using pooled samples of VHLSSs 2004, 2008, 2010, and 2014. Tables A12.6 to A12.8 of the Appendix present the regression results. Figures 12.7 to 12.9 present the estimates of intergenerational elasticity or the intergenerational coefficient for different groups of people.

Figure 12.7 presents the intergenerational elasticity between fathers and sons/daughters and intergenerational elasticity between mothers and sons/daughters. It shows that intergenerational elasticity is quite similar between different pairs of parents and children. However, intergenerational elasticity is higher between parents and sons than between parents and daughters. It means that girls tend to have higher income mobility than boys.

In Figure 12.8, we estimate the intergenerational elasticity of children's wages with respect to the parent with higher wages. Intergenerational elasticity is 0.36, which implies that if the parents' wage

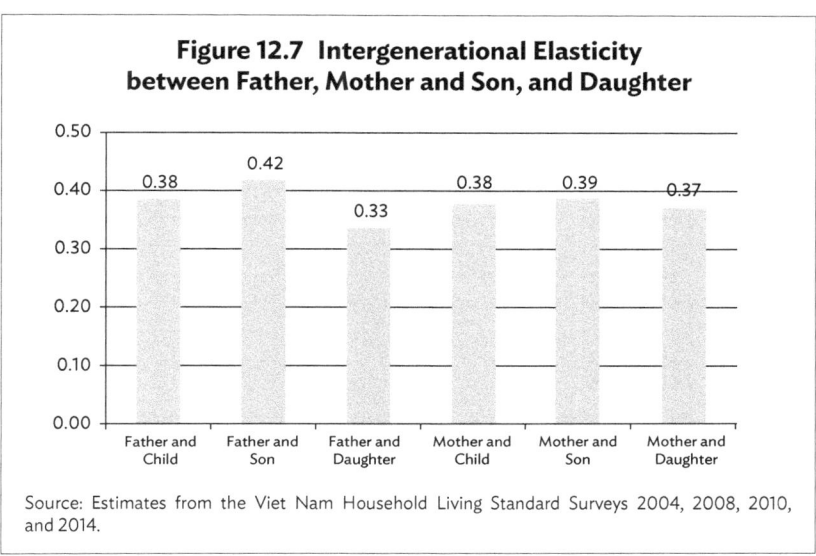

Figure 12.7 Intergenerational Elasticity between Father, Mother and Son, and Daughter

Source: Estimates from the Viet Nam Household Living Standard Surveys 2004, 2008, 2010, and 2014.

increases by 1%, their children's wage increases by 0.36%. The higher value of the intergenerational elasticity means low intergenerational mobility. This value is similar to several developed countries, such as Germany and Japan, but lower than France, the United Kingdom, and the US, and higher than Canada, Australia, and the Nordic countries (according to the estimates in Corak 2013a). Viet Nam also has a lower intergenerational elasticity than, for example, the People's Republic of China (0.62 according to Gong, Leigh, and Meng 2012), Brazil (0.58 according to Ferreira and Veloso 2006), and Malaysia (0.54 according to Grawe 2004).

Figure 12.8 shows that intergenerational mobility was slightly higher in 2014 than in 2004. Intergenerational mobility is higher for urban and Kinh/Hoa people than for rural and ethnic minority people.

Figure 12.9 shows a higher intergenerational mobility for women than men. Intergenerational elasticity is very similar between young and older people. Figure 12.9 shows the important role of education in improving intergenerational mobility. The intergenerational elasticity for children without education degrees and those with post-secondary degrees is 0.51 and 0.17, respectively.

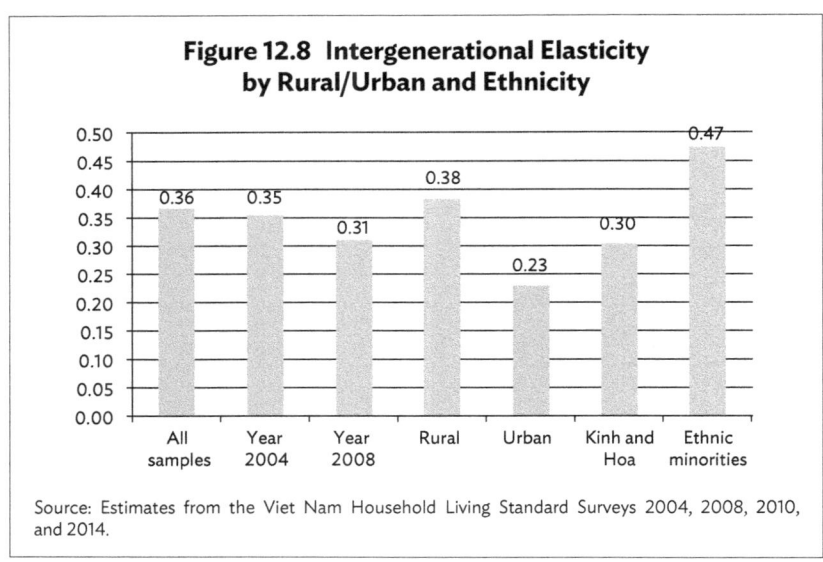

Figure 12.8 Intergenerational Elasticity by Rural/Urban and Ethnicity

Source: Estimates from the Viet Nam Household Living Standard Surveys 2004, 2008, 2010, and 2014.

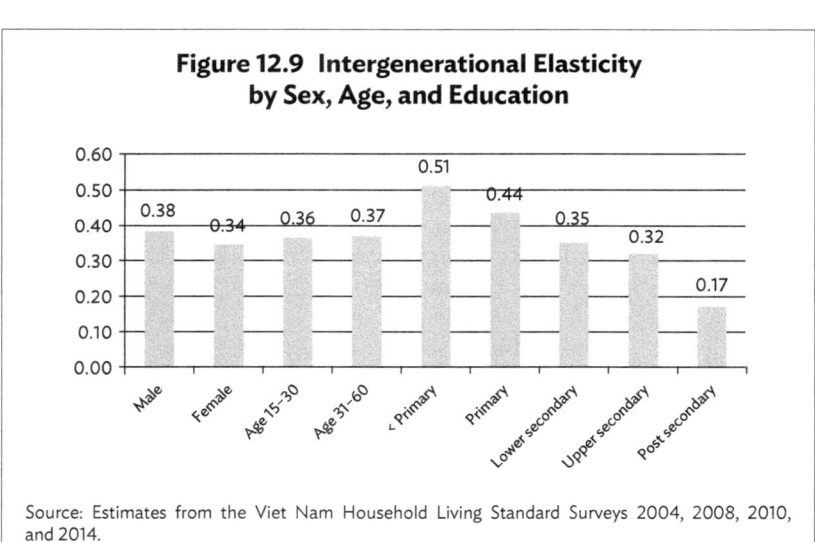

Figure 12.9 Intergenerational Elasticity by Sex, Age, and Education

Source: Estimates from the Viet Nam Household Living Standard Surveys 2004, 2008, 2010, and 2014.

12.5.3 Regression of Intergenerational Mobility of Employment

Finally, Table 12.8 presents the OLS regression of intergenerational employment mobility using pooled samples of VHLSSs 2004, 2008, 2010, and 2014. It shows that men are less likely to have upward intergenerational mobility and more likely to have downward intergenerational mobility than women. There is an inverted-U shape between upward intergenerational mobility and age. As age increases, the probability of having a better job than their parents increases. However, after achieving a peak, the probability of having a better job than their parents decreases with age.

Table 12.8 Regression of Intergenerational Employment Mobility

	Dependent Variables		
Explanatory Variables	Skill Upward: Skilled Children and Unskilled Parents	Skill Downward: Unskilled Children and Skilled Parents	Employment Upward: Wage Children and Self-employed Parents
Male = 1, female = 0	−0.0263***	0.0241**	0.0210**
	(0.0080)	(0.0114)	(0.0087)
Age	0.0400***	−0.0837***	0.0585***
	(0.0056)	(0.0119)	(0.0071)
Age squared	−0.0006***	0.0015***	−0.0011***
	(0.0001)	(0.0002)	(0.0001)
Ethnic minorities (yes = 1; Kinh, Hoa = 0)	−0.1128***	0.1838***	−0.1522***
	(0.0121)	(0.0317)	(0.0165)
Having primary education	0.0670***	−0.1158***	0.0329*
	(0.0118)	(0.0361)	(0.0172)
Having lower-secondary degree	0.0899***	−0.1324***	0.0202
	(0.0130)	(0.0360)	(0.0182)
Having upper-secondary degree	0.1446***	−0.1800***	0.0546***
	(0.0169)	(0.0371)	(0.0210)
Having college, university	0.5079***	−0.3592***	0.3227***
	(0.0181)	(0.0356)	(0.0221)
Gender of parent (father = 1, mother = 0)	−0.0201*	0.0277	−0.0512***
	(0.0118)	(0.0199)	(0.0140)

continued on next page

Table 12.8 *continued*

Explanatory Variables	Skill Upward: Skilled Children and Unskilled Parents	Skill Downward: Unskilled Children and Skilled Parents	Employment Upward: Wage Children and Self-employed Parents
Age of parent	−0.0019	0.0003	−0.0119
	(0.0092)	(0.0202)	(0.0112)
Age of parent squared	0.0000	−0.0000	0.0001
	(0.0001)	(0.0002)	(0.0001)
Parent with primary education	0.0303***	0.0367	−0.0024
	(0.0115)	(0.0247)	(0.0138)
Parent with lower-secondary degree	0.0430***	0.0051	−0.0105
	(0.0136)	(0.0250)	(0.0155)
Parent with upper-secondary degree	0.0228	−0.0128	−0.0221
	(0.0241)	(0.0290)	(0.0274)
Parent with college, university	0.0494**	0.0161	−0.0759***
	(0.0227)	(0.0262)	(0.0229)
Household size	−0.0008	−0.0025	0.0002
	(0.0031)	(0.0053)	(0.0037)
Proportion of children below 15	−0.0267	0.0623	−0.1207***
	(0.0342)	(0.0592)	(0.0425)
Proportion of members above 60	0.0528	0.0089	−0.0381
	(0.0627)	(0.0845)	(0.0662)
Log of annual crop land	−0.0030**	0.0152***	−0.0097***
	(0.0015)	(0.0027)	(0.0020)
Log of perennial crop land	−0.0051***	0.0049*	−0.0113***
	(0.0013)	(0.0027)	(0.0016)
Urban (urban = 1, rural = 0)	0.0336*	−0.0120	−0.0116
	(0.0190)	(0.0218)	(0.0212)
Northeast	−0.1652***	0.0751***	−0.1746***
	(0.0192)	(0.0258)	(0.0197)
Northwest	−0.1824***	0.1864***	−0.2094***
	(0.0199)	(0.0444)	(0.0225)
North Central Coast	−0.1989***	0.2184***	−0.1941***
	(0.0195)	(0.0270)	(0.0202)
South Central Coast	−0.0607***	−0.0223	−0.0313
	(0.0231)	(0.0213)	(0.0235)

continued on next page

Table 12.8 *continued*

Explanatory Variables	Dependent Variables		
	Skill Upward: Skilled Children and Unskilled Parents	Skill Downward: Unskilled Children and Skilled Parents	Employment Upward: Wage Children and Self-employed Parents
Central Highlands	−0.1895***	0.2782***	−0.1838***
	(0.0239)	(0.0339)	(0.0238)
Southeast	−0.0348	−0.0457**	−0.0248
	(0.0228)	(0.0226)	(0.0257)
Mekong River Delta	−0.1427***	0.0500**	−0.1298***
	(0.0192)	(0.0225)	(0.0195)
Dummy year 2008	0.0434***	−0.0662***	0.0220
	(0.0106)	(0.0216)	(0.0134)
Dummy year 2010	0.1154***	−0.1228***	0.0396***
	(0.0129)	(0.0205)	(0.0141)
Dummy year 2014	0.1321***	−0.1279***	0.0547***
	(0.0137)	(0.0205)	(0.0152)
Constant	−0.2872	1.5431***	0.0301
	(0.2175)	(0.4735)	(0.2674)
Observations	12,268	6,082	13,387
R-squared	0.308	0.267	0.224

Explanatory Variables	Dependent Variables		
	Employment Downward: Self-employed Children and Wage Parents	Sector Upward: Nonagricultural Children and Agricultural Parents	Sector Downward: Agricultural Children and Nonagricultural Parents
Male = 1, female = 0	−0.0522***	−0.0394***	0.0006
	(0.0127)	(0.0092)	(0.0091)
Age	−0.0986***	0.0590***	−0.0830***
	(0.0143)	(0.0072)	(0.0094)
Age squared	0.0019***	−0.0009***	0.0015***
	(0.0003)	(0.0002)	(0.0002)
Ethnic minorities (yes = 1; Kinh, Hoa = 0)	0.0507*	−0.1702***	0.1543***
	(0.0285)	(0.0159)	(0.0340)

continued on next page

Table 12.8 continued

Explanatory Variables	Dependent Variables		
	Employment Downward: Self-employed Children and Wage Parents	Sector Upward: Nonagricultural Children and Agricultural Parents	Sector Downward: Agricultural Children and Nonagricultural Parents
Having primary education	0.0273	0.0929***	−0.0680***
	(0.0224)	(0.0143)	(0.0240)
Having lower-secondary degree	0.1064***	0.1156***	−0.0526**
	(0.0257)	(0.0157)	(0.0247)
Having upper-secondary degree	0.0663**	0.1530***	−0.0684***
	(0.0297)	(0.0195)	(0.0259)
Having college, university	−0.1322***	0.4229***	−0.1519***
	(0.0282)	(0.0199)	(0.0252)
Gender of parent (father = 1, mother = 0)	0.0245	−0.0235*	0.0113
	(0.0192)	(0.0142)	(0.0124)
Age of parent	−0.0144	−0.0111	−0.0090
	(0.0171)	(0.0109)	(0.0137)
Age of parent squared	0.0002	0.0001	0.0001
	(0.0002)	(0.0001)	(0.0001)
Parent with primary education	0.0582***	0.0153	0.0148
	(0.0214)	(0.0140)	(0.0175)
Parent with lower-secondary degree	0.0817***	0.0137	0.0456**
	(0.0245)	(0.0161)	(0.0188)
Parent with upper-secondary degree	0.1315***	0.0139	0.0460**
	(0.0318)	(0.0280)	(0.0223)
Parent with college, university	0.1214***	0.0344	0.0743***
	(0.0263)	(0.0264)	(0.0206)
Household size	0.0109**	0.0014	0.0038
	(0.0053)	(0.0036)	(0.0040)
Proportion of children below 15	−0.0355	−0.1015**	0.0481
	(0.0573)	(0.0418)	(0.0437)
Proportion of members above 60	−0.0523	−0.0564	−0.0345
	(0.0994)	(0.0702)	(0.0666)
Log of annual crop land	0.0197***	−0.0084***	0.0194***
	(0.0026)	(0.0019)	(0.0022)
Log of perennial crop land	0.0222***	−0.0083***	0.0174***
	(0.0032)	(0.0016)	(0.0029)

continued on next page

Table 12.8 *continued*

Explanatory Variables	Employment Downward: Self-employed Children and Wage Parents	Sector Upward: Nonagricultural Children and Agricultural Parents	Sector Downward: Agricultural Children and Nonagricultural Parents
	Dependent Variables		
Urban (urban = 1, rural = 0)	0.0480**	0.0629**	−0.0327**
	(0.0191)	(0.0250)	(0.0133)
Northeast	0.1775***	−0.2347***	0.1119***
	(0.0298)	(0.0210)	(0.0224)
Northwest	0.3084***	−0.2574***	0.0208
	(0.0515)	(0.0239)	(0.0533)
North Central Coast	0.2158***	−0.2605***	0.2164***
	(0.0291)	(0.0224)	(0.0238)
South Central Coast	0.0191	−0.1121***	0.0567***
	(0.0246)	(0.0266)	(0.0186)
Central Highlands	0.0862**	−0.3025***	0.1394***
	(0.0394)	(0.0271)	(0.0317)
Southeast	−0.0388*	−0.1004***	0.0074
	(0.0222)	(0.0276)	(0.0144)
Mekong River Delta	−0.0079	−0.1790***	0.0481***
	(0.0237)	(0.0214)	(0.0172)
Dummy year 2008	−0.0270	0.0293**	−0.0042
	(0.0190)	(0.0129)	(0.0143)
Dummy year 2010	−0.0221	0.0320**	−0.0328**
	(0.0195)	(0.0147)	(0.0149)
Dummy year 2014	−0.0646***	0.0395**	−0.0374***
	(0.0197)	(0.0156)	(0.0138)
Constant	1.5362***	−0.0216	1.4027***
	(0.3937)	(0.2599)	(0.3261)
Observations	4,963	11,629	6,721
R-squared	0.229	0.276	0.235

Notes: Robust standard errors in parentheses; *** $p<0.01$, ** $p<0.05$, * $p<0.1$.
Source: Estimates from the Viet Nam Household Living Standard Surveys 2004, 2008, 2010, and 2014.

Ethnic minorities have a lower probability of upward intergenerational mobility and a higher probability of downward intergenerational mobility than the Kinh and Hoa. Education plays an important role in intergenerational employment. Better education increases upward intergenerational mobility and reduces downward intergenerational mobility, especially holding post-secondary degrees improves the intergenerational employment substantially compared with holding other lower educational degrees.

Urban and regional variables also contribute to intergenerational mobility. Compared with rural people, urban people are more likely to have skilled occupations when having unskilled parents. They are also more likely to transition from agricultural to nonagricultural employment. Compared with people in Red River Delta (the reference group), people in other regions such as in the Northwest, Northeast, Central Coast, Central Highlands, and Mekong River Delta have a higher probability of downward intergenerational mobility and a lower probability.

12.6 Conclusions

In this study, we examine intragenerational and intergenerational mobility of employment and income in Viet Nam from 2004 to 2008 and from 2010 to 2014. We find rather high mobility across income quintiles—45% of households in the bottom quintile in 2004 moved to a higher income quintile in 2008. However, income mobility decreased over time; and 37% of households in the bottom quintile in 2010 were able to move to a higher income quintile in 2014.

Compared with the Kinh and Hoa, ethnic minorities are more likely to move down but less likely to move up across income quintiles. Households with higher education heads are more likely to move up and less likely to move down. They are also more mobile than households with lower education heads. Households with more children and more elderly people tend to have lower income mobility. They are less likely to move up to a higher quintile, but more likely to move down to a lower income quintile. Agricultural land is not important for income mobility. Having more lands might restrict households to agricultural production, and they are less likely to move.

There was high mobility by occupational skills but less mobility by employment status and sectors. Among the unskilled workers in 2004, 17% of them had become skilled manual or nonmanual workers in 2008. The upward mobility of occupation increased from 2010–2014. Of the unskilled workers in 2010, 24% had a skilled manual or nonmanual job in 2014. Men are less likely to move down from skilled and nonmanual occupation to unskilled occupation than women and they are more likely to move from self-employed to wage work than women. Education plays an important role in labor mobility from unskilled to skilled employment. Compared with people with no education, having a post-secondary degree increases the probability of moving up from unskilled to skilled or nonmanual occupation by 0.19. It also reduces the probability of moving down from skilled and manual occupation to unskilled occupation by 0.23. Having more agricultural land increases the movement from employed to self-employed work and the movement from nonagricultural to agricultural work.

The intergenerational elasticity of earnings for parents and children is estimated at around 0.36. Intergenerational elasticity is very similar for 2004 and 2014. Intergenerational mobility is higher for urban and the Kinh/Hoa than for rural and ethnic minority people. The analysis shows the important role of education in improving intergenerational mobility. Intergenerational elasticity for children without education degrees and for those with post-secondary degrees is 0.51 and 0.17, respectively.

Intergenerational mobility of occupation has improved in Viet Nam. In 2004, among children who had a parent with unskilled occupation, 19% were able to find skilled or nonmanual jobs. In other words, 81% of children had unskilled occupations like their parents. Occupation mobility greatly improved in 2014—38% of children with unskilled parents found skilled or nonmanual occupation. One reason for this upward mobility is the increase in skilled and nonmanual employment from 2004–2014. Education plays an important role in improving intergenerational mobility of occupational skills. With a post-secondary degree, 80% of people whose parents are unskilled have skilled or nonmanual occupation. The urban and Kinh/Hoa people are more likely to have skilled and nonmanual occupation than rural and ethnic minorities.

References

Baulch, B., and D. Vu. 2010. *Poverty Dynamics in Vietnam, 2002–2006*. Ha Noi: Chronic Poverty Research Centre and Prosperity Initiative and Centre for Analysis and Forecasting, Viet Nam Academy of Social Sciences.

Behrman, J. 200. Social Mobility: Concepts and Measurement. In *New Markets, New Opportunities? Economic and Social Mobility in a Changing World*, edited by N. Birdsall and C. Graham, Washington, DC Brookings, pp. 69–100.

Black, S., and P. Devereux. 2010. Recent Developments in Intergenerational Mobility. NBER Working Paper 15889. Cambridge, MA: National Bureau of Economic Research.

Brand-Weiner, I., F. Francavilla, and M. Olivari. Globalisation in Viet Nam: An Opportunity for Social Mobility? *Asia & the Pacific Policy Studies* 2(1): 21–33.

Corak, M. 2013a. Income Inequality, Equality of Opportunity, and Intergenerational Mobility. *Journal of Economic Perspectives* 27(3): 79–102.

———. 2013b. Inequality from Generation to Generation: The United States in Comparison. In *The Economics of Inequality, Poverty, and Discrimination in the 21st Century*, edited by R. S. Rycorft. Santa Barbara, CA: ABc–cLIO.

Emran, M. S., and F. Shilpi. 2011. Intergenerational Occupational Mobility in Rural Economy Evidence from Nepal and Vietnam. *Journal of Human Resources* 46: 427–458.

Ferreira, S. G., and F. A. Veloso. 2006. Intergenerational Mobility of Wages in Brazil. *Brazilian Review of Econometrics* 26: 181–211.

Fields, G., and E. Ok. 1996. *The Meaning and Measurement of Income Mobility*. Journal of Economic Theory 71: 349–377.

———. 1999. *The Measurement of Income Mobility: An Introduction to the Literature*. Ithaca, NY: Cornell University, ILR School.

Gong, H., A. Leigh, and N. Meng. 2012. Intergenerational Income Mobility in Urban China. *Review of Income and Wealth* 58: 481–503.

Grawe, N. 2004. Intergenerational Mobility for Whom? The Experience of High-and Low-earning Sons in International Perspective. In *Generational Income Mobility in North America and Europe*, edited by M. Corak. Cambridge, United Kingdom: Cambridge University Press.

Hertz, T., T. Jayasundera, P. Piraino, S. Selcuk, N. Smith, and A. Verashchagina. 2008. The Inheritance of Educational Inequality: International Comparisons and Fifty-year Trends. *The B. E. Journal of Economic Analysis & Policy* 7(2): 1–48.

Lanjouw, P., M. Marra, and C. Nguyen. 2013. Vietnam's Evolving Poverty Map: Patterns and Implications for Policy. Policy Research Working Paper 6355. Washington, DC: The World Bank.

Nguyen, C. 2011. Poverty Projection Using a Small Area Estimation Method: Evidence from Vietnam. *Journal of Comparative Economics* 39(3): 368–382.

———. 2012. Poverty Dynamics: The Structurally and Stochastically Poor in Vietnam. MPRA Paper 45738. Munich, Germany: University Library of Munich.

Nguyen, C., and A. Tran. 2014. Poverty Identification: Practice and Policy Implications in Vietnam. *Asian–Pacific Economic Literature* 28(1): 116–136.

Nguyen, C., T. Phung, and D. Westbrook. 2015. Do the Poorest Ethnic Minorities Benefit from a Large-scale Poverty Reduction Program? Evidence from Vietnam. *The Quarterly Review of Economics and Finance, Elsevier* 56(C): 3–14.

Psacharopoulos, G., and H. A. Patrinos. 2004. Returns to Investment Education: A Further Update. *Education Economics* 12(2): 111–134.

Schultz, T. P. 1997. Assessing the Productive Benefits of Nutrition and Health: An Integrated Human Capital Approach. *Journal of Econometrics* 77(11): 141–148.

———. 2002. Why Governments Should Invest More to Educate Girls. *World Development* 30(2): 207–225.

Solon, G. 2013. Cross-Country Differences in Intergenerational Earnings Mobility. *Journal of Economic Perspectives* 16(3): 59–66.

Torche, F. 2015. Analyses of Intergenerational Mobility: An Interdisciplinary Review. *ANNALS, AAPSS* 657.

World Bank. 2013. *Well Begun, Not Yet Done: Vietnam's Remarkable Progress on Poverty Reduction and the Emerging Challenges.* Washington, DC: The World Bank.

Appendix

Table A12.1 Income Mobility of Households from 2004–2008

	% Moving Up from the 20% Bottom in 2004 to a Higher Quintile in 2008	% Moving up from the 40% Bottom in 2004 to a Higher Quintile in 2008	% Moving Down from the 40% Top in 2004 to a Lower Quintile in 2008
Sex of household head			
Male	52.2	14.4	15.3
Female	42.6	14.0	13.9
Age of household head			
Age 15–30	33.0	8.2	20.0
Age 31–60	45.7	14.4	13.9
Education of household head			
< Primary	37.5	9.1	20.1
Primary	42.9	13.3	13.7
Lower-secondary	52.5	14.6	15.5
Upper-secondary	74.7	19.6	7.1
Postsecondary	82.4	22.5	3.2
Rural/urban			
Rural	43.8	13.2	16.2
Urban	55.6	17.6	6.9
Ethnicity of household head			
Kinh and Hoa	56.8	14.4	13.3
Ethnic minorities	17.3	10.2	25.7
Total	**44.7**	**14.1**	**14.3**

continued on next page

Table A12.1 *continued*

	% Moving Down from the 20% Top in 2004 to a Lower Quintile in 2008	Absolute Change in per Capita Income 2004–2008 (Fields and Ok Index)	Relative Change in per Capita Income 2004–2008
Sex of household head			
Male	41.0	3,763.0	55.5
Female	46.3	3,693.6	63.3
Age of household head			
Age 15–30	60.0	3,310.4	63.4
Age 31–60	44.0	3,735.2	60.9
Education of household head			
< Primary	57.6	2,819.9	58.2
Primary	54.7	3,357.7	63.7
Lower-secondary	52.5	4,004.0	69.4
Upper-secondary	29.2	4,140.1	**52.5**
Postsecondary	32.5	5,342.0	55.8
Rural/urban			
Rural	53.6	3,346.4	64.3
Urban	32.5	4,966.0	54.7
Ethnicity of household head			
Kinh and Hoa	44.3	3,944.0	60.9
Ethnic minorities	63.5	1,898.0	64.0
Total	**44.6**	**3,711.6**	**61.1**

Source: Estimates from the Viet Nam Household Living Standard Surveys 2004 and 2008.

Table A12.2 Regression of Income Mobility of Households from 2004–2008

Explanatory Variables	Moving Up from the 20% Bottom in 2010 to a Higher Quintile in 2014	Moving Up from the 40% Bottom in 2010 to a Higher Quintile in 2014	Moving Down from the 40% Top in 2010 to a Lower Quintile in 2014
Gender of household head (male = 1, female = 0)	−0.0449	−0.0378	0.0211
	(0.0678)	(0.0311)	(0.0276)
Age of household head	−0.0024	−0.0005	0.0022*
	(0.0027)	(0.0013)	(0.0013)
Ethnicity of head (Kinh, Hoa = 0; ethnic minorities = 1)	−0.3669***	−0.0088	0.1358***
	(0.0672)	(0.0462)	(0.0515)
Household head with primary education	0.0370	0.0454	−0.0424
	(0.0665)	(0.0317)	(0.0335)
Household head with lower-secondary degree	0.1104	0.0744**	−0.0532
	(0.0775)	(0.0332)	(0.0344)
Household head with upper-secondary degree	0.3073**	0.1382**	−0.1319***
	(0.1425)	(0.0538)	(0.0408)
Household head with college, university	0.3583***	0.1466***	−0.1675***
	(0.1104)	(0.0467)	(0.0353)
Household size	0.0300*	0.0101	−0.0187**
	(0.0155)	(0.0088)	(0.0079)
Proportion of children below 15	−0.6010***	−0.2120***	0.1321**
	(0.1418)	(0.0649)	(0.0600)
Proportion of members above 60	−0.2995*	−0.1001*	0.0610
	(0.1632)	(0.0556)	(0.0672)
Log of annual crop land	0.0003	0.0005	−0.0060
	(0.0102)	(0.0041)	(0.0038)
Log of perennial crop land	−0.0040	0.0103**	−0.0047
	(0.0101)	(0.0045)	(0.0037)
Urban (urban = 1, rural = 0)	0.0333	0.0280	−0.0904***
	(0.1191)	(0.0403)	(0.0333)
Northeast	−0.0598	−0.0413	−0.0648*
	(0.0964)	(0.0447)	(0.0389)

continued on next page

Table A12.2 *continued*

Explanatory Variables	Moving Up from the 20% Bottom in 2010 to a Higher Quintile in 2014	Moving Up from the 40% Bottom in 2010 to a Higher Quintile in 2014	Moving Down from the 40% Top in 2010 to a Lower Quintile in 2014
Northwest	−0.0526	−0.1849***	0.1826*
	(0.1085)	(0.0417)	(0.1007)
North Central Coast	−0.1233	−0.0762**	0.0784
	(0.0813)	(0.0331)	(0.0500)
South Central Coast	0.0979	−0.0300	−0.1004***
	(0.0947)	(0.0388)	(0.0364)
Central Highlands	−0.0787	0.0542	−0.0099
	(0.1230)	(0.0733)	(0.0578)
Southeast	0.0352	0.0792	−0.0911**
	(0.1148)	(0.0499)	(0.0422)
Mekong River Delta	0.1021	0.0186	−0.0970***
	(0.1042)	(0.0387)	(0.0326)
Constant	0.7651***	0.1381*	0.1926**
	(0.1917)	(0.0838)	(0.0801)
Observations	397	1,092	1,092
R-squared	0.238	0.062	0.090

continued on next page

Table A12.2 *continued*

Explanatory Variables	Moving Down from the 20% Top in 2010 to a Lower Quintile in 2014	Absolute Change in per Capita Income 2010–2014 (Fields and Ok Index)	Relative Change in per Capita Income 2010–2014
Gender of household head (male = 1, female = 0)	0.0727	7.88	0.0139
	(0.0647)	(378.68)	(0.0570)
Age of household head	0.0009	–18.98	–0.0025
	(0.0034)	(15.38)	(0.0023)
Ethnicity of head (Kinh, Hoa = 0; ethnic minorities = 1)	0.2378	–960.57*	–0.1546*
	(0.1593)	(500.02)	(0.0843)
Household head with primary education	–0.0093	591.31	–0.0781
	(0.1019)	(419.33)	(0.0652)
Household head with lower-secondary degree	–0.0926	1,340.62*	–0.0447
	(0.1037)	(745.91)	(0.1008)
Household head with upper-secondary degree	–0.3114***	1,399.68*	–0.1377
	(0.1140)	(766.52)	(0.0946)
Household head with college, university	–0.2855***	2,299.0***	–0.1156
	(0.0993)	(657.70)	(0.0940)
Household size	–0.0515**	–198.00	0.0285
	(0.0236)	(134.35)	(0.0221)
Proportion of children below 15	0.3392*	–2,782.8***	–0.3227**
	(0.1823)	(990.49)	(0.1384)
Proportion of members above 60	0.2406	–2,044.7***	–0.3078***
	(0.1464)	(679.32)	(0.0977)
Log of annual crop land	0.0107	56.13	0.0054
	(0.0089)	(115.07)	(0.0133)
Log of perennial crop land	–0.0080	113.50*	0.0088
	(0.0112)	(66.44)	(0.0103)
Urban (urban = 1, rural = 0)	–0.0636	1,454.04**	–0.0423
	(0.0747)	(703.23)	(0.0863)
Northeast	–0.0415	–293.16	0.0018
	(0.0887)	(545.66)	(0.0820)

continued on next page

Table A12.2 *continued*

Explanatory Variables	Moving Down from the 20% Top in 2010 to a Lower Quintile in 2014	Absolute Change in per Capita Income 2010–2014 (Fields and Ok Index)	Relative Change in per Capita Income 2010–2014
Northwest	-0.4281***	-1,075.02*	-0.0587
	(0.1070)	(558.51)	(0.1209)
North Central Coast	0.0240	-1,335.1***	-0.0382
	(0.1504)	(441.48)	(0.0755)
South Central Coast	-0.0548	-602.60	-0.0460
	(0.1074)	(534.14)	(0.0776)
Central Highlands	-0.1219	53.86	0.0625
	(0.1874)	(772.70)	(0.1084)
Southeast	-0.0461	1,172.40	-0.0661
	(0.0844)	(842.05)	(0.1049)
Mekong River Delta	-0.1104	2,126.85	0.1912
	(0.0840)	(1,305.45)	(0.1428)
Constant	0.6591***	4,689.8***	0.8377***
	(0.2207)	(1,083.05)	(0.1632)
Observations	328	1,817	1,816
R-squared	0.142	0.060	0.024

Notes: Robust standard errors in parentheses; *** $p<0.01$, ** $p<0.05$, * $p<0.1$.
Source: Estimates from the Viet Nam Household Living Standard Surveys 2004 and 2008.

Table A12.3 Employment Mobility of Individuals from 2004-2008

	Moving Up from Unskilled to Skilled and Nonmanual	Moving down from Skilled and Nonmanual to Unskilled	Moving from Self-employed to Wage Jobs
Sex			
Male	23.04	24.61	23.22
Female	11.99	26.43	13.60
Age			
Age 15–30	22.56	24.99	34.25
Age 31–60	15.38	25.43	12.77
Education			
Less primary	10.70	55.72	16.11
Primary	15.72	32.05	18.49
Lower secondary	19.60	31.71	17.19
Upper secondary	25.50	21.99	22.73
Post secondary	27.78	12.10	13.99
Rural/urban			
Rural	16.82	29.00	17.88
Urban	20.16	18.61	16.66
Ethnicity			
Kinh and Hoa	20.13	25.14	17.60
Ethnic minorities	3.28	28.92	18.18
Total	**17.24**	**25.31**	**17.69**

continued on next page

Table A12.3 continued

	Moving from Wage Jobs to Employed	Moving from Agricultural to Nonagricultural	Moving from Nonagricultural to Agricultural
Sex			
Male	24.06	19.52	14.31
Female	24.59	15.46	14.43
Age			
Age 15–30	19.70	23.76	11.47
Age 31–60	26.33	15.33	15.49
Education			
Less primary	32.37	9.87	19.79
Primary	25.69	16.45	17.15
Lower secondary	30.91	20.47	17.58
Upper secondary	18.64	27.18	11.10
Post secondary	12.12	30.21	7.22
Rural/urban			
Rural	27.25	17.27	19.96
Urban	15.08	19.80	4.13
Ethnicity			
Kinh and Hoa	21.98	20.78	13.65
Ethnic minorities	44.90	5.41	34.77
Total	**24.24**	**17.42**	**14.36**

Source: Estimates from the Viet Nam Household Living Standard Surveys 2004 and 2008.

Table A12.4 Regression of Employment Mobility of Individuals from 2004–2008

Explanatory Variables	Moving Up from Unskilled to Skilled and Nonmanual	Moving Down from Skilled and Nonmanual to Unskilled	Moving from Self-employed to Wage Jobs
Male = 1, female = 0	0.0890***	−0.0351	0.0878***
	(0.0165)	(0.0328)	(0.0171)
Age	−0.0085*	−0.0242*	−0.0289***
	(0.0049)	(0.0128)	(0.0057)
Age squared	0.0001	0.0004**	0.0003***
	(0.0001)	(0.0002)	(0.0001)
Ethnic minorities (yes = 1; Kinh, Hoa = 0)	−0.1264***	−0.0194	−0.0080
	(0.0246)	(0.0907)	(0.0421)
Having primary education	0.0241	−0.2184***	−0.0201
	(0.0225)	(0.0738)	(0.0263)
Having lower-secondary degree	0.0895***	−0.2403***	−0.0454
	(0.0255)	(0.0811)	(0.0280)
Having upper-secondary degree	0.1303***	−0.3370***	−0.0167
	(0.0382)	(0.0885)	(0.0421)
Having college, university	0.1844***	−0.4214***	−0.0400
	(0.0528)	(0.0758)	(0.0436)
Household size	0.0063	−0.0040	−0.0162**
	(0.0058)	(0.0138)	(0.0066)
Proportion of children below 15	0.0403	0.0557	0.0228
	(0.0562)	(0.0992)	(0.0566)
Proportion of members above 60	0.1006	−0.1303	−0.0034
	(0.0873)	(0.1158)	(0.0906)
Log of annual crop land	−0.0089**	0.0092	−0.0006
	(0.0044)	(0.0063)	(0.0034)
Log of perennial crop land	0.0014	0.0033	−0.0042
	(0.0044)	(0.0089)	(0.0036)
Urban (urban = 1, rural = 0)	−0.0710	−0.0207	−0.0122
	(0.0438)	(0.0515)	(0.0358)

continued on next page

Table A12.4 *continued*

Explanatory Variables	Moving Up from Unskilled to Skilled and Nonmanual	Moving Down from Skilled and Nonmanual to Unskilled	Moving from Self-employed to Wage Jobs
Northeast	−0.0326	0.1206*	−0.0699*
	(0.0336)	(0.0687)	(0.0381)
Northwest	−0.0062	−0.0686	−0.0830
	(0.0361)	(0.1289)	(0.0709)
North Central Coast	−0.0519	0.0834	−0.0109
	(0.0324)	(0.0722)	(0.0394)
South Central Coast	0.0517	−0.0087	−0.0241
	(0.0451)	(0.0509)	(0.0395)
Central Highlands	−0.0074	0.0191	0.0151
	(0.0497)	(0.1018)	(0.0507)
Southeast	0.1083*	0.0132	0.0202
	(0.0598)	(0.0591)	(0.0428)
Mekong River Delta	0.0390	−0.0374	−0.0670**
	(0.0380)	(0.0598)	(0.0310)
Constant	0.3240***	0.9156***	0.9777***
	(0.1017)	(0.2483)	(0.1189)
Observations	2,264	809	1,898
R-squared	0.100	0.109	0.106

continued on next page

Table A12.4 *continued*

Explanatory Variables	Dependent Variables		
	Moving from Wage Jobs to Employed	Moving from Agricultural to Nonagricultural	Moving from Nonagricultural to Agricultural
Male = 1, female = 0	−0.0391	0.0319*	−0.0148
	(0.0255)	(0.0184)	(0.0173)
Age	−0.0102	−0.0112**	−0.0065
	(0.0090)	(0.0051)	(0.0077)
Age squared	0.0002*	0.0001	0.0001
	(0.0001)	(0.0001)	(0.0001)
Ethnic minorities (yes = 1; Kinh, Hoa = 0)	0.1705***	−0.1428***	0.1540*
	(0.0550)	(0.0263)	(0.0793)
Having primary education	−0.0342	0.0249	−0.0067
	(0.0463)	(0.0258)	(0.0384)
Having lower-secondary degree	−0.0126	0.0465	−0.0093
	(0.0494)	(0.0285)	(0.0405)
Having upper-secondary degree	−0.1246**	0.1031**	−0.0679
	(0.0568)	(0.0445)	(0.0416)
Having college, university	−0.2088***	0.1945***	−0.1021***
	(0.0475)	(0.0620)	(0.0380)
Household size	0.0062	0.0212***	−0.0014
	(0.0096)	(0.0073)	(0.0074)
Proportion of children below 15	−0.1420*	−0.0039	−0.0110
	(0.0771)	(0.0566)	(0.0611)
Proportion of members above 60	0.0343	−0.0508	0.0097
	(0.1124)	(0.1012)	(0.0774)
Log of annual crop land	0.0036	−0.0085**	0.0106**
	(0.0048)	(0.0042)	(0.0048)
Log of perennial crop land	0.0266***	−0.0101***	0.0097
	(0.0059)	(0.0032)	(0.0063)
Urban (urban = 1, rural = 0)	−0.0195	−0.0887	−0.0886***
	(0.0411)	(0.0576)	(0.0321)
Northeast	0.0898**	−0.1170***	0.1441***
	(0.0443)	(0.0370)	(0.0525)
Northwest	0.0518	−0.1553***	−0.0668
	(0.0990)	(0.0414)	(0.0904)

continued on next page

Table A12.4 *continued*

Explanatory Variables	Dependent Variables		
	Moving from Wage Jobs to Employed	Moving from Agricultural to Nonagricultural	Moving from Nonagricultural to Agricultural
North Central Coast	0.1304**	−0.1820***	0.1309***
	(0.0551)	(0.0394)	(0.0485)
South Central Coast	−0.0141	−0.1072**	0.0075
	(0.0461)	(0.0515)	(0.0315)
Central Highlands	0.0651	−0.1467***	0.1325**
	(0.0616)	(0.0464)	(0.0635)
Southeast	0.0328	−0.0965	−0.0085
	(0.0485)	(0.0592)	(0.0275)
Mekong River Delta	−0.0120	−0.1447***	0.0664*
	(0.0442)	(0.0388)	(0.0376)
Constant	0.3120*	0.5364***	0.1678
	(0.1622)	(0.1076)	(0.1363)
Observations	1,175	1,778	1,295
R-squared	0.129	0.104	0.120

Notes: Robust standard errors in parentheses; *** $p<0.01$, ** $p<0.05$, * $p<0.1$.
Source: Estimates from the Viet Nam Household Living Standard Surveys 2004–2008.

Table A12.5 Intergenerational Mobility of Employment in 2004

Characteristics of Children	Skill Upward: Skilled Children and Unskilled Parents	Skill Downward: Unskilled Children and Skilled Parents	Employment Upward: Wage Children and Self-employed Parents
Sex			
Male	18.88	43.16	37.18
Female	18.39	45.12	28.85
Age			
Age 15–30	18.34	44.60	33.59
Age 31–60	28.14	31.23	37.06
Education			
Less primary	6.17	68.21	24.96
Primary	13.27	57.67	29.61
Lower secondary	13.59	63.28	26.11
Upper secondary	22.35	42.56	39.58
Post secondary	77.88	7.98	77.73
Rural/Urban			
Rural	15.66	53.66	30.43
Urban	36.43	27.48	54.44
Ethnicity			
Kinh and Hoa	21.96	41.97	39.22
Ethnic minorities	4.39	72.65	9.35
Total	**18.67**	**43.98**	**33.73**

continued on next page

Table A12.5 *continued*

Characteristics of Children	Employment Downward: Self-employed Children and Wage Parents	Sector Upward: Nonagricultural Children and Agricultural Parents	Sector Downward: Agricultural Children and Nonagricultural Parents
Sex			
Male	24.94	32.96	20.41
Female	36.67	31.17	23.47
Age			
Age 15–30	30.36	31.78	22.39
Age 31–60	15.15	47.76	9.46
Education			
Less primary	17.14	18.71	28.12
Primary	29.05	29.21	22.17
Lower secondary	48.86	28.44	35.06
Upper secondary	37.88	37.45	19.94
Post secondary	11.75	84.91	2.85
Rural/Urban			
Rural	36.08	30.41	33.18
Urban	19.19	55.34	5.98
Ethnicity			
Kinh and Hoa	28.39	38.69	19.80
Ethnic minorities	45.74	9.49	61.42
Total	29.94	32.22	21.71

Source: Estimates from the Viet Nam Household Living Standard Survey 2004.

Table A12.6 Regression of Log of Children's Wages on Father's and Mother's Wages

Explanatory Variables	Dependent Variable is Log of Wages of Children					
	All Samples	Male	Female	All Samples	Male	Female
Log of father's wage	0.3835***	0.4168***	0.3347***			
	(0.0216)	(0.0253)	(0.0297)			
Log of mother's wage				0.3753***	0.3870***	0.3698***
				(0.0260)	(0.0310)	(0.0352)
Age	0.2606***	0.2560***	0.2670***	0.2114***	0.1997***	0.2322***
	(0.0256)	(0.0309)	(0.0442)	(0.0305)	(0.0348)	(0.0513)
Age squared	−0.0039***	−0.0039***	−0.0039***	−0.0029***	−0.0027***	−0.0035***
	(0.0005)	(0.0006)	(0.0009)	(0.0006)	(0.0007)	(0.0011)
Dummy year 2008	0.1652***	0.1707***	0.1417*	0.1851***	0.2151***	0.0950
	(0.0476)	(0.0561)	(0.0742)	(0.0579)	(0.0714)	(0.0879)
Dummy year 2010	0.2448***	0.2282***	0.2766***	0.2297***	0.2195***	0.2259**
	(0.0473)	(0.0568)	(0.0731)	(0.0614)	(0.0762)	(0.0876)
Dummy year 2014	0.2808***	0.2572***	0.3211***	0.3215***	0.2688***	0.3787***
	(0.0492)	(0.0580)	(0.0754)	(0.0659)	(0.0792)	(0.0947)
Constant	1.4111***	1.2973***	1.5832***	2.1512***	2.2668***	1.9066***
	(0.3250)	(0.3972)	(0.5171)	(0.3716)	(0.4490)	(0.5820)
Observations	3,774	2,407	1,367	2,577	1,568	1,009
R-squared	0.400	0.420	0.380	0.391	0.390	0.401

Notes: Robust standard errors in parentheses; *** $p<0.01$, ** $p<0.05$, * $p<0.1$.
Source: Estimates from the Viet Nam Household Living Standard Surveys.

Table A12.7 Regression of Log of Children's Wages on Parent's Wages for Different Groups

Explanatory Variables	Dependent Variable is Log of Wages of Children						
	All Samples	Year 2004	Year 2014	Male	Female	Age 15–30	Age 31–60
Log of parental wages	0.3648***	0.3537***	0.3087***	0.3838***	0.3435***	0.3640***	0.3674***
	(0.0183)	(0.0348)	(0.0445)	(0.0215)	(0.0258)	(0.0187)	(0.0744)
Age	0.2516***	0.2562***	0.2643***	0.2436***	0.2640***	0.2319***	0.5901*
	(0.0217)	(0.0416)	(0.0413)	(0.0253)	(0.0380)	(0.0336)	(0.3117)
Age squared	−0.0037***	−0.0038***	−0.0039***	−0.0036***	−0.0039***	−0.0032***	−0.0082*
	(0.0005)	(0.0009)	(0.0008)	(0.0005)	(0.0008)	(0.0007)	(0.0044)
Dummy year 2008	0.1263***			0.1507***	0.0640	0.1334***	−0.1129
	(0.0418)			(0.0495)	(0.0654)	(0.0420)	(0.2091)
Dummy year 2010	0.2242***			0.2207***	0.2261***	0.2297***	0.0812
	(0.0424)			(0.0502)	(0.0648)	(0.0428)	(0.1674)
Dummy year 2014	0.2760***			0.2554***	0.2969***	0.2756***	0.2147
	(0.0436)			(0.0508)	(0.0680)	(0.0443)	(0.1764)
Constant	1.6981***	1.7471***	2.3187***	1.7080***	1.6410***	1.8999***	−4.4625
	(0.2720)	(0.5132)	(0.6553)	(0.3266)	(0.4439)	(0.3915)	(5.4997)
Observations	4,959	1,217	1,235	3,129	1,830	4,724	235
R-squared	0.390	0.342	0.317	0.402	0.378	0.382	0.264

Notes: Robust standard errors in parentheses; *** $p<0.01$, ** $p<0.05$, * $p<0.1$.
Source: Estimates from the Viet Nam Household Living Standard Surveys.

Table A12.8 Regression of Log of Children's Wages on Parent's Wages for Different Groups

Explanatory Variables	Dependent Variable is Log of Wages of Children				
	Less than Primary	Primary	Lower Secondary	Upper Secondary	Post Secondary
Log of parental wages	0.5107***	0.4354***	0.3526***	0.3198***	0.1729***
	(0.0545)	(0.0381)	(0.0349)	(0.0428)	(0.0286)
Age	0.1325***	0.2164***	0.3684***	0.5528***	0.3320***
	(0.0357)	(0.0347)	(0.0564)	(0.1030)	(0.0629)
Age squared	−0.0021***	−0.0033***	−0.0062***	−0.0094***	−0.0046***
	(0.0007)	(0.0007)	(0.0012)	(0.0021)	(0.0012)
Dummy year 2008	−0.0700	0.0908	0.1929**	−0.0052	0.2433***
	(0.0858)	(0.0777)	(0.0889)	(0.1022)	(0.0762)
Dummy year 2010	0.1932*	0.2271***	0.2666***	0.0325	0.2308***
	(0.1047)	(0.0764)	(0.0885)	(0.1076)	(0.0682)
Dummy year 2014	0.1229	0.2337**	0.4146***	0.0754	0.2716***
	(0.1070)	(0.0925)	(0.0864)	(0.1052)	(0.0665)
Constant	2.2645***	1.6888***	0.4495	−1.6510	2.1560***
	(0.5701)	(0.4900)	(0.6957)	(1.2350)	(0.8187)
Observations	635	1,213	1,133	629	1,349
R-squared	0.363	0.375	0.341	0.303	0.234

continued on next page

Table A12.8 *continued*

Explanatory Variables	Dependent Variable is Log of Wages of Children			
	Rural	Urban	Kinh and Hoa	Ethnic Minorities
Log of parental wages	0.3825***	0.2277***	0.3022***	0.4738***
	(0.0231)	(0.0321)	(0.0183)	(0.0503)
Age	0.2806***	0.2324***	0.2776***	0.0719
	(0.0257)	(0.0440)	(0.0231)	(0.0648)
Age squared	−0.0046***	−0.0030***	−0.0042***	−0.0007
	(0.0005)	(0.0009)	(0.0005)	(0.0015)
Dummy year 2008	0.1653***	0.0906	0.1803***	−0.0409
	(0.0493)	(0.0717)	(0.0431)	(0.1035)
Dummy year 2010	0.2527***	0.2185***	0.2533***	0.2997***
	(0.0512)	(0.0682)	(0.0454)	(0.1007)
Dummy year 2014	0.3359***	0.2092***	0.3230***	0.3594***
	(0.0540)	(0.0706)	(0.0435)	(0.1264)
Constant	1.2758***	3.1428***	1.9500***	2.8291***
	(0.3327)	(0.5703)	(0.2916)	(0.7873)
Observations	3,488	1,471	4,257	702
R-squared	0.355	0.304	0.362	0.387

Notes: Robust standard errors in parentheses; *** $p<0.01$, ** $p<0.05$, * $p<0.1$.
Source: Estimates from the Viet Nam Household Living Standard Surveys.

13

Foreign Direct Investment and Wage Inequality: Evidence from the People's Republic of China

Cen Chen, Hongmei Zhao, and Yunbo Zhou

13.1 Introduction

The wage gap caused by foreign direct investment (FDI) between foreign firms and domestic firms in the host country has been a hot topic in labor economics research and development economics research. Many studies have sought to explain this (Feenstra and Hanson 1997; Markusen and Venables 1997). Some studies showed that foreign firms attract many high-skilled workers because of their high technological level, advanced management systems, and high wage levels, which widens the wage gap between foreign firms and domestic firms in the host country (Feenstra and Hanson 1997; Figini and Görg 1999). Other research found that the technology spillover effect of foreign firms can improve the technological level for domestic firms, which narrows the wage gap (Xu, Qi, and Li 2009). We think foreign firms in the host country would have dynamic effects on the wage gap, following expansion of the FDI scale and FDI market. The effect of foreign firms could be different at different stages. Regretfully, there is no existing theoretical framework that allows us to analyze the affecting mechanism of FDI on the wage gap between foreign firms and domestic firms in the host country, which leads to diverging of explanations of the effect of FDI on the wage gap in the host country. Moreover, many empirical studies have estimated the effect of FDI on the wage gap, but there have been few studies focusing on the contribution of FDI to the wage gap and the development tendency of the effect of FDI.

The People's Republic of China (PRC) has attracted much FDI since the early 1980s. Foreign firms usually pay higher wages than domestic firms to attract the highly qualified labor force they need. According to Chinese official statistics, the average wage paid by foreign firms, from 1998 to 2013, was 14.45% higher than that paid by domestic firms. Using the Chinese Manufacturing Enterprises Database, we find that foreign firms paid about 5.76% higher wages than domestic firms after controlling for enterprise scale, productivity, profits, per capita investment, industry, and location. Therefore, we were wondering about the impact of large inflows of foreign capital will bring to the PRC and the changing trend of this impact. Through this study, we hope to offer some suggestions for improving income inequality and lowering the risk of the PRC falling into the middle-income trap.

The objective of this chapter is to investigate effects of FDI on the wage gap in the host country. We first construct a theoretical model, attempting to describe the effects of FDI on the wage gap between domestic firms and foreign firms. We then use the Shapley value decomposition method to compute the contributions of the observed factors, including FDI to Gini coefficient and Theil index. Our theoretical results show that the overall effect of foreign investment leads first to an expansion of the wage gap and then to a narrowing of it. This implies that the contribution of FDI to the wage gap in the host country follows an inverted U-shaped track. Our empirical results show that contributions of FDI to wage inequality between enterprises tend to fall during the period of observation.

The chapter proceeds as follows. In Section 13.2, we provide an overview of the existing literature on the wage effects of FDI in the host country. In Section 13.3, we construct a two-sector model to calculate the effects of FDI on the wage gap between domestic firms and foreign firms. In Section 13.4, we describe our data and estimation method. We then discuss our main findings in Section 13.5, and Section13.6 concludes the chapter.

13.2 Literature Review

There has been extensive research on the impact of FDI on the economy in the host country, both theoretical and empirical research. Regarding the affecting mechanism of FDI on the wage gap, most studies conclude that FDI affects the wage level and wage gap in the host country in two ways: through a labor transfer effect and through a technology spillover effect. On one hand, foreign firms entering the host country increase the demand for labor. The labor force prefers to transfer from lower-wage domestic firms to higher-wage foreign firms, which inevitably leads to wage increases in the host country. However, analysis using the competition model of the labor market suggests that the wage gap would not be sustained indefinitely (Brown, Deardorff, and Stern 2003;

Lipsey and Sjoholm 2004; Driffield and Taylor 2006). On the other hand, domestic firms can benefit from the presence of foreign multinationals through positive spillovers as it allows them to improve their productivity through technology transfer, labor mobility, and product mobility. The extent of horizontal spillover depends on the research and development activities of foreign firms and the absorption capacity of domestic firms (Todo and Miyamoto 2006); the extent of vertical spillover depends on participation of domestic firms in the supply chain of foreign firms (Saggi 2002). But there are contrary opinions suggesting that when economic development level and technological level in the host country are low, the negative crowding-out effect of FDI on domestic firms may be greater than the positive spillover effect. This even hurts the technological development of domestic firms (Wang 2009).

Studies of the impact of FDI on the wage gap can be classified into two groups. In the first group of studies it is argued that inflow of FDI enlarges the wage gap between domestic firms and foreign firms. Foreign firms have higher technological and managerial levels, which increases relative demand for skilled workers. To prevent losing highly skilled workers, foreign firms tend to pay higher wages. Therefore, foreign investment enlarges the wage gap between low-skilled workers and high-skilled workers (Lipsey and Sjoholm 2004; Lipsey 2004), which is supported by much empirical evidence. Feenstra and Hanson (1997) argued that multinationals from developed countries always outsource production to developing countries, such as Mexico. This leads to an increase of relative demand for skilled workers and the relative wage of skilled workers in the developing country in question increases as well. Chen, Ge, and Lai (2011) investigated the wage premium and wage spillover effect of foreign firms in the PRC's manufacturing sector. Their results indicated that expansion of foreign investment increases inter-firm wage inequality.

In the second group of studies it is argued that the direction of FDI influence on the wage gap is uncertain. Wu (2001) argued that this impact depends on whether the technology transfer effect of FDI is skill oriented or labor oriented, and this is relevant to which sector will receive FDI. Analysis shows that FDI with relatively labor-oriented technology will decrease the wage gap, whereas relatively skill-oriented technology will increase the profit margin of exports and then the wage gap in the host country. Das (2002) found that there are short-run effects of FDI entering skilled-labor intensive sectors. Faced with the wage gap between foreign firms and domestic firms, domestic firms would be encouraged to sustain increased demand for skilled labor. This raises the relative wage of domestic firms. In the long run, more FDI would increase the supply of skilled labor and reduce relative wage. Driffield and Taylor (2006) used industrial- and regional-level panel data for the United Kingdom to conclude that foreign firms have significant wage spillover effects on domestic firms. Such wage spillover effects are more widespread for skilled workers than for unskilled workers, and they are weaker in sectors with high unemployment.

Using the PRC as an example, there are numerous studies about the effects of FDI on wage disparities across different industries and regions. Bao and Shao (2008) argued that wage spillover effects of FDI are closely related to industrial characteristics. They set up the simultaneous equations model and used the PRC's manufactured industrial data and found that FDI enlarges the wage gap within the industry through the wage spillover effect. However, researchers have obtained different conclusions about the impact of foreign investment on the wage gap between industries due to differing industrial characteristics.

Industries that can absorb more foreign investment have higher wage levels. So foreign investment enlarges the wage gap between industries (Chen and Xie 2004). Some researchers (Xuan and Zhao 2005) also found that regions where foreign investments gather have the ability to offer higher wages. Imbalanced distribution of foreign investments across different regions is the main reason for the wage gap between regions.

To sum up, the findings of research on the effects of FDI on the wage gap between domestic firms and foreign firms in the host country are not conclusive. Empirical results even go against the theoretical conclusions. There has not been any study so far that provides a theoretical framework to analyze the affecting mechanism of FDI on the wage gap in the host country. The affecting mechanism of FDI on the wage gap is a relatively complicated process, which includes both labor transfer effects and technology spillover effects. The direction and extent of the effect could be different at different stages. This chapter attempts to improve existing research, both theoretically and empirically, to obtain more convincing results.

13.3 Model

We incorporate two affecting mechanisms of FDI on the wage gap into a theoretical model. Specifically, by analyzing the change of Theil index caused by the labor transfer effect and technology spillover effect, we construct a two-sector model to calculate the effect of FDI on wage inequality between domestic firms and foreign firms. First, workers employed in domestic firms will surely be attracted to higher wages paid by foreign firms. We then calculate the change of Theil index caused by the labor transfer effect. Second, the relative wage between foreign firms and domestic firms can be derived from the technology spillover model. We then introduce this relative wage into the Theil index and the variation of inequality along with the increase of FDI technology spillover can be calculated. Based on our overall analysis of the two affecting mechanisms, we then present our final theoretical results.

The model follows Acemoglu (1998, 2002) and is developed based on the two-sector model used by Robinson (1976), Glomm and Ravikumar (1992), and Zhou (2009).

Assumption 1: There are two sectors, Y_d (domestic sector) and Y_f (foreign sector), that use capital (K) and labor (L); Y is the total output of society, which is expressed as follows:

$$Y = \left(Y_d^\rho + \gamma Y_f^\rho\right)^{\frac{1}{\rho}}.$$

where the elasticity of substitution between Y_d and Y_f is $1/(1-\rho)$; γ is the importance of Y_f to Y.

Assumption 2: The production functions of two sectors are as follows:

$$Y_f = A_f K_f^\alpha L_f^\beta$$

$$Y_d = A_d K_d^\alpha L_d^\beta$$

where A_f and A_d denote technology parameter. The labor market is competitive and clear, and people can move across the sector. $L_d + L_d = L$, labor's shares of domestic sector and foreign sector, are $1 - \eta$ and η, respectively.

Assumption 3: W_d and W_f represent wages of the domestic sector and foreign sector, respectively. The average wage of the whole country can be expressed as $(1 - \eta)W_d + \eta W_f$. The wage of the two sectors depends on the technical level and is also an increasing function of it. This is expressed is as follows:

$$w_f = f(A_f), \quad \frac{\partial w_f}{\partial A_f} > 0$$

$$w_d = f(A_d), \quad \frac{\partial w_d}{\partial A_d} > 0,$$

The level of technology in the foreign sector is higher than in the domestic sector, so $w_f > w_d$, $w = \dfrac{w_f}{w_d} > 1$.

Assumption 4: There is no wage gap within each sector.

13.3.1 Effect of Labor Transfer on Wage Inequality

In this section, we ignore the effect of technology spillover and only analyze the effect of the labor transfer on the wage gap. Assumption 5 then is as follows:

Assumption 5: There is no technology spillover between two sectors; thus, the wage gap, depending on technical level, is a constant.

Theil index is selected as the analyzing tool as it is more sensitive to income difference between groups.[1] The formula of Theil index is as follows:

$$T = \sum \left(\frac{I_i}{I} Ln \frac{I_i/I}{N_i/N} \right) \quad (1)$$

where I_i denotes total income of group i, N_i denotes number of individuals of group i and I and N are gross income and total number of individuals, respectively. The Theil index between domestic sector and foreign sector can be calculated as follows:

$$T = \frac{L_d w_d}{L((1-\eta)w_d + \eta w_f)} \ln \frac{L_d w_d / L((1-\eta)w_d + \eta w_f)}{1-\eta}$$

$$+ \frac{L_f w_f}{L((1-\eta)w_d + \eta w_f)} \ln \frac{L_f w_f / L((1-\eta)w_d + \eta w_f)}{\eta} \quad (2)$$

$$= \frac{(1-\eta)w_d \ln w_d + \eta w_f \ln w_f}{(1-\eta)w_d + \eta w_f} - \ln((1-\eta)w_d + \eta w_f)$$

To determine the effect of the labor transfer on wage inequality, the first derivative of Equation (2) on η is as follows:

---

[1] Theil index is sensitive to transfers of income from poor to rich.

$$\frac{\partial T}{\partial \eta} = \frac{(w_f \ln w_f - w_f \ln w_d)((1-\eta)w_d + \eta w_f) - (w_d - w_f)\big((1-\eta)w_d \ln w_d + \eta w_f \ln w_f - ((1-\eta)w_d + \eta w_f)\big)}{((1-\eta)w_d + \eta w_f)^2}$$

$$= \frac{-\eta(w_d - w_f)^2 + w_d w_f (\ln w_f - \ln w_d) + w_d(w_d - w_f)}{((1-\eta)w_d + \eta w_f)^2} \quad (3)$$

η^* is obtained to make the value of Equation (3) zero.

$$\eta^* = \frac{w_d w_f (\ln w_f - \ln w_d) + w_d(w_d - w_f)}{(w_d - w_f)^2}$$

$$= \frac{\dfrac{w_f}{w_d} \ln \dfrac{w_f}{w_d} - \dfrac{w_f}{w_d} + 1}{\left(1 - \dfrac{w_f}{w_d}\right)^2} \quad (4)$$

Hence, if $\eta = \eta^*$, then $\dfrac{\partial T}{\partial \eta} = 0$

Since $\dfrac{w_f}{w_d} > 1$, it is easy to find that $\eta^* \in (0,1)^2$.

Workers who are employed by domestic firms will surely be attracted by higher wages paid by foreign firms. So labor will transfer from the domestic sector to the foreign sector. This means η will increase. According to derivation result, if $0 < \eta < \eta^*$, then $\dfrac{\partial T}{\partial \eta} > 0$, which means the wage gap between the two sectors will increase gradually, along with the labor transfer, before η arrives at the critical point η^*. While $\eta^* < \eta < 1$, $\dfrac{\partial T}{\partial \eta} > 0$. This means the labor transfer from the domestic sector to the foreign sector will narrow the gap after η exceeds the critical point η^*. In summary, the wage gap between the two sectors first increases and then decreases with the labor transfer, which is an inverted U-shaped variation.

---

[2] let $f\left(\dfrac{w_f}{w_d}\right) = \dfrac{w_f}{w_d} \ln \dfrac{w_f}{w_d} - \dfrac{w_f}{w_d} + 1$, $f'_{w_f/w_d} = \ln \dfrac{w_f}{w_d} > 0$, $f(1) = 0$, so $f\left(\dfrac{w_f}{w_d}\right) > 0$;

let $g\left(\dfrac{w_f}{w_d}\right) = 1 - \dfrac{w_f}{w_d} + \ln \dfrac{w_f}{w_d}$, $g'_{w_f/w_d} = \dfrac{w_d}{w_f} - 1 < 0$, $g(1) = 0$, so $g\left(\dfrac{w_f}{w_d}\right) < 0$, $\dfrac{w_f}{w_d}\left(1 - \dfrac{w_f}{w_d} + \ln \dfrac{w_f}{w_d}\right) < 0$,

that is $\eta^* < 1$.

To determine the specific feature and shape of the U-shaped curve, the second derivative of Equation (2) on η is given as follows:

$$\frac{\partial^2 T}{\partial \eta^2} = \frac{\left(\frac{w_f}{w_d}-1\right)\left(1-\frac{w_f}{w_d}\right)\left(1-\eta+\eta\frac{w_f}{w_d}\right)+2\eta\left(1-\frac{w_f}{w_d}\right)^2-2\left(\frac{w_f}{w_d}\ln\frac{w_f}{w_d}-\frac{w_f}{w_d}+1\right)}{\left(1-\eta+\eta\frac{w_f}{w_d}\right)^3}$$

$$= \frac{\left(\frac{w_f}{w_d}-1\right)\left[\left(2\frac{w_f}{w_d}-2\right)\eta-2\ln\frac{w_f}{w_d}-1\right]}{\left(1-\eta+\eta\frac{w_f}{w_d}\right)^3}$$

(5)

η^{**} is obtained to make the value of Equation (5) zero:

$$\eta^{**} = \frac{2\ln\frac{w_f}{w_d}+1}{2\left(\frac{w_f}{w_d}-1\right)}$$

(6)

Since,

$$\eta^{**} - \eta^* = \frac{2\ln\frac{w_f}{w_d}+1}{2\left(\frac{w_f}{w_d}-1\right)} - \frac{\frac{w_f}{w_d}\ln\frac{w_f}{w_d}-\frac{w_f}{w_d}+1}{\left(1-\frac{w_f}{w_d}\right)^2} > 0 \quad ^3$$

(7)

Namely, $\eta^* < \eta^{**}$

Figure 13.1 depicts a process that occurs when the wage gap moves along with the labor transfer from the domestic sector to the foreign sector. At the beginning, the wage gap between the two sectors gradually expands following the increase of the labor's share of the foreign sector (Stage 1). Increasingly, labor moving into the foreign sector reduces the wage gap (Stage 2). Once η exceeds η^{**}, the wage gap decrease starts to slow down (Stage 3). According to Equation (4) and Equation (6), the values of η^*, and η depend on $\frac{w_f}{w_d}$.

---

3 let $h\left(\frac{w_f}{w_d}\right) = 3\frac{w_f}{w_d} - 2\ln\frac{w_f}{w_d} - 3$, $h(1) = 0$, $h'_{\frac{w_f}{w_d}}\left(\frac{w_f}{w_d}\right) = 3 - 2\frac{w_d}{w_f} > 0$ so $h\left(\frac{w_f}{w_d}\right) > 0$, that is $\eta^{**} - \eta^* > 0$.

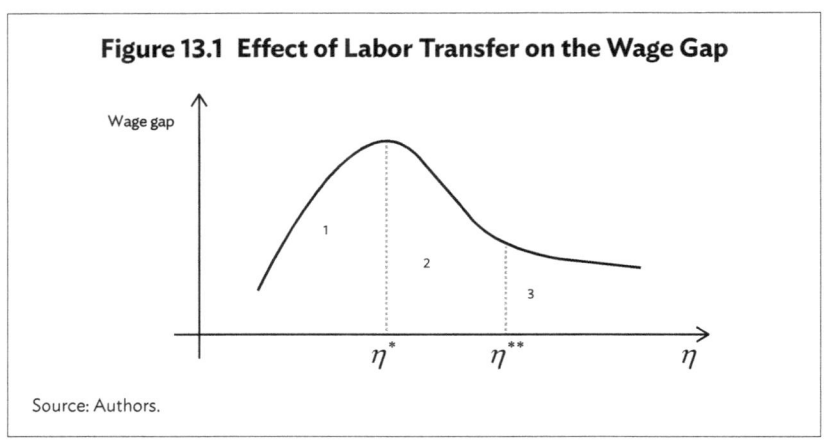

Figure 13.1 Effect of Labor Transfer on the Wage Gap

Source: Authors.

13.3.2 Effect of Technology Spillover on Wage Inequality

All descriptions in the preceding section of the effect of labortransfer from the domestic sector o the foreign-invested sector on the wage gap are assume there is no technology spillover. To determine the effect of technology spillover on wage inequality, there is a need to relax Assumptions 5 and 6.

Assumption 6: The foreign sector could affect the productivity of the domestic sector through technology spillover. The level of technology in the domestic sector will increase with higher foreign-invested capital, due to possible technology spillovers (Saglam and Sayek 2011), A_f, $= AK^{\delta}_{f}$, where K_f denotes foreign-invested capital. A denotes the net foreign-invested sector's technology spillovers on the domestic sector's productivity; σ denotes the extent of technology spillovers from K_f, and σ is an increasing function of K_f, $\frac{\partial \delta}{\partial K_f} > 0$. Normalize the price of the final good Y to 1.

According to Assumption 1, competitive pricing gives a standard relative demand equation for the domestic sector and the foreign sector:

$$\frac{P_f}{P_d} = \gamma \left(\frac{Y_d}{Y_f} \right)^{1-\rho}$$

where P_d and P_f denote the prices of the two sectors. The wage premium between the domestic sector and the foreign sector is W:

$$w = \frac{W_f}{W_d} = \frac{K_f^{\rho(\alpha-\delta)}}{\gamma K_d^{\alpha\rho}} \left(\frac{A_f}{A}\right)^{\rho} \left(\frac{L_f}{L_d}\right)^{\beta\rho-1} \quad (8)$$

Equation (2) can be converted as follows:

$$T = \frac{\eta \frac{W_1}{W_2}\left[\ln\frac{W_1}{W_2} - \ln\left(1-\eta+\eta\frac{W_1}{W_2}\right)\right] - (1-\eta)\ln\left(1-\eta+\eta\frac{W_1}{W_2}\right)}{1-\eta+\eta\frac{W_1}{W_2}} \quad (9)$$

To simplify the process of the deduction, let $J = \frac{1}{\gamma}\left(\frac{K_f}{K_d}\right)^{\alpha\rho}\left(\frac{A_f}{A}\right)^{\rho}\left(\frac{L_f}{L_d}\right)^{\beta\rho-1}$, $\frac{W_f}{W_d} = JK_f^{-\rho\delta}$ substitute $\frac{W_f}{W_d}$ in Equation (9),

$$T = \frac{\eta JK_f^{-\rho\delta}\left[\ln JK_f^{-\rho\delta} - \ln(1-\eta+\eta JK_f^{-\rho\delta})\right] - (1-\eta)\ln(1-\eta+\eta JK_f^{-\rho\delta})}{1-\eta+\eta JK_f^{-\rho\delta}} \quad (10)$$

To determine the technology spillover effect of the foreign sector on wage inequality, the first derivative of Equation (10) on δ is given as follows:

$$\frac{\partial T}{\partial \delta} = \frac{-(1-\eta)\rho\eta JK_f^{-\rho\delta}\ln K_f \ln JK_f^{-\rho\delta}}{(1-\eta+\eta JK_f^{-\rho\delta})^2} \quad (11)$$

Since $\frac{\partial T}{\partial \delta} < 0$, improvements in the extent of technology spillovers will reduce the wage gap between the two sectors, which is in line with conventional wisdom.

Similarly, to determine the specific features and shape of the curve, the second derivative of Equation (10) on δ is given as follows:

$$\frac{\partial^2 T}{\partial \delta^2} = \frac{(1-\eta)\rho^2\eta JK_f^{-\rho\delta}(\ln K_f)^2\left[(1-\eta)(\ln JK_f^{-\rho\delta}+1) - \eta JK_f^{-\rho\delta}\ln JK_f^{-\rho\delta} + \eta JK_f^{-\rho\delta}\right]}{(1-\eta+\eta JK_f^{-\rho\delta})^3}$$

$$= \frac{(1-\eta)\rho^2\eta(\ln K_f)^2\frac{W_f}{W_d}\left[(1-\eta)\left(\ln\frac{W_f}{W_d}+1\right) - \eta\frac{W_f}{W_d}\ln\frac{W_f}{W_d} + \eta\frac{W_f}{W_d}\right]}{\left(1-\eta+\eta\frac{W_f}{W_d}\right)^3} \quad (12)$$

The sign of Equation (12) depends on the following function:

$$L\left(\frac{W_f}{W_d}\right) = (1-\eta)\left(\ln\frac{W_f}{W_d}+1\right) - \eta\frac{W_f}{W_d}\ln\frac{W_f}{W_d} + \eta\frac{W_f}{W_d}$$

The image of $L\left(\frac{W_f}{W_d}\right)$ is depicted in Figure 13.2.

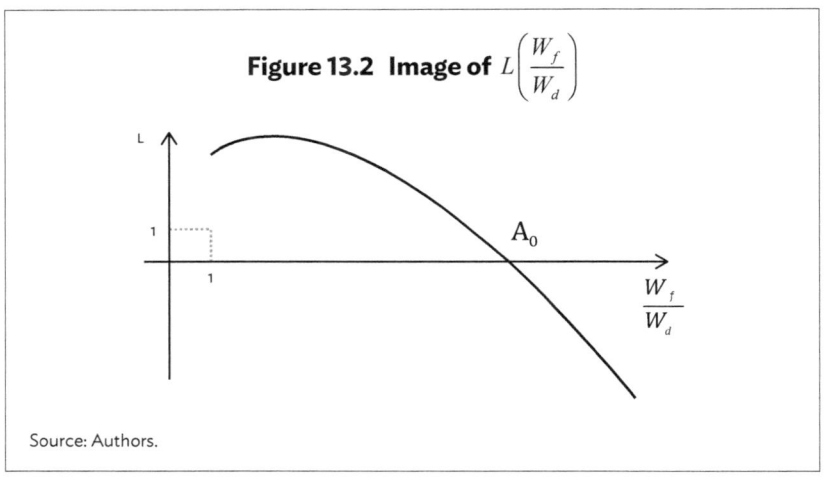

Figure 13.2 Image of $L\left(\frac{W_f}{W_d}\right)$

Source: Authors.

In Figure 13.2, If $\frac{W_f}{W_d} = A_0$ [4], $L\left(\frac{W_f}{W_d}\right) = 0$, $\delta = \delta^* = \frac{\ln(J/A_0)}{\rho \ln K_f}$, then $\frac{\partial^2 T}{\partial \delta^2} = 0$. If $1 < \frac{W_f}{W_d} < A_0$, then $L\left(\frac{W_f}{W_d}\right) > 0$, that is $\delta < \delta^*$, $\frac{\partial^2 T}{\partial \delta^2} > 0$. If $\frac{W_f}{W_d} > A_0$, then $L\left(\frac{W_f}{W_d}\right) < 0$, that is $\delta > \delta^*$, $\frac{\partial^2 T}{\partial \delta^2} < 0$.

---

[4] A_0 depends on η.

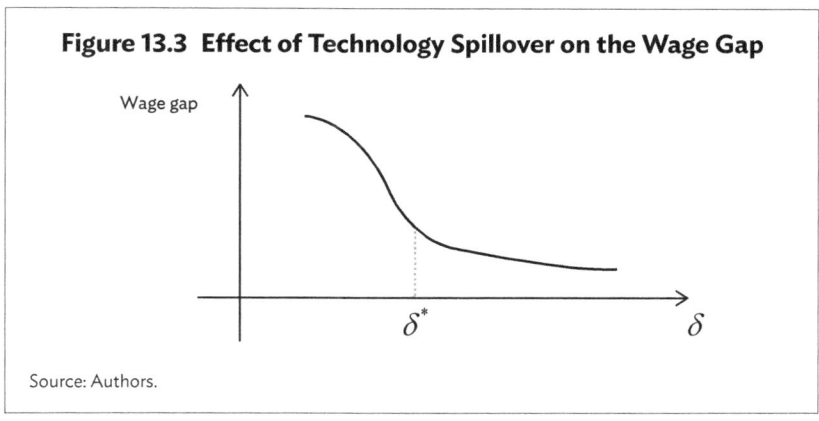

Figure 13.3 Effect of Technology Spillover on the Wage Gap

Source: Authors.

These analyses lead to the conclusion that technology spillovers can reduce the wage gap between the two sectors with increasing speed under the condition of $\delta > \delta^*$; once δ exceeds δ^*, the speed of reduction will start to slow down. Figure 13.3 depicts this process.

13.3.3 Overall Influence of Labor Transfer and Technology Spillover

Generally, higher wages and higher welfare paid by foreign firms will surely induce the local qualified labor force to transfer away from other sectors, if there are no obstacles to labor mobility. Therefore, the effect of labor transfer will play a role in determining the wage gap. Hence, due to restrictions arising from technical barriers, the patent system, as well as the absorptive capacity of local enterprises, the technology spillover effect lags the labor transfer effect. But lag length is influenced by many factors. In theory, there are two situations.

First, the effect of technology spillover occurs before the wage gap caused by labor transfer reaches the inflection point. This process is depicted in Figure 13.4. This means that the technology spillover effect has already started to play a role in reducing the wage gap when it is in the expansion phase that the labor-transfer effect occurs. This may have two consequences. The first is that the expansion phase of the wage gap caused by labor transfer is shortened; the second is a reduction in the maximum value of the wage gap caused by labor transfer, and the reduction occurs earlier. The overall result is that the technology spillover effect leads to an overall reduction of the inverted U-shaped curve compared to the curve caused by the labor transfer effect.

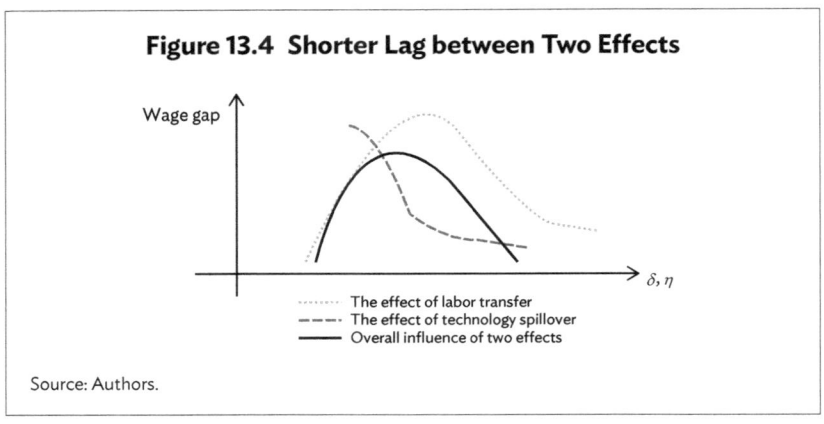

Figure 13.4 Shorter Lag between Two Effects

.... The effect of labor transfer
----- The effect of technology spillover
——— Overall influence of two effects

Source: Authors.

Second, the technology spillover effect occurs after the wage gap caused by the labor transfer effect reaches the inflection point. This process is depicted in Figure 13.5, which shows that the effect of technology spillover does not affect the first half and vertices of the inverted U-curve. But it speeds up the declining rate of the latter part of the curve, which is caused by labor transfer.

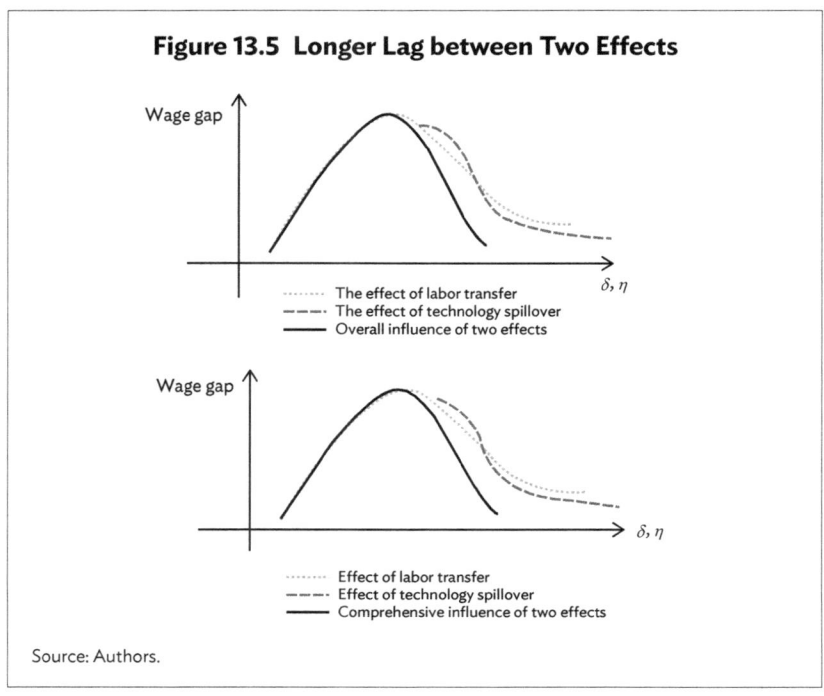

Figure 13.5 Longer Lag between Two Effects

.... The effect of labor transfer
----- The effect of technology spillover
——— Overall influence of two effects

.... Effect of labor transfer
----- Effect of technology spillover
——— Comprehensive influence of two effects

Source: Authors.

In general, theoretical analysis shows that the wage gap between two sectors first increases and then decreases as labor transfers from the domestic sector to the foreign sector. This implies an inverted U-shaped track. Meanwhile, increased technological spillovers reduce the wage gap between the two sectors. Finally, the overall effect of foreign investment leads the wage gap between two sectors first to increase and then to decrease. This means the overall effect of foreign investment on the wage gap also implies an inverted U-shaped track.

Using the Chinese Manufacturing Enterprises Database, the rest of this paper uses a regression-based inequality decomposition approach to explore determinants of the wage gap in the PRC. A comparison between the empirical results and the theoretical results could be helpful to examine the robustness of our assumptions.

13.4 Empirical Method and Data

Current research about inequality decomposition includes Oaxaca Decomposition, Cotton Decomposition, Neumark Decomposition, Brown Decomposition, and Appleton Decomposition. Each method has its own limitations. We use a regression-based Shapley Decomposition Approach, which has been improved by Wan (2004), to calculate the contributions of explanatory variables to income inequality. The basic idea of this method is that in the regression function we replace each variable by its mean value. The new fitted value can be considered as assessed income inequality ruling out the effect of that variable on inequality. The difference between assessed inequality and actual inequality can be considered as the contribution of that variable.

To implement the decomposition method, we first construct the decomposition function, as below, following the income function proposed by Shorrocks and Wan (2004):

$$lnW_{it} = \alpha + \beta_{1t}FCC_{it} + \beta_{2t}DR_{it} + \beta_{3t}EXP_{it} + \beta_{4t}CLA_{it} + \beta_{5t}PCP_{it} + \beta_{6t}OLP_{it} + \beta_{7t}MON_{it} + \beta_{8t}SCAL_{it} + \beta_{9t}NPR_{it} + \beta_{10t}X_i + \varepsilon_{it} \quad (13)$$

Where W is the average annual wage per worker, which encompasses the accrued payroll and welfare; fcc (Foreign-capital corporations) is the core dummy variable, which is identified as 1 if the enterprise is a foreign investment, 0 otherwise. Other control variables include: dr is debt ratio, reflecting the viability of enterprises; exp is export performance, measuring the degree of export dependency; clr is capital–labor ratio, which is used to distinguish labor intensity; pcp is per capita profit as assessment of economic efficiency; olp is overall labor productivity, reflecting the level of production and technology; *mon* is also a dummy variable, identified as 1 if the enterprise belongs to a monopoly industry;[5] *sca* is total assets, which indicates enterprise scale; *pnp* is proportion of new products, which indicates innovation capacity. We also include regional dummy variables. According to the different levels of development, the PRC could be divided into three regions: the eastern, central, and western regions. To compute the contribution to income inequality, we solve the estimated model to get the income level value. As a consequence, the constant term becomes a scalar so that it does not contribute to inequality. Hence, both the constant and dummy variable terms can be removed without affecting the decomposition results (Wan 2004).

$$W_i = \exp(\alpha) \times \exp(\beta_i X_i) \times \exp(T) \times \exp(u) \qquad (14)$$

Second, according to the regression result, we adopt the Shapley Decomposition Approach to calculate the contributions of explanatory variables to income inequality by using the Java program developed by the United Nations University World Institute for Development Economics Research.

The database we use consists of a panel of PRC manufacturing enterprises from 1999 to 2007. This dataset comes from the National Bureau of Statistics Enterprise Dataset. The National Bureau of Statistics of the PRC (NBSC) obtains annual reports from most state enterprises and large and medium-sized non-state enterprises (with annual sales of more than CNY 5 million). These annual reports contain the firm's financial statements and some non-financial information, such as the entry date, district code, industry code, and the main products of the enterprise. This database is used as the base for compiling the statistical data for the aggregate manufacturing sector, which is collected in the China Statistical Yearbook (NBSC 2000–2008). In this database, statistics on two-digit manufacturing industries are collected in the China Industry Economy Statistical Yearbook (NBSC 2000–2008). The sample size of 160,000 in 1999 was increased to 330,000 in 2007.

---

[5]   According to Ding (2010), Petroleum and Natural Gas Extraction; Petroleum Processing and Coking; Coal Mining and Processing; Mining and Processing of Non-Ferrous Metal Ores; Manufacture of Tobacco; Production and Supply of Electric Power and Heat Power; Production and Supply of Gas; Production and Supply of Water are classified as the monopoly industries.

Table 13.1 Descriptive Statistics

Variable	Number of Observations	Mean	SD	Min	Max
W	116,028	17,555.26	16,282.34	81.27	1478,836
fcc	116,028	0.41	0.4918	0	1
dr	116,028	57.74	38.58	−46.32	4,846.23
exp	116,028	26.86	39.56	0	104.67
clr	116,028	313.58	695.96	0.17	147,886.4
pcp	116,028	13.44	53.92	−5,501.61	2,678.385
olp	116028	88.77	196.03	−8,801.03	22,506.07
mon	116028	0.07	0.25	0	1
sca	116028	80,251.62	147,725.9	171	2,921,800
pnp	116028	3.68	14.48	0	100

Max = maximum, Min = minimum, SD = standard deviation.
Source: Authors.

We eliminate outliers according to the methods of Cai and Liu (2009)[6] and deflate price separately by consumer price index, producer price index, and Price Indices of Investment in Fixed Assets I and finally pick up 12,892 enterprises consisting of 7,726 domestic enterprises and 5,116 foreign-invested enterprises from 1999 to 2007.

There might be multicollinearity among these variables. But none of the Pearson correlation coefficients was larger than 0.4. Variance inflation factors fell from the band of 1.03 to 1.41. This evidence could prove that there is no multiple co-linear relation among variables. Descriptive statistics of primary variables are shown in Table 13.1.

We use data of 12,892 companies to calculate the wage ratio between foreign firms and domestic firms (W_f/W_d); the proportion of foreign firms' workforce in the total labor force (η), and the corresponding η^* and η^{**} from 1999 to 2007 (results are reported in Table 13.2). As can be seen from the table, η exceeds η^* in 2004. This means that the wage gap between the domestic sector and the foreign sector caused by the labor transfer effect has entered the declining phase, as we predict in our theoretical analysis.

---

[6] The following data observations have been excluded from the sample: those with missing value, those for the enterprises not meeting the criterion of above designated size' and those outliers in the key variables.

Table 13.2 Results of W_f/W_d, η, η^*, η^{**}

	W_f/W_d	η	η^*	η^{**}
1999	1.6401	0.3564	0.4182	0.8725
2000	1.6301	0.3752	0.4192	0.8748
2001	1.5146	0.3936	0.4312	0.9020
2002	1.5288	0.4140	0.4297	0.8986
2003	1.4805	0.4307	0.4349	0.9101
2004	1.4237	0.4580	0.4414	0.9237
2005	1.3978	0.4658	0.4444	0.9299
2006	1.3887	0.4733	0.4455	0.9321
2007	1.3456	0.4596	0.4507	0.9423

Source: Authors.

We also calculate the value of Theil index between domestic firms and foreign firms (according to Equation [9]), Theil index for all the companies' average wage, and the changing rate of Theil index from 1999 to 2007. The results are reported in Table 13.3.

In Table 13.3, the overall wage gap between domestic and foreign enterprises in the PRC shows a shrinking trend from 1999 to 2007. This might be because supply and demand in the labor market have undergone structural changes. Labor supply increasingly exceeds labor demand. Faced with increasing competition in the labor market, some enterprises that used to pay low wages have to increase them to attract workers. This leads to a decrease in the wage gap.

Second, the overall wage gap between domestic and foreign enterprises is quite significant in the PRC—Theil index of all companies' average wage is within the range of 0.2 to 0.25. The average wage is about 0.22. Theil indexes between domestic firms and foreign firms range from 0.01 to 0.03. The proportions of the Theil indexes between domestic firms and foreign firms accounting for the Theil index of all companies range from 5% to 12%. The average value of this proportion is more than 8%. The contribution of the wage gap between domestic firms and foreign firms to Theil index of all companies is obvious, therefore. However, the proportion is declining, implying FDI is no longer the main reason for the wage gap between enterprises.

Finally, Table 13.2 shows that the turning point in the wage gap caused by labor transfer effect takes occurs in 2004. Table 13.3 shows that the overall wage gap declined from 1999, which means the

Table 13.3 Theil Index between Domestic Firms and Foreign Firms and All Companies' Average Wage

	Theil Index between Domestic and Foreign Firms T_{two}	Rates of Change (%)	Theil Index of All Companies' Average Wage T_{all}	Rates of Change (%)	T_{two}/T_{all} (%)
1999	0.0300	NA	0.24115	NA	12.44
2000	0.0295	−1.67	0.24052	−0.26	12.27
2001	0.0214	−27.46	0.2344	−2.54	9.13
2002	0.0224	4.67	0.24623	5.05	9.10
2003	0.0192	−14.29	0.22288	−9.48	8.61
2004	0.0156	−18.75	0.21027	−5.66	7.42
2005	0.0140	−10.26	0.20417	−2.90	6.86
2006	0.0134	−4.29	0.20774	1.75	6.45
2007	0.0110	−17.91	0.20977	0.98	5.24
Average	0.01961	−11.24	0.22413	−1.63	8.61
1999–2007		−63.33		−7.05	

NA = not available.
Source: Authors.

technology spillover effect occurred before 2004. In other words, the overall influence of the labor transfer effect and technology spillover effect on the wage gap in the PRC supports the first case of our theoretical analysis. The effect of technology spillover occurs before the wage gap caused by the labor transfer effect reaches the turning point.

13.5 Empirical Results

Table 13.4 presents the estimation results of Equation (13). Column (1) shows the estimation results of the Fixed Effect Model with the log average wage of enterprises as dependent variable. The presence of significant heteroscedasticity and serial correlation can be tested using the Wooldridge test and the Wald test. Therefore, we report Driscoll–Kraay standard errors that are robust to heteroscedasticity and serial correlation (see Driscoll and Kraay 1998). Column (2) of Table 13.4 shows the results.

Table 13.4 Results of Estimating Equation (13)

	Estimation Results of the Fixed Effect Model	Estimation Results of the Fixed Effect Model with Driscoll and Kraay Standard Errors
fcc	0.0545***	0.0545**
dr	−0.0985**	−0.0985
exp	−0.5273***	−0.5273
cla	0.0351***	0.0351
pcp	0.4072***	0.4072***
olp	0.2355***	0.2355***
mon	0.1688***	0.1688***
sca	0.0282***	0.0282**
npr	0.0123	0.0123
Central region	−0.1491	−0.1491***
Western region	0.0167	0.0167
Constant	9.1262***	9.1262***
Wooldridge text	594.849 (0.000)	
Wald text	5,300,000 (0.000)	
R^2	0.2981	0.2981
Prob>F	(0.000)	(0.000)
Number of observations	116,028	116,028

Note: Time dummies are all significant at the 1% level. For convenience, they are not reported.
*** $p < 0.01$, ** $p < 0.05$, * $p < 0.1$.
Source: Authors.

After standard errors have been corrected, estimated coefficients of the foreign-capital company, per capita profit, overall labor productivity, monopoly, and scale of enterprise are statistically significant at least at the 5% level. The estimated coefficient of the foreign-capital company is significantly positive at the 5% level. This suggests that FDI has a significant impact on the wage level of the PRC. This also indicates that foreign-capital companies pay a 5.6% higher wage than domestic companies. There is a significant wage gap between foreign-capital and domestic companies.

Per capita profit, enterprise scale, and monopoly have significantly positive coefficients. This means that these variables are important factors for wage determination in the PRC. According to the profit-sharing model (Kahneman, Knetsch, and Thaler 1986), companies with higher profits are more willing to pay their employees high wages. The cost of supervision, organization, management, and coordination is usually high in large-scale enterprises; a high level of wages can help companies reduce these costs on the basis of the theory of efficiency wages (Shapiro and Stiglitz 1984). Monopoly industries with benefits from the government and monopoly prices pay a higher level of wages to employees. This result has been recognized by many studies.

The impacts of debt ratio and export on the wage level are negative in the PRC. It is clear that a high debt ratio means a bad financial situation. Regarding export, the PRC still exports labor-intensive products, and export enterprises usually pay relatively lower wages to maintain export advantages. Both variables have insignificant coefficients.

According to neoclassical theory, a high capital–labor ratio means higher marginal products of labor. This means that only enterprises with higher returns have the ability to conduct research and development for new products and then pay the higher level of wage for workers, but both variables have insignificant coefficients, implying that neither of them is a crucial factor in the wage-determination process.

To decompose the annual wage gap, we also need to obtain the annual income estimation equation from 1999 to 2007. That means running the regression on annual cross-sectional data. The regression results can be found in the Appendix table.

We compute contributions of each explanatory variable in the regression model using the Shapley value-based approach (decomposition results are shown in Table 13.5). Since the decomposition results are influenced by the choice of the inequality index, decomposition results are presented for two inequality measures: Gini index and Theil index. The table shows the contributed percentage of explanatory variables to total inequality. Decomposition results of Gini coefficient and Theil index are very similar. This shows that the method generates a robust result. Degrees of explanation remain at 50% to 60%, indicating that the results are quite reliable.

Table 13.5 shows that the contributions of all explanatory variables have obviously changed from 1999 to 2007. This is because the PRC was experiencing a rapid transformation of its economic structure.

The impact of foreign-capital companies on the wage gap between domestic companies and foreign companies is quite significant over the period of study. Decomposition results of Gini coefficient show that the contribution of foreign-capital companies ranges from 11% to 17%. The decomposition results of Theil index show that the contribution of foreign-capital companies ranges from 5% to 8%, which is the second-

Table 13.5 Factor Contributions to Inequality Using the Shapley Method
(%)

	1999		2000		2001	
	Gini Coefficient	Theil Index	Gini Coefficient	Theil Index	Gini Coefficient	Theil Index
Debt ratio	2.14	0.67	3.98	1.07	1.69	0.41
Export	0.53	−0.01	0.64	0.07	1.53	0.49
Capital-labor ratio	17.56	20.14	15.14	20.12	13.24	21.73
Per capita profit	3.03	2.83	4.88	7.56	4.98	10.79
Overall labor productivity	4.48	6.45	0.97	2.12	5.16	11.93
Monopoly	0.74	0.74	1.04	0.97	1.97	1.56
Foreign-capital companies	17.11	8.05	15.71	6.79	14.07	4.98
Region	9.69	4.11	10.06	4.05	9.28	0.96
Scale	2.24	2.18	2.85	3.07	3.90	3.29
Proportion of new products	0.71	0.22	1.30	0.35	1.04	0.30
Total degrees of explanation	58.22	45.38	56.59	46.19	56.84	56.45
	2002		2003		2004	
	Gini Coefficient	Theil Index	Gini Coefficient	Theil Index	Gini Coefficient	Theil Index
Debt ratio	12.86	5.59	1.10	0.38	2.65	0.78
Export	1.00	−0.29	1.31	0.46	2.70	0.89
Capital-labor ratio	14.58	25.43	19.12	23.38	10.29	16.80
Per capita profit	5.36	9.38	2.74	7.95	3.94	5.24
Overall labor productivity	4.80	10.67	6.55	15.22	3.35	5.04
Monopoly	1.88	1.76	1.86	1.01	2.22	2.37
Foreign-capital companies	13.12	7.89	12.60	7.21	12.95	4.85
Region	8.26	3.78	8.88	4.55	8.13	3.27
Scale	3.54	3.32	2.62	2.06	4.92	5.30
Proportion of new products	1.31	0.47	1.69	3.01	1.63	0.64
Total degrees of explanation	66.71	67.99	58.48	65.23	52.78	45.18

continued on next page

Table 13.5 continued

	2005		2006		2007	
	Gini Coefficient	Theil Index	Gini Coefficient	Theil Index	Gini Coefficient	Theil Index
Debt ratio	2.08	0.61	2.57	0.46	2.16	0.57
Export	2.20	0.33	1.89	0.26	1.72	0.36
Capital–labor ratio	7.70	10.50	7.06	10.83	8.68	13.66
Per capita profit	1.96	2.58	1.89	2.02	2.14	1.05
Overall labor productivity	4.62	4.60	6.39	9.11	2.46	5.82
Monopoly	2.17	1.66	2.59	1.20	2.45	1.30
Foreign-capital companies	13.34	5.30	13.55	5.41	11.73	4.98
Region	7.68	3.32	7.33	3.12	8.83	4.09
Scale	5.38	4.04	6.56	4.14	7.23	4.99
Proportion of new products	1.63	0.70	1.47	0.48	1.10	0.40
Total degrees of explanation	48.76	33.62	51.30	37.04	48.51	37.22

Source: Authors.

highest contribution to total inequality. In the long run, the contribution for the foreign-capital companies shows a declining trend. The Gini coefficient decomposition results show that it declined from 17.11% in 1999 to 11.73% in 2007. Theil index decomposition results show that it declined from 8.05% to 4.98%. The most likely reason for this declining trend is that labor transfer and technological spillover effects together impact the wage gap between domestic companies and foreign companies. Another reason could be that the management level of domestic enterprises has improved rapidly following the development of the PRC's economy. The wage gap between domestic enterprises and foreign enterprises is gradually narrowing.

The capital–labor ratio has the highest level of contributions to total inequality; Gini coefficient decomposition results show that it ranges from 13% to 20%. Theil index decomposition results show that it ranges from 8% to 17%. This means that the capital–labor ratio is still the most important factor in the wage determination process. Overall, the unbalanced development of regional has made the third largest contribution to the total inequality, reflecting the fact that regional barriers to the flow of labor in PRC is always exist. The average scale of the enterprise has increased contributions totaling inequality. Gini coefficient decomposition results show it ranges from 2.24% in 1999 to 7.23% in 2007. Theil index decomposition results show that it ranges from 2.18% to 4.99%. This result indicates that economic scale has become the main determining factor for the wage gap.

The contribution of monopoly to the wage gap is small. This result is different from that of previous research. Gini coefficient decomposition results show that it ranges from 1% to 2.5%. Theil index decomposition results show that it ranges from 1% to 2%. The main reason is that data used in this paper come from the Industrial Enterprises Database, where most observations are from the manufacturing sector. However, most of the PRC's monopoly companies are concentrated in the non-manufacturing sectors.

Regarding the other variables, the contribution of export to the wage gap is not very high, implying that the wage bonus arising from export tends to disappear in the PRC. The contribution of the new products proportion remains at a low level. This is probably because there are fewer innovative companies in the database or that the innovation ability of industrial enterprises in the PRC is still at a low level. The difference in per capita profits plays only a minor role in the wage gap. This probably implies that enterprises always try to get higher profits by cutting wages.

13.6 Conclusion

Most developing countries have experienced a sharp increase in income inequality during the process of globalization. This study presents evidence that the inflow of FDI is closely associated with inter-enterprise wage inequality. Two mechanisms through which FDI impacts the wage gap between foreign firms and domestic firms in the host country are identified from the existing literature: the labor transfer effect and the technology spillover effect. We set up a model including these two mechanisms to analyze the overall effects of FDI on the wage gap. Our theoretical results show that the inflow of FDI in the host country at first results in an increase in wage inequality and subsequently a decrease. Using data obtained from the Chinese Industrial Enterprises Database, we investigate the contributions of the observed factors to the wage gap. The turning point of the wage gap caused by the labor transfer effect occurred in 2004 in the PRC. The technology spillover effect occurred before 2004 in the PRC. The results of Shapley-value decomposition reveal a declining trend for the contribution of FDI to the wage gap. According to our deduction conclusion, the technology spillover effect of FDI would help to narrow the wage gap between enterprises, suggesting that market-access barriers in the PRC should be eliminated to attract more high-technology companies.

References

Acemoglu, D. 1998. Why Do New Technologies Complement Skills? Directed Technical Change and Wage Inequality. *The Quarterly Journal of Economics* 113: 1055–1089.

———. 2002. Technical Change, Inequality, and the Labor Market. *Journal of Economic Literature* 40: 7–72.

Bao, Q., and M. Shao. 2008. Foreign Investment and the Wage Gaps in Host Countries: An Empirical Study Based on China's Industrial Panel Data. *Management World* 5: 46–54.

Brown, D., A. Deardorff, and R. Stern. 2003. The Effects of Multinational Production on Wages and Working Conditions in Developing Countries. NBER Working Paper 9669. Cambridge, MA: National Bureau of Economic Research.

Cai, H., and Q. Liu. 2009. Competition and Corporate Tax Avoidance: Evidence from Chinese Industrial Firms. *The Economic Journal* 119: 764–795.

Chen, L., and H. Xie. 2004. The Impacts of the Foreign Direct Investments to the Salary Level in China. *Review of Economy and Management* 20: 31–35.

Chen, Z., Y. Ge, and H. Lai. 2011. Foreign Direct Investment and Wage Inequality: Evidence from China. *World Development* 39: 1322–1332.

Das, S. P. 2002. Foreign Direct Investment and the Relative Wage in a Developing Economy. *Journal of Development Economics* 67: 55–77.

Driffield, N., and K. Taylor. 2006. Wage Spillovers, Inter-regional Effects and the Impact of Inward Investment *Spatial Economic Analysis* 1: 187–205.

Driscoll, J. C, and A. C. Kraay. 1998. Consistent Covariance Matrix Estimation with Spatially Dependent Panel Data. *Review of Economics and Statistics* 80: 549–560.

Feenstra, R. C., and G. H. Hanson. 1997. Foreign Direct Investment and Relative Wages: Evidence from Mexico's Maquiladoras. *Journal of International Economics* 42: 371–393.

Figini, P., and H. Görg. 1999. Multinational Companies and Wage Inequality in the Host Country: The Case of Ireland. *Review of World Economics* 135: 594–612.

Glomm, G., and B. Ravikumar.1992. Public versus Private Investment in Human Capital: Endogenous Growth and Income Inequality. *Journal of Political*

Kahneman, D., J. L. Knetsch, and R. Thaler. 1986. Fairness as a Constraint on Profit Seeking: Entitlements in the Market. *American Economic Review* 76: 728–741.

Lipsey, R. E. 2004. Home-and Host-Country Effects of Foreign Direct Investment. *Nber Chapters* 2: 333–382.

Lipsey, R. E., and F. Sjoholm. 2004. Foreign Direct Investment, Education and Wages in Indonesian Manufacturing. *Journal of Development* 73: 415–422.

Markusen, J. R., and A. J. Venables. 1997. The Role of Multinational Firms in the Wage-Gap Debate. *Review of International Economics* 5: 435–451.

Robinson, S. 1976. A Note on the U Hypothesis Relating Income Inequality and Economic Development. *American Economic Studies* 66: 437–440.

Saggi, K. 2002. Trade, Foreign Direct Investment, and International Technology Transfer: A Survey. *World Bank Research Observer* 17: 191–235.

Saglam, B. B., and S. Sayek. 2011. MNEs and Wages: The Role of Productivity Spillovers and Imperfect Labor Markets. *Economic Modelling* 28: 2736–2742.

Shapiro, C., and J. E. Stiglitz. 1984.Equilibrium Unemployment as a Worker Discipline Device. *American Economic Review* 74: 433–444.

Shorrocks, A., and G. Wan. 2004. Spatial Decomposition of Inequality. UNU-WIDER Discussion Paper No. 2004/01.

Todo, Y., and K. Miyamoto. 2006. Knowledge Spillovers from Foreign Direct Investment and the Role of Local R&D Activities: Evidence from Indonesia. *Economic Development and Cultural Change* 55: 173–200.

Wan, G. 2004. Accounting for Income Inequality in Rural China: A Regression Based Approach. *Economic Research Journal* 8: 117–127.

Wang, Y. 2009. The Influence of FDI on the Technical Progress in China's Industry. *World Economy Study* 2: 66–73.

Wu, X. 2001. The Impact of Foreign Direct Investment on the Relative Return to Skill. *Economics of Transition* 9: 695–715.

Xu, H., P. Qi, and H. Z. Li. 2009. Foreign Direct Investment, the Labour Market, and the Wage Spillover Effect. *Management World* 9: 53–68.

Xuan, Y., and S. Zhao. 2005. The Effect of FDI on Wage Rate—An Empirical Study of Jiangsu Province. *Nankai Economic studies* 12: 72–78.

Zhou, Y. 2009. Urbanization, Urban–Rural Income Gap and Overall Income Inequality in China: An Empirical Test of the Inverse-U Hypothesis. *China Economic Quarterly* 8: 1239–1256.

Appendix

Table A13.1 Regression Results of Annual Cross-sectional Data

	1999	2000	2001	2002	2003
Foreign-capital companies	0.3144***	0.2978***	0.2915***	0.2833***	0.2677***
Debt ratio	−0.1179***	−0.1942***	−0.0908***	−0.0507***	−0.0618***
Export	−0.0714***	−0.0832***	−0.1206***	−0.1184***	−0.0997***
Capital-labor ratio	0.0429***	0.0367***	0.0282***	0.0321***	0.0431***
Per capita profit	0.1563***	0.0171***	0.1475***	0.1611***	0.0669***
Overall labor productivity	0.5342***	0.0888***	0.4545***	0.4183***	0.4945***
Monopoly	0.1206***	0.1530***	0.2380***	0.2357***	0.2319***
Central region	−0.3669***	−0.4001***	−0.4004***	−0.3800***	−0.3738***
Western Region	−0.2242***	−0.2216***	−0.1965***	−0.2044***	−0.1802***
Scale	0.0342***	0.0396***	0.0492***	0.0464***	0.0295***
Proportion of new products	0.0019***	0.0030***	0.0025***	0.0034***	0.0031***
Constant	2.1057***	2.2771***	2.2761***	2.2932***	2.3400***
R^2	0.2718	0.2605	0.2477	0.2621	0.2643
Adjusted R2	0.2712	0.2599	0.2471	0.2615	0.2637

continued on next page

Table 13.1 *continued*

	2004	2005	2006	2007
Foreign-capital companies	0.2977***	0.2902***	0.3011***	0.2649***
Debt ratio	−0.1295***	−0.1029***	−0.1215***	−0.1119***
Export	−0.1930***	−0.1593***	−0.1462***	−0.1431***
Capital–labor ratio	0.0193***	0.0147***	0.0121***	0.0147***
Per capita profit	0.0114***	0.0053***	0.0028***	0.0038***
Overall labor productivity	0.2693***	0.3444***	0.2625***	0.1364***
Monopoly	0.2421***	0.2416***	0.2854***	0.1833***
Central region	−0.3595***	−0.3173***	−0.3437***	−0.3825***
Western Region	−0.1651***	−0.1720***	−0.1360***	−0.1799***
Scale	0.0468***	0.0470***	0.0531***	0.0508***
Proportion of new products	0.0033***	0.0027***	0.0026***	0.0019***
Constant	2.5590***	2.6247***	2.7556***	2.8926***
R2	0.2706	0.2417	0.2397	0.2274
Adjusted R2	0.27	0.241	0.2391	0.2268

Source: Authors.

14

Impacts of Rural Dual Economic Transformation on the Inverted-U Curve of Rural Income Inequality: An Empirical Study of Tianjin and Shandong Provinces in the People's Republic of China

Zongsheng Chen, Ting Wu, and Jian Kang

14.1 Introduction

The dual economic structure of different provinces and regions in the People's Republic of China (PRC) represents different trends. Gao (2005) has attributed this difference to the different labor transfer costs among regions. Limited to the purpose of the research, Gao did not analyze the difference of the dual economic transformation. It is true that some scholars have also undertaken research on the overall dual economic transformation in the rural areas and its influence on the overall expansion of rural income inequality; further, it is believed that the different income groups have different degrees and change rates of dependence on agricultural and non-agricultural income, which inevitably leads to the expansion of the income inequality in the current stage (Lin, Cai, and Li 1998; Chen and Chen 1999; Ma 2001). Among these scholars, Li (1999) has emphasized that the transfer of surplus labor force from the traditional sector has different effects on rural income inequality in different regions. Despite its being valuable, Li's research didn't connect the dual economic transformation with the declining trend of income inequality because it is too early, which makes it limited to a certain extent.

The existing literature has either focused on regional differences in the large-scale dual economic transformation in the national economy, or only paid attention to the influence of the rural dual economic transformation on the expansion of rural income inequality (Xue 2005; Wan, Zhou, and Lu 2005; Yao and Wang 2009; Chen and Liu 2011). This overlooks that the difference of dual economic transformation in different regions may lead to the regional differences of rural income inequality; thus, it is impossible to focus on the resident income inequality in some areas of the PRC having already entered the decline stage of the so-called "income inequality inverted-U curve in public ownership economy". The change track of rural income inequality in Tianjin studied in this paper presents such an inverted-U shape. In our research, a case analysis on rural Tianjin and other provinces can explain how rural dual economic transformation leads to the income inequality inverted-U curve,[1] and how it affects income inequality in rural areas, especially with regard to the inverted-U transition in some developed areas in the PRC. We choose rural Tianjin as representative of developed provinces because it depends more on the urban economy and its technological and human resources infrastructure. In addition, the degree of rural labor transfer and agricultural specialization, modernization, and economic intensity in Tianjin is higher.[2] As a result, rural income inequality has surpassed the turning point of the income inequality inverted-U curve. With a higher proportion of the population being rural and a significant dual economic structure, Shandong represents the general situation of agricultural provinces dominated by the traditional mode; thus, rural income inequality increases constantly, just as in most rural areas of the PRC to some extent. Through this empirical and comparative study, we can make some policy suggestions to both grow rural income and reduce income inequality in rural PRC, that is, to pass the inverted-U curve turning point.

The data of our research are mainly from *Tianjin rural social and economic survey data in 1994–2008*, the quintile-grouped data of disposable income from *Tianjin Rural residents in 2003–2014*, and *Shandong rural economic and social economy survey data in 2007–2009*. Among these, indicators in the rural economic and social survey data

---

[1] As to the general principle of dual economic transformation's impact on income inequality, we have stated it as an "income inequality inverted-U curve in public ownership economy". See Chen (1991), p. 164.

[2] The term "urban agriculture" was first seen in "Agricultural Economic Geography" from Japanese scholar Shiro Aoshika. Urban agriculture is scattered within the business district and residential areas in the city, or scattered around urban peripheral areas in a special form.

are comprehensive, and data have high accuracy and comparability in comparison with the corresponding packet data. In addition, the national statistics used in this paper are mainly from the *China Statistical Yearbook 1994–2014*. With reference to Shorrocks and Wan (2008), we decompose the income-grouped data of national rural residents in 1994–2013 and Tianjin rural residents in 2003–2014 into the data of personal income. From this perspective, we calculate the Gini coefficient of per capita income in rural Tianjin and rural PRC, respectively.[3] In comparison with the Gini coefficient of income inequality in rural Tianjin calculated from different data and different methods, we find that there are very small differences between these results; therefore, the calculations have high reliability.

14.2 The Evolution of Dual Economic Transformation and Income Inequality in Rural Areas

14.2.1 Changes in Income Inequality in Rural Tianjin and the People's Republic of China

Through the analysis of related data (as shown in Figure 14.1), we can find, from 2003 to 2013, the rural-resident income Gini in Tianjin dropped from 0.4036 to 0.2974, with an average decrease of 2.92% per year, while from 1994 to 2013, the rural-resident income Gini in the PRC rose from 0.33 to 0.36, an increase of 7.99%. The change tendency of the Gini in Tianjin before 2003 is consistent with that in the PRC, and rural-resident income Gini also expanded rapidly with the rapid economic growth and improvement of household income (Figure 14.1). However, after crossing the vertex in 2003, the rural-resident income Gini in Tianjin began a decline phase, showing an inverted-U curve, which is much different from the situation in Shandong and the whole of the PRC. If the change in Tianjin is sustainable, it must contain some important variables and information that may be applied for prompting changes in income inequality in other provinces of the PRC.

---

[3] For Shandong, depending on the available data, we can only calculate several years Gini by *Shandong rural socio-economic survey in 2007–2009*.

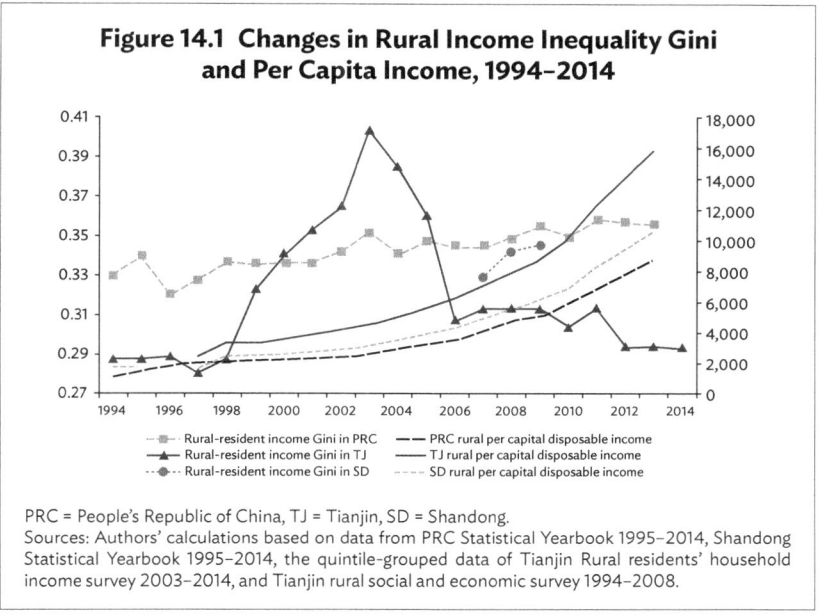

Figure 14.1 Changes in Rural Income Inequality Gini and Per Capita Income, 1994–2014

PRC = People's Republic of China, TJ = Tianjin, SD = Shandong.
Sources: Authors' calculations based on data from PRC Statistical Yearbook 1995–2014, Shandong Statistical Yearbook 1995–2014, the quintile-grouped data of Tianjin Rural residents' household income survey 2003–2014, and Tianjin rural social and economic survey 1994–2008.

To make a more intuitive analysis, we also calculate the income share that constitutes Gini and the average within each group. Further, we list the changes in the income share by quintiles of rural household income in Tianjin and the PRC, as well as the average within each group from 2003 to 2013 (Table 14.1). In this way, we may observe whether the changes in income share in each group are abrupt or smooth, and determine whether they are sustainable.

Table 14.1 shows that the rural income inequality both in Tianjin and the PRC is still relatively high: 20% of top-income households retain about 40% of the income, while the bottom 20% retains less than 8% of the income; further, it shows that the declining trend of income share in the highest-income group in Tianjin is more significant in most years, and, comparatively, it decreased by 17.41% from 2003 to 2013. At the same time, the income shares of the lowest-income group and lower-middle-income group increased year-by-year, and increased by 65% in total for the lowest group, that is, the relative poverty of the 20% lowest-income family eased to a certain extent. By contrast, despite the slight decrease in the income share of the highest-income group in the whole PRC, the income share of the lowest-income group and middle-income group exhibits a significant decline, indicating that

Table 14.1 The Income Share (%) and Average Income (CNY) of Rural Households by Quintile

Income Quintile Groups		Bottom		Lower		Middle	
Categories		Average	Share	Average	Share	Average	Share
2003	Tianjin	1,092.7	4.58	2,697.2	11.30	3,884.1	16.27
	PRC	865.9	6.06	1,606.5	11.23	2,273.1	15.90
2004	Tianjin	1,351.8	5.19	3,121.0	11.98	4,340.1	16.65
	PRC	1,006.9	6.31	1,842.0	11.54	2,578.5	16.15
2005	Tianjin	1,531.3	5.14	3,371.5	11.32	4,976.1	16.70
	PRC	1,067.2	6.03	2,018.3	11.41	2,851.0	16.12
2006	Tianjin	2,416.8	7.33	4,225.2	12.81	5,608.3	17.00
	PRC	1,182.5	6.07	2,222.0	11.41	3,148.5	16.17
2007	Tianjin	2,694.1	7.38	4,837.4	13.24	6,287.9	17.22
	PRC	1,346.9	5.98	2,581.8	11.47	3,658.8	16.26
2008	Tianjin	3,227.1	7.78	5,521.1	13.30	7,017.9	16.91
	PRC	1,499.8	5.8	2,935.0	11.35	4,203.1	16.26
2009	Tianjin	3,365.7	7.29	6,107.5	13.23	8,031.4	17.39
	PRC	1,549.3	5.54	3,110.1	11.13	4,002.1	16.11
2010	Tianjin	3,947.1	7.44	6,993.5	13.19	9,540.7	17.99
	PRC	1,869.8	5.81	3,621.2	11.24	5,221.7	16.21
2011	Tianjin	4,285.6	6.97	8,306.9	13.51	10,843.0	17.64
	PRC	2,000.5	5.25	4,255.7	11.16	6,207.7	16.28
2012	Tianjin	5,811.1	8.25	9,462.6	13.43	12,394.0	17.59
	PRC	2,316.2	5.35	4,807.5	11.10	7,041.0	16.26
2013	Tianjin	5,961.7	7.54	10,977.9	13.88	14,274.0	18.05
	PRC	2,583.2	5.31	5,516.4	11.33	7,942.1	16.31
Change rate (2013/2003)	Tianjin	445.59%	64.63%	307.01%	22.83%	267.50%	10.94%
	PRC	198.33%	12.38%	243.38%	0.89%	249.40%	2.58%

Income Quintile Groups		Higher		Top		Income Ratio (Top/Bottom)
Categories		Average	Share	Average	Share	
2003	Tianjin	5,374.7	22.52	108,201	45.33	9.90
	PRC	3,206.8	22.43	6,346.9	44.39	7.33
2004	Tianjin	5,918.1	22.71	11,330	43.48	8.38
	PRC	3,607.7	22.6	6,930.7	43.41	6.88

continued on next page

Table 14.1 continued

Income Quintile Groups Categories		Higher		Top		Income Ratio (Top/Bottom)
		Average	Share	Average	Share	
2005	Tianjin	7,160.1	24.03	12,757	42.81	8.33
	PRC	4,003.3	22.63	7,747.4	43.8	7.26
2006	Tianjin	7,714.1	23.39	13,020	39.47	5.39
	PRC	4,446.6	22.83	8,474.8	43.52	7.17
2007	Tianjin	8,198.2	22.44	14,508	39.72	5.39
	PRC	5,129.8	22.79	9,790.7	43.5	7.27
2008	Tianjin	9,207.9	22.19	16,527	39.82	5.12
	PRC	5,928.6	22.93	11,290	43.66	7.53
2009	Tianjin	10,628.	23.02	18,038	39.07	5.36
	PRC	6,467.6	23.14	12,319	44.08	7.95
2010	Tianjin	12,321	23.23	20,230	38.15	5.13
	PRC	7,440.6	23.11	14,050	43.63	7.51
2011	Tianjin	13,971	22.72	24,078	39.16	5.62
	PRC	8,893.6	23.32	16,783	44.00	8.39
2012	Tianjin	15,990	22.69	26,812	38.05	4.61
	PRC	10,142	23.41	19,009	43.88	8.21
2013	Tianjin	18,264	23.09	29,607	37.44	4.97
	PRC	11,373	23.36	21,273	43.69	8.24
Change rate (2013/2003)	Tianjin	239.81%	2.53%	−72.64%	−17.41%	−49.80%
	PRC	254.65%	4.15%	235.17%	−1.58%	12.41%

PRC = People's Republic of China.
Note: The ratio of the last column is that between the average in the highest income group and that in the lowest income group.
Sources: Authors' calculations based on data from China Statistical Yearbook 1995–2014, Shandong Statistical Yearbook 1995–2014, the quintile grouped data of Tianjin Rural residents' household income survey 2003–2014, and Tianjin rural social and economic survey 1994–2008.

the relative poverty of low-income people is getting higher and higher. Finally, Table 14.1 shows that, from the view of the ratio of the average household income between the top and bottom groups (income ratio), rural income inequality in Tianjin appears to decrease significantly after 2003. The income ratio decreased by 49.80% until 2013, indicating that the relative income inequality between Tianjin high-income and low-income households is shrinking. While the rural income inequality in the PRC generally increased, the income ratio rose by 12.41% from 2003 to 2013, which is broadly consistent with the change tendency of income inequality demonstrated by the Gini coefficient.

The above grouping decomposition analysis indicates that rural income inequality in Tianjin evolved from expansion to reduction, while rural resident income inequality in the PRC continued to expand gradually. Both processes occurred without any abrupt change, which means they are both part of a general trend, and thus may be sustainable.

14.2.2 The Evolution of the Rural Dual Economy in the People's Republic of China and Tianjin

The trends in rural income inequality in Tianjin and the PRC can be attributed to the changes in rural dual economic transformation over the past 20 years. Changes in the deep relationship between the urban sector and the rural sector led to the rural inequality. For instance, the development of urban agriculture and the growing number of small-scale farmers migrating to urban areas have increased rural income inequality. As a consequence, the rural dual economic transformation can be treated as a very important part of the structural change between rural and urban sectors, which is also an important driving force of overall income inequality.

The rural dual economic transformation reflects the reallocation of output and labor force among several sectors. Correspondingly, it contributes to a decrease in the proportion of output and employment in the traditional sector, but to an increase in both proportions in the modern sector. Some scholars constructed a comprehensive dual index, which can make up the shortcomings of the existing indicators measuring the dual structure, such as comparative labor productivity, dual contrast coefficient, or dual contrast index, etc. These indices may only measure the difference among labor productivities without overcoming their shortages. But the comprehensive dual index can better measure the economic growth performance in dual economic transformation (Gao 2007). Hence, we adopt its exponential form to estimate the extent of the dual economy in rural areas as follows:

$$r = [(E_{rm} / E_{rt}) \times (W_{rt} / W_{rm})]^{\frac{1}{2}} \qquad (1)$$

Where E_{rm} refers to the labor productivity of the non-agricultural sector, and E_{rt} to the labor productivity of the traditional agriculture sector in the rural economy. E_{rm} is the rural-resident per capita non-agricultural income, including employment wage income from rural enterprises, non-agricultural business income, and property income.

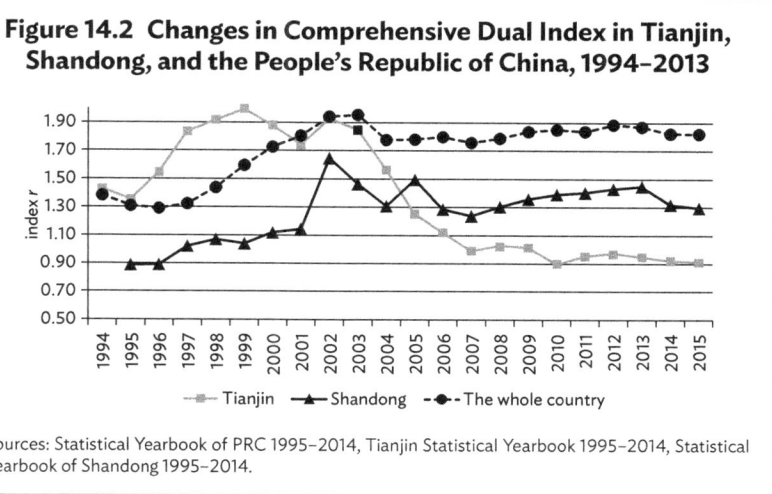

Figure 14.2 Changes in Comprehensive Dual Index in Tianjin, Shandong, and the People's Republic of China, 1994–2013

Sources: Statistical Yearbook of PRC 1995–2014, Tianjin Statistical Yearbook 1995–2014, Statistical Yearbook of Shandong 1995–2014.

E_{rt} is the rural-resident per capita agricultural income and mainly refers to the household income of agricultural management. The ratio between E_{rm} and E_{rt} reflects the comparison of labor productivity between the two sectors. W_{rt} refers to the proportion of the labor force in the traditional agriculture sector, and W_{rm} to the proportion of the labor force in the non-agricultural sector in the rural economy. W_{rt} is the number of rural residents engaging in primary agriculture, and W_{rm} is the number of rural residents engaging in non-agricultural industry. The ratio between W_{rt} and W_{rm} reflects the sectoral structure of labor force, and there is also a positive correlation between this ratio and the structural intensity of rural dual economy. In addition, we adopt the form of the square root to stabilize the excessive influence that may be caused by multiplication of these two factors. Typically, the smaller the index r, the lower the extent of the dual economy.

In Figure 14.2 and Table 14.2, we see that, after 1994, the evolution of the dual economy in Tianjin differed from that of rural PRC. The dual economy in rural PRC was intensified and still maintains overall stability, while the transformation of the dual economy in Tianjin can be divided into two stages.

The first stage is from 1994 to 2002. In this period, the dual economy was almost the same as rural PRC. The comprehensive dual indices in Tianjin, Shandong, and the PRC showed a growth trend, and the rural dual economic structure was intensified constantly. Unemployed rural laborers mostly chose to work in the non-agricultural sector as part of the tide of migrant workers. However, due to the constraints of the household registration system, small-scale farmers can only be migrant workers and their remittances are included in the non-agricultural income, which exacerbates the rural income inequality to a greater extent. In addition, the labor productivity divide between the non-agricultural and agricultural sectors expands continuously in the rural economy, for the migrant workers first transferring to the non-agricultural sector must be skilled with high productivity. Therefore, the labor force transfer also increases the productivity differences between the traditional agriculture sector and the non-agricultural sector in the rural economy, resulting in a significant expansion in income inequality within rural areas.[4] At this stage, the intensity of the dual economy in rural Tianjin is significantly higher than in Shandong and the PRC, and was closely related to the relatively high level of non-agricultural labor in Tianjin.

The second stage was from 2002 to 2013. The evolution of the dual economic structure within rural areas began to vary with the regions. Located along the coast and relatively lacking in land, Tianjin's rural labor force began to move from traditional agriculture to modern industry and urban agriculture in 2000, which led to a slowdown or even stagnation in rural surplus labor. Due to a higher degree of specialization and modernization, and more capital, technology, equipment, and other elements, the labor productivity in industry and urban agriculture is relatively higher. As a result, it contributed to the steady decline in difference of labor productivity between the agricultural sector and the non-agricultural sector. The comprehensive dual index in Tianjin dropped rapidly; it was lower than that in rural PRC after 2002, as well as lower than that in Shandong province after 2004. From 2002, the comprehensive dual index in Shandong and the PRC stopped rising and slightly decreased. However, as a traditional agricultural province, Shandong has more land resources and larger arable land per capita, so most of the rural residents are still in the traditional agriculture sector. On the other hand, the development of the non-agricultural sector is much slower than that in Tianjin, so the proportion of non-agricultural income and employment in Shandong is relatively lower (Table 14.2). Taking into consideration the income share of the two sectors and the labor force structures, the intensity of the dual economy in Shandong is still bigger than in Tianjin in 2004, and its change path is roughly the same as rural PRC. One of the specific reasons is the *hukou* system, which seriously hindered many surplus labors to transfer. Furthermore, the difference of labor productivity in rural economy inevitably becomes

---

[4] This is consistent with the conclusions of our past study. See Chen and Zhou (2002).

Table 14.2 The Non-agricultural Income Share and Employment Share of Rural Residents

	The Proportion of Non-agricultural Income			The Proportion of Non-agricultural Employment		
Years	Tianjin	Shandong	Rural PRC	Tianjin	Shandong	Rural PRC
1994	60.70	—	61.15	46.54	—	24.95
1995	55.95	25.03	60.62	45.46	29.84	27.53
1996	62.66	26.12	59.57	45.63	30.91	28.98
1997	70.67	31.52	58.38	45.83	30.65	28.95
1998	72.30	34.05	55.15	45.72	31.08	28.24
1999	74.65	37.11	51.53	46.24	35.28	26.98
2000	69.78	41.76	48.40	44.70	36.44	26.34
2001	64.00	41.48	47.61	43.36	35.13	25.22
2002	68.65	44.16	45.85	43.47	22.60	23.86
2003	68.23	43.57	45.60	44.24	26.53	23.79
2004	64.85	41.31	47.61	46.48	29.14	25.85
2005	72.60	53.57	45.15	56.53	34.05	27.71
2006	73.74	46.11	42.41	59.90	34.14	29.57
2007	68.90	45.91	42.15	60.03	35.65	30.74
2008	75.40	46.68	40.88	62.98	34.04	31.15
2009	71.90	48.93	38.58	64.97	34.19	32.03
2010	69.74	50.31	37.69	74.89	34.58	32.56
2011	74.25	51.93	36.12	76.03	36.29	34.35
2012	78.79	54.38	34.39	77.36	37.52	34.92
2013	74.72	57.85	33.02	78.34	39.88	35.52

PRC = People's Republic of China.
Sources: Statistical Yearbook of China 1995–2014, Tianjin Statistical Yearbook 1995–2014, Statistical Yearbook of Shandong 1995–2014.

much wider. Correspondingly, the change in rural income inequality must show the same tendency.

14.2.3 The Relationship between Rural Dual Transformation and Income Inequality

Based on the above analysis, we can make the summary in Table 14.3: the comprehensive dual index is an earlier or prior index, which would lead

Table 14.3 The Relationship between Rural Dual Transformation and Income Inequality

	Tianjin	Shandong	Country
Gini coefficient turning point	2003	No	No
dual index turning point	2002	No	No
Non-agricultural income share over 50%	Before 1994	No	No
Non-agricultural employment share over 50%	2005	No	No

Sources: Statistical Yearbook of China 1995–2014, Tianjin Statistical Yearbook 1995–2014, Statistical Yearbook of Shandong 1995–2014.

to the change in rural income inequality. Concretely, the Gini coefficient of rural income inequality in Tianjin began to decline in 2003, but the comprehensive dual index decreased in 2002. Further, the proportion of rural residents' non-agricultural income exceeded the proportion of agricultural income before 1994, but the proportion of non-agricultural employment exceeded agricultural employment in 2005. However, in Shandong and rural PRC, both proportions of non-agricultural income and employment are below 50%. Their comprehensive dual indexes also fluctuated within a narrow range in 2002, but did not pass the turning point, and there was no obvious sign to lead the Gini coefficient to decline.

Here, we further conduct a basic regression analysis, revealing the relationship between the income inequality, income growth, and dual economic transformation in rural Tianjin and the PRC. The outcome is shown in Table 14.4.

In this regression model, the Gini coefficient (Gini) is related with the independent variables such as rural per capita income (income) and

Table 14.4 Regression Estimation Results

Variable	Ln Income	Ln Income2	Ln Income L1	Ln Index	_cons	R^2
Ln Gini (Tianjin)	3.082*** (0.947)	−0.201*** (0.054)	0.539*** (0.211)	0.283*** (0.083)	−17.375*** (4.132)	0.7370
Ln Gini (PRC)	0.031*** (.008)	–	–	0.087*** (0.034)	−1.363*** (0.059)	0.7850

PRC = People's Republic of China.
Sources: Statistical Yearbook of PRC 1995–2014, Tianjin Statistical Yearbook 1995–2014, Statistical Yearbook of Shandong 1995–2014.

comprehensive dual index (index). The rural per capita income represents the level of rural economic development, and the comprehensive dual index is to measure the extent of rural dual economic transformation. The study sample contains two parts: Tianjin and the PRC, and the time span is from 1994 to 2013. Gini and income are the same as the resource of Figure 14.1, and index is calculated in section 2.2. Taking into account that the data sample is small, we only make a basic regression estimation, and the outcome (shown in Table 14.4) is basically consistent with theoretical predictions.

As for Tianjin, the linear term coefficient is positive, and the quadratic term coefficient per capita income is negative, and also the dual index coefficient is positive, which means a positive effect on income inequality according to the change path of the dual index itself, which first goes up and then goes down. All the estimations indicate that Tianjin rural income inequality exhibits an inverted-U curve change tendency. As for the general situation for the whole rural PRC, the linear term is positive, as are the dual indexes, which means that income inequality in rural PRC still enlarges with a linear feature.

Both in Tianjin and the PRC, the dual economic transformation in total has a positive effect on income inequality, which corresponded to the evolution path of rural income inequality. Thus, we still need to conduct a more detailed analysis to calculate the sectoral effects of income inequality, as well as the "structure effect" and "distribution effect" of rural dual economic transformation on the rural income.

14.3 Impact of Dual Economic Transformation on Rural Income Inequality

Through the analysis of the previous section, we observe directly that, after 2003, the evolution of the internal dual economy in rural areas began to vary in Tianjin, Shandong, and throughout the PRC, which corresponded to the evolution of rural income inequality. However, the analysis did not answer to what extent the dual economy transformation leads to the regional differences of income inequality in rural PRC.

To answer that, we conducted a decomposition analysis between and within sectors for total income inequality according to the Fei–Ranis method. Rural income inequality can be divided into two parts: between the rural modern non-agricultural and traditional agricultural sectors, and within each sector. Calculation is as follows: firstly, we calculate the sectoral Gini coefficient of each sector's income according to the sorting of total income per capita of rural households,[5] and then we calculate the total Gini coefficient by combining with the sectoral Gini coefficient and the proportion of each sector's income. The formula is

$$G = \sum G_i \times Y_i . \; G = \sum G_i \times Y_j \qquad (2)$$

Here is the total rural income inequality, is the income inequality of sector i, and is the proportion of total income. is calculated according to the sorting of net income of rural residents, and is the Gini coefficient mainly reflecting the relationship between the sectoral income inequality and total income inequality: (i) if the sectoral Gini coefficient is positive and greater than the Gini coefficient of total income, it indicates that the sectoral income inequality is the determinant to expand total income inequality; (ii) if the sectoral Gini coefficient is positive, but less than the Gini coefficient of total income, it indicates that sectoral income inequality is the determinant relatively to reduce the total income inequality; (iii) if the sectoral Gini coefficient is negative, it indicates that the sectoral income inequality is absolutely the determinant to reduce the total income inequality (Chen 1991).

Second, based on the analysis, we studied the contribution rate of the traditional agricultural and modern non-agricultural sectors' income inequality to the total inequality. The formula is

$$\Phi_j = G_i \times Y_j / G. \qquad (3)$$

$$\sum_i \Phi_i = 1. \qquad (4)$$

Here Φ_i is the contribution rate of the sectoral income inequality to the total income inequality.

It should be noted that the application of the Fei–Ranis decomposition method has a high requirement of the data. In particular, it is necessary to distinguish agricultural from non-agricultural income. Therefore, we only adopt the fully available data in the *Tianjin Rural Socio-economic Survey* in 1994–2008. We know that the income inequality in rural Tianjin reached the inverted U-curve turning point in 2003. Therefore, even without the data after 2009, the reliability of this study should not be affected. The results are shown in Table 14.5.

---

5   The sectoral Gini, or Pseudo Gini, is the coefficient calculated from income inequality within each sector, according to the order and sorting of household income per capita. The reason why we adopt it is based on its good decomposability. On the other hand, it allows a better observation and comparison of the influence of each sector's income inequality to total income inequality.

Table 14.5 The Decomposition of Total Gini Coefficient by Sectoral Inequality in Tianjin and Shandong

Year	Tianjin			
	Agricultural Gini	Non-agricultural Gini	Transfer Gini	Total Gini
1994	0.3492 (58.74)	0.2318 (40.07)	0.1852 (1.18)	0.2878 (100)
1995	0.3583 (68.83)	0.2040 (30.37)	0.1275 (0.82)	0.2879 (100)
1996	0.3920 (69.53)	0.1813 (29.34)	0.1671 (1.11)	0.2891 (100)
1997	0.4158 (65.98)	0.1766 (33.51)	0.0813 (0.54)	0.2817 (100)
1998	0.3887 (58.22)	0.2138 (40.80)	0.1503 (0.98)	0.2881 (100)
1999	0.4530 (57.06)	0.2389 (42.48)	0.0817 (0.45)	0.3233 (100)
2000	0.4160 (54.89)	0.2788 (42.46)	0.3108 (2.64)	0.3416 (100)
2001	–	–	–	–
2002	0.4069 (35.47)	0.3318 (60.22)	0.4564 (4.31)	0.3596 (100)
1994–2002 Average	0.3975 (58.59)	0.1977 (39.91)	0.2200 (1.50)	0.3074 (100)
2003	0.4604 (36.8)	0.3735 (61.57)	0.2833 (1.63)	0.3981 (100)
2004	0.3768 (35.06)	0.3562 (61.48)	0.4695 (3.46)	0.3778 (100)
2005	0.4001 (31.57)	0.3640 (68.16)	0.0707 (0.27)	0.3801 (100)
2006	0.3494 (29.76)	0.3073 (68.83)	0.1921 (1.42)	0.3187 (100)
2007	0.3911 (36.98)	0.2691 (61.06)	0.4258 (1.96)	0.3149 (100)
2008	0.33409 (36.68)	0.3724 (60.88)	0.2107 (2.43)	0.3113 (100)
2009	–	–	–	–
Average	0.3854 (34.66)	0.3224 (63.35)	0.2754 (1.99)	0.3501 (100)

continued on next page

Table 14.5 continued

Year	Shandong			
	Agricultural Gini	Non-agricultural Gini	Transfer Gini	Total Gini
1994				
1995				
1996				
1997				
1998				
1999				
2000				
2001				
2002				
1994–2002 Average	–	–	–	–
2003	–	–		–
2004	–	–		–
2005	–	–		–
2006	–	–		–
2007	0.3144 (43.25)	0.3254 (54.72)	0.3491 (2.03)	0.3252 (100)
2008	0.3503 (45.49)	0.3568 (51.84)	0.3561 (2.87)	0.3526 (100)
2009	0.3333 (41.05)	0.3480 (57.01)	0.3461 (1.94)	0.3393 (100)
Average	0.3327 (43.26)	0.3434 (54.52)	0.3504 (2.28)	0.3390 (100)

Note: The number in the bracket is the contribution rate of each sector's income inequality to total income inequality.
Source: Authors' calculations based on data from Tianjin Rural Socio-economic Survey in 1994–2008 and Shandong Rural Socio-economic Survey in 2007–2009.

14.3.1 Income Inequality in the Traditional Agriculture Sector

It was shown that the sectoral Gini coefficient of traditional agricultural income in Tianjin is greater than the total Gini, which implies that the development of urban agriculture leads more residents to enter the higher-income class, thus expanding the total inequality. It is much different in Shandong and rural PRC, where the distribution of agricultural income is generally more equal than total income. Some literature shows that the inequality of agricultural income plays an important role in reducing total rural income inequality. The reason why Tianjin is different is that the characteristics of urban agricultural development, including input elements, output function, and mode of operation, are much different from general agriculture in Shandong and other traditional agricultural provinces.

From the perspective of input factors, the development of urban agriculture, less dependent on labor and land resources, mainly relies on capital and technology, which determines that the richer family has easier access to and gets higher income from it, thus increasing rural income inequality. However, Shandong and other traditional agricultural provinces, which are more dependent on rural unskilled labor and land resources, have relatively lower labor productivity in rural areas. Thus, income inequality in agricultural labor is relatively small.

From the perspective of the output function, urban agriculture not only provides fresh, non-staple food commodities and some other tangible products for the city, but also provides a green environment, beautiful scenery, and other intangible products. Therefore, urban agriculture has a production function, an ecological function, and a cultural function. However, the endowment difference of intangible products is large (Chen and Li 2004); thus, it will exacerbate the total income inequality in rural areas.

In terms of location of production and business mode, since the rural area in Tianjin is just around the big city, small-scale farmers have more opportunities to come into cities and engage in selling flowers or vegetables, as well as other nontraditional agricultural businesses. Through rental markets, professional contractors, family farms, and some other channels, agricultural land and other productive resources gradually concentrate in large-scale growing and breeding farmers, as well as some other non-agricultural professional producers. By means of the development of large-scale operation of grain, export agriculture, characteristic agriculture, and animal husbandry, or a combination of production and sales, some small-scale farmers transform into large-scale mechanization and modernization. As a result, they become wealthy in rural areas in various ways, which widens the income gap between them and ordinary agricultural households.

14.3.2 Income Inequality in the Rural Non-Agricultural Sector

The sectoral Gini coefficient of non-agricultural income in Tianjin is lower than the total Gini, indicating the non-agricultural economy driven by the development of urban agriculture is an important determinant to decrease income inequality. In contrast, in Shandong and most parts of rural PRC, the non-agricultural sector not only contributes to improving the level of total income, but also exacerbates rural income inequality, no matter how small-scale farmers choose to work, whether in the rural township enterprises or as migrant workers.

In Tianjin, urban agriculture cultivates diverse forms of non-agricultural economy, such as facility horticulture, planting bases, agricultural products logistics, and agricultural leisure tourism, which can absorb surplus labor widely. According to the Tianjin survey, 80% of rural households participated in non-agricultural activity in 2007 and 90% in 2008. It is due to the universality of this distribution that non-agricultural income becomes a major factor in reducing income inequality. But in Shandong and most parts of rural PRC, small-scale farmers mostly rely on being engaged in township enterprises, working as a migrant, or some other traditional forms of non-agricultural work, so the less-developed non-agricultural economy may exacerbate income inequality in rural areas. The main reason is that large enterprises in cities substantially reduce the township enterprises' ability to absorb rural labor, and the participation rate of rural residents. On the other hand, without urban agriculture in most areas, the highly educated and capable small-scale farmers usually choose to serve as migrant workers to get higher income, which leads to the expansion of rural income inequality.

14.3.3 Transfer Income Inequality

The Gini coefficient of transfer income distribution mainly reflects some redistributive policies, and usually should be negative and absolutely reduce total inequality. Most Gini coefficients of transfer income are lower than the total Gini coefficient in Tianjin, indicating that transfer income contributes to relatively reducing total income inequality. It is surprising, however, that the transfer income Gini in Shandong is slightly higher than the total Gini coefficient, implying that the redistribution policy expands rural income inequality to some extent. It is difficult to explain this because transfer income is usually the subsidy for the poorest families. One possibility is that some special subsidies were distributed to richer people to encourage them to invest in enterprises or some special industry, or the living subsidy for poorer people is so small and dispersed that the distribution of transfer income itself is unequal to the total income inequality. In short, we need to further collect data and conduct a deeper research, and distinguish the productive subsidies from living ones, which should be guaranteed to go to the poorer strata.

14.3.4 Contribution Rate of Sectoral Income Inequality: Sectoral Effects

The influence of Tianjin agricultural income inequality on the total income inequality suffered a significant decline. The average contribution rate from 2003 to 2008 is only 34.66%, but is close to 60% in the first stage from 1994 to 2002. In 2002 in particular, during the initial stage of Tianjin urban agricultural development, the contribution rate of non-agricultural income inequality exceeded that of the agricultural, reaching more than 50%, which reflects the rapid development of Tianjin modern non-agricultural sector; subsequently, its sectoral income inequality replaced the traditional agriculture sector to become the main determinant of total inequality in rural Tianjin. As for Shandong, the average contribution rate of the modern non-agricultural sector to total inequality is slightly higher (54.52%), but the contribution rate of agricultural inequality still accounts for nearly half the share. In addition, both in rural Tianjin and Shandong, the contribution rates of transfer inequality are so small that they may be negligible.

In short, we can clearly observe that dual economic transformation constrains the change of rural income inequality, and the process of dual economic transformation is consistent with the process of income inequality change in different regions. The turning moment of the income inequality inverted-U curve in rural Tianjin occurred roughly and consistently with the dual economic transformation, in which non-agricultural income inequality accounts for most of total inequality instead of agricultural inequality. However, the income inequality in Shandong and rural PRC did not exhibit an inverted-U curve transition, which is also consistent with their dual economic transformations, in which agricultural income inequality still holds the dominant position in total inequality.

14.4 The Structural and Distribution Effects of Dual Economic Transformation on Rural Income Inequality

Further research is needed to know, in the process of rural dual economic transformation, which is the main determinant to lead to total income inequality change (either increase or decrease): the change in the proportion of sectoral income caused by the dual economic transformation or the change of sectoral income inequality; and further, to what extent these determinants lead to this change. To answer these questions, we need more detailed marginal decomposition analysis on total Gini coefficient of income inequality. Thus, formulas (2) and (4) can be expanded as follows:

$$G = Y_1 G_1 + Y_2 G_2 + Y_3 G_3 \tag{5}$$

$$1 = Y_1 G_1/G + Y_2 G_2/G + Y_3 G_3/G \tag{6}$$

Here, formulas (5) and (6) show that total income inequality is a weighted sum of the sectoral income inequality, and the weight is the proportion of sectoral income in total. In other words, the contribution rate of sectoral income inequality to total inequality is the combined result of the changes of sectoral income shares in total and sectoral income inequality. Based on this, we get a derivative with respect to t in the above formula to obtain marginal decomposition formula as follows:

$$dG/dt = \alpha + \beta \tag{7}$$

$$\alpha = dY_1/dtG_1 + dY_2/dtG_2 + dY_3/dtG_3 \text{ (structural effect)} \tag{8}$$

$$\beta = dG_1/dtY_1 + dG_2/dtY_2 + dG_3/dtY_3 \text{ (distribution effect)} \tag{9}$$

From the perspective of dual economic transformation, we divide the change in total income inequality into two parts: (i) the structural effect, which is the change in total Gini coefficient caused by the proportional changes in agricultural and non-agricultural income (and transfer income);[6] (ii) the distribution effect, which is the change in the total Gini coefficient caused by the changes in sectoral Gini coefficients. If both effects are positive (negative), the increment of total Gini coefficient must be positive (negative); on the contrary, if the signs of the two effects are just opposite to each other, the direction of the marginal Gini coefficient change depends on a comparison between them.

---

[6] Here, structural effect is different from sectoral effect. Sectoral effect is the contribution rate of sectoral income Gini to total Gini in the stationary condition, while structural effect deals with changing sectoral income proportion in the dynamic condition, namely the change of total Gini coefficient caused by changes in proportion of sectoral incomes over time.

We adopt data in the *Tianjin Rural Socio-economic Survey* in 1994–2008 and the *Shandong Rural Socio-economic Survey* in 2007–2009 to study the influence of rural dual economic transformation on the change in rural income inequality in 1994–2002 (rising stage of inverted-U curve) and 2003–2008 (decline stage of inverted-U curve) respectively, depending on the evolution path of income inequality invert-U curve in rural Tianjin. The results are shown in Table 14.6.

Table 14.6 Structural Effects and Distribution Effects of Dual Economic Transformation on Changes in Rural Income Inequality (Tianjin 1994–2002, 2003–2008; Shandong 2007–2009)

Provinces (Time)/Sectors		Structural Effect = α		Distribution Effect = β		Total	
		Gini Change	Share (%)	Gini Change	Share (%)	Gini Change	Share (%)
Tianjin (1994–2002)	Agriculture	−0.0596	−96.27	0.0280	45.16	−0.032	−51.11
	Non-agricultural	0.0360	58.06	0.0498	80.36	0.0857	138.42
	Transfer	0.0029	4.68	0.0050	8.01	0.0079	12.70
	Total	−0.0208	−33.53	0.0827	133.53	0.0619	100
Tianjin (2003–2008)	Agriculture	−0.0332	30.82	−0.040	37.29	−0.073	68.11
	Non-agricultural	0.0221	−20.48	−0.072	67.01	−0.050	46.53
	Transfer	0.0037	−3.43	0.0121	−11.21	0.0158	−14.64
	Total	−0.0074	6.91	−0.100	93.09	−0.108	100
Shandong (2007–2009)	Agriculture	−0.0091	−62.07	0.0079	53.73	−0.001	−8.33
	Non-agricultural	0.0064	43.69	0.0059	40.35	0.0123	84.05
	Transfer	0.0037	25.04	−0.000	−0.75	0.0036	24.29
	Total	0.0010	6.67	0.0137	93.33	0.0146	100

Source: Authors' calculations based on data from Tianjin Rural Socio-economic Survey in 1994–2008 and Shandong Rural Socio-economic Survey in 2007–2009.

14.4.1 The Distribution Effects Can Better Explain Total Inequality Changes in both Shandong and Tianjin Than the Structural Effects of Dual Economic Transformation[7]

Our previous research in Tianjin in the 1980s and 1990s also showed that the distribution effect accounts for 88.4% of rural income inequality in Tianjin from 1984 to 1988 (Chen 1991; Chen, Zhou, and Ren 2006), while here the distribution effect is as high as 108.25% from 1984 to 1988. Hence, though the distribution effect varies at different periods of time, it always occupies the dominant position and is the fundamental factor determining the change in rural income inequality. It implies that dual economic transformation always changes the sectoral structure of labor to further change the total income inequality. In other words, dual economic transformation can affect the income inequality of residents directly by changing the labor force participation and, further, affect the total income inequality. Without changing the labor participation rate, simply adjusting the income proportion between two sectors would have little effect on the total income inequality.

By comparing the expansion stage (1994–2002) and reduction stage (2003–2008) of rural income inequality in Tianjin, the distribution effect is always the most important factor, and the expansion and reduction of income inequality depend on the changes in sectoral income inequality. Meanwhile, though the structural effect is relatively small, it always contributes to reducing the internal rural income inequality. By comparing the different stages of dual economic transformation in the same area, we can see that the essential ingredient to reverse the direction of change in rural income is to reduce the non-agricultural income inequality (described in detail below). Of course, it is necessary to adjust the income proportion between the two sectors to reduce income inequality. Especially when the income inequality is expanding,

---

[7] Because reduced agricultural income proportion ($d\Phi_{rt} < 0$) offsets the increases in non-agricultural income proportion ($d\Phi_{rt} > 0$), the structure effects, which are the sum of them, would be relatively smaller. Despite that, there is no mathematical logic problem in formulas (8) and (9), assuming that changes of transfer income ($d\Phi_T$) are exogenous, meaning there is a trade-off between proportions of agricultural income and non-agricultural income. In other words, under the condition that Pseudo Gini is greater than 0, the signs of $d\Phi_{rt}/dtG_{rt}$ and $d\Phi_{rm}/dtG_{rm}$ are inevitably just opposite each other. It is, in general, $d\Phi_{rt}/dtG_{rt} < 0$ and $d\Phi_{rm}/dtG_{rm} > 0$ that determine that the structural effect may be small after they are summed. Due to the technical limitations, when we analyze the structural effect on the contribution rate of rural income inequality, we should only focus on the absolute value of each factor's contribution rate, rather than the structural effect.

the absolute value of the contribution rate of agricultural income's structural effect on income inequality is as high as 96.27%.

By further comparison with the situation in Tianjin (2003–2008) and Shandong (2007–2009), we find that no matter whether the rural income inequality is rising or reducing, the distribution effect still dominates. This implies that dual economic transition must change the sectoral labor structures and, thus, sectoral income inequality, and further to change total income inequality in different stages of dual economic transformation in different regions. In other words, the dual economic transformation must affect sectoral income inequality through changing labor participation rate directly, and further to change the total income inequality in different stages. This further explains that only when the labor participation rate reaches a certain level would the total income inequality begin to decrease after rising initially in the period of inverted-U curve transition. For instance, when the labor participation rate in the non-agricultural sector reaches at least 50% (just as in Tianjin, and at that time its proportion of income even was higher than 70%; see Table 14.2), the inverted-U transition automatically occurs. Again, adjusting the income proportion of two sectors without changing the labor participation results in a very small overall impact on total income inequality.

14.4.2 The Decline of the Modern Non-agricultural Income Inequality in Tianjin is the Most Important Factor in Reducing the Total Income Inequality (The Contribution Rate is 67.01%)

First, dual economic transformation allows almost all small-scale farmers to participate in the non-agricultural economy. In 2008, for example, more than 90% of small-scale farmers were involved in non-agricultural production derived from urban agriculture. Among them, 75.83% chose to engage in non-agricultural production activities in the township, while only 0.8% chose to be migrant workers. Second, the contribution rate of the reduction of agricultural income inequality was 37.29% in 2003–2008. Regardless of its being less significant than non-agricultural income, the contribution rate still plays an important role in reducing total income inequality. Third, the change in proportion of agricultural income reduces total income inequality by 30.82%, but the change in proportion of non-agricultural income expands income inequality by 20.48%. As a result, the total income inequality decreases by 7% in total. Thus, when the development of dual economy enters into a certain stage, such as when non-agricultural income in Tianjin occupies the dominant position (about 70% in 2003, while the share of employment was 50% [see Table 14.2]), both structural effect and distribution effect are conducive to reducing income inequality in rural areas, which constitutes just the beginning of the inverted-U transition of rural income inequality. It has a significant reference for rural PRC that the rapid development of dual economy in the rural areas around big cities would accelerate rural income inequality to cross the turning point, then to enter the process of reduction. (Here, the transfer income inequality exhibits an evolutionary expansion. However, because of its relatively smaller proportion, it is not discussed.)

14.4.3 The Expansion of Rural Income Inequality in Shandong is First Attributed to the Expansion of Income Inequality in the Traditional Agriculture Sector; Its Contribution Rate is 53.73%

Second, the contribution rate of non-agricultural income to the expansion of total inequality is 43.69%. For instance, in 2009, 31.32% of rural residents in Shandong chose to go out to work. Third, the expansion of non-agricultural income inequality itself is the reason for the increase in total inequality, and its contribution rate is 40.35%. Fourth, the proportion change of agricultural income is the factor to reduce income inequality, and its contribution rate is 62.07%, which is smaller than other factors' greater influence; thus, total income inequality in Shandong is continuously expanding (transfer income ignored). In other words, for rural areas in Shandong and rural PRC, the surplus labor transferring from the agriculture sector to the non-agricultural sector still expands rural income inequality in the current stage of dual economic transformation, which implies that there is still a long way to go to reach the inverted-U turning point. Even to achieve the target as with Tianjin in 2003, the non-agricultural income of rural residents of Shandong still needs to increase by about 30%, and non-agricultural employment needs to increase by 25%. According to the current speed of labor transfer and non-agricultural income growth in Shandong, we forecast that the earliest date that the non-agricultural labor participation rate can reach 50% with the non-agricultural income proportion growing by 70% is at least 2020, when it will likely be able to reach the turning point of inverted-U transition.[8]

---

[8] We adopt exponential smoothing method to forecast it according to the time series of non-agricultural employment and the proportion of non-agricultural income in Shandong during 1995–2013.

14.5 Conclusions and Suggestions

After the 1980s, the PRC's dual economic transformation exhibited different evolutionary characteristics, and the dual economy in rural areas began to vary with the regions. Tianjin's rural dual economic transformation entered a higher stage in which the proportions of non-agricultural employment and income held the dominant position, and the rural duality declined gradually. The rural dual economy in Shandong and rural PRC are still at the stage in which agriculture holds a predominant role. Correspondingly, changes in rural income inequality constrained by dual transformation also exhibit regional differentiation. Rural income inequality in Shandong and most of rural PRC is still rising, though at a slower pace, so it may indicate that they are in the latter part of the rising stage of an inverted-U curve. In areas similar to Tianjin, where the urban agriculture and non-agricultural sector have developed rapidly, income inequality has exhibited an obvious public economic income inequality inverted-U curve process; therefore, it is important to study the variable factors so that we may predict and promote the evolution of income inequality in rural PRC.

The development of the modern non-agricultural sector in rural Tianjin, unlike Shandong or other parts of the PRC, became the major determinant to reduce income inequality. The development of urban agriculture is an important factor in reducing income inequality. In contrast, in most rural areas of the PRC and Shandong, despite residents' choice to work in township enterprises or to be migrant workers, their non-agricultural income not only contributes to improving the level of total income, but also exacerbates the rural income inequality, thus becoming the main factor in expanding income inequality. While the distribution of agricultural incomes is more equal relative to the total income, its overall influence is to reduce total inequality.

There are some differences between Tianjin and Shandong provinces in terms of stages of dual economic transformation, and the directions of influence exerted by determinants of income inequality. In Tianjin, with the development of the modern non-agricultural sector entering a higher stage, its sectoral income inequality exhibited an evolution path of decrease and led total inequality in rural areas to a narrowing trend. Whether from the perspective of the distribution effect or the structural effect, urban agricultural income is also conducive to reducing rural income inequality. Correspondingly, in Shandong and other parts of the PRC, such dual economies are still in the transition stage in which the transfer of rural surplus labor from the agriculture sector to the non-agricultural sector is still the most important determinant of expanding rural income inequality. Besides, the rising proportion of non-agricultural income, as well as the expansion of the non-agricultural inequality itself, causes rural income inequality to increase, notwithstanding the decrease in magnitude (Figure 14.1).

In total, by the comparative analysis of Tianjin and Shandong provinces, as well as the whole of rural PRC, we studied the relationship between rural dual economic transformation and rural income inequality changes. In order to prompt total income inequality of rural PRC to pass the turning point of a public-ownership economic inequality inverted-U curve as soon as possible, we make the following three suggestions:

- In suburbs around small and medium-sized cities, government should encourage small-scale farmers to join the non-agricultural sector. At the same time, policy should induce urban enterprises to accelerate urban agricultural investment and attract more labor transfer.
- In the large agricultural provinces, especially the central and western provinces of the PRC, urbanization should be accelerated to develop the non-agricultural sector sustainably. Provinces around big cities with good conditions should develop urban agriculture, and encourage foreign and domestic investment and enterprise from eastern regions to expand into western regions, thus to establish modern rural non-agricultural economic sectors closely related with agricultural production with relatively high maturity and various forms.
- The western region should attract their rural migrant workers back to their hometowns and guide the transfer of surplus labor into the local non-agricultural economy, so that they can get incomes from local industries.

A continued implementation of such basic strategic initiatives must accelerate growth so that rural economies can progress from total inequality towards the reduction stage of a public-ownership economic inequality inverted-U curve.

References

Chen, D., and J. Liu. 2011. The Empirical Analysis on the Rural Residents' Income Gap in China. *Review of Industrial Economics* 10(1):75–86.

Chen, Z. 1991. *Income Distribution in Economic Development*. Shanghai: Shanghai Joint Publishing.

Chen, Z., and X. Chen. 1999. Research on the Income Inequality of Rural Residents in China. *Economic Outlook of Bohai Sea* 6:37–42.

Chen, Z., and D. Li. 2004. A Growth Model of Dual Economy with Endogenous Agricultural Technology Progress—The Re-Analysis of "East Asian Miracle" and Chinese Economy *Economic Research Journal* 11:16–27.

Chen, Z., and Y. Zhou. 2002. Re-study on the Income Distribution in Reform and Development. Beijing: Economic Science Press.

Chen, Z, Y. Zhou, and G. Ren. 2006. A Research of the Major Factors of Impacting the Three Kinds of Off-farm Employment Paths—An Empirical Analysis Based on Tianjin Case. *Journal of Finance and Economics* 32(5):4–18.

Gao, F. 2005. A Study on the Transform Tendency of Dual Economic Structure. *Economic Research Journal* 9:91–102.

———. 2007. The Synchronization of the Transformation of Dual Economic Structure in the Provinces of China: An Empirical Study--With Additional Studies on the Relationship between the Transformation of Regional Economic Structure and the Gap of Economic Growth. *Management World* 9:27–36.

Li, S. 1999. Rural Labor Mobility with Income Growth and Distribution in China. *Social Sciences in China* 2:16–33.

Lin, Y., F. Cai, and Z. Li. 1998. An Analysis of Regional Inequality in China's Economic Transition Period. *Economic Research Journal* 6:3–10.

Ma, J. 2001. Agriculture, the Adjustment of Rural Industrial Structure and the Change of Rural Income Gap. *Reform* 6:92–101.

Shorrocks, A., and G. Wan. 2008. Spatial Decomposition of Inequality. *Journal of Economic Geography* 5(1):59–81.

Wan, G., Z. Zhou, and Q. Lu. 2005. Income Inequality in Rural China: The Regression Decomposition by Using the Peasant Household Data. *Chinese Rural Economy* 5:4–11.

Xue, Y. 2005. An Empirical Analysis of the Income Difference of Rural Areas and Its Geographical Features in China. *Journal of Finance and Economics* 31(5):133–144.

Yao, H., and X. Wang. 2009. Labor Mobility, Educational Standards, Pro-poor Policies and Rural Income Gap–A Micro Empirical Study based on Logit Multinomial Model. *Management World* 9:80–90.

Index

Figures, notes, and tables are indicated by f, n, and t following the page number.

A

ADB. *See* Asian Development Bank
Advantaged regions. *See* disadvantaged/advantaged regions
Africa, middle class in, 180, 181t. *See also specific countries and regions*
age
  employment and, 286, 289–90
  income mobility and, 279–80
  intergenerational employment mobility and, 295, 301
  inter-group inequalities and, 46, 60
  per capita income and, 264, 266, 268
agricultural sector
  employment in, 34, 117–18, 286
  inclusive growth and, 34
  intergenerational employment mobility and, 298
  market access for, 34, 52
  social mobility and, 285
  urban, 357, 357n2, 362, 371–72
Arellano–Bond test, 121, 182–83
Asia. *See also specific countries and regions*
  educational attainment in, 136–39, 136–38f
  Gini coefficient average in, 113–14, 142
  global GDP, Asian share of, 12
  income inequality in. *See* income inequality
  middle class in, 180, 181t
  OECD country inequality compared, 142, 143f
  opportunity inequality in, 38–39
Asian Development Bank (ADB), 172n7
Asian financial crisis (1997–1998), 216, 218, 221, 226–27n1, 239–40, 248–49
Atkinson Index, 269
automation. *See* technological improvements

B

Bangladesh, increasing inequality in, 127
banking sector. *See* financial sector
between-country income inequality
  in Asia, 6–7, 6f, 133f
  defined, 133
  intergenerational transmission of poverty and, 40
between-group inequalities. *See* inter-group inequalities
Bhutan, education in, 10
Blinder–Oaxaca decomposition, 44–46

C

Cambodia, education in, 10
Canada
  earnings inequality in, 116
  income inequality and inflation in, 117
capital formation, 123, 127, 183
Caucasus region, post-communist economic growth in, 154. *See also specific countries*
Central Asia, 2, 154–65. *See also specific countries*
  economic growth statistics, 162–63f
  Gini coefficient of countries in, 7t, 141, 156, 157f
  income distribution in transition economies of, 158–59
  income distribution statistics for, 164–65f
  income inequality and economic growth in, 156–57, 157–58f
  literature review, 155–56
  policy recommendations for, 159–60
  role in Soviet Union, 156
  transition strategies in, 156–57
China. *See* People's Republic of China
consumption
  agriculture and, 34
  conspicuous, 13
  decile ratio and, 21, 23, 23–24f
  employment and, 34–35
  growth incidence curves and, 17–21, 24–28, 25–27f, 28n5, 29f
  inflation and, 123, 125–26
  middle class and, 168, 173, 174–76, 175f, 184
  taxation of, 112
corruption, 118–19, 124t, 127
Corruption Perception Index, 118–19

D

debt ratios, 347
decentralization of Indonesia, 226–27, 226–27n1, 228f, 239–42, 240n14, 248–49
decile ratio, 21, 23, 23–24f
democratization, 118, 135
demographic group inequalities, 117–18, 123–25, 124t. *See also* inter-group inequalities; *specific demographic factors*
development banks, 166. *See also specific development banks*
disadvantaged/advantaged regions
 disposable household income per capita and, 105t, 107t
 expenditure inequality and, 226–59. *See also* expenditure inequality
 globalization and, 142
 income inequality gap, 49–50, 59–65, 59n6, 60–64t
 intergenerational employment mobility and, 306
 structural differences and, 39
 summary statistics by income quintile, 106t
 Viet Nam, 274, 285–86, 295
discrimination, 39, 52, 65, 87n7. *See also* ethnic minorities; gender inequality
distribution effects
 pro-poor growth and, 200
 rural dual economic transformation and, 373–77, 375t
dual economic transformation. *See* rural dual economic transformation

E

economic consequences of inequality, 11–12, 40, 111
economic freedom, 145, 148–49
economic growth
 education and, 150
 fair redistribution of, 128, 150, 158–59
 inclusive, 17–37. *See also* inclusive growth
 inequality resulting from, 111–12, 261
 inequality undermining, 40
 infrastructure and stimulation of, 116
 middle-class growth and, 168–69, 181–87, 185–86t
 pro-poor, 199–225. *See also* pro-poor growth
education, 2, 132–53
 attainment and inequality in, 136–39, 136–38f

disposable household income per capita and, 105t, 107t
as driver of income inequality, 10, 13, 117, 134–36, 262, 267–68
employment and, 125, 279, 286, 294
expenditure inequalities and, 246
family resources and, 273
gender and, 96–97, 98
human development and, 12
income inequality gap and, 65–67, 67–75t, 98, 125, 127
intergenerational employment mobility and, 295, 306
Kuznets inverted-U hypothesis on, 144–49, 147–48t
literature review, 134–36
middle class and, 183–84
policy recommendations for, 13, 98, 149–50, 160
in rural areas, 52, 59
social mobility and, 10, 280, 282
summary statistics by income quintile, 106t
unequal access to, 112
in urban areas, 65–66
emerging economies, 9, 13–14, 166
employment. *See also* self-employment
 defined, 286
 disposable household income per capita and, 105t, 107t
 as driver of income inequality, 10, 117–18, 123, 126
 education and, 125, 279, 286, 294
 family resources and, 273
 in foreign firms, 328–55. *See also* foreign direct investment
 gender and, 96–97, 98, 264, 266, 286, 289–90
 human development and, 12
 inclusive growth and, 17, 34–35
 income inequality gap and, 76–86, 76–84t, 106t
 informal, 10, 76
 labor unions and, 268
 migration and, 158, 249, 362–64, 372
 policy recommendations for, 98–99
 return to skills, 40
 in rural areas, 34, 52, 59, 117–18. *See also* rural dual economic transformation
 skilled vs. unskilled, 9, 10, 65, 142, 149, 286, 288, 288f, 289–90t
 social mobility and, 39, 273–327. *See also* intragenerational and intergenerational mobility
 taxation of income from, 112

technological improvements and automation, 10
wage inequality, 10
environmental protection and sustainability, 12–13
ethnic minorities
 employment mobility of, 288, 290
 income gap and, 276, 277f
 income mobility and, 278–80, 282
 intergenerational employment mobility and, 295–96, 299, 300f, 306
 skilled occupations of, 288, 295
expenditure inequality, 3, 226–59
 data on, 235–38, 237f
 findings on, 247–51
 literature review, 229–31
 method for determining, 231–35
 region–province–district frameworks, 243–46, 244–45f, 247f, 258–59
 urban and rural sector–district frameworks, 238–43, 238–39f, 241f, 256–59

F

families. *See also* household head characteristics
 composition of, 50, 51, 285, 294
 intergenerational employment mobility and, 295–306, 296–98t, 296f, 299–300f, 301–5t
 resources of, 273
family planning, 98
farming. *See* agricultural sector
FDI. *See* foreign direct investment
Fei–Ranis decomposition method, 367–68
FGT indexes, 202n3
financial sector
 as driver of income inequality, 9, 262
 financial inclusion and, 9, 112
 globalization and, 134
 inclusive growth and, 35
fiscal policy. *See also* taxation
 as driver of income inequality, 10–11
 fair redistribution of economic growth through, 128, 150
 middle class and, 184
 for poverty alleviation, 13, 184, 186
floating class
 consumption levels of, 180
 defined, 172
 economic development and, 173, 174t, 186–87
foreign aid, 118
foreign direct investment (FDI), 3, 328–55
 as driver of income inequality, 9, 39, 184

empirical method and data for, 341–45, 343–45t
empirical results for, 345–50, 346t, 348–49t, 354–55t
globalization and, 135
influence of labor transfer and technology spillover, 339–41, 340f
labor transfer and, 333–35, 336f
literature review, 329–31
model for, 331–32
technology spillover and, 336–39, 338–39f
Freedom House, 145, 148

G

G20. *See* Group of 20
GDP. *See* gross domestic product
gender inequality
 disposable household income per capita and, 105t, 107t
 education and, 96–97, 98
 employment and, 96–97, 98, 264, 266, 286, 289–90
 household heads and, 279–80
 income inequality gap, 86–97, 87–95t, 87n7
 intergenerational employment mobility and, 295, 298–99, 299–300f, 301
 inter-group inequalities and, 46, 60
 summary statistics by income quintile, 106t
generalized method of moments (GMM) estimation technique, 121–22, 182
Gini coefficient
 Asia compared to OECD countries, 142, 143f
 Asian average, 113–14, 142
 of Central Asian countries, 7t, 141, 156, 157f
 by country, 7–9, 7–8t, 113–15, 113–14t, 139–41, 139–40t
 of education and inequality, 146–49, 147–48t
 as equality measure, 21, 22, 22t, 41, 41n1, 145, 267
 of foreign direct investment effects, 347–50, 348–49t
 growth rate by country, 114–15, 115f
 macroeconomic factors, effects of, 120, 124t
 of middle-class income distribution, 176–77, 176n10, 176t, 177–78f
 of rural per capita income in PRC, 358–59, 359f, 366–68, 368n5, 369–70t
 of transfer income distribution, 372
global income inequality, 133, 133f, 167n1

globalization
  as driver of income inequality, 9, 111, 116–17, 142, 149, 350
  education levels and, 134, 135–36, 145
  increase in, 134
  Kearney globalization index, 135
  KOF globalization index, 145–46, 148, 150
  middle class and, 174, 175t
  to reduce inequality, 116
GMM. *See* generalized method of moments
government debt, 123, 127
Great Gatsby curve, 273
great U-turn hypothesis, 132–33, 149
gross domestic product (GDP)
  global, Asian share of, 12
  income inequality, effect on, 11, 123, 125, 127
  middle-class income distribution and, 167, 170, 183–87, 185–86t
  poverty reduction and, 32
Group of 20, 260
growth incidence curves, 17–21, 24–28, 25–27f, 28n5, 29f
growth with equity, 142

H

Hansen test, 182–83
healthcare, 112, 267, 273
Heritage Foundation, 145, 148
high-income countries, middle class in, 173–80, 173f, 174t
horizontal mobility, 201
household head characteristics
  education, 70–75t
  employment, 76, 76–84t
  expenditure inequalities and, 246
  gender, 86–87, 87–95t
  inclusive growth data and, 22
  income mobility and, 279, 280–84t, 310–12t, 314t
  inter-group inequality and, 46, 52, 67
household surveys
  inter-group inequality measured by, 41, 44–45, 47–48, 104t
  as measures of equality, 21–22, 38
  middle-class data from, 167
human capital and development, 12, 13, 267
human capital theory, 134

I

IMF. *See* International Monetary Fund
immigration. *See* migration
inclusive growth, 1, 17–37

  defined, 17
  growth incidence curves for, 24–28, 25–27f, 29f
  measures of equality and data issues for, 21–22
  policies to increase, 33–35
  poverty and inequality estimates for, 29–32, 30t, 31–32f
  Senegal case study, 22–23, 22f, 23–24t
  theoretical considerations for, 17–21, 20b
income inequality, 1, 6–16
  between-country. *See* between-country income inequality
  Central Asia, 154–65. *See also* Central Asia
  confronting, 13–14
  drivers of (generally), 9–11, 111–12, 116
  economic consequences of, 11–12, 40, 111
  education and globalization effects, 132–53. *See also* education
  education as driver of, 10, 13, 117, 134–36, 262, 267–68
  employment as driver of, 10, 117–18, 123, 126
  expenditure inequality and, 226–59. *See also* expenditure inequality
  FDI as driver of, 9, 39, 184
  financial deepening, 9
  financial sector as driver of, 9, 262
  fiscal policy as driver of, 10–11
  foreign direct investment, effect of, 328–55. *See also* foreign direct investment
  Gini coefficient data on, 139–42, 139–40t, 141–43f
  globalization as driver of, 9, 111, 116–17, 142, 149, 350
  inclusive growth, lessons from, 17–37. *See also* inclusive growth
  inter-group inequality and, 38–107. *See also* inter-group inequalities
  intragenerational and intergenerational mobility and, 273–327. *See also* intragenerational and intergenerational mobility
  Kuznets hypothesis on. *See* Kuznets inverted-U hypothesis
  labor market imperfections, 10
  literature review, 134–36
  macroeconomic factor effects, 111–31. *See also* macroeconomic factors
  market-oriented reforms as driver of, 111, 142
  middle class and, 166–95. *See also* middle-class

population growth as driver of, 118, 127, 132
profile of, 6–9, 6f, 7–8t
public opinion on, 1
in rural areas, 356–81. *See also* rural dual economic transformation
social and political consequences of, 12–13, 40
Sustainable Development Goals on, 277
taxation as driver of, 10, 112, 184
technological change, 10
technological improvements as driver of, 10, 111, 135, 142, 149
trade as driver of, 116–17, 135
types of, 133–34, 134f
urban areas as driver of, 132
within-country. *See* within-country income inequality
income tax, 150, 160
India
as developing economy, 111
disadvantaged vs. advantaged region inequality in, 49, 59–60, 63–64t, 65
education in, 10, 40, 65–66, 67–68t, 98
employment in, 10, 40, 76, 76–77t, 85
financial deepening in, 9
gender inequality in, 86, 87–88t, 96
income distribution in, 104t
increasing inequality in, 127
middle class in, 167n1
rural vs. urban inequality in, 41, 42–43t, 51–52
individual rate of pro-poor growth (RPPG), 201
Indonesia, 3, 260–72
cash transfer program in, 242–43, 242n18
data and methodology for, 263–66, 264t
decentralization in, 226–27, 226–27n1, 228f, 239–42, 240n14, 248–49
education in, 264, 267–70
fuel prices in, 242, 242–43nn17–19
GDP of, 226, 229–30, 260, 261f
increasing inequality in, 127
Indonesia Family Life Survey (IFLS), 214–15, 261, 263–64, 264t
infrastructure deficit in, 250
literature review, 261–62
National Socio-Economic Survey (*Susenas*), 228, 230, 235–36, 247, 249
natural resources in, 249–50
overview, 260–62, 261f
pro-poor growth in, 214–19, 215t, 216f, 217–20t

public expenditures and regional inequality in, 226–59. *See also* expenditure inequality
results and discussion for, 266–70, 266–69t
industrialization, 168
inflation, 117, 123, 125–28
infrastructure
disadvantaged/advantaged regions and, 39
economic growth stimulation and, 116, 125
inter-group inequalities, 1–2, 38–107. *See also specific demographic factors*
contributions of study on, 41–44, 42–43t
data on, 47–50
disadvantaged/advantaged region gap, 59–65, 60–64t
disposable household income per capita and, 105t, 107t
as drivers of inequality, 117–18, 123–25, 124t
education gap and, 65–67, 67–75t
employment gap and, 76–86, 76–84t
gender gap and, 86–97, 87–95t
income distribution by country, 104t
Indonesia, 261–62
means of explanatory variables of interest and, 105t
method of study for, 44–46
motivation for study on, 38–41
results overview for, 50–51
rural/urban income gap and, 51–59, 53–58t
summary statistics by income quintile, 106t
international income inequality. *See* between-country income inequality
International Monetary Fund (IMF), 9, 33–34, 118
international poverty line, 28–29, 29f
intertemporal poverty, 202–9
intragenerational and intergenerational mobility, 3, 273–327
data sets for, 275
defined, 273
employment mobility and, 288–90, 288f, 289–90t
employment mobility regression, 290–95, 291–94t, 318–23t
employment structure and, 286, 287t
income inequality and, 276–78, 276–78f
income mobility and, 278–86, 278f, 280–85t, 310–15t

intergenerational correlations of
earnings and, 298–300, 299–300f,
324–27t
intergenerational employment mobilitd,
295–98, 296–98t, 296f
intergenerational employment mobility
regression, 301–6, 301–5t
intragenerational employment mobilitd,
286–95, 287–94t, 288f, 316–17t
transmission of poverty and, 40

J

Japan
disadvantaged vs. advantaged region
inequality in, 49, 59–60, 63–64t, 65
education in, 65–66, 69t, 150
employment in, 10, 76, 77–78t, 85–86,
87n7
gender inequality in, 87, 87n7, 89t, 96
income inequality in, 40, 98, 104t
increasing inequality in, 127
rural vs. urban inequality in, 41, 42–43t,
51–52

K

Kazakhstan
economic growth in, 163f
income distribution in, 164f
Kearney globalization index, 135
KOF globalization index, 145–46, 148, 150
Kuznets inverted-U hypothesis
arguments against, 112, 116, 132, 155
education inequality and, 144–49,
147–48t
expenditure inequality and, 241, 241f
great U-turn hypothesis and, 132–33,
149
income inequality and, 141, 142f
studies supporting, 132–33
urban-rural gap and, 13–14
Kyrgyz Republic
economic growth in, 163f
education in, 160
income inequality in, 141, 142f, 164f
role in Soviet Union, 156

L

labor market. *See* employment
labor transfer effects, 329, 333–35, 336f,
339–41, 340f, 341, 343–45, 349
labor unions, 268
LIS. *See* Luxembourg Income Study
Lorenz curve, 17–19, 18n1
low-income countries

agricultural sector in, 34–35
Gini coefficients of, 114, 115t
middle class in, 168, 172–73, 173f, 174t,
180
Luxembourg Income Study (LIS), 41, 44,
47–48, 47n3

M

macroeconomic factors, 2, 111–31
existing knowledge on, 115–18
Gini coefficient trends for, 113–15,
113–14t, 115f
inclusive growth and, 33
methodology and model specification
for, 118–22, 119t
middle-class effect on, 167–68
policy recommendations for, 127–28
results and discussion for, 122–26, 124t,
126t
Malaysia
decreasing inequality in, 127
financial deepening in, 9
marital status, 46, 60
market access for agricultural products,
34, 52
market-oriented reforms, 111, 142
mean log deviation (MLD), 21–22, 21n4,
22t
men. *See* gender inequality
middle class, 2, 166–95
configurations of, 179–81, 179t, 181t
countries by region, 194–95t
data and methodology for, 169–70, 193t
growth of, 166
heterogeneity of, 175–78, 176t, 177–78f
income growth, impact on, 181–87,
185–86t
income inequality within, 167
living standards measures, 174, 175t
size and economic weight, 171, 171t
subcategories of, 172–74, 173–74f
middle-income trap, 12, 329
migration
employment and, 158, 249, 362–64, 372
globalization and, 135
remittances and, 76, 86, 364
minorities. *See* ethnic minorities; gender
inequality
MLD. *See* mean log deviation
mobility. *See* intragenerational and
intergenerational mobility; social
mobility
mobility as equalizer, 201
monopolies, 347, 350

N

national-registration laws, 39, 98, 364
Nepal, education in, 10

O

obesity, 13
OECD. *See* Organisation for Economic Co-operation and Development
official development assistance (ODA), 123, 125, 126, 127–28
oil and fuel prices
  global, 250
  Indonesia, 242–43, 242–43nn17–19, 248
opportunity, equality of, 14, 38–39, 274
Organisation for Economic Co-operation and Development (OECD), 117, 118, 142, 143f, 155

P

Pakistan, decreasing inequality in, 127
Penn World Table GDP, 170
People's Republic of China (PRC)
  Chinese Household Income Survey Project, 47
  Chinese Manufacturing Enterprises Database, 329, 341
  as developing economy, 111
  disadvantaged vs. advantaged region inequality in, 49, 59–60, 63–64t, 65
  economic consequences of inequality in, 11
  education in, 60, 65–66, 67–68t
  employment in, 76, 76–77t, 85
  ethnic minorities in, 39
  exports of, 347
  foreign direct investment in, 9, 39, 328–55. *See also* foreign direct investment
  gender inequality in, 86–87, 87–88t
  income inequality in, 98, 104t
  increasing inequality in, 127
  middle class in, 167n1
  National Bureau of Statistics (NBSC), 342
  rural dual economic transformation in, 356–81. *See also* rural dual economic transformation
  rural vs. urban inequality in, 41, 42–43t, 51–52, 262
Pew Research Center, 1
Philippines
  financial deepening in, 9
  fiscal policy in, 10
  government expenditures and inequality in, 116

polarization, 13, 40
policy recommendations
  for Central Asian transition economies, 159–60
  for education, 13, 98, 149–50, 160
  for equality of opportunity, 14
  for inclusive growth, 33–35
  macroeconomic factor impacts and, 127–28
  for reducing inequality, 98–99
  for rural dual economic transformation, 379–80
  for urbanization, 13–14
political economy
  consequences of inequality for, 12–13, 40
  income inequality, effect on, 118–19, 123, 124t, 127
political freedom, 135, 145, 148–49
Political Risk Index, 118–19
population growth, 118, 127, 132
populism, 12
post-communist economic growth, 154. *See also* Central Asia
PovcalNet, 29, 167, 169, 174, 178
poverty and poverty reduction
  economic growth and inequality, 111
  financial sector access and, 35, 262
  GDP increases and, 32
  inclusive growth for, 17–37. *See also* inclusive growth
  intergenerational transmission of, 40
  international poverty line, 28–29, 29f
  intertemporal poverty assessment, 202–9
  policy recommendations for, 33
  pro-poor growth for, 199–225. *See also* pro-poor growth
  social programs for, 184, 186
Poverty and Social Impact Analysis, 33–34
poverty gap, 30
poverty indexes, 200–201
poverty line, 28–29, 29f
poverty traps, 40
PRC. *See* People's Republic of China
privatization, 154, 156–57, 159
property rights, 34
pro-poor growth, 2–3, 199–225
  anonymous vs. non-anonymous perspectives on, 199–201
  decompositions of, 209–14, 225
  defined, 30
  intertemporal poverty assessment for, 202–6
  measurement of pro-poorness in intertemporal settings, 206–9

middle-class growth and, 169, 184, 186
  Senegal, 30–32, 32f
protectionism, 12
PRS Group, 119
public housing, 98
public transfers, 159, 242, 242n18, 372

R

rank mobility, 219
rate of pro-poor growth (RPPG), 200, 201
re-centered influence function (RIF) method, 45–46
redistribution of economic growth. *See also* policy recommendations
  channels for, 158–59
  fiscal policy for, 128, 150
regional inequality. *See* disadvantaged/advantaged regions; expenditure inequality; within-country income inequality
remittances, 76, 86, 364
rent seeking, 12
Republic of Korea
  decreasing inequality in, 127
  disadvantaged vs. advantaged region inequality in, 59, 63–64t, 65
  education in, 65–66, 69t, 150
  employment in, 10, 76, 77–78t, 85–86
  gender inequality in, 86, 87n7, 89t, 96
  globalization and, 142
  income inequality in, 40, 98, 104t
  rural vs. urban inequality in, 41, 42–43t, 48–49, 49n5, 52
RIF. *See* re-centered influence function
risk management, 34
RPPG. *See* rate of pro-poor growth
rule of law, 34
rural areas. *See also* agricultural sector
  discrimination of rural poor and, 52
  disposable household income per capita and, 107t
  education in, 52, 59, 65–66
  employment in, 34, 52, 59, 117–18.
    See also rural dual economic transformation
  employment mobility in, 288, 290, 295
  expenditure inequality compared with urban areas, 238–39f, 238–46, 241f, 244–45f, 247f
  inclusive growth and, 24, 26–28, 27f
  income gap with urban areas, 48–49, 51–59, 53–58t, 98, 262, 266, 276
  intergenerational employment mobility and, 299, 300f, 306

poverty reduction for, 33, 34
urban-rural gap, 9, 13
rural dual economic transformation, 3–4, 356–81
  agricultural sector and, 370–71
  impact on income inequality, 367–70, 369–70t
  income inequality, relationship between, 365–67, 366t
  income inequality in Tianjin, 358–62, 359f, 360–61t
  non-agricultural sector and, 371–72
  policy recommendations for, 379–80
  sectoral effects and, 373
  structural and distribution effects of, 373–78, 375t
  transfer income inequality and, 372
  trends in income inequality in Tianjin, 362–65, 363f, 365t
Russian Federation
  cross-regional inequality in, 39
  disadvantaged vs. advantaged region inequality in, 49–50, 59–60, 63–64t, 65
  education in, 59, 65–67, 69–72t
  employment in, 79–81t, 85–86
  gender inequality in, 87, 90–92t, 96–97
  household surveys from, 47–48, 47n4
  income inequality in, 98, 104t
  increasing inequality in, 127
  rural vs. urban inequality in, 41, 51–52, 53–55t, 59

S

Sargan test, 122, 125
sectoral effects, 373, 374n6
self-employment
  age and, 290
  among rural and ethnic minority people, 286
  disadvantaged regions and, 295
  education and, 294
  employment mobility and, 288
  gender and, 98, 307
  intergenerational employment mobility and, 298
Senegal
  growth incidence curves in, 24–28, 25–27f
  income inequality in, 22–23, 23–24t
  poverty and inequality estimates in, 29–32, 30t, 31–32f
Serial Correlation test, 122, 125
services, unequal access to, 112
shadow economy, 10, 76

Shandong province, PRC, 356–81. *See also* rural dual economic transformation
Shapley value decomposition framework
  on foreign direct investment, 329, 341, 342, 347, 348t, 349–50
  on income inequality in Indonesia, 261, 262, 265–68, 268t
  on pro-poor growth, 213n18, 214
Singapore
  globalization and, 142
  increasing inequality in, 127
social consequences of inequality, 12–13, 40
social exclusion, 112
social mobility. *See also* intragenerational and intergenerational mobility
  defined, 273
  education and, 10, 280, 282
  employment and, 39
  as equalizer, 201
  intertemporal pro-poorness and, 217–18
  measuring, 199–201
  middle class and, 172, 187–88
social status, 156, 175
South Asia, middle class in, 180, 181t. *See also specific countries*
spatial inequality. *See* expenditure inequality
squared poverty gap, 21–22, 21n2, 22t
Sri Lanka, increasing inequality in, 127
Stopler-Samuelson theorem, 142
structural effects, 373–77, 374n6, 375t, 376n7
sub-Saharan Africa
  middle class in, 180, 181t
  poverty levels in, 28, 30–31, 31f
Sustainable Development Goals, 277

T

Taipei,China
  disadvantaged vs. advantaged region inequality in, 50, 59–60, 59n6, 65
  education in, 40, 59, 65–67, 73–75t, 86, 150
  employment in, 82–84t, 85
  gender inequality in, 40, 86, 93–95t, 97
  globalization and, 142
  income inequality in, 40, 98, 104t
  rural vs. urban inequality in, 41, 48–49, 49n5, 51–52, 56–58t, 59
Tajikistan
  economic growth in, 162f
  education in, 160
  income distribution in, 165f
  role in Soviet Union, 156

taxation
  as driver of income inequality, 10, 112, 184
  evasion of, 154, 160
  policy recommendations for, 150
technological improvements
  for agriculture, 34
  as driver of income inequality, 10, 111, 135, 142, 149
  influence of labor transfer and technology spillover, 339–41, 340f
  productivity and, 10
  technology spillover and, 329–30, 336–39, 338–39f
Thailand, financial deepening in, 9
Theil index of inequality
  on expenditure inequality, 227–28, 231–35, 231n5
  on foreign direct investment, 329, 331–33, 344, 347–50, 348–49t
  on global, between-, and within-country inequality, 133f
  on income inequality sources in Indonesia, 269
  on inequality in Asia, 6, 6f
  on urban vs. rural expenditure inequality, 230–31, 238, 238–39f
Tianjin province, PRC, 356–81. *See also* rural dual economic transformation
trade
  benefits of, 126
  as driver of inequality, 9, 116–17, 135
  globalization and, 134
  North-South, 135
transition economies, 158–59. *See also* Central Asia
Transparency International, 119
transportation sector, 250
Turkmenistan, economic growth in, 162f

U

unconditional quantile regression (UQR) decomposition, 44–45
unemployment, 117, 123, 126, 156
United Kingdom
  consumption inequality in, 117
  earnings inequality in, 116
  foreign direct investment in, 331
  middle class and industrialization in, 168
United States
  consumption inequality in, 117
  income inequality and inflation in, 117
  middle class in, 170
upper-middle-income countries
  GDP of, 170

income gap in, 38
middle class in, 173–74, 173f, 174t, 180
urban agriculture, 357, 357n2, 362, 371–72
urban areas
  Asian financial crisis (1997–1998), 239–40
  disposable household income per capita and, 105t, 107t
  as drivers of income inequality, 132
  economic activity concentration in, 123
  education in, 65–66
  employment mobility in, 288, 290, 295
  expenditure inequality with rural areas, 238–46, 238–39f, 241f, 244–45f, 247f
  inclusive growth in Senegal and, 24–25, 26f, 28
  income gap with rural areas, 48–49, 51–59, 53–58t, 98, 262, 266, 276
  intergenerational employment mobility and, 299, 300f, 306
  migration to, 249, 362–64
  policy recommendations for, 13–14
  summary statistics by income quintile, 106t
urban-rural gap, 9, 13, 112
Uzbekistan
  economic growth in, 163f
  employment in, 160
  role in Soviet Union, 156

V

Viet Nam
  economic growth and poverty reduction in, 273–74
  education in, 275, 279, 288
  ethnic minorities in, 274–75, 276, 276n2, 277f, 282, 288, 290
  intragenerational and intergenerational mobility in, 273–327. See also intragenerational and intergenerational mobility
Viet Nam Household Living Standard Surveys (VHLSS), 274–75, 278, 298

W

wage inequality, 10. See also foreign direct investment
Watts index, 21, 21n3, 22, 22t
WDIs. See World Development Indicators
wealth accumulation, 264–65, 267, 270
West African Economic and Monetary Union (WAEMU), 31
WIID. See World Income Inequality Database
within-country income inequality. See also disadvantaged/advantaged regions
  Asia, 6–7, 6f
  defined, 133
  Indonesia. See expenditure inequality trends in, 133f
within-economies income inequality, 6–7, 6f
women. See gender inequality
World Bank
  agricultural earnings, policies for, 34
  on income inequality in Indonesia, 262
  on inequality and economic growth, 155
  middle-class measures, data for, 167, 169, 174, 178
  Poverty and Social Impact Analysis of, 33–34
  poverty measures, data for, 29, 119
World Development Indicators (WDIs), 145, 174
World Income Inequality Database (WIID), 118, 139, 145–46

Lightning Source UK Ltd.
Milton Keynes UK
UKHW041122210319
339591UK00005B/374/P